CW01011142

AMERICA'S MOST VICIOUS CRIMINALS

AMERICA'S MOST VICIOUS CRIMINALS

Carl Sifakis

Checkmark Books®
An imprint of Facts On File, Inc.

America's Most Vicious Criminals

Copyright © 2001 by Carl Sifakis
The material in this book, except for the introduction, was previously published as part of
The Encyclopedia of American Crime (Facts On File, 2000)
by Carl Sifakis and is reprinted here with permission.

All rights reserved. No part of this book may be reproduced or utilized in any form or by any means, electronic or mechanical, including photocopying, recording, or by any information storage or retrieval systems, without permission in writing from the publisher. For information contact:

Checkmark Books
An imprint of Facts On File, Inc.
132 West 31st Street
New York NY 10001

Library of Congress Cataloging-in-Publication Data

Sifakis, Carl.
America's most vicious / Carl Sifakis
p. cm.
Originally published as part of: The encyclopedia of American crime.
New York: Facts On File, 2000, in series: Facts On File crime library.
Includes bibliographical references and index.
ISBN 0-8160-4423-6 (pbk. : alk. paper)
1. Crimes—United States—Encyclopedias. 2. Criminals—United States—Biography.
I. Sifakis, Carl. Encyclopedia of American Crime. II. Title.
HV6789 .S537 2001
364.1'092'273—dc21
[B] 2001028660

Checkmark Books are available at special discounts when purchased in bulk quantities for businesses, associations, institutions or sales promotions. Please call our Special Sales Department in New York at (212) 967-8800 or (800) 322-8755.

You can find Facts On File on the World Wide Web at http://www.factsonfile.com

Text design by Cathy Rincon
Cover design by Nora Wertz

Printed in the United States of America

VB FOF 10 9 8 7 6 5 4 3 2 1

This book is printed on acid-free paper.

Contents

INTRODUCTION	vii
ENTRIES A–Z	1
PHOTO CREDITS	227
BIBLIOGRAPHY	229
INDEX	233

Introduction

Among America's most vicious killers of the last couple of decades, Robert Hansen has to make any Top Ten list. As a serial killer he operated in Alaska and reveled in its wide expanses of nothingness offering so many places to bury his victims, all women, where they could not be found. Hansen made a sport out of his killings, luring women to his home and sometimes killing them there. The fact that he had a wife and kids never got in the way of his murder games. He played the part of a wonderful husband who packed his family off to trips to visit relatives in the lower 48, or he sent them off to see the sights in Europe. Hansen had the convenience of owning his own private Piper Super Cub bush plane and simply loaded some of the bodies on board and took off after studying his aviation chart to pick out likely burial spots in forsaken areas of snow and ice. Often he did not dispatch the women beforehand but took them for a joyride into the white wilderness. Hansen had achieved considerable fame as an outdoorsman and pilot—hunt stalking Dahl sheep, wolves and bears with a rifle and bow and arrow.

He longed to hunt human prey the same way and on landing he would inform his joyriding passenger that she was in the game of her life. He gave her a headstart and then stalked her with his trusty rifle or his more challenging bow and arrow. His victims ran for their lives—with nowhere to go. There were no survivors in that sporting game.

After he was finally caught, Hansen admitted to murdering at least 17 women as he trailblazed Alaska for serial killing.

The annals of American crime are filled with mass murderers and "serial killers," a term that came into vogue in the last few decades of the past century. There are names like Charles Whitman, Leonard Lake and his partner Charles Ng, the "Hillside Stranglers"—not one but two cousins working in concert, John Graham, Harvey Glatman, Billy Gohl, Richard Speck, Dean Corll, Juan Corona, Jeffrey Dahmer, and many more of that ilk.

If Robert Hansen had a unique way of disposing of his victims, he had nothing on Joe Ball, the Texas lover who got rid of his unwanted females by feeding them to his pet alligators. Two of America's more accomplished bluebeards, J. P. Watson and Alfred Cline, who had dispatched possibly 40 or 50 women between them had a certain exasperation with the law. How, each complained, could they both be expected to remember *all* the names of their victims?

Then there are the horrid cases of American cannibals, such as the frightful Albert Fish. Another cannibal, Alfred Packer, gained a measure of popularity in American lore as "The Man Who Ate Democrats." Packer killed and devoured five of his victims, causing the judge who sentenced him to 40 years for his awesome appetite, to exclaim, "Packer, you depraved Republican son of a bitch, there were only five Democrats in Hinsdale County, and you ate them all!"

Professional killers like to say their crimes are all strictly business. Bugsy Siegel once told a worried builder working on his Flamingo hotel in Las Vegas, he had no cause to fear all the threatening characters hanging around because "We only kill each other." It was a pungent piece of philosophy, but untrue. Siegel killed many times and not only among his colleagues. The fact is Bugsy loved killing anyone. That it could be considered business made his mad dog acts somewhat more tolerable. Murder, Inc.'s most prolific killer, Pittsburgh Phil, killed at least 100 persons, and probably more. Once he was not present when the murder troop dispatched a victim, and he was heartbroken. "Aw," Phil moaned, "I want to lend a hand."

Another mobster type who may have had a bigger death toll than Pittsburgh Phil was Pretty Amberg, noted for his horrid looks. He was quite horrid about killing as well, and planted laundry bags with corpses all over the streets of Brooklyn. His need for laundry bags was so great that Pretty, as immortalized in stories by Damon Runyon, went out and bought a laundry just to fill his need for bags.

Quite naturally, the female of the species can be just as vicious as the male. The list of vicious women criminals is long and deadly, and includes Kate Bender, Martha Beck, Bonnie Parker, Belle Gunness, Anna Hahn, Mary Jane Jackson, Duchess Spinelli, and Lydia Struck, among others. And the most heinous? Let us defer to the opinion of Ellery Sedgwick, the distinguished editor of *Atlantic Monthly* who leans to Jane Toppan, the murdering nurse who may have killed at least 100 persons. As Sedgwick protests: "When it came to evaluating the histories of famous murderers, Jane Toppan has never received proper recognition. Without the slightest doubt, she outranks both Bluebeard and Jack the Ripper." Sedgwick's interest in Toppan stemmed from the fact that he had been nursed by her through a siege of pneumonia and allowed to live. Many other patients did not survive her ministrations. It was a matter of whom she took a fancy to and whom not.

Still, it would be wrong not to discover in many of these more than 140 selections from the *Encyclopedia of American Crime*, that even the most vicious killers could show occasional bouts of good cheer. Even Robert Hansen sometimes let some of his intended victims go untouched. There was no accounting for his varying attitudes. The same could be said for Samoots Amatuna, a noted and feared Chicago gangster of the 1920s. He killed without the slightest restraint, seldom showing pity, but Samoots was also a fop, the proud possessor of 200 monogrammed silk shirts, and once took off in murderous pursuit of a driver on a Chinese laundry delivery wagon after one of his shirts was returned scorched. Samoots pulled his gun to shoot the frightened delivery driver, but at the last moment he was overcome with a spark of humanity. He shot the driver's horse instead.

Entries A - Z

Abbandando, Frank "the Dasher"
(1910–1942) Murder, Inc. killer

One of Murder, Inc.'s most prolific killers, Frank "the Dasher" Abbandando got his nickname, according to one version, on one of his early hits. He pointed his gun at a huge waterfront character and pulled the trigger, but the weapon didn't fire. Abbandando then made a mad dash to get away, with his intended victim lumbering after him. According to the story, Abbandando ran around a building so fast that he actually came up behind the man. This time he got him with three slugs in the back. Even if this story is legend, it is matter of fact that during the 1930s, Abbandando did a remarkable job of littering the streets of Brooklyn with corpses. No accurate statistics on his kills were ever kept, but he was known to have been involved in probably 50 or so. When he wasn't knocking off mob victims, the Dasher spent his free time raping young girls in the Brownsville and Ocean Hill sections of Brooklyn. In one case he "squared up" with a girl's family by tossing them $25, "or otherwise I buy you all tombstones."

When finally brought to justice as a result of the testimony of informer Abe Reles and several other gang members who turned into stoolies, Abbandando was probably the most unrepentant of the hired killers in court. At one stage in the Dasher's trial, the judge ordered a court officer to stand between himself and Abbandando on the witness stand after the defendant threatened to kill him right in his own court. Still, the Dasher's lawyer tried to cast him in the best possible light, pointing out he had indeed been a star at second base for the Elmira team—the Elmira Reformatory team that was. In his summation he pleaded for the Dasher in the fair name of baseball, arguing: "Ballplayers don't kill people. In all my experience I cannot think of a single baseball player who ever killed anybody—at least so viciously as in this case."

The athletic assassin went to the electric chair on February 19, 1942.

See also: MURDER, INC.; ABE RELES.

Abrams, Big Mike (?–1898) murderer

While the Chinese of New York's Chinatown have fought many savage tong wars among themselves, through the years they have tried to avoid violent conflicts with whites. The opposite was not the case, however. White killers were familiar denizens of the Chinatown alleys, always ready to eliminate any man's enemy for a shockingly reasonable price. The most notorious of this ilk was Big Mike Abrams, who roamed the area performing beatings and killings for pay. When work was slow, Abrams would take to street muggings, which, besides earning his keep, further enhanced his reputation.

Big Mike sometimes operated opium-smoking dens on Pell Street and in Coney Island and in his later years settled for a small percentage from such establishments, while contributing nothing to their operation. The fact that a man was a client of one of these dens, however, did not afford him protection in the event Big Mike was offered cash to slug or kill him. Big Mike's most celebrated murders were the knife decapitations of three Chinese before the horrified eyes of onlookers on Pell Street.

Even the dread hatchet men of the tongs feared Big Mike, but finally one of them, Sassy Sam of the Hip Sing Tong, got drunk on rose wine and rice brandy and attacked the awesome killer. Big Mike happened to be unarmed at the time and fled down Pell Street, with Sassy Sam in hot pursuit waving a long ceremonial sword.

Big Mike lost considerable stature after that display of vulnerability. While he did regain a measure of respect by removing the head of Ling Tchen, one of the chiefs of the Hip Sing Tong, the unthinkable—the elimination of Big Mike—began to be considered. Within a month of the death of Ling Tchen, police found Big Mike dead in bed, his room filled with gas. The windows and door to his room had been sealed from the outside and a line of thin hose from a gas jet in the hall had been stuffed in the keyhole of Big Mike's door.

The Hip Sings were generally credited with killing Big Mike, but the Tongs never acknowledged the deed, apparently fearful of retribution from other white gangsters.

Accardo, Anthony Joseph (1906–1992)

Chicago mob leader

Today, it may be somewhat hard to believe that someone like "Joe Batters," who, as a young tough, gained his sobriquet for his proficiency with a baseball bat and who served as one of Al Capone's bodyguards, could become the boss of the Chicago mob and be described by his syndicate supporters as having "more brains before breakfast than Al Capone had all day."

Accardo's rise in the Chicago underworld was rapid. When Capone first went to jail for a brief stay in 1929 and named Jake Guzik in charge of administration and Frank Nitti in charge of operations, Accardo was installed as the head of "enforcement." Under him were such brutal characters as Machine Gun Jack McGurn, Tough Tony Capezio, Screwy John Moore, Sam "Golf Bag" Hunt, Red Forsyth and Jimmy Belcastro, the King of the Bombers. Accardo continued to grow in stature in the gang, and when Nitti committed suicide in 1943 rather than go to prison, he became the acknowledged head of the Chicago mob.

At various stages in the 1950s and 1960s, Accardo reportedly had his powers wrested away by Sam "Momo" Giancana, but it is unclear how much Accardo gave up under force and how much he relinquished willingly.

Accardo was always reputed as a leader who believed in iron-clad obedience in the lower ranks but a sharing of power at the top. Under his rule the level of violence in the Chicago underworld dropped to near zero, especially compared to the old Capone days. However, enforcement against alleged informers and those who tried to steal from the syndicate remained strict and awesome. Such was the fate in 1961 of one William "Action" Jackson, a collector for the mob who had developed "sticky" fingers. Action got particularly brutal treatment, ending up stripped naked and hanging by his chained feet from a meat hook in the basement of a Cicero gambling joint. He was beaten on the lower body and genitals with a baseball bat, carved up with a razor and had his eyes burned out with a blowtorch. Following that treatment he was further dissected, and then pictures were taken of his corpse (he had died, according to the coroner's report, not of his wounds but of shock) and distributed in mob centers as a warning of what was in store for a thief.

Accardo's personal fairness, by underworld standards, was of the same sort that inspired so much loyalty in many of Capone's adherents. Noted for his pool playing, Accardo was once victimized in a $1,000 bet by a pool hustler who had wedged up the table and then adjusted his technique accordingly to beat the crime chief. When the hustler was exposed, Accardo blamed only himself. "Let the bum go," he said. "He cheated me fair and square." Accardo's behavior in such matters won him a great amount of affection.

But Accardo also proved most resourceful in dealing with the drug problem, which

Tony Accardo, nicknamed Joe Batters for his proficient use of a baseball bat in the service of Al Capone, became the most enduring boss of the Chicago outfit.

much of the national syndicate and the Mafia had ruled out of bounds. Some families disobeyed the rule but others enforced it rigorously, killing any who disobeyed or cutting them off from legal and support aid if they were caught. Accardo's solution was to ban all narcotics dealings, but he also ordered that all those involved in dope be given $200 a week out of family funds to help make up their losses.

This "taking care of everybody" approach helped to pacify the Chicago mob; by comparison, gangland murders became much more common in New York, with its five greedy Mafia families. This record of peace may well have been shattered by the 1975 murder of Sam Giancana, but a number of underworld sources insist Accardo was not behind the murder. According to them, the Giancana killing was "a CIA operation all the way," designed to prevent him from speaking about the agency's use of the underworld in a Castro assassination plot.

By the late 1970s Accardo, a multimillionaire, was in semiretirement, living the good life as he traveled from Florida to the West Coast to Chicago looking after his enormous legitimate investments. According to the FBI, the mob's operational authority in Chicago had shifted to Joe Aiuppa, an Accardo gunman buddy from the old days. After that, Joe Batters returned to approve further new leaderships when Aiuppa went to prison. Accardo died in 1992, never having spent a night in jail.

See also: SAM "MOMO" GIANCANA.

Joe Adonis, longtime power in organized crime and sidekick of Lucky Luciano and Meyer Lansky, takes "voluntary deportation" to Italy in aftermath of revelations at the Kefauver hearings. He abandoned his real name, Joseph Doto, for the Adonis moniker in honor of his self-proclaimed good looks.

Adonis, Joe (1902–1972) **syndicate gangster**

A member of the governing board of the national crime syndicate from its inception in the early 1930s, Joe Adonis, or simply Joey A., remained a power until he was deported in 1956. While Adonis always insisted that he was born in this country, he was, in fact, born in Montemarano, Italy, on November 22, 1902. Joseph Doto entered the country illegally and adopted the name Adonis to pay tribute to what he regarded to be his handsome looks. After joining a New York street gang, Adonis formed a teenage friendship with the future big names in American crime—Albert Anastasia, Vito Genovese and Lucky Luciano. By the mid-1920s Adonis was the head of the Broadway Mob, which controlled the flow of bootleg liquor in mid-Manhattan, the richest market in the country. While he was the operating head of the mob, he may not have been the real brains, since his partners included Luciano and Frank Costello. However, Adonis continued to rise in the hierarchy of organized crime because he was loyal and never overambitious. He became a trusted member of the board of the national syndicate, settling disputes between various criminal factions and issuing murder contracts, among other duties. Abe Reles, the informer in the Murder, Inc. case, once told authorities, "Cross Joey Adonis and you cross the national combination." When Luciano went to prison, he left Adonis in nominal charge of the combination's affairs, but he added, "Cooperate with Meyer." Meyer was Meyer Lansky, who became the chief officer in the combination. Adonis proved smart enough to know how to take orders.

Following the end of Prohibition, Adonis extended his domain to include not only the waterfront and gambling rackets in Manhattan but those in Brooklyn and New Jersey as well. He also masterminded a number of jewel thefts, an avocation that amused his big-time confederates. It seemed like a dangerous enterprise but it made Adonis happy. Despite a long career in crime, he did not go to jail until 1951, when, after the Kefauver Committee hearings, he pleaded guilty in New Jersey to violation of the state's gambling laws and received a two-year sentence. In 1956, Adonis, facing federal perjury charges, accepted a deportation order, after his true birthplace had been discovered. Thereafter, he lived out his days lavishly in Milan, Italy, still maintaining ties with the underworld in America and occasionally meeting with Luciano, who resided—also in exile—in Naples.

Aiello, Joseph (1891–1930) Chicago mobster

Joseph Aiello and his brothers, Dominick, Antonio and Andrew, were enemies of Al Capone in the struggle for control of organized crime in Chicago. Aiello tried to have Capone killed in somewhat novel ways, e.g., attempting to bribe a restaurant chef $10,000 to put prussic acid in Capone's soup and, on another occasion, offering a reward of $50,000 for Big Al's head. These efforts called for extraordinary vengeance on Capone's part, and he ordered his enemy killed "real good." On October 23, 1930 Aiello was gunned down on North Kolmar Avenue, struck by 59 bullets, weighing altogether well over a pound.

See also: LOUIS "LITTLE NEW YORK" CAMPAGNA.

Alderisio, Felix "Milwaukee Phil" (1922–1971) hit man

Regarded by many as the top hit man of the Chicago mob, Felix "Milwaukee Phil" Alderisio was popularly given credit for designing the "hitmobile," a car especially geared for committing murder with the least possible interference. Among what may be called its optional features were switches that would turn out the car's front or rear lights to confuse police tails. Another innovation was a secret compartment in a backrest that not only held murder weapons but contained clamps to anchor down handguns, shotguns or rifles for more steady shooting while the vehicle was in motion. Although the Chicago police insisted that Milwaukee Phil was the executioner in well over a dozen gangland hits, no murder charge against him was ever proven. He was, however, finally convicted of extortion and died in prison in 1971.

Allen, Bill (?–1882) murderer

A Chicago black man named Bill Allen had the distinction of being hunted by the largest "posse" in American history. On November 30, 1882 Allen killed one black and wounded another, and later that evening he murdered Patrolman Clarence E. Wright, who tried to arrest him. Three days after the incident Allen was located in the basement of a house by Patrolman Patrick Mulvihill, but the fugitive shot Mulvihill through a window and fled. Soon, 200 policemen were scouring the black district of Chicago for Allen. By mid-afternoon, according to a contemporary account, "Upwards of 10,000 people armed with all sorts of weapons from pocket pistols and pitchforks to rifles, were assisting the police in the hunt." At 3:30 that afternoon, Sgt. John Wheeler found Allen in the backyard of a house on West Kinzie Street and killed him in a gunfight. Allen's body was taken in a patrol wagon to the Desplaines police station, and somehow the rumor started that he had been arrested rather than killed. A lynch mob of thousands quickly formed, and when a few officers tried to break up the crowd, they were threatened. "The crowd," one report of the event said, "became frenzied and threatened to tear down the station. Threats and promises were all in vain, and a serious riot seemed inevitable. Chief Doyle mounted the wagon and assured the crowd that the Negro was really dead. They hooted and yelled, shouting that the police were concealing the man and encouraging each other to break in the windows of the station."

The police chief then came up with a way of placating the mob. Allen's body was stripped, laid out on a mattress and put on view through a barred window where it could be seen at the side of the station. A line was formed, and "the crowd passed in eager procession, and were satisfied by a simple glance at the dull, cold face. All afternoon that line moved steadily along, and the officers were busily occupied in keeping it in order. The crowd increased rather than diminished, and until darkness settled down, they were still gazing at the dead murderer. After dark a flaring gas jet at the head of the body brought it out in strong relief, and all night long the line of curious people filed by for a glimpse of the dead." It was 48 hours before Allen's body could be taken off display.

Allison, Clay (1840–1887) gunfighter

One of the most notorious of the western gunfighters, Clay Allison was not an outlaw in the ordinary sense of the word. He called himself a "shootist," apparently in an attempt to indicate he was a professional, like an artist or a dentist. Allison lived on the fringe of the law and according to a personal code governed more by his own belief in honor than by the strictures of the law. Invariably, this meant he killed men "that deserved killin'." In a morbid sense, he may have contributed some of the most entertaining—to observers rather than to victims—shootings in western lore.

One of his more famous duels was with a gunman named Chunk Colbert in 1874. The pair sat eyeball to eyeball in a New Mexico Territory eatery, staring each other down and stirring their coffee with the muzzles of their six-guns. Soon each reholstered his piece and continued to eat. Colbert made the first move to draw but Allison shot him dead just above the right eye. On another occasion Allison led a lynching party against a man named Kennedy who was suspected of killing his own young daughter. Some bones were found on the Kennedy ranch, but there was no definite determination that the bones were human. The matter was still in dispute after the lynching, but that didn't stop Allison from cutting off the dead man's head, impaling it on a pike and riding 29 miles to Cimarron, Kan. to his favorite watering hole, Henry Lambert's saloon.

Allison could best be described as a part-time maniac, since between his vicious killings he was generally a well-mannered rancher. There might have been some excuse for his behavior, however. He had joined the Confederate Army in his native Tennessee

Contemporary drawing depicts Clay Allison's famous shoot-out with another notorious gunman, Chunk Colbert.

but was discharged after sustaining a blow on his skull, which was said to have made him intermittently epileptic and at other times maniacal. After the Civil War, he punched cattle and finally set up the first of his several ranches.

What troubled other men about Allison was his unpredictability. In 1875, although a rancher, he sided with the homesteaders in their battles, clearly out of a sense of fair play, an attitude that enraged other ranchers and stock associations. At the same time Allison was a bitter racist, and in New Mexico he killed a number of Mexican "outlaws." Few, however, even considered challenging him for any of his deeds.

Allison continued to devise duels that bordered on lunacy. He once indulged in a fast-draw contest with a gunman named Mace Bowman. After Bowman continually outdrew him, Allison suggested they pull off their boots, strip down to their underwear and take turns shooting at each other's bare feet to see who danced best under fire. Remarkably, the confrontation ended without bloodshed after several hours, each man giving in to exhaustion.

When he got into yet another dispute, Allison arranged to do battle naked in a grave in which each adversary would be armed with a Bowie knife. Both agreed to purchase a tombstone and the winner would see to it that the stone of the loser was suitably engraved. While waiting for the delivery of the tombstone, Allison picked up a wagonload of supplies from Pecos, Tex. to bring back to his ranch. When a sack of grain fell from the moving wagon, he tried to grab it and toppled to the ground. A wagon wheel rolled over his neck, breaking it and killing him.

It was a bizarre ending to a violent life for a man credited, by various counts, with the deaths of 15 to 21 men. A Kansas newspaper had a difficult time trying to evaluate the life of Clay Allison and whether he was "in truth a villain or a gentleman." That was "a question that many never settled to their own satisfaction. Certain it is that many of his stern deeds were for the right as he understood that right to be."

Allman, John (?–1877) the cavalryman killer

The prototypical western cavalryman bad guy, according to a Hollywood historian, "Bad John Allman did as much to make John Ford a great movie director as did John Wayne." The point may have been stretched, but John Allman was just about the worst killer the U.S. Army contributed to the West.

A native of Tennessee, Allman was a violent character throughout his army career. There is some speculation that Allman was not his original name, that he had served elsewhere in uniform under another identity or two until it became wise to change it.

There is no record of exactly how many men Allman killed—"not countin' injuns," as they said in the cavalry. In any case, his last spree substantially reduced the population of the Arizona Territory. In the summer of 1877 Allman got into an argument during a poker game in the cavalry barracks at Prescott, Ariz. When the pistol smoke cleared, Allman and the pot were gone and two army sergeants were dead. A posse soon started out after Bad John and got close to him, close enough for two of its members, Billy Epps and Dave Groat, to be killed by him. Still on the run, Allman was recognized, or at least thought he had been recognized, by two woodcutters, and he promptly shot them dead. Late in August, about two weeks after he had killed the woodcutters, Allman, tired, hungry and broke, rode into Yuma. When he rode out, a bartender named Vince Dundee was dead, and Allman had the contents of the till and as many bottles of whiskey as a man could tote. In Williams, Ariz. Deputy Sheriff Ed Roberts spotted Allman in a saloon, but Bad John's gun was quicker; on his way out, the cavalryman killer stepped right over the dying lawman.

Sheriff Ullman of Coconino County turned over the job of apprehending Allman to a bizarre group of bounty hunters referred to by the press as Outlaw Exterminators, Inc. The Exterminators consisted of five bounty hunters who specialized in going after "dead or alive" quarries and bringing them in dead rather than alive. However, Allman was a hard man to run to ground. Low on bullets, he killed a sheepherder named Tom Dowling for his gun and ammunition. Next he kidnapped a 13-year-old white girl named Ida Phengle and a 12-year-old Hopi girl and raped them both. Allman eventually freed his two young captives but soon found himself pursued by various lawmen, the Exterminators and a Hopi war party. In the end, it was Clay Calhoun, one of the Exterminators, who located Allman among some deserted Indian cliff dwellings on October 11, 1877. According to Calhoun, whose version of what happened was the only one reported, he brought down Allman in a stirring gun fight. This dramatic scenario is hard to credit since Allman had been shot four times, in the mouth, chest, stomach and groin, all in a nice neat line. Any of those shots would have grounded Allman, making the alignment of wounds most unusual for a shoot-out. Some speculated that Allman had more likely been shot while asleep. But speculation aside, the important thing was that Bad John Allman's bloody reign of terror was over, and the particulars of how it happened didn't trouble many people in Arizona.

See also: OUTLAW EXTERMINATORS, INC.

Alterie, Louis "Two Gun" (1892–1935)

gangster

The Dion O'Banion gang that dominated Chicago's North Side during the early years of Prohibition was particularly noted for its zaniness (it once "rubbed out" a horse for killing one of its members in a riding mishap), but even for this bunch, Louis "Two Gun" Alterie was wacky. Alterie, whose real name was Leland Verain, owned a ranch in Colorado but came east to join up with O'Banion's gambling and bootlegging operations. He wore two pistols, one on each hip, Wild West–style, and always boasted of his perfect marksmanship with either his left or right hand, often shooting out the lights in saloons to prove his point.

It was Alterie, it was said, who insisted that revenge was required after a leading member of the gang, Nails Morton, had been thrown by a horse in Lincoln Park and kicked to death. He led the gang to the riding stable, and there they kidnapped the horse, took it to the scene of Morton's demise and shot it to death. Alterie was so incensed by the "murder" of his comrade that he first punched the hapless horse in the snout before turning his gun on it.

When Dion O'Banion was assassinated by Capone gunmen, Two Gun Alterie went wild. In a tearful performance at the funeral, Alterie raged to reporters: "I have no idea who killed Deanie, but I would die smiling if only I had a chance to meet the guys who did, any time, any place they mention and I would get at least two or three of them before they got me. If I knew who killed Deanie, I'd shoot it out with the gang of killers before the sun rose in the morning." Asked where the duel should be fought, he suggested Chicago's busiest corner, Madison and State Streets, at noon. Mayor William E. Dever was enraged when he heard of Alterie's words. "Are we still abiding by the code of the Dark Ages?" he demanded.

Earl "Little Hymie" Weiss, successor to O'Banion as head of the mob, ordered Alterie to cool off, stating that because of his rantings political and police pressure was being put on the gang's operations on the North Side. Alterie nodded grandly with a big wink and stayed quiet for about a week. Then he swaggered into a Loop nightclub frequented by reporters and gangsters and, brandishing his two pistols, boasted loudly: "All 12 bullets in these rods have Capone's initials carved on their noses. And if I don't get him, Bugs, Hymie or Schemer will."

For Weiss, who was trying to keep peace with Capone until the right time to strike, Alterie's blustering was just too much. He ordered Bugs Moran to "move" Alterie. Moran went to the cowboy gangster and growled: "You're getting us in bad. You run off at the mouth too much."

Alterie recognized an invitation to leave town when he heard one and returned to his ranch in Colorado, ending his participation in the Chicago gang wars. When he finally came back to Chicago on a visit in 1935, the O'Banion gang had been wiped out except for Moran, and he was no longer a power. Apparently, just for old time's sake, somebody shot Alterie to death.

See also: CHARLES DION "DEANIE" O'BANION.

Amatuna, Samuzzo "Samoots"

(1898–1925) Chicago gangster and murderer

One of Chicago's most colorful and brutal gangsters during the 1920s, Samuzzo "Samoots" Amatuna for a time held a power base from which he challenged Al Capone's control of crime in the city. In the end, however, Samoots was more remembered for the changes his death brought about in the practices of Chicago-area barber shops.

A professional fiddler and a fop, Samoots was one of the first to conceal a weapon in an instrument case, using this technique with three confederates in the attempted murder of a musicians' union business agent. The proud possessor of 200 monogrammed silk shirts, he once took off in pursuit of the driver of a Chinese laundry delivery wagon after one of his shirts was returned scorched. Samoots pulled his gun to shoot the frightened driver, but at the last moment he was overcome by a spark of humanity and shot the driver's horse instead.

Samoots became the chief bodyguard for the notorious Terrible Gennas, who controlled much of the city's homemade bootleg racket. As they were wiped out or scattered one by one, Samoots moved up in power and in 1925 he seized control of the Unione Siciliana. This group had been a lawful fraternal organization up to the turn of the century, but from then on, it became more and more a front for the criminal operations of Mafia forces. Chicago had the largest number of branches of the Unione, whose 40,000 members represented a potent force as well as an organization to be looted through various rackets, such as manipulation of pension funds. For years the Unione was under the control of Mike Merlo, who knew how to keep peace among the various criminal combines, but after his death in 1924 the Unione presidency became a hot seat. Bloody Angelo Genna took over as president, only to be murdered in May 1925.

Al Capone, who was not a Sicilian and thus not eligible for membership, wanted to place his *consigliere,* Tony Lombardo, in the office but decided to wait for an election. In the meantime Samoots walked into the Unione's offices with two armed confederates, Abe "Bummy" Goldstein and Eddie Zion, and declared himself elected. Capone was furious at the effrontery, but he soon had more reason to hate Samoots as the latter moved to open a chink in Capone's booze and other operations.

However, Samoots had other enemies such as the O'Banion Irish gang, which was still in power on the North Side even after the death of its leader. On November 13, 1925 Samoots, planning to go to the opera with his fiancée, Rose Pecorara, dropped into a Cicero barbershop for a shave. He was reclining in a barber's chair with a towel over his face when two assassins, believed to be Jim Doherty and Schemer Drucci of the O'Banions, marched in. One of the gunmen fired four shots but, remarkably, missed Samoots with every shot. The frightened target bolted from the barber's chair and tried to dodge four bullets from the second gunman. Each of these shots hit home, and the assassins strode out, leaving their victim near death. Rushed to a hospital,

Samoots asked to marry his fiancée from his hospital bed but died before the ceremony started.

Within a few weeks Samoots' aides, Goldstein and Zion, were also killed, and the way was open for Capone's man, Lombardo, to take over the Unione. After Samoots' death, which was the second recent Chicago barbershop assassination, it became common practice for barbers dealing with a gangster clientele never to cover their faces with a towel and to position the chair so that it always faced the entrance. This local custom did not spread to New York, where some two decades later Albert Anastasia was gunned down under similar circumstances.

Amberg, Louis "Pretty" (1898–1935)

racketeer and murderer

From the late 1920s until his own violent demise in 1935, Louis "Pretty" Amberg was New York's best-known killer, having dispatched more than 100 victims. Thanks to cunning and dumb luck, however, he was never so much as saddled with a stiff fine for any of his or his brother Joe's murders, although his achievements were common knowledge. His technique of stuffing victims into laundry bags, alive but trussed up in such a way that they strangled themselves, was immortalized by Damon Runyon in several stories in which Pretty Amberg was featured in a thinly fictionalized form.

Pretty, so named because of his ugliness, was brought to America from Russia by his fruit peddler parents. By the age of 10 he was terrorizing his home territory of Brownsville in Brooklyn, New York City, an area that bowed only to genuine toughness and meanness. Young Pretty developed a unique fruit-selling technique: he would kick on a door until the resident opened up and then shove handfuls of fruit and vegetables forward and snarl, "Buy." People bought.

Pretty Amberg, often described as the worst Jewish criminal ever raised in America, was immortalized by Damon Runyon in his short stories as the racketeer who bought a laundry business because he needed bags to stuff all his corpses in.

By the time he was 20, Pretty was *the* terror of Brownsville. He was now so ugly that a representative from Ringling Brothers offered him a job with the circus as the missing link. It is the mark of Pretty's intellect or sense of humor that he often bragged about the offer. However, Pretty didn't accept the job because of his involvement in the loansharking business with his brother. Unlike the banks of Brownsville, the Ambergs turned no one down for a loan, but at 20 percent interest a week. Pretty would watch his brother count out the amount of the loan and growl, "I will kill you if you don't pay us back on time."

The Amberg brothers soon became so successful in loansharking that they shifted their operations to around Borough Hall in downtown Brooklyn. The brothers did not desert Brownsville, however. Pretty stalked Pitkin Avenue; for amusement he would walk into a cafeteria and spit in someone's soup. If the diner protested, Pretty would spill the whole bowl in his lap. Even Buggsy Goldstein, shortly to become a prize killer in the fledgling Murder, Inc., once took the soup treatment in silence. Famous Murder, Inc. informer Abe Reles later said, "The word was that Pretty was nutty."

Pretty Amberg's continuing ties with Brownsville were not based solely on sentiment. He took control of all bootlegging in the area, and speakeasies took Pretty's booze or none at all, a business practice Pretty established with a few bombings and frequent use of a lead pipe.

Soon, Pretty was wallowing in money, and he became a lavish-spending, if rather grotesque, figure in New York's nightlife. Waiters fawned over him because he never tipped less than $100. He was a regular at the Central Park Casino, where in time he became a nodding acquaintance of the city's playboy mayor, James J. Walker. It was Runyon who reported that when the mayor first saw Pretty, he vowed to stay off booze.

Pretty expanded his rackets to include laundry services for Brooklyn businesses. His rates were rather high, but his sales approach was particularly forceful. It was at this time that laundry bags stuffed with corpses started littering Brooklyn streets. One victim was identified as a loanshark debtor of the Ambergs who owed a grand total of $80. Pretty was arrested for that one, but he just laughed: "I tip more than that. Why'd I kill a bum for a lousy 80 bucks?" In fact, it was Pretty's philosophy to kill men who were indebted to him for small amounts so that their loss of life would not cause him to have to write off a major capital investment. It also made an excellent object lesson for more substantial debtors. And while the police knew the particulars, they could not prove them in court and Pretty went free.

By the early 1930s Pretty was considered among the most successful racketeers in the city, one who could withstand any inroads by other kingpins, such as Dutch Schultz and Legs Diamond. Once, Schultz told him, "Pretty, I think I'm going to come in as your partner in Brooklyn."

"Arthur," Pretty was quoted as replying, "why don't you put a gun in your mouth and see how many times you can pull the trigger."

Pretty was famous for such pithy comments. Another big racketeer, Owney Madden, mentioned to Pretty one day that he'd never visited Brownsville in his life and thought he would come out some time and "let you show me the sights." Pretty was carving up a steak at the moment. "Tell you what, Owney," he said matter-of-factly while continuing his meal, "if I ever see you in Brownsville, I'll cut your heart out on the spot." He was even more direct with Legs Diamond, whom he buddied around with. "We'll be pals, Jack," Pretty told Diamond, "but if you ever set foot in Brownsville, I'll kill you and your girlfriend and your missus and your whole damn family."

With the end of Prohibition, however, such threats proved insufficient. Dutch Schultz, without his former bootleg rackets, was down to only a multimillion dollar numbers racket centered in Harlem, and he kept casting greedy glances over at Brooklyn and the Amberg loanshark operations around Borough Hall. Pretty had by now firmly established himself in the laundry business, but loansharking remained his principal source of funds. He was therefore hardly overjoyed in 1935 when Schultz ensconced his top lieutenants, Frank Dolak and Benny Holinsky, in a new loan office just a block away from the Amberg enterprise. When Pretty stormed into the place, the pair glared back at him defiantly. "We ain't afraid of you," Holinsky said, and Dolak echoed, "That's right, we ain't afraid of you." The statements qualified as famous last words because 24 hours later their bodies, riddled with bullets, were found on a Brooklyn street.

The Ambergs and the Schultz forces faced off for total war. The first to go was Joey Amberg, who was ambushed by Schultz's gunmen. In October 1935 both Amberg and Schultz died. Some historians have insisted that each man was responsible for the other's death. According to this theory Amberg had paid professional killers $25,000 down to kill Schultz and promised them $25,000 more upon completion of the job. In the meantime, however, the fire department, responding to an alarm, found a blazing automobile on a Brooklyn street. In the back seat of the car was the body of a man roasted beyond all recognition, with wire wrapped around his neck, arms and legs. It took a few days for a positive identification: it was Pretty Amberg. But by the time the identification was made, a couple of killers had gunned down Dutch Schultz in a Newark chop house.

Despite the war, it is not certain that Amberg was killed by Schultz. A more convincing theory attributed Pretty's passing to a gang of armed robbers he had joined and offended by insisting on taking virtually all the loot for himself. Another view held that both Amberg and Schultz were "put to sleep" by the increasingly dominant national crime syndicate bossed by Lucky Luciano and Meyer Lansky.

But whoever was to blame, Pretty Amberg was dead, and as a *Brooklyn Eagle* reporter observed, "There was joy in Brownsville."

Anastasia, Albert (1903–1957) syndicate gang leader and murderer

The Lord High Executioner of Murder, Inc., Albert Anastasia rose to the top levels of the national crime syndicate and remained there until he himself was murdered in a hit as efficient as any of the countless ones he carried out or planned.

Immediately upon his arrival in the United States in 1920, Anastasia and his brother, Tough Tony Anastasia, became active on the crime-ridden Brooklyn docks and gained a position of power in the longshoremen's union. He demonstrated a penchant for murder at the snap of a finger, an attitude that was not altered even after he spent 18 months in the Sing Sing death house during the early 1920s for killing another longshoreman. He was freed when, at a new trial, the four most important witnesses against him could not be located, a situation that proved permanent.

For Anastasia the solution to any problem was homicide. So it was hardly surprising that he and Louis "Lepke" Buchalter were

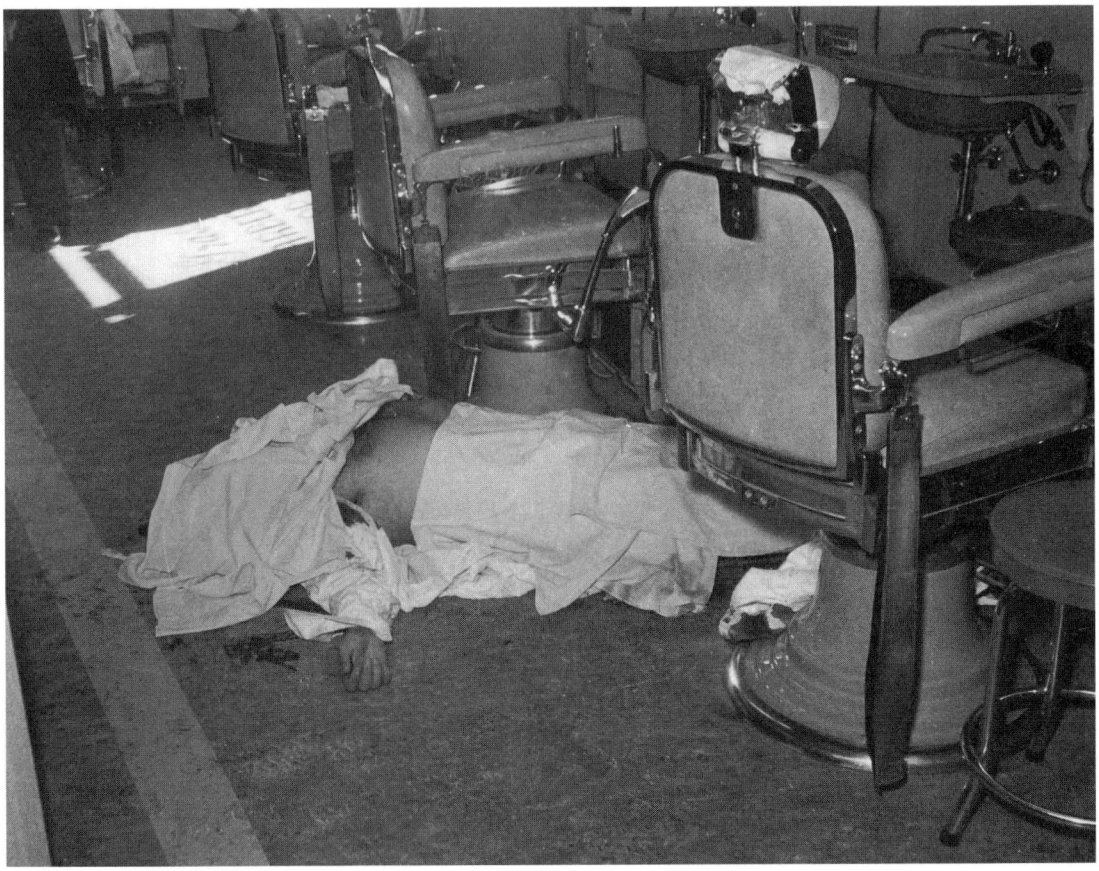

Albert Anastasia, Lord High Executioner of Murder, Inc., was gunned down in a Manhattan hotel barbershop with all the efficiency he himself exhibited in numerous killings.

installed as the executive heads of the enforcement arm of Murder, Inc. The victim toll of Murder, Inc. has been estimated as low as 63 and as high as 400 or 500. Unlike Lepke and many other members of the operation, Anastasia escaped punishment. In a "perfect case" against him, the main prosecution witness—again—vanished. This disappearance of witnesses was a regular occurrence in the Anastasia story, as were killings to advance his career. When in 1951 Anastasia aspired to higher things, he took over the Mangano family, one of New York's five crime families, by murdering Phil Mangano and making Vincent Mangano a permanent missing person.

Anastasia became known as the Mad Hatter because his killings were so promiscuous. He had always been a devoted follower of others, mainly Lucky Luciano and Frank Costello. His devotion to Luciano was legendary. In 1930, when Luciano decided to take over crime in America by destroying the two old-line Mafia factions headed by Giuseppe "Joe the Boss" Masseria and Salvatore Maranzano, he outlined his plan to

Anastasia because he knew the Mad Hatter would kill for him. Anastasia promptly grabbed Luciano in a bear hug and kissed him on both cheeks. He said: "Charlie, I been waiting for this day for at least eight years. You're gonna be on top if I have to kill everybody for you. With you there, that's the only way we can have any peace and make the real money."

Anastasia's killer instincts could be contained as long as Luciano and Costello were around to control him, but Luciano was deported in 1946 and a few years later Costello became bogged down by continuous harassment from the authorities. Now in charge of his own crime family, Anastasia really turned kill-crazy. In 1952 he even had a young Brooklyn salesman named Arnold Schuster killed after watching Schuster bragging on television about how he had recognized bank robber Willie Sutton and brought about his capture. "I can't stand squealers!" Anastasia screamed and then ordered his men, "Hit that guy!"

The Schuster killing violated a principal rule of the underworld: we only kill each other. Outsiders—prosecutors, reporters, the general public—were not to be killed unless the very life of the organization was threatened. That clearly was not the case in the Schuster murder. The rest of the underworld, even Anastasia's friends Luciano (now in Italy) and Costello, were horrified, but they dared not move on him because they needed him as a buffer against a new force within the crime structure. Vito Genovese, long number two under Luciano, was making a grab for greater power. Between him and that goal stood Anastasia, a man who had hated him for years. Secretly, Genovese brought to his banner Anastasia's underboss, Carlo Gambino, a frail-looking mobster with unbridled ambition of his own, who in turn recruited Joe Profaci and his Brooklyn crime family.

Before Genovese could move against Anastasia, he needed more support, and he could not move without the tacit agreement of Meyer Lansky, the highest-ranking Jewish member of the national syndicate. Normally, Lansky would not have supported Genovese under any circumstances; their ethnic bitterness was one of the underworld's longest-standing feuds. But Anastasia had recently given Lansky reason to hate him even more. In 1957 Lansky was in full control of gambling in Cuba through his close personal and financial arrangements with that country's dictator, Fulgencio Batista. As was his style of always enhancing his own base within the underworld, Lansky gave a piece of the action to Miami crime boss Santo Trafficante and a number of other Italian-American mobsters. When Anastasia learned of Lansky's largesse, he started to put pressure on him for a huge cut.

Under these circumstances Lansky, who previously had preferred to let Genovese and Anastasia bleed each other to death, okayed the elimination of the latter.

Early on the morning of October 25, 1957 Anastasia entered the barbershop of the Park Sheraton Hotel in New York City and sat down for a quick haircut, shutting his eyes. Anastasia's bodyguard took his car to an underground garage and then conveniently went off for a little stroll. Moments after Anastasia sat down in the barber's chair, two men entered the shop with scarves over their faces. Arthur Grasso, the shop owner, was standing at the entrance by the cash register. He was told, "Keep your mouth shut if you don't want your head blown off." The two men moved to Anastasia's chair and shoved the barber aside. If Anastasia's eye had been open, he would have seen them in the mirror. Suddenly, both guns roared.

Anastasia leaped out of the chair with the first volley and weaved on his feet. Then he saw his attackers and lunged at them—in the mirror. He took several more shots, one in the back of the head, and collapsed dead on the floor.

Officially, the Anastasia killing remains unsolved, although it is known that Joe Profaci gave the contract for the killing to the three homicidal Gallo brothers from Brooklyn.

The double-dealing continued after the Anastasia murder, with Gambino breaking off from Genovese and making his peace with Luciano, Costello and Lansky. A desperate Genovese called an underworld summit meeting at Apalachin, N.Y. to justify the elimination of Anastasia, who, he said, had become so murder-crazed that he had imperiled the entire organization. That meeting ended in disaster following a state police raid, and six months after that, Genovese was arrested on a narcotics rap, one which much of the underworld regarded as a setup. The inside word was that the setup was arranged by Gambino, Luciano, Costello and Lansky. At any rate, Genovese was effectively removed from the scene.

See also: VITO GENOVESE; MURDER, INC.

Anselmi and Scalise gangsters

It is impossible to record the criminal activities of Albert Anselmi without also discussing those of John Scalise, the worst pair of killers during the bloody 1920s. Anselmi and Scalise grew up together, played together, worked together, killed together and, fittingly, were slaughtered together. The two resembled that other inseparable pair Mutt and Jeff; Anselmi was short and bulky, Scalise tall and thin. It was this duo who brought to the Chicago underworld the old Sicilian custom of rubbing bullets with garlic; if the shots failed to kill, the resulting gangrene allegedly would. Anselmi and Scalise's medical knowledge was somewhat faulty, although the same could not be said about their homicidal prowess, which was proficient even by Chicago standards.

While in their twenties, Anselmi and Scalise were forced to flee their native Marsala because of a murder charge. The pair turned up in Chicago during the early 1920s and went to work for the Terrible Gennas, a family of killers who had established themselves as the leading bootleggers in the Midwest. Since the Gennas also hailed from Marsala, they welcomed the two to their bosom, having a constant need for reliable torpedoes. Anselmi and Scalise were single-minded of purpose: they planned to make a million dollars each, which they felt would give them enough to fix the case against them in Sicily and allow them to return as rich men. Their killing services came high, but they were extremely efficient. For one killing the Gennas rewarded each of the pair with $10,000 and a $3,000 diamond ring. Scalise, the more romantic of the two, sent his ring to his sweetheart in Sicily. Anselmi reportedly sold his to a jeweler at the point of a gun for $4,000.

Anselmi and Scalise introduced a degree of double-dealing unknown even in the Chicago underworld. True innovators, they introduced the "handshake hit," whereby the short, fat Anselmi would shake hands with the unsuspecting victim and lock his right hand in a tight grip. With the victim's gun hand incapacitated, the taller Scalise would quickly step forward and shoot him in the head. The shorter Anselmi always did the holding because he had a grip of iron and Scalise did the shooting because his height enabled him to get in a head shot regardless of how tall the victim was. Anselmi and Scalise were definitely two of three killers involved in the 1924 assassination of Dion O'Banion, the leading Irish gangster of the era, in which the usually careful gang leader was caught off guard in a handshake just before the funeral of a leading Italian underworld figure.

Some of their other killings were legendary. One victim held his hands in prayer and begged to be spared. They shot off his hands before putting a bullet in his brain. Anselmi and Scalise probably sprayed more pedestrian-mobbed streets than any other pair of kill-happy gunners. They gunned down gangland rivals and police officers with equal ferocity. Once, in the company of several other killers, they noticed that their bullet-filled victim lying on a street managed to raise his head. Chagrined that he was not dead, the two rushed back across the street and, before dozens of witnesses, finished the job.

The only time Anselmi and Scalise wavered in obeying the orders of the Gennas was when they were told to kill Al Capone, for they realized their ultimate reward for such an act would be their own deaths. Instead, they informed Capone of the Gennas' plan and became Capone men while ostensibly still working for the Gennas. When it finally came time for Capone to erase the Gennas, Anselmi and Scalise "set up" one of the brothers and took an active part in killing another.

Capone now welcomed the pair openly into his organization, making them two of his most important bodyguards and gunners. When the mob boss offered to make peace with Hymie Weiss and the rest of the O'Banion gang, his terms proved entirely acceptable. Weiss made only one stipulation: Anselmi and Scalise had to be turned over to the gang for killing Dion O'Banion. Capone rejected the deal, declaring, "I wouldn't do that to a yellow dog."

Several legal attempts were made to get Anselmi and Scalise. They were once charged with the killing of two police detectives, but after three trials, involving a great number of threats against witnesses and jurors, they went free, remarkably, on the ground that they had merely been resisting unwarranted police aggression.

In 1929 they were arrested for taking part in the infamous St. Valentine's Day Massacre, but by the time their trial date arrived, they too had been murdered. How they died is no secret. Capone staged a party in honor of the pair and Joseph "Hop Toad" Giunta, whom he had recently installed as president of Unione Siciliana. At the height of the banquet, Capone stopped the festivities, accused the trio of plotting to murder him and, after having them tied up, beat all three to death with a heavy Indian club. They may well have been conspiring against Capone, but it is just as possible that Capone decided to kill the trio because he feared they were getting too important. Anselmi and Scalise had been appointed as bodyguards for Giunta in his new rule, but Scalise had quickly relegated Giunta to the background and had taken direct charge of the organization's affairs. He was heard to brag, "I am the most powerful man in Chicago." And Anselmi chimed in, "We the big shot now."

It was a fitting collective singular. Anselmi and Scalise, who had so often killed together, died together.

See also: ALPHONSE "SCARFACE AL" CAPONE, GENNA BROTHERS, CHARLES DION "DEANIE" O'BANION.

Apache Kid (1867–?) rapist, robber, murderer

The Apache Kid conducted the worst one-man reign of terror the Arizona Territory and perhaps the entire West ever saw. Until age 20 the Apache Kid adapted well to the white man's world, becoming a sergeant of scouts at the San Carlos Agency under Al Sieber, Arizona's famed Indian fighter. When his father was murdered, tribal law required the young Indian to avenge the crime, and under that law, it would be a legal execution. Although Sieber warned him that such revenge would be illegal under the white man's law, the Apache Kid slipped away with a few followers, located his quarry near a creek and stabbed him to death. The young Indian then surrendered to Sieber, but becoming fearful of his treatment in a hostile white court, he escaped with his followers. After two years on the run, the Apache Kid returned to face a court-martial. He was convicted but won a pardon from President Grover Cleveland. Incensed by this action, the local Indian haters promptly indicted the Kid and several of his band on charges of having killed a whiskey drummer who was trying to sell "fire water" to their people. The Apache Kid was found guilty and given

Originally a sergeant of scouts, the Apache Kid (center) later went on an orgy of robbery, rape, kidnapping and murder, becoming the most-hunted Indian outlaw in the Arizona Territory.

seven years in prison, a remarkably short sentence that indicated the case against him was either weak or that the crime itself was considered by many to be justified. On November 1, 1889 the Apache Kid was being escorted to the prison at Yuma when he overwhelmed his two guards, Sheriff Glen Reynolds and Deputy Bill Holmes, killed them and made his escape. From then on, the Apache Kid became the scourge of the state, leaving a bloody trail of robbery, rape and murder. He struck blindly, victimizing Indians as well as whites. He took many Indian women, and when he tired of them, he cut their throats. Prospectors were robbed and murdered in their mountain cabins; lonely ranches were attacked and their inhabitants killed. It was impossible to get an accurate count of the number of white girls he kidnapped, raped and killed because he was blamed whenever a lone Indian committed a crime, but there was no doubt that most such victims were his. Even a $5,000 bounty on his head failed to stop him, although several whites and Indians alike tried and died in the effort.

The terror ended abruptly in 1894. One night Ed Clark, a prospector and former chief of Wallapai Scouts, awakened at his camp north of Tucson to see two young Indians trying to steal his horse. Clark shot the woman and badly wounded the man, who fled. Clark, whose partner, Billy Diehl, had been killed by the Apache Kid five years earlier, was sure he recognized him. He was equally positive that he had gotten in a killing shot and that the Apache Kid had crawled in some hole to die. Clark's story was plausible, but it was more likely that the Apache Kid realized the tale of his fate gave him the perfect opportunity to fade away. There seems little doubt that he took an Indian woman, went into the Sierra Madre in Mexico and raised a family. He was recognized and spoken to by a number of reliable witnesses well into the 20th century.

Further reading: *Lone War Trail of Apache Kid* by Earle F. Forrest and Edwin B. Hill.

Atlanta Centennial Park bombing

case of the wrong suspect

Early in the morning hours of July 27, 1996, television cameras swayed during Olympic Games interviews, and a loud report sounded. It was an explosion. It was a deafening blast that flooded out the rock music in the park. Shrapnel and debris rained down on dancers and onlookers. Bodies were riddled as more than 100 persons were hit. Luckily, only one person, Alice Hawthorne, a 43-year-old African-American businesswoman, was fatally wounded. Another 111 persons were treated at local hospitals or at the scene but all recovered. A second death claimed as a result of the explosion was that of Turkish TV cameraman Melih Uzanyol, who suffered a fatal heart attack while attempting to videotape the bombing scene.

The death toll would have been much higher had not a private security firm guard, Richard Jewell, spotted a suspicious looking knapsack and, with other guards, hustled numerous people from the area before the pipebomb in the knapsack exploded. Jewell's alert action was credited with probably saving scores of lives. Television interviewers flocked to the hero guard who said, "I just happened to be at the right place at the right time, and doing the job I was trained to do."

Jewell's day in the sun did not last long. Investigators soon zeroed in on a chief suspect—Richard Jewell. The president of Piedmont College in Demorest, Ga., informed authorities that Jewell had previously been employed there as a campus security guard but had been fired for "infractions," such as once on his own flagging down motorists to give them sobriety tests. Before that Jewell had been a deputy for the Habersham County sheriff's department where following a reprimand for his behavior, he was reduced in rank to jail guard. Since that time he had worked in security guard positions at Piedmont and for other security companies, including the Olympic post he held at the time of the explosion.

It soon became clear that the FBI was determined to nail Jewell for the terrorist bombing (although FBI agents apparently made it appear to Jewell they considered him an ally in the hunt for the culprit). The open speculation fostered by the authorities' actions was that Jewell had himself planted the bomb, then spotted it so that he could then be credited with saving many innocent lives.

Emphasizing the FBI's belief that they had their man, agents made a very public search of the two-bedroom apartment Jewell shared with his mother, taking out box after box of material they found there, including scores of videotapes. Despite this busy-bee activity, the FBI did not charge Jewell with any crime, but he was left twisting in the wind by the agency, which did not dismiss him as a suspect. Eventually Jewell's mother wrote in protest to President Bill Clinton, pointing out her son "is a prisoner in my home."

Attorneys hired by Jewell now went on the offensive, demanding that the government either charge the security guard or that he be given an apology. The most picturesque quote came from one of Jewell's lawyers who raged, "These jerks need to get up off their butts and tell the truth." It took another two months, until October 26, before the Department of Justice officially declared that Jewell was no longer a suspect in the case. It could not be regarded as one of the FBI's most shining hours.

In early 1997 a suburban Atlanta abortion clinic was bombed, and the following month a gay and lesbian bar was similarly hit, so similarly in fact that investigators believed it was the work of the same terrorist. And they had indications that the suspect in the first two cases and probably the Centennial Park bombing was Eric Robert Rudolph. Rudolph was a suspect in other cases as well, but, an adept survivalist, he vanished somewhere in the wilds of the southeastern states. At present the Centennial Park bombing remains in the unsolved files.

Atlanta children murders

Over a period of 24 months, from mid-1979 to mid-1981, a total of 29 young blacks, most of whom were considerably under the age of 20, disappeared in Atlanta, Ga. Twenty-eight of them were found dead. The string of murders terrified the city and galvanized the rest of the country into outpourings of support and sympathy. The main national effort came in the form of green ribbons, "symbolizing life," which appeared on millions of lapels everywhere, worn by blacks and whites. Even shopping bag ladies in New York City were seen wearing the ribbons as well as green-lettered buttons proclaiming "SAVE THE CHILDREN."

Vice President George Bush journeyed to Atlanta to demonstrate an extraordinary degree of national concern. President Ronald Reagan announced the authorization of a $1.5 million grant to aid the investigation, and huge rewards were offered for information leading to the capture of the killer or killers. Celebrities, such as Frank Sinatra and Sammy Davis, Jr., contributed money to pay for investigations and aid to the families of the victims, and thousands of letters containing checks, dollar bills and even coins streamed into Atlanta.

The official manhunt was marked by bickering between local and federal investigators. FBI director William H. Webster riled local feelings when he announced that four of the cases, apparently unrelated to the others, had been solved. The next day a bureau agent in Macon, Ga. said the four children had been killed by their parents. This brought an angry outcry from the public, demanding to know why no arrest had been made. None was made, Atlanta mayor Maynard Jackson said, because there was not enough evidence to justify an arrest. He complained the FBI head had undermined the public's confidence in the investigation.

A large proportion of the deaths were so similar they indicated the likelihood that many of the victims had died by the same hand or hands. Nineteen of the 28 were believed to have died from strangulation or other forms of asphyxiation. Nine were found in rivers, nude or almost nude. More than a dozen had traces of similar fibers, from a blanket or carpet, on their bodies. Evidence of dog hairs was found on a number of the bodies.

Numerous suspects, some found thousands of miles from Atlanta, were quizzed, but without success. Finally, on June 3, 1981 23-year-old Wayne B. Williams was standing in an Atlanta phone booth when FBI agents appeared and "insisted," according to Williams, that he come downtown for questioning. Word of his interrogation spread quickly through Atlanta, and for the first time many felt the hunt for the mass killer might be over. However, after being held for 12 hours, Williams, who had worked as a TV cameraman and part-time talent scout and booking agent, was released. Publicly, officials said there was insufficient evidence to hold him, but privately they implied he was still a definite suspect.

It appears that Williams was picked up because investigators feared he might destroy suspected criminal evidence. During his interrogation Williams submitted to three lie detector tests, which, he later said he was told, indicated "all my answers were deceptive." The findings, Williams explained to the press, might have been caused by his nervousness. Following his release, authorities obtained a warrant to search Williams' home and confiscated a yellow blanket and a purple robe and collected samples of dog hairs and fibers from a bedspread and carpet.

Williams had first come to police attention on May 22. Around 3 A.M. officers staking out a bridge across the Chattahoochee River stopped his car after hearing a loud splash in the water. According to the police, when asked if he had thrown anything into the river, Williams said he had dumped some garbage. However, he subsequently insisted, "I told them I had dropped nothing in the river." Two days later, the body of 27-year-old Nathaniel Cater floated to shore about a mile downstream from the bridge, within 500 yards of where the body of 21-year-old Jimmy Ray Payne had been found the month before.

On June 21 Williams was arrested and charged with murdering Cater. An Atlanta grand jury indicted him on July 17 for both the Payne and Cater slayings. Clearly, the authorities acted as though several of the killings had been solved. In August, Williams pleaded not guilty to the charges.

By September, when the new school year started, there had been no further unaccountable murders of young blacks. Teachers reported that unlike the previous year there was hardly any talk among the pupils about the unsolved murders. A 12-year-old boy, Owen Malone, was quoted as saying: "It seems like it's over. Last year we talked a lot about the case; we got safety tips. The students were afraid of getting snatched." But this year, he observed, "It was all right."

On February 27, 1982 Williams was convicted of the two murders and sentenced to life imprisonment.

Baker, Cullen M. (1838–1868) outlaw and murderer

A sallow-faced killer, Cullen Baker did most of his "Civil War fighting" as the head of a Texas gang of outlaws who called themselves Confederate Irregulars in the years immediately after Appomattox. The band was really little more than a group of farm looters, but they pacified their fellow Texans by occasionally killing some Yankee soldiers or upstart "nigger police."

Baker hadn't been much of a patriot during the war. He had been drafted into the Confederate Army in Cass County, where he had lived since the age of four. Actually, being drafted had its advantages: since he had killed a man in Arkansas two years earlier, the army provided a good hiding place for Baker. He soon deserted, however. After killing two Union soldiers in Spanish Bluffs, Tex., Baker figured a good place to hide would be in Lincoln's army, so he joined the Union cause. Not long after, he deserted again and joined a group of Confederate irregulars. After the war Baker saw no reason to stop his activities. He and his gang of vicious gunmen terrorized much of Texas, preying mostly on local farmers. They were still regarded in some circles as local heroes because they were pursued by Northern troops and black police, several of whom they killed in various fights.

Late in 1867, Bill Longley, a young gunfighter on the run from the law, joined the irregulars. He was to become the infamous Wild Bill Longley. Young Longley stayed with Baker about a year, leaving just before Baker's death. During that period Baker had developed a strong liking for a girl named Belle Foster, who did not return his attention but instead focused her affection on a crippled schoolteacher named Thomas Orr. In December 1868 Baker kidnapped Orr at gunpoint and hung him from a tree. Fortunately for Orr, he was found before he strangled to death. This act set local opinion against Baker. Trying to hang Orr hardly qualified as an anti-Yankee act. Orr and a posse of local citizens took off after Baker, and when they cornered him, Orr was given the privilege of shooting him full of holes, permanently dissolving Baker's Confederate Irregulars.

Ball, Joe (1892–1938) mass murderer

When it came to ghoulishness, an ex-bootlegger and tavern owner named Joe Ball, of Elmendorf, Tex., was exceptional even for a mass murderer.

In the 1930s Ball ran the Sociable Inn, a watering hole famous for two tourist attractions: the most beautiful waitresses for miles around and the pet alligators Ball kept in a pond in back of the establishment. The high point of the day was feeding time for the alligators, which Ball turned into a regular show, often feeding a live stray dog or cat to the slithering reptiles. It was a performance that could drive even the strongest men to drink, which made the gators as good for business as the pretty waitresses.

Ball's waitresses seemed to be a fickle lot, disappearing without a word to any of the customers. Naturally, they told Ball. Some were getting married, others had sick mothers, still others left for new jobs. Ball was never very enlightening. He merely shrugged and said philosophically, "They come, they go."

Exactly how many really went was never fully established. Later, police were able to find some of the waitresses alive, but 12 or 14 were never found. Most or all of the missing women were murdered by Ball so he would not be hampered in his constant search for a new romance. Some of them had become pregnant and demanded that Ball "do the right thing." His concept of the right thing was to ax them to death. Then, as later evidence would show, he often chopped up the body and fed the incriminating pieces to the alligators.

In 1937 the family of Minnie Mae Gotthardt wrote the local police complaining they had not heard from her for a long time. Some officers dropped in to see Ball. He set up drinks for them and explained that Minnie Mae had left to take another job. A short while later, the police came around again, wondering what happened to another waitress named Julia Turner. She left for the same reason, Ball said. That didn't wash too well because Julia had not packed any of her belongings. However, when Ball explained Julia had had a fight with her roommate and left without packing because he had given her $500 to help out, the law was placated. Then two more waitresses were listed among the missing and the Texas Rangers entered the case. They began compiling a list of Ball's former waitresses and found quite a few who could not be accounted for; their relatives had no idea of where they were.

The investigators were clearly suspicious of Ball but failed to break him down. However, an old black handyman and cook who had worked for Ball for years proved less resistant to the lawmen's questions and confessed helping his boss kill some of the women and dispose of their bodies. He said he did so because he was fearful that Ball would kill him if he refused. When the lawmen showed up at the inn on September 24, 1938 seeking the barrel in which Ball said he kept meat for feeding the alligators, the tavern owner realized the game was up. Before the officers could stop him, Ball rang up a "no sale" on the cash register, pulled out a revolver and shot himself in the head, dying instantly.

The handyman got two years for being an accessory after the fact, and the alligators were carted off to the San Antonio Zoo.

Barker, Arizona Clark "Kate" or "Ma" (1871?–1935) outlaw or mother of outlaws

Kate, or Ma, Barker remains one of the enigmas of the underworld. Was she the brains, indeed the queen mother, of one of the most violent gangs of the 1930s, or was she just a dumpy little old lady whom many of the gangsters of the era considered just plain "Mom"? One version, which belongs to Hollywood and the FBI, presents us with an iron mistress who was feared by her murderous sons as well as numerous other members of the Barker-Karpis gang and who died, tommy gun in hand, in a fabled shoot-out with federal agents. A different viewpoint, held by other members of the underworld, portrays a doting, worried—although at times ill-tempered—mother whose sole concern was always the safety of her brood. Whatever the truth was, the fact is that Ma Barker was never on any official list of public enemies and indeed was never charged with a crime during her lifetime.

Born to Scotch-Irish parents about 1871 in the Ozark Mountain area near Springfield, Mo.—the area that nurtured Jesse and Frank James—she was saddled with the unlikely name of Arizona, which friends soon shortened to "Arrie" and she herself later switched to Kate. One of her greatest experiences in childhood was seeing Jesse James ride by one day, and she cried with youthful anguish when "that dirty coward" Bob Ford killed Jesse in 1882. The year 1892 was doubly bad for Kate: the Dalton gang was cut down at Coffeyville, Kan., and Kate married an itinerant farm laborer named George Barker. It was not a happy marriage. Kate realized that a penniless sharecropper could never be much of an inspiration for the four boys—Herman, Lloyd, Arthur and Fred—who were born of the union. As the boys grew up in a series of tar paper shacks, Kate made it clear to Barker that she would run the family and she would guide the boys' upbringing. George Barker merely shrugged.

Ma Barker was either "a veritable beast of prey," as J. Edgar Hoover claimed, or just a dumpy little old mom to a bunch of gangsters, as the latter said.

Brought up in this impoverished environment, the boys soon started turning up regularly on police blotters. Ma Barker frequently managed to get her sons released, sometimes weeping hysterically and at other times screaming. As late as 1915, Ma was able to get her eldest, Herman, freed from a highway robbery charge. In the following years the Barkers turned to bank robbery. According to later FBI accounts, Ma planned all the jobs, and the boys and their buddies executed them. Ma supposedly ran things with iron discipline, making the boys memorize a "getaway chart." She herself was said to drive around all the surrounding roads, checking the times needed on them under all weather conditions. During the actual commission of a crime, Ma would once more become the doting mother, weeping for fear that her sons might be hurt. Ma was also said to dominate the gang's personal lives, refusing to allow the presence of any girlfriends. This, to be sure, was nonsense. All of the gang's hideouts were always awash with whores, and Ma did nothing about it. Things hardly could have been otherwise, given the character of her sons and the other top gangsters she sheltered, such as Al Spencer, Ray Terrill, Earl Thayer, Frank Nash, Francis Keating, Tommy Holden and Alvin "Creepy" Karpis. Karpis probably best presented the underworld version of the real Ma Barker. He wrote in his memoirs:

> *Ma was always* somebody *in our lives. Love didn't enter into it really. She was somebody we looked after and took with us when we moved from city to city, hideout to hideout.*
>
> *It's no insult to Ma's memory that she just didn't have the brains or know-how to direct us on a robbery. It wouldn't have occurred to her to get involved in our business, and we always made a point of only discussing our scores when Ma wasn't around. We'd leave her at home when we were arranging a job, or we'd send her to a movie. Ma saw a lot of movies.*

In 1927 son Herman was stopped by police near Wichita, Kan. after a robbery. When one officer leaned down to look in Herman's car window, Herman grabbed the policeman around the neck and fired a pistol into his head. A cop on the other side of the car cut loose at Barker, so filling him with bullets that the gangster turned his weapon on himself and finished the job. This development, according to J. Edgar Hoover in a bit of colorful prose, caused Ma to change "from an animal mother of the she-wolf type to a veritable beast of prey." Thereafter, according to the FBI version of events, Ma planed a near-endless string of bank robberies, the kidnappings of millionaires William A. Hamm, Jr. and Edward George Bremer and the murder of her "loving man," Arthur Dunlop. The best evidence indicates that Dunlop was murdered by Ma's sons and other members of the gang, with total disregard for Ma's feelings, because they suspected him of being a "squealer." The FBI claim that Ma was the brain behind the Hamm kidnapping is somewhat tarnished by the fact that the agency first arrested and caused the wrongful prosecution of Roger Touhy and his "Terribles" for the offense before discovering its mistake and correctly pinning the charge on the Barker-Karpis gang.

By 1935 the gang was being intensively pursued by the FBI and other law inforcement agencies. On January 16, Ma and her youngest and favorite son, Freddie, were traced to a cottage hideout at Lake Weir, Fla. A four-hour gun battle ensued, and both Freddie and Ma were shot to death. The official version had Ma manning a submachine gun in the battle, but this is debatable. Freddie was found with 14 bullets in him, indicating he was obviously in the line of fire. There is a discrepancy on how many bullets were in Ma, however. Some accounts said three and others only one—and that one self-inflicted. Cynics have charged that the FBI, having killed a dumpy, insignificant middle-aged woman, quickly promoted her into "Bloody Mama."

See also: BARKER BROTHERS, SHOTGUN GEORGE ZIEGLER.

Barker brothers public enemies

Easily the worst collection of criminal brothers in 20th- century America were the Barkers, or the "Bloody Barkers," as the newspapers not inappropriately called them. Indeed J. Edgar Hoover called the Barker-Karpis gang "the toughest mob we ever cracked." This characterization was close to the truth, whether or not Ma Barker herself, the so-called Bloody Mama, was included. There is considerable controversy over whether Ma Barker was really much of a criminal, but there is no doubt that her brood of four boys—Herman, born 1894; Lloyd, born 1896; Arthur—or "Doc" or "Dock"—born 1899; and Fred, born 1902—were a bloodthirsty lot. Of the four, Doc Barker was probably the leader, the one who commanded the respect of other prominent gangsters of the day.

Doc was both fearless and cold blooded and often killed without provocation or warning. Once when his brother Freddie and a few others of the gang wanted another gang member, William J. Harrison, rubbed out, Doc jumped at the assignment. He took Harrison at gunpoint to an abandoned barn near Ontarioville, Ill., shot him to death and after saturating him and the surrounding area of the barn with gasoline, set fire to the whole thing. He then wrote a note to several of the gang members hiding out in Florida: "I took care of that business for you boys. It was done just as good as if you had did it yourself. I am just like Standard Oil—always at your service. Ha, Ha!"

After several brushes with the law on minor—by Barker family standards—charges, Doc was sentenced to life imprisonment at the Oklahoma State Penitentiary for the murder of a night watchman during a robbery in 1920. In 1927 Herman Barker took his own life after being severely wounded in a shoot-out with police following a robbery. The next severe blow to the Barker family came when Lloyd Barker was arrested for a 1932 mail robbery and sentenced to 25 years in Leavenworth. This left only Freddie free.

Next to Doc, Freddie was the deadliest of the Barkers. He had a rather loose attitude toward killing. Once in Monett, Mo., he and another gangster, Bill Weaver, broke into a garage to steal a car for use in a job. Freddie got behind the wheel, and Weaver slid the garage door open to find himself facing a policeman with gun drawn. Freddie leaned out of the window and promptly shot the officer dead. He later moralized, "That's what comes from stealing these goddamn cars all the time." Freddie did a considerable amount of time for that killing, but he was eventually freed after Ma Barker haunted the parole board, wardens and governors and reputedly spent a significant amount of money.

When Freddie rejoined his mother following his release, he brought with him Alvin "Creepy" Karpis, who proved to be the most important leader of the gang. Each had a mutual respect for the other and they worked well as a team. Ma Barker was equally taken with Karpis and treated him almost as another son, perhaps because she now only had Freddie on the loose. In the meantime, however, Ma also worked on freeing Doc. Remarkably, Doc won a banishment pardon from the governor, which meant he could go free provided he left the state of Oklahoma. J. Edgar Hoover raged over the pardon and even more over the treatment afforded Doc's partner-in-crime, Volney Davis, who was granted an unbelievable "two-year leave of absence."

The Barker-Karpis gang, headed by Creepy, Doc and Freddie, was now ready for full operation. They pulled off an unparalleled number of bank robberies and the like and then moved into the lucrative new field of kidnapping. Their two major jobs were the abductions of William A. Hamm, Jr. and Edward George Bremer, which netted the gang a total of $300,000 in ransoms. Many have claimed Ma Barker was the master planner of both crimes, but none of the facts support this conclusion. Hoover credited the plan to a member of the Barker-Karpis gang named Jack Peifer, while according to Karpis, the Bremer job was the brainchild of Harry Sawyer, a flamboyant character who ran much of the crime in St. Paul, Minn. In all, there were about 25 or 26 members of the Barker-Karpis gang, and Doc and Freddie Barker were only slightly more equal than the rest. None regarded Ma Barker as their leader but did feel she was valuable for renting hideouts and handling payoffs to corrupt officials.

The Hamm and Bremer kidnappings were to prove the downfall of the Barkers and the rest of the gang, triggering one of the most persistent manhunts in history, during which the members were picked off one by one.

On January 8, 1935 Doc Barker was captured by FBI agents led by the legendary Melvin Purvis, the man who got Dillinger. The authorities located Doc by shadowing women he was known to have been in contact with. Eight days later, Freddie Barker was traced to a cottage at Lake Weir in northern Florida, where he was hiding with Ma Barker. Both were killed in a four-hour shoot-out, although there are some reports that Ma Barker actually shot herself when she saw her favorite son riddled with bullets.

In January 1939, Doc Barker, long a troublemaker at Alcatraz, attempted an escape from what was known as America's Devil's Island. He made it into the water before his skull was smashed and his left leg broken by guards' bullets. In the prison hospital he murmured: "I was a fool to try it. I'm all shot to hell." He died the following day, January 14, and was buried in a potter's field on the California mainland.

That left Lloyd Barker the last living brother. He remained in prison until 1947. Two years later, after returning home from his job at a filling station–snack shop, he was shot to death by his wife, with whom he had been feuding.

See also: ARIZONA CLARK "KATE" OR "MA" BARKER, SHOTGUN GEORGE ZIEGLER.

barrel murders early Mafia execution style

The "barrel murders" started turning up in America around 1870. The modus operandi of these killings, which occurred in several large cities, was always the same. A victim, invariably an Italian, would be killed—either shot, strangled or stabbed—and then stuffed into a barrel, which was then either deposited on a street corner or empty lot or else shipped by rail to a nonexistent address in another city.

It was the barrel murders that first alerted authorities to the existence of the Mafia. The murder technique started by coincidence with the arrival of a fierce pack of brothers, half brothers and brothers-in-law from Corleone, Sicily, the Morellos. Over the next three decades more than 100 barrel murders were traced to the Morellos, who finally abandoned the technique because all such murders merely advertised their criminal activities. Even worse, freelance non-Italian murderers were using the barrel method to divert suspicion from themselves to Italian gangsters.

Battaglia, Sam "Teets" (1908–1973)

syndicate gangster

Perhaps the craziest and certainly the deadliest of the four notorious Battaglia brothers who were members of the Chicago mobs, Sam Battaglia was a graduate of the notorious juvenile 42 Gang.

A burglar from the age of 16 and later a muscleman for the mob, he was arrested 25 times, beginning in 1924, on various armed robbery charges and at least seven homicide charges. A huge barrel of a youth, nicknamed Teets because of his muscular chest, Battaglia gained his first major notoriety when he was arrested in the fall of 1930 on a charge of robbing at gunpoint $15,500 worth of jewelry from the wife of the mayor of Chicago, Mrs. William Hale Thompson. Adding insult to injury, Teets appropriated the gun and badge of her policeman chauffeur. However, a positive identification could not be made, and Teets went free when he insisted he was watching a movie at the time of the robbery and a half-dozen witnesses insisted they were watching him watching the movie.

The robbery occurred on November 17, and, between then and the end of the year, Teets was involved in one fatal killing and one attempted killing. In ensuing years he became one of the mob's most reliable machine gunners and, despite a reputation for being a bit zany, moved steadily up the syndicate ladder. By the 1950s he was the virtual king of the mob's "juice," or loansharking, rackets and supervised a number of gambling joints and prostitution rings.

Sam Battaglia, a tough out of Chicago's Patch district who was always considered stronger on brawn than brains, became a millionaire and the owner of a luxury horse-breeding farm and country estate in Kane County, Ill. In 1967 Battaglia was finally sent away for 15 years on extortion charges, yet he was considered, pending his release, the likely head of the Chicago mob.

Bayonne-Abriel gang New Orleans

waterfront killers

A small band of burglars, wharf rats and professional murderers that terrorized New Orleans in the 1860s, the Bayonne-Abriel gang made up in viciousness what they lacked in numbers. According to one story, the gang once stole a row boat and, after discovering the boat was missing an oar, went out and killed another sailor just for his oars. While they occasionally functioned as shanghaiers, their main operation was a lucrative racket supplying seamen with everything from women and drugs to murder services. It was such a murder-for-hire service that eventually eliminated both leaders, Vincent Bayonne and Pedro Abriel, and led to the gang's dissolution.

Early in June 1869 the mate of a Spanish bark offered Bayonne and Abriel the kingly sum of $6 to kill a sailor who had earned his enmity. With such a prize at stake, Bayonne and Abriel decided to handle the job themselves rather than share it with any of their followers. The pair lured the sailor into a dive for a few drinks and then all three headed down to the levee "for some fun." Fun for the sailor turned out to be getting batted over the head with a club wielded by Bayonne. When Bayonne raised his arm to strike the unconscious man again, Abriel stopped him and said, "Let me finish him."

Bayonne refused, and Abriel struck him in assertion of his rights. The pair struggled fiercely for several minutes until Abriel knocked Bayonne out. By that time the sailor was stirring. Abriel then stabbed him 17 times and heaved the body into the river. Abriel and Bayonne reconciled afterwards but made the mistake of revealing the details of their vicious crime to a man named Isadore Boyd. Boyd's testimony was instrumental in getting the pair convicted and on May 14, 1871, hanged.

Beck, Martha (1920–1951) Lonely Hearts Killer

Together with Raymond Martinez Fernandez, 280-pound Martha Beck became infamous in the 1940s as one of the Lonely Hearts Killers. Although the pair was charged with only three murders, they were suspected of committing 17 others.

Both Fernandez and Beck were social misfits who joined several lonely hearts clubs seeking companionship. In addition to companionship, Fernandez sought money from women he became acquainted with. When Fernandez and Beck met through the auspices of a club, they teamed up to make a business of swindling women. While Fernandez wooed the women, Martha played the role of his sister. They mulcted scores of women and simply killed those who proved uncooperative or troublesome. The murders that tripped the pair up were those of Mrs. Janet Fay, a 60-year-old Albany, N.Y. widow, and Mrs. Delphine Downing, an attractive 41-year-old widow from Grand Rapids, Mich., and her 20-month-old child.

Mrs. Fay traveled as fast as she could to Valley Stream, Long Island to meet her husband-to-be (Fernandez) and his sister (Beck) after selling her home in Albany. Once the pair was sure they had all the woman's money, they beat her to death with a hammer and buried her in the cellar of a rented house. The killers then traveled to Grand Rapids and similarly stripped Mrs. Downing of much of her wealth. After feeding her sleeping pills, Fernandez then shot her to death. A few days later Martha Beck drowned the woman's child in the bathtub. The murderous pair then buried both corpses under cement in the cellar.

That chore completed the couple went off to a movie. When they returned, they found the police inside the Downing home. Suspicious neighbors had not seen the woman around for a few days and notified the authorities. Since the cement in the cellar had not yet dried, the bodies were quickly found. The police also discovered traces of the late Mrs. Fay's belongings in the couples' possession and soon obtained a confession to the New York murder as well. Since New York had a death penalty and Michigan did not, the two were tried for the Fay killing. After a 44-day trial, in which the sexual aberrations of Fernandez and Beck provided a field day for the sensational press, they were sentenced to death. On March 8, 1951—their final day of life—Fernandez received a message from Beck that she still loved him, news he exclaimed, that made him "want to burst with joy." Martha Beck was granted her last request. Before she was executed in Sing Sing's electric chair, she had her hair meticulously curled.

The lonely hearts murders led to the tightening of restrictions on the operations of lonely hearts clubs, but most lawmakers conceded little safeguards could be established to protect foolish and romantic people from being swindled and even killed for love's sake.

Becker, Charles E. (1869–1915) corrupt policeman and murderer

In the 1890s novelist Stephen Crane witnessed a tall, brawny policeman walk up to a prostitute and start beating her to a pulp when she refused to share the proceeds of her last business transaction. Crane would write about this brutish patrolman in his novel titled *Maggie: A Girl of the Streets,* but the real-life officer, Charles Becker, would go on to commit far worse offenses. Becker was known as "the crookedest cop who ever stood behind a shield," no mean accomplishment in the sordid history of New York City police corruption.

He rose to the rank of lieutenant, became personal assistant to dapper police commissioner Rhinelander Waldo, perhaps the most inept holder of that office before or since, and was in charge of the department's special crime squad. In addition to his police function, Becker was also the protégé of Tammany Hall leader Tim Sullivan and aspired to succeed him. Becker used his position to handle all payoffs to the police and politicians from gamblers, prostitutes and other vice operators. His special squad as well as outside gangsters were employed to enforce the payoff rules, providing protection to those who paid and retribution to those who refused.

One gambler who attempted to stand up to Becker was Herman Rosenthal, who ran a betting joint on West 45th Street. Fearful that Rosenthal would set a bad example for other gamblers, Becker kept intensive pressure on him, but the tactic boomeranged. Rosenthal started telling his troubles to reporter Herbert Bayard Swope of the *New York World* and to Charles S. Whitman, Republican district attorney of Manhattan. Soon, Becker realized his position was threatened. He turned to his top underworld henchman, Big Jack Zelig, to take care of Rosenthal before he did any more talking. At the moment, Zelig was in jail, but Becker used his influence to free him. Zelig then arranged for four gunmen—Gyp the Blood, Lefty Louie, Dago Frank and Whitey Lewis—to handle the hit.

The four botched a few attempts, and the frightened Rosenthal sent word to Becker and Zelig that he was finished talking and would leave New York. However, Rosenthal had already talked too much, and on July 16, 1912 the four killers brought him down in a fusillade of bullets outside the Hotel Metropole on West 43rd Street.

An investigation was ordered, and Commissioner Waldo put Becker in charge. With amazing nerve, Becker instructed the police to "lose" the license number of the murderers' car and even attempted to hide an eyewitness to the crime in a police station jail cell. Through a tipster, District Attorney Whitman learned of the witness and, with the help of his own investigators, seized him in a scuffle in the station house.

Eventually, the killers were caught and, in hope of saving their own necks, talked, implicating Zelig. Zelig, in turn, realized his best chance to avoid execution also lay in talking, and he informed on Becker. Allowed free on bail, Zelig was shot and killed by another gangster. However, Whitman, who saw the Rosenthal case as a way of purging police graft and perhaps promoting himself into the governorship, still presented enough evidence to have the four killers convicted and sentenced to death and convicted Becker of being the instigator of the killing.

Becker was granted a new trial amid clear indications that Whitman had promised rewards to various prosecution witnesses in return for their aid in convicting a police officer. Nonetheless, he was found guilty once again and was sentenced to death. As Becker's execution date drew near, his only hope was to obtain clemency from the governor, but unfortunately for him, Whitman had since been elected to that office. He ignored a plea from Becker's wife, who remained faithful to her husband to the end.

Becker's friends insisted that he had been "jobbed" and, whatever his sins, had not masterminded the Rosenthal murder. After Becker was electrocuted on July 7, 1915, in what was probably Sing Sing's clumsiest execution, his wife had attached to the top of his coffin a silver plate with the following inscription:

CHARLES BECKER
MURDERED JULY 7, 1915
BY GOVERNOR WHITMAN

The plate was finally removed when the police convinced Mrs. Becker that she could be prosecuted for criminal libel.

Bender family mass murderers

The Hell Benders, as they came to be called, were the most murderous family America ever produced. They robbed as a family, killed as a family and may well have been slaughtered together as a family. When the Benders moved into Cherryvale in southeastern Kansas during the early 1870s, no one thought ill of them, and in fact, most of the young blades around were much impressed by the beauty of young Kate Bender, whose age was around 18 or 20.

The family consisted of Old Man William John, aged about 60, Ma Bender (no Christian name has ever been ascribed to her), young Kate and her brother, John, who, while older in years, was certainly less mature mentally than his sister. He was actually a moron whose main activity in life appeared to be cackling insanely.

The family maintained a log cabin outside of town consisting of one large room divided by a canvas curtain. They served drink and meals to travelers on one side of the curtain and slept on the other side. At night, they set up some beds on the public side to put up travelers wishing to stay the night. If they served meals to someone they knew, the Benders were most hospitable and sent them cheerfully on their way. However, if the patron was a lone traveler and looked like he had money, he never left the Bender cabin alive. Kate would sit him down on a bench against the canvas curtain and presumably flirt with him until he was smitten—in the most literal sense of the word. Either Old Man Bender or moronic John would be on the other side of the canvas, and when they made out the outline of the man's head, they would bash it in with a sledgehammer.

The dead man would be taken down to the cellar through a trap door and stripped of all money and valuables. Later, the victim would be buried on the grounds around the house, and Ma Bender would plant flowers over the spot.

The Benders' last victim was a Dr. William H. York of Fort Scott, Kan. Passing through Cherryvale in March 1873, he asked for a place where he could eat and perhaps stay the night and was directed to the Benders'. When he disappeared, his brother, a lawyer named Col. A. M. York, followed his trail. He traced Dr. York to Cherryvale and no further. The Benders told Col. York that his brother had never come to their place. Kate Bender invited the colonel to sit a while and she would fix him a cup of tea. She offered him a seat by the canvas, but York said he wanted to ride on past Cherryvale to see if he could pick up his brother's trail. Then John came in with a jug of cider and suggested the lawyer have a swig before leaving. York refused the offer and said he wanted to cover some ground before night fell. If he failed to pick up his brother's trail, he announced, he would be coming back.

The next day a neighbor rode past the Bender place and noted the door was open and the family wagon nowhere in sight. He went inside and discovered the Benders had gone, belongings and all. When Col.York returned to Cherryvale, the trail gone cold, he was informed of the facts. A group of men went out to the Bender place. They looked in the cellar and found some loose dirt there. They dug and discovered the body of Dr. York.

They started digging around the cabin and found 10 other bodies, all with their skulls crushed. The Benders had something like a two-day start, but if they were in their wagon, they still might be caught. A posse of seven men headed by Col. York started out to scour the surrounding area in the hopes of finding the fugitive family. When they came back some weeks later, they said they had failed to find the Benders. But the posse members were downright uncommunicative about where they had been; they didn't seem to want to talk about it. Col. York lost interest in hunting for the murderous family and took his brother's body with him for reburial.

The news of the Hell Benders spread from coast to coast. Souvenir hunters descended on Cherryvale and soon leveled the Bender place to the ground. Nails and boards said to be from the Benders' house sold for high prices in New York and San Francisco. Months passed, then years, but none of the four Benders turned up. Of course, there was a rash of false identifications. In 1889 Leroy Dick of Cherryvale traveled to Michigan and identified Mrs. Almira Griffith and her daughter, Mrs. Sarah Eliza Davis, as Ma Bender and Kate. They were returned to Kansas, and out of 13 persons, seven agreed with Dick's identification. Proof was then produced that one of the women had been married in Michigan in 1872, and the case against the two women was dropped. There were a number of other false identifications, all of which proved unreliable.

In 1909 George Downer lay dying in a Chicago suburb. He called for his lawyer, and in his last hour, Downer told the lawyer and his wife that he had been a member of the posse that had killed the Benders. After catching up with them, the posse had butchered the family so badly they felt they could not reveal the facts; they therefore buried the Benders in a 20-foot well and covered them over with dirt. In 1910 a man named Harker, dying in a New Mexico cow camp, confessed he too had helped kill the Benders. He also mentioned the 20-foot well—at that time Downer's confession had not yet become common knowledge. Harker said the posse had taken several thousand dollars from the bodies of the Benders, money they believed to have been stolen from the victims. As late as 1940 the same story surfaced from another source, George Stark, who said his late father had made an identical confession to him but had pledged him to secrecy until after his death.

Were the confessions true? After the 1909 and 1910 confessions a search was made for the well in the area identified by Downer and Harker. But the area had long since been planted with corn. If the Benders were there, they had been plowed under.

Of all the missing members of the Hell Benders, William "Old Man" Bender (c. 1813–1884?) is worth special mention since, if any of the family did survive the manhunt for them and was not killed, it was the elder Bender. If that was what happened, Old Man Bender died in 1884, 11 years after he had fled Kansas. In that year an aged individual who answered to his description and spoke with a German accent, as Bender had, was seized in the Montana Territory for a murder near Salmon, Idaho Territory. The victim's skull had been crushed from behind with a blunt instrument. The method, plus the suspect's physical appearance and the fact that he grew sullen when the name Bender was mentioned, convinced the arresting officers that they had the much-sought Old Man Bender.

The suspect was clamped in ankle irons and tossed in the Salmon jail while the authorities back in Kansas were notified to send someone to make an identification. The next morning the old man was dead. In a desperate effort to escape, he had tried to cut off his foot and had bled to death. Since there was no ice house in town, the sheriff's deputies tried to preserve the body in a calcifying pool. It didn't work, and by the time witnesses arrived from Kansas, identification was no longer possible.

However, since it seemed like a waste to give up such an attraction as a heinous murderer, the dead man's skull, identified as "Bender's skull," was put on display in the Buckthorn Saloon in Salmon, where it remained, an object of many toasts, until the onset of Prohibition in 1920. Then it, like the rest of the Benders, disappeared.

Billington, John (?–1630) America's first murderer

Even before the Pilgrims landed at Plymouth Rock in 1620, Capt. Miles Standish had already had his fill of one John Billington aboard the *Mayflower*. Standish reprimanded Billington, a foul-mouthed brawler from the London slums, and eventually was forced to make an example of the man by having his feet and neck tied together. There is no evidence that this punishment had any lasting effect on Billington, who became the scourge of the Plymouth colony, starting feuds with a number of settlers.

One Pilgrim who refused to knuckle under to Billington's bullying was John Newcomen, a neighbor, and the pair became mortal enemies. Finally, one day in 1630 Billington ambushed Newcomen while he was out in the woods hunting, shooting him dead with a blunderbuss from behind a rock. Billington was quickly seized, tried by the Pilgrims and summarily hanged. Ironically, many Americans today proudly trace their ancestry back to the *Mayflower* and Billington, the American colonies' first murderer.

Blackbeard (?–1718) pirate

No pirate in American history enjoys quite as ferocious a reputation as Edward Teach (or Thack or Thatch) of the 14 wives and the pigtailed beard. A contemporary pirate historian, Capt. Charles Johnson, offered the following description:

> *This beard was black, which he suffered to grow of an extravagant length, as to breadth,*

An old print depicts the bloody end of Blackbeard the Pirate.

> *it came up to his eyes. He was accustomed to twist it with ribbons, in small tails . . . and turn them about his ears. In time of action he wore a sling over his shoulders, with three brace of pistols hanging in holsters like bandoliers, and stuck slow-burning lighted matches under his hat, which, appearing on each side of his face, his eyes naturally looking fierce and wild, made him altogether such a figure that imagination cannot form an idea of a fury from hell to look more frightful.*

Not much is known about Blackbeard's early life. He was generally believed to have been born in Bristol, England, although some claimed he was from Jamaica or the Carolinas and "of very creditable parents." Blackbeard himself boasted his parents were even bigger rascals than he, keeping a grogshop and specializing in giving sailors knockout drops and then shanghaiing them. In any event, Blackbeard went to sea at a young age and served on English privateers during Queen Anne's War (1702–13), eventually gathering a group of cutthroats on a ship of his own. When peace came, Blackbeard turned pirate and came to command five ships and crews totaling 400 to 500. By 1716 Blackbeard enjoyed the protection of Gov. Charles Eden of Carolina, who thereafter shared in a portion of the booty taken. Blackbeard preyed on shipping all along the American coast line from New England down to the West Indies. In one of his more daring raids, he once blockaded the port of Charleston,

S.C., finally accepting a ransom in drugs and medications.

Under a pardon granted by Gov. Eden, Blackbeard became a familiar figure in what is now North Carolina. At the time he had 13 wives, scattered around various ports. In Bath, N.C. he took bride number 14, a blond-haired girl just turned 15. The marriage barely outlasted the honeymoon when Blackbeard brought a number of his ruffians along for a visit at his new in-laws' plantation. His young wife finally fled and hid with friends. Despite the pirates' lavish spending, the people of Bath soon were disenchanted with Blackbeard, finding that he and his crew made free with their houses and women and demanded all kinds of requisitions from them. Despairing because of the pirate's close ties to the royal governor, several Carolinians appealed to Gov. Alexander Spotswood of Virginia for help. Spotswood could not interfere in another colony but resolved to do something about Blackbeard at sea, since the pirate was notorious for attacking Virginian shipping. Spotswood commissioned a young lieutenant named Robert Maynard to conduct a hunt. Maynard finally located the pirate at anchor near Ocracoke Island, off North Carolina. On November 21, 1718 Blackbeard was killed in a fierce battle in which he took five bullets and 25 cutlass wounds before a seaman struck him from behind and sliced his head off. When Maynard sailed back to Virginia, Blackbeard's bloody head was hung by the hair from the bowsprit of his ship for all to see.

Stories of Blackbeard's buried treasure have tantalized fortune hunters for 250 years. Legend places some of his many hoards in such locations as Ocracoke Island; the Isles of Shoals off New Hampshire; Plum Point, N.C.; under the Blackbeard Tree on the island of New Providence in the Bahamas; Ossabaw Island, Ga.; under a walnut in Burlington, N.J.; and the island of Trinidad. None has ever been found.

Bolber-Petrillo murder ring

The Bolber-Petrillo murder ring, which reaped a fortune from insurance killings in the Italian community of Philadelphia during the 1930s, is an excellent example of why murder statistics are not to be trusted. The ring disposed of an estimated 30 to 50 victims before police suspicions over just one or two brought about the killers' downfall. From a statistical viewpoint, the case is often cited as an indication that the generally accepted figure of 20,000 murder victims a year may be greatly understated and that a truer figure would be 20,000 known homicides a year and 20,000 undiscovered ones.

Neither Dr. Morris Bolber nor his two cousins, Paul and Herman Petrillo, were much interested in such a statistical overview, being content to rake in a goodly income from the occupation of murder during the Depression, a period when most forms of business were hardly rewarding.

The original murder scheme was hatched by Dr. Bolber and Paul Petrillo in 1932, when they decided to have Petrillo seduce Mrs. Anthony Giscobbe, the wife of one of the doctor's patients. The woman had often complained to Dr. Bolber of her husband's infidelities. When she fell in love with Petrillo, she also rather enthusiastically agreed to a plan to kill her husband for the $10,000 insurance on his life. Since the errant Mr. Giscobbe often staggered home dead drunk, it was a relatively simple matter to undress him and leave him all night by an open window in the dead of winter. Eventually, the husband succumbed to pneumonia, and the grieving widow and Dr. Bolber each netted $5,000. Perhaps the only sad development for the widow was that immediately upon completion of this financial transaction, Paul Petrillo lost all amorous interest in her. The slick-haired Petrillo had moved on to conquer new lonely wives, all of whom had husbands not long for this world.

Since the plotters found that few Italian husbands carried much, if any, insurance, they decided to add a new wrinkle to the operation by recruiting Petrillo's cousin, Herman Petrillo, an actor of some accomplishment with church groups, to impersonate the husbands and apply for insurance. Naturally, the wives were required to screen their husbands' mail and weed out all insurance correspondence. After a few premium payments were made, the husbands were efficiently dispatched. A roofer named Lorenzo was heaved off an eight-story building by the Petrillos in an on-the-job accident that doubled the payment on his life. To make the death more convincing, the Petrillos gave the roofer some French postcards before shoving him off the roof, making it rather obvious that the victim had been distracted by them when he misstepped.

After a dozen or so murders, the plotters recruited a valuable new accomplice, Carino Favato, a faith healer known as the Witch in her own bailiwick. The Witch had murdered three of her own husbands and apparently been consulted by female clients who wished to be rid of their spouses. The Witch poisoned them for a price. However, when Dr. Bolber pointed out that she had erred grievously by not adding the insurance wrinkle to the operation, the Witch was duly impressed, readily agreed to a liaison and was able to supply the names of quite a few potential victims.

The ring went busily about committing murder, most often by poison or by Dr. Bolber's favorite method, "natural means," a canvas bag filled with sand that, when artfully applied, caused a fatal cerebral hemorrhage without any telltale marks. By 1937 the ring's death toll may easily have approached 50, at least 30 of which were rather well documented later on.

A recently released convict in need of money called on Herman Petrillo with a scheme by which they could both make money. Herman was not impressed, mainly because he already had a very good thing going. "Dig up somebody we can murder for some insurance and you can make some dough with us," he told the ex-convict earnestly. The ex-con was frightened of murder and informed the police. The ring's members were rounded up, and with unseemly eagerness, each agreed to inform on all the others in the hope of gaining leniency. Although some wives went to prison, others were permitted to turn state's evidence. Dr. Bolber and the Witch were sentenced to life imprisonment and the Petrillos were executed.

Bonnie and Clyde public enemies

As professional thieves, Bonnie and Clyde—Bonnie Parker and Clyde Barrow—never qualified as public enemies. Most of their thefts were of the minor-league variety: grocery stores, filling stations, luncheonettes and a few small-town banks. Their greatest haul was no more than $3,500. But they were brutal, killing at least 13 persons and escaping police ambushes with incredible pluck.

In a sense, Clyde Barrow was cut from a heroic mold, unlike many other gangsters of the 1930s, such as Baby Face Nelson, Pretty

Bonnie and Clyde are snapped in a playful mood. Gag photos such as these did much to capture the public's attention.

Boy Floyd and even John Dillinger. When trapped, he never abandoned his woman, often fighting his way back to her and leading her to safety. It was an odd relationship: a homosexual and a near nymphomaniac.

Born in extreme poverty in Texas in 1909, Clyde followed his older brother into crime, first stealing turkeys and then graduating to cars. The pair committed several robberies in the Dallas area. Finally, after holding up a gas station in Denton, Tex., they were forced to make a 90-mile-an-hour run from the police with Clyde behind the wheel. Buck was shot during the chase, and when Clyde wrecked the car in a ditch, he left Buck for the law, fearing his brother would bleed to death otherwise. Buck got five years.

In January 1930 Clyde met 90-pound, golden-haired 19-year-old Bonnie Parker, who was "sort of married" to a convict, Roy Thornton, serving 99 years for murder. Bonnie described herself in that period as "bored crapless." They started living together, and Clyde tried to support them by playing the saxophone. It was a futile effort and he quickly reverted to robbery. It wasn't long before Dallas lawmen arrested Clyde for a burglary in Waco: he had left his fingerprints behind. The judge sentenced him to two years.

Buck Barrow escaped from prison, and he and his wife, Blanche, joined up with Bonnie. On a visit soon afterwards, Bonnie passed a narrow-handle .38 Colt through the jail bars to Clyde. After he made his break, Bonnie stayed put for a while to keep the law occupied. The law caught up with Clyde in Ohio.

This time Barrow was sent to the prison farm at Eastham, Tex., one of the most brutal institutions in the state. Clyde endured many tortures there and became a far more hardened criminal and a confirmed homosexual. He served 20 months, gaining a pardon after his mother tearfully pleaded his cause with Gov. Ross Sterling. Clyde Barrow said he would never see the inside of a prison again. "I'll die first," he said, and he was right.

Following Clyde's release, Bonnie teamed up with him on various robberies, but after a confrontation with the police, they became separated and Bonnie was caught. She served three months for the robbery of a car the couple had seized trying to escape. Clyde went on committing robberies and killed his first two lawmen in Atoka, Okla.

When Bonnie rejoined him, they fell in with a gunman named Ray Hamilton, an incorrigible young thief and killer who in many ways was a more spectacular criminal than Clyde. His relationship with Bonnie and Clyde, however, was more meaningful than just the addition of greater firepower on their holdups. Hamilton regularly slept with Bonnie and at times with Clyde as well. It was, by all accounts, a well-adjusted triangle, at least for brief periods. Eventually, the sexual pressures probably became too much for the three, and Hamilton broke away. Both Bonnie and Clyde apparently needed a more submissive love partner; Hamilton was just too tough to give them their way. After leaving them the last time, he pulled off a long string of crimes and several jailbreaks before finally dying in the electric chair in 1935.

While Bonnie and Clyde's robberies continued to be on the minor side, their escapades were often extremely violent. They stuck up a butcher, and when the man came at Clyde with a cleaver, Clyde avoided the blow and emptied his gun into him. In November 1932 the pair held up a filling station and kidnapped the attendant, William Daniel Jones. After learning who his captors were, Jones joined up with them and replaced Ray Hamilton in their affections. He later described his experience as "18 months of hell."

Meanwhile, Buck Barrow had been in and out of jail again, this time pardoned by the new governor, Mrs. Miriam "Ma" Ferguson, who had granted pardons to some 2,000 felons during an earlier term. With Buck and Blanche in tow, the gang now numbered five and was ready for the big time. Brandishing newly obtained machine guns, they held up a loan company office in Kansas City. They had been identified, and their exploits made front-page news from coast to coast, which pleased Bonnie no end. She deluged newspapers with samples of her "poetry." Editors eagerly printed her poem "The Story of Suicide Sal." They also printed pictures of her smoking a cigar and brandishing a machine gun. Bonnie said these were "horsing around" pictures and resented the light in which the newspapers had put them. During their getaways the gang often kidnapped lawmen, one of whom was chief of police Percy Boyd. When they let him go, Bonnie told Boyd: "Tell the public I don't smoke cigars. It's the bunk."

They fought their way out of a trap in Joplin, Mo., killing two officers, but it was apparent that the gang could not continue to escape capture or death. In July 1933 the gang was hiding out in the deserted fair grounds in Dexter, Iowa when a posse closed in. Buck Barrow was fatally wounded and Blanche captured. Bonnie and Jones were also wounded, but Clyde got both of them away.

In the next few months, Bonnie and Clyde killed four more lawmen. During this period Jones took the first opportunity to desert them. When picked up in late 1933, he told of his incredible career of crime and suffering with the pair and begged to be sent to prison, where he would be safe from Bonnie and Clyde. The law obliged.

Bonnie knew the end was near. She mailed newspapers "The Ballad of Bonnie and Clyde," which concluded:

The road gets dimmer and dimmer,
Sometimes you can hardly see,
Still it's fight man to man,
And do all you can,
For they know they can never be free.

If they try to act like citizens,
And rent them a nice little flat,

About the third night they are invited
to fight,
By a submachine-gun rat-tat-tat.

They don't think they are too tough or
desperate,
They know the law always wins,
They have been shot at before
But they do not ignore
That death is the wages of sin.

From heartbreaks some people
have suffered,
From weariness some people have died,
But take it all and all,
Our troubles are small,
Till we get like Bonnie and Clyde.

Some day they will go down together,
And they will bury them side by side.
To a few it means grief,
To the law it's relief
But it's death to Bonnie and Clyde.

The pair stayed on the run until May 23, 1934, when they attempted to hook up with Henry Methvin, a convict they had freed once while busting out Ray Hamilton in a daring prison raid. With the law closing in on all sides, they felt Methvin was the only one left outside of family whom they could trust. But Methvin sold them out, informing the law about a roadside rendezvous he was to have with them. In exchange, he was not prosecuted for charges pending against him in Louisiana and Texas.

A trap was set up at Gibland, La., near the Texas border, under the command of Capt. Frank Hamer of the Texas Highway Patrol, an ex–Texas Ranger who for the past three and a half months had been assigned exclusively to tracking down Bonnie and Clyde. Hamer and five other lawmen waited at an embankment armed with a Browning automatic rifle, three automatic shotguns and two rifles.

Bonnie and Clyde drove up to the rendezvous site. Clyde was driving in his socks; Bonnie was munching on a sandwich. They had in their car a shotgun, a revolver, 11 pistols, three Browning automatic rifles and 2,000 rounds of ammunition.

There is some argument about whether they were given a chance to surrender or even knew they had run into a trap. The lawmen opened fire and the pair died instantly. They dug 25 bullets out of Clyde and 23 out of Bonnie.

Botkin, Cordelia (1854–1910) poisoner

A poisoner convicted in one of the most sensational trials of the 1890s, Cordelia Botkin may well have been, as the Sunday supplement writers later referred to her, the original Red Hot Mama. Certainly her triangle love affair earned her a reputation as a truly wanton woman as well as a murderess.

A stocky, fleshy woman living in San Francisco, she nonetheless seemed to have all the charms necessary to lure a successful journalist named John Presley Dunning away from his wife and child for a life of gambling and whoring. In 1896 Dunning's wife had had enough and returned to her parents in Dover, Del. While that should have pleased Botkin, she still feared Dunning's wife might someday lure him back, and she deluged Mrs. Dunning with anonymous threatening letters, advising her against trying to rejoin her husband.

In 1898 Dunning got an assignment covering the Spanish-American War, and Botkin grew more certain he would not return to her. Her depression gave way to murderous thoughts. She went out and bought a box of chocolates, a lace handkerchief and two ounces of arsenic. She spent several hours inserting arsenic into each piece of candy. She enclosed the handkerchief and a note that read "With love to yourself and baby—Mrs. C." and tied up the whole package with pink ribbons. The next day she mailed the "gift" to Mrs. Mary Dunning in Delaware.

When the box arrived, Mrs. Dunning puzzled over the identity of the "Mrs. C." who had sent the candy. She thought of several people it might have been. But having a sweet tooth, she didn't hesitate long before polishing off the box. Her sister, Mrs. Joshua Deane, joined in. Twenty-four hours later both women were dead. The deaths did not help Botkin's lovelife, however, because the box of candy was eventually traced back to her in San Francisco.

After a lurid trial that satisfied even the most avid readers of the sensational press, she was found guilty of murder on December 31, 1898 and sentenced to life imprisonment. She died in San Quentin in 1910.

Brady gang public enemies

Although they are little remembered now, the Brady gang were the most sought criminals in the United States following the fall of such 1930s gangsters as Dillinger, Baby Face Nelson, Pretty Boy Floyd, Bonnie and Clyde, and the Barker-Karpis mob. By eradicating the Brady gang, the FBI disarmed the critics of its methods. Before that, J. Edgar Hoover had been attacked on the floor of the U.S. Senate as being a personal coward, the FBI had been criticized for killing John Dillinger without giving him a "chance"; and when Hoover made his famed foray to New Orleans to arrest Alvin Karpis personally, the newspapers gleefully reported that none of the host of FBI agents making the arrest had thought of bringing along a pair of handcuffs.

The Brady gang began in Indiana during the early 1930s, when three former lonewolves—Al Brady, Clarence Shaffer and James Dalhover—teamed up to terrorize the Midwest. While the other public enemies fell one by one, Brady and his two friends left a trail of holdups of banks and other establishments during which they killed two clerks and three police officers. They had been captured once but had escaped jail and by the end of 1937 were the most hunted men in the country. Feeling the "heat," the trio moved into virgin territory in Maine. In October 1937 they entered a sporting goods store in Bangor and asked for two revolvers of a certain make. The clerk waiting on them recognized the three as the Brady gang and said the weapons would be in stock the following week. On October 12, 1937 the trio returned and were recognized by an employee, who immediately pulled a hidden cord that caused a suspended show card to drop in the store window. At that instant four FBI men, guns drawn, jumped from hiding places under the counter and surprised the gangsters, who turned and charged out the door. They were immediately hit with a hail of bullets fired by 16 other FBI agents hidden across the street. Brady and Shaffer died instantly; Dalhover lived long enough to be executed. More important, the FBI received no criticism for the ambush of the gang. In part, that was because none of the gangsters ever exhibited the verve and flair of John Dillinger. But it was also true that the public took the Brady gang for what they were, brutal murderers. The days of romanticizing public enemies were over.

Briggen, Joseph (c. 1850–1903) mass murderer

One of this country's most awesome mass murderers, Joseph Briggen committed his crimes for many years on a small ranch in a remote California valley.

Briggen barely made a living on his Sierra Morena Ranch. Certainly he was never prosperous enough to keep more than one hired hand at a time. In fact, were it not for his prime Berkshire swine, for which he almost invariably won the coveted blue ribbon at the state fair in Sacramento, Briggen's ranching would probably have been considered a total loss.

At state fair time, however, he was in his glory, his prize swine attracting top dollar. When he was asked about how he raised them, Briggen would say the secret was all in their care and feeding. But his recipe for the latter was something he would share with no one, other than to say they got prime feed only.

There was good reason for Briggen to guard his secret. The truth was a grisly story. He hired homeless men as his helpers, recruiting them on a customary trip to the Embarcadero section of San Francisco. A down-and-outer would jump at the chance for a good job with room and board, and Briggen could keep him several weeks if not months before the man would demand his back pay. Then Briggen would kill him, chop up the body and feed it to his prize swine. In his twisted mind, Briggen had become convinced it was this diet of human flesh that made his swine prize winners. He was finally exposed in early 1902, when his newest hired hand, a youth named Steve Korad, who had arrived very enthusiastic about finding work, looked around his room and found two severed human fingers from a previous victim that Briggen had carelessly dropped behind the bed. Korad raced off in the night and notified the law. When authorities dug up Briggen's ranch, their search turned up the bones of at least a dozen victims, but they were sure they had not found them all. The pigpen itself yielded up several bones, including one dead man's skull.

Briggen was convicted in August 1902 and sentenced to life. He died in San Quentin shortly thereafter.

Buccieri, Fiore "Fifi" (1904–1973)

syndicate killer

A top enforcer for the Chicago syndicate, Fiore "Fifi" Buccieri was considered to be mob leader Sam Giancana's personal hit man. No complete record of Fifi's kills have been recorded, although federal agents who had bugged a house in Florida being used to plan a murder heard Buccieri reminisce about a number of killings. Among other principles he espoused was that ammunition for shotguns used in an assassination should be "fresh." Fifi was particularly lighthearted about the gruesome demise of William "Action" Jackson, a 300-pound collector for the mob's loansharking operation who was suspected of holding out some of the money and of being an informant for federal authorities. Jackson was hung from a meat hook, stripped and shot in the knee. Then, Buccieri recalled, the boys decided "to have a little bit of fun." Jackson was worked over with ice picks, baseball bats and a blow torch. Fifi got hold of an electric cattle prod and jammed it up Jackson's rectum. The fat victim lived for two days, but even at that, Fifi was "sorry the big slob died so soon." Buccieri took photographs of the mutilated corpse and passed them around as reminders to other mobsters not to stray from mob rule.

Fifi was a graduate of Chicago's worst juvenile gang, the 42ers. He was a hulking, gravel-voiced punk who attracted younger kids by his dapper dress and his affection of wearing wide-brimmed hats similar to those worn by movie gangsters. He attached himself to another up-and-coming 42er, Sam Giancana, who eventually rose to the top position in the Chicago outfit. Fifi became Giancana's personal executioner and his loyal ally during the power struggles for mob leadership.

The law never made Buccieri crack. During one federal probe investigators tried to elicit mob information by questioning Fifi about his brother Frank, also involved in mob affairs. They even questioned Fifi about the fact that his brother had a girlfriend who had been a Playboy bunny and a centerfold nude in *Playboy* magazine and that he had given her a horse as a present. Fifi's answer, which became a classic in underworld circles was, "I take the Fifth on the horse and the broad."

Fifi died of cancer in 1973, and Giancana was assassinated two years later. There was speculation at the time that the mob—if the Giancana killing was a mob caper and not a CIA operation, as the underworld has insisted—would never have dared move against Giancana while Fifi Buccieri was alive.

Buchalter, Louis "Lepke" (1897–1944)

syndicate leader and murderer

The only national crime czar and kingpin of the rackets ever to go to the electric chair, Louis "Lepke" Buchalter graduated from sneak thievery during his youth on New York's Lower East Side to become one of the founders of the national crime syndicate.

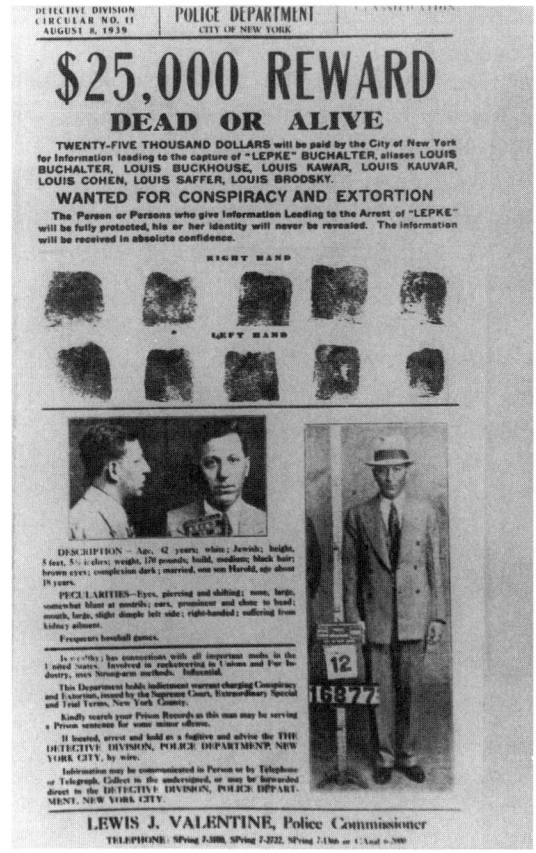

DETECTIVE DIVISION
CIRCULAR NO. 11
AUGUST 8, 1939

POLICE DEPARTMENT
CITY OF NEW YORK

$25,000 REWARD

DEAD OR ALIVE

TWENTY-FIVE THOUSAND DOLLARS will be paid by the City of New York for Information leading to the capture of "LEPKE" BUCHALTER, aliases LOUIS BUCHALTER, LOUIS BUCKHOUSE, LOUIS KAWAR, LOUIS KAUVAR, LOUIS COHEN, LOUIS SAFFER, LOUIS BRODSKY.

WANTED FOR CONSPIRACY AND EXTORTION

The Person or Persons who give Information Leading to the Arrest of "LEPKE" will be fully protected, his or her identity will never be revealed. The information will be received in absolute confidence.

RIGHT HAND

LEFT HAND

DESCRIPTION – Age, 42 years; white; Jewish; height, 5 feet, 5½ inches; weight, 170 pounds; build, medium; black hair; brown eyes; complexion dark; married, one son Harold, age about 18 years.

PECULIARITIES—Eyes, piercing and shifting; nose, large, somewhat blunt at nostrils; ears, prominent and close to head; mouth, large, slight dimple left side; right-handed; suffering from kidney ailment.

Frequents baseball games.

Is wealthy; has connections with all important mobs in the United States. Involved in racketeering in Unions and Fur Industry, uses Strongarm methods. Influential.

This Department holds indictment warrant charging Conspiracy and Extortion, issued by the Supreme Court, Extraordinary Special and Trial Terms, New York County.

Kindly search your Prison Records as this man may be serving a Prison sentence for some minor offense.

If located, arrest and hold as a fugitive and advise the THE DETECTIVE DIVISION, POLICE DEPARTMENT, NEW YORK CITY, by wire.

Information may be communicated in Person or by Telephone or Telegraph. Collect to the undersigned, or may be forwarded direct to the DETECTIVE DIVISION, POLICE DEPARTMENT, NEW YORK CITY.

LEWIS J. VALENTINE, Police Commissioner

TELEPHONE: SPring 7-3000, SPring 7-2222, SPring 7-1300 or CAnal 6-3000

The manhunt for Louis "Lepke" Buchalter was among the most intensive ever, one that ended only when other leaders of organized crime betrayed him.

Through control of the tailors and cutters unions, Lepke milked millions from the New York garment industry. Part of Lepke's power sprung from his control of Murder, Inc., the Brooklyn "troop" of specialist killers who serviced the syndicate. Thus, Thomas E. Dewey referred to Lepke as "the worst industrial racketeer in America," and J. Edgar Hoover called him "the most dangerous criminal in the United States."

In the early 1920s, while most gangsters were attracted by the huge fortunes to be made in booze, Lepke chose a different route to underworld fame and wealth. He and another thug, Jacob "Gurrah" Shapiro, linked up with the era's top labor racketeer, "Little Augie" Orgen, to offer strike-breaking services to garment industry employers. Little Augie was shot dead in 1927, but Lepke and Shapiro prospered, especially after refining their operations so that they could serve both sides, assuming the added duties of union organizers and eventually taking control of union locals.

The union racketeers extended their operations to control the bakery drivers' union and levied a penny "tax" per loaf on bakers to guarantee their products got to market fresh. To greater or lesser degrees, Lepke moved into other industries, especially in league with Tommy Lucchese, a mobster with close ties to Lucky Luciano. Their extortion rackets expanded to tough on such businesses as handbags, shoes, millinery, poultry, cleaning and dyeing, leather, restaurants and others until it was estimated legitimate businesses were paying Lepke up to $10 million a year just so they could operate without trouble.

The Lucchese connection gave Lepke an "in" with the budding crime syndicate being formed by Luciano, Meyer Lansky, Frank Costello, Joe Adonis, Dutch Schultz and others. The new organization recognized the need for an enforcement branch within its framework. Lepke was put in charge of it, with Albert Anastasia as second in command. The choice of Anastasia was obvious; he was a madman whose philosophy could be summed up in three words—kill, kill, kill. And the election of Lepke over him was equally logical. Lepke was the greatest exponent of violence in the rackets; an associate once noted, "Lep loves to hurt people." Under Lepke and Anastasia the enforcement branch, later dubbed Murder, Inc. by the newspapers, carried out hundreds of hits for the syndicate.

Lepke courted trouble with the law, living lavishly and relishing the spotlight. Thomas Dewey, then an ambitious special prosecutor, zeroed in on him once he had convicted Luciano. And while Dewey went after him for bakery extortion, the federal government stalked him for restraint-of-trade violations. Then the federal Narcotics Bureau began gathering proof that Lepke was the head of a narcotics-smuggling operation that was involved in massive bribing of U.S. customs agents. Free on bail, Lepke decided to go into hiding. While a nationwide manhunt was organized to catch him, he continued to control his union rackets from various Brooklyn hideouts, where he was being hidden by Anastasia.

The continued manhunt, however, put extraordinary pressure on the entire syndicate and hamstrung their operations. Mayor Fiorello LaGuardia turned the screw even tighter by ordering his police commissioner, Lewis Valentine, to go to war on "hoodlums." The problem got so bad that it was brought to the attention of Luciano, then confined at Dannemora Prison but still the top voice in the organization. Luciano agreed that Lepke had to give himself up, but there was a problem: Lepke realized Dewey could convict him of enough charges to keep him in prison for life. Therefore, Luciano decided that Lepke would have to be fooled into surrendering. He arranged for an emissary Lepke trusted, Moe "Dimples" Wolensky, to carry a message that a deal had been worked out with J. Edgar Hoover whereby if he surrendered directly to the FBI chief, he would be tried on the federal narcotics charge only and not handed over to Dewey.

Lepke bought the story and surrendered on a Manhattan street to gossip columnist Walter Winchell and Hoover. As soon as he entered their car and Hoover spoke to him, Lepke realized he had been double-crossed. Lepke was convicted on federal charges of narcotics conspiracy and sentenced to 14 years at Leavenworth but was then turned over to Dewey who succeeded in getting another conviction that resulted in a 39-year-to-life sentence.

Unfortunately for Lepke, while he was behind bars, the story of Murder, Inc. broke, mainly because of information supplied by squealer Abe Reles, one of the group's leading killers. Lepke was tied in as the leader of the killer troop and was specifically linked to the 1936 murder of a Brooklyn candy store owner named Joe Rosen, a former trucker in the garment district who had been forced out of business by Lepke. Instead of bearing his loss in silence, Rosen began making noise about going to the district attorney's office. Lepke handed out a contract on Rosen to two of his chief aides, Mendy Weiss and Louis Capone, and to Pittsburgh Phil Strauss. Rosen ended up with 17 bullets in his corpse.

Even though Reles was killed in a mysterious fall from a window in a hotel where he was being kept under police guard, authorities had more than enough evidence to convict Lepke, Weiss and Capone (Strauss had already been sentenced to death for another murder). Through various appeals, Lepke staved off execution until March 1944. Shortly before his death the newspapers were filled with speculation that Lepke was talking about corrupt political and labor officials he had had dealings with and that if he really "opened up" he could blow the roof off the country, among other things delivering what one newspaper called "a prominent labor leader, powerful in national politics, as a man who had inspired several crimes." In thinly disguised sidebar stories, that labor leader was readily identifiable as Sidney Hillman, then an intimate adviser to President Franklin D. Roosevelt. Lepke himself was quoted as saying: "If I would talk, a lot of big people would get hurt. When I say big, I mean big. The names would surprise you." The *New York Mirror* reported, "It is said Lepke offered material to Governor Dewey that would make him an unbeatable presidential candidate."

On the afternoon of the execution, Lepke released his version of the facts. He had his wife read a statement that he had dictated: "I am anxious to have it clearly understood that I did not offer to talk and give information in exchange for any promise of commutation of my death sentence. I did not ask for that! . . . The one and only thing I have asked for is to have a commission appointed to examine the facts. If that examination does not show that I am not guilty, I am willing to go to the chair, regardless of what information I have given or can give."

Clearly Lepke had given some information, but it had not been enough, and now he was eager to inform the syndicate he was not going to talk about crime matters. If he did, he realized, no member of his family would be spared.

On March 4, 1944 Lepke silently followed Capone and Weiss to the chair.

See also: MURDER, INC.

Bundy, Ted (1947–1989) the charming human monster

The standard description of the average serial killer is that he has, especially in the eyes of neighbors, the behavior patterns of a

Ted Bundy struck a "Dracula" pose as the judge left the courtroom following a jury recommendation that Bundy be sentenced to die in the electric chair.

"creep." In some atypical instances, however, the serial killer comes across differently. Ted Bundy certainly belongs to this "different" class. As one journalist noted: "The moment he stepped into the courtroom in Utah . . . those who saw him for the first time agreed with those who had known him for all of his twenty-eight years. There must have been some terrible mistake."

It was no mistake, as Robert Keppel, an expert who worked on serial killer investigations, noted: "Bundy [later] said he had a Ph.D. in serial killing. He taught us that a serial killer can appear to be absolutely normal, the guy next door. It's very simple. He liked to kill."

Ted Bundy was to leave a scar on the American psyche from 1974 to 1989, when he was finally executed in Florida. His first batch of kills, eight of them, started in 1974, as young women disappeared from Seattle streets. They had been lured into a beige Volkswagen by a presentable young man named Ted. A police computer search turned up nearly 3,000 owners of light-colored Volkswagens in Seattle, and Bundy's name cropped up among them. But while many were questioned and checked on, Bundy was not. Why should he have been? He was of impeccable character, with numerous good points:

- He had worked as a counselor at a crisis clinic.
- He had become an assistant director of the Seattle Crime Prevention Advisory Commission.
- He had written a rape prevention pamphlet for women.
- He had gotten a letter of commendation from the governor of Washington for once capturing a purse snatcher in a shopping mall.

Bundy was very active in the Republican Party and won the title of Mr. Up-and-Coming Republican. A former state party chairman who knew Bundy well and recruited him as his assistant said: "If you can't trust someone like Ted Bundy, you can't trust anyone—your parents, your wife, anyone."

Presumably, Seattle lost a fine resource when Bundy left the area and moved on to Salt Lake City and became a Mormon. The killings followed him.

Bundy's first arrest came in October 1975 when a 19-year-old woman identified him in a police lineup as the man who had tried to handcuff her and pull her into his car one night in Murray, Utah. Bundy had been picked up for a traffic violation, and when handcuffs were found in the car, police thought back to the attempted kidnapping of the young woman. Bundy was convicted in the case and given a one- to 15-year prison sentence. While the case was pending, police in Colorado became convinced Bundy had murdered Caryn Campbell, a nurse who had been vacationing in Aspen almost a year earlier. Campbell had been missing for five weeks before her body turned up in a snowbank. She had been raped, bludgeoned to death and then ravaged almost beyond recognition by wild animals.

Bundy was extradited to Colorado but was never to stand trial for the Campbell murder. Instead he escaped twice. The first break occurred when Bundy was alone in a room in the county courthouse in Aspen. He jumped from a second-story window and disappeared, not to be recaptured until a week later. Although Bundy was charged with a vile crime, his exploit made him a folk hero in some quarters, a perverse public reaction expressed on future occasions. Six months later, still awaiting trial, Bundy outwitted his jailers again, this time wiggling through a lighting panel in the ceiling of his cell. The opening was only 18 inches wide, and in order to make good his escape, Bundy had managed to lose 35 pounds.

While authorities pressed their search for the fugitive, Bundy made his way across the country to Tallahassee, Fla. Using a phony name and stolen cars and credit cards, he moved into a rooming house on the outskirts of Florida State University. The lodging was just four blocks from the Chi Omega sorority house.

Less than two weeks after arriving in Florida, Bundy invaded the sorority house. He was dressed in black and carried a heavy wooden club. Two coeds were to die in the house. They were found to have been gnawed badly, but unlike Campbell, they bore bite marks not from wild animals but from their wild *human* attacker. Particularly gnawed up was Lisa Levy, who bore teeth marks on one of her breasts and on her buttocks. She had been beaten, bitten, and strangled in her bed. Another sorority member, Margaret Bowman, met the same grisly fate. The bite marks, investigators realized, were appalling evidence of the killer's psychotic fervor at the moment of the kills.

Levy and Bowman were not the only victims in the Chi Omega house that night. Another coed was also attacked and beaten unconscious, but she recovered. Meanwhile, Bundy moved on like a wraith in the night, and six blocks farther on, a young actress was beaten and raped in her bed. She also survived but could offer no description of her attacker.

During the ensuing investigation, several residents in Bundy's rooming house were suspected of the killings, although Bundy was not. Evidently, he was considered a cut above the rest. At the time, the fact that Bundy had very crooked teeth went unnoticed.

Three weeks after the sorority house invasion, Bundy stole a white van and drove to Jacksonville, where he attempted to abduct a 14-year-old girl. He was forced to drive off when the girl's brother appeared. The brother and sister were quick enough to make a note of the van's license plate.

Three days later, 12-year-old Kimberly Leach disappeared from her Lake City junior high school in the middle of the day. Her corpse was not found for two months. When it was discovered, Kimberly was described as having been the victim of "homicidal violence to the neck region."

By now, police in Washington State, Utah, Colorado and Florida were coming to grasp that a *single* killer was responsible for at least 18 murders in their jurisdictions. Bundy had been the prime suspect in the Campbell murder in Colorado, and he was now being sought for many others as well. He moved on to Pensacola, driving yet another stolen VW and unaware that the FBI had just listed him on its Ten Most Wanted list. The car Bundy was driving was recognized by police as a stolen vehicle, and he was seized when he tried to flee on foot. At first, the police did not know whom they had caught, as Bundy gave a false name. But they did know that he was involved somehow in other cases: They found the plates from the van in which the 14-year-old Jacksonville girl had nearly been abducted.

Thirty-six hours after Bundy's arrest, he was identified. The authorities had hit the jackpot.

Florida law officials charged Bundy with the murders of Lisa Levy and Margaret Bowman. An impression made of Bundy's teeth showed that his crooked bite marks matched perfectly those found on Lisa Levy's buttocks.

Bundy pleaded not guilty to the Chi Omega murders and once again was perversely celebrated by those with a twisted and maudlin viewpoint when, as an ex–law student, he conducted part of his own defense. It took the jury just seven hours to find Bundy guilty on a variety of counts. The teeth bite evidence was the most damning, but in addition, a hair in the panty hose mask worn during the attack on the actress the same night as the sorority house killings was found to be indistinguishable from Bundy's.

When asked if he had anything to say before sentencing, Bundy, with tears in his eyes, declared: "I find it somewhat absurd to ask for mercy for something I did not do. The sentence is not a sentence of me. It's a sentence of someone who is not standing here today." Bundy's mother was quoted as saying, "There will be appeal after appeal after appeal."

Even the judge exhibited a certain sympathy for Bundy when passing the death sentence, saying: "Take care of yourself, young man. I say that to you sincerely. It's a tragedy to this court to see such a total waste of humanity. You'd have made a good lawyer. I bear you no animosity, believe me. But you went the wrong way, partner. Take care of yourself." On a radio talk show one commentator wondered if the judge would have been pleased to have Bundy give his daughter driving lessons.

A year later, Bundy was convicted of the murder of Kimberly Leach, whose body had been found half-buried near a state park. The van he was driving at the time contained leaves and soil matching samples near the burial site. Also, bloodstains in the van matched the blood type of the murdered girl.

There were a number of appeals put forward by Bundy. In the process, he accumulated a large body of supporters, including a number of lawyers and journalists who had followed the trials.

The string ran out at last for Bundy in 1989. In a final interview, Bundy confessed to 28 additional murders. On the night of his electrocution, there were 100 newspeople circulating the crowd outside the prison. It was one of a few cases where those favoring execution far outnumbered those opposed.

Signs raised in celebration bore messages such as "Buckle up, Bundy, it's the law" and "roast in peace."

Burrow, Rube (1856–1890) train robber and murderer

Reuben Houston Burrow, the leader of the notorious Burrow gang of the 1880s, developed the same sort of mystique that Jesse James enjoyed. The balladeers and legend-makers, for instance, celebrated the time Rube and brother Jim drove off the miserly banker out to foreclose on a widow's mortgage; of course, they also robbed him for their own gain.

A daring criminal, Rube several times pulled off one of the most difficult of criminal endeavors: robbing a train single-handed. Generally, however, he worked with a gang that included his brother, James, another pair of brothers, Will and Leonard Brock, and various other "hard cases."

The Burrow brothers were born in Alabama and eventually moved to Texas, where they led rather tranquil existences as small farmers for about 14 years before suddenly turning to crime, perhaps because of tales they had heard about a so-called glamorous and lately lamented outlaw named Sam Bass. In any event, they went about robbing trains until they became the subject of ballads, especially after the brothers made a habit of robbing the same train at the same spot on a number of occasions. In February 1888 the Burrows were captured, but Rube broke jail and escaped. With an accomplice named Lewis Waldrip, who may have been Leonard Brock, Rube spent most of the next several months trying to break Jim Burrow out of his Little Rock, Ark. prison, but his brother died there from consumption in December. Forced eastward by his pursuers, Rube Barrow continued his train-robbing activities in Florida and Alabama. In 1890 he pulled one of his lone wolf jobs. As he confidently strode to his horse to ride off once more into the darkness, a Southern Express detective took his head off with a shotgun blast.

Campagna, Louis "Little New York"
(1900–1955) gangster

Considered by Al Capone to be his most reliable bodyguard, Louis "Little New York" Campagna was a stubby little mobster who, thanks more to his steel nerves than his brainpower, rose to the top echelon of syndicate crime.

During the Chicago mob's movie studio extortion days, Campagna walked into a jail and stiffened a wilting gang member, Willie Bioff, who had announced he wanted to quit the rackets. In a menacing voice few could equal, Campagna said, "Whoever quits us, quits feet first." Later, after Bioff cracked, sending several top syndicate men, including Campagna, to prison, Little New York always bemoaned the fact that his associates had vetoed a "feet first" proposal regarding Bioff.

Al Capone had imported Campagna in 1927 from New York, where he had cut his criminal teeth as a teenager in the Five Points Gang and been convicted of bank robbery at 19. Capone dubbed him Little New York merely to demonstrate his ability to import all the gunners he needed. Campagna soon demonstrated his nerve following an unsuccessful plot by the Aiello brothers to assassinate Capone. Shortly thereafter, Joseph Aiello and one of his gunmen were taken to the Chicago Detective Bureau lockup. Campagna promptly surrounded the bureau with a dozen gunmen, and he and two others approached the building, shifting weapons from holsters to side pockets. A policeman recognized Campagna and, realizing he was laying siege to the building, sounded the alarm. A score of detectives rushed out to seize the trio and hustled them into the building before their accomplices could come to their aid.

Campagna was lodged in a cell next to Aiello while a detective who understood the Sicilian dialect posed as a prisoner in another cell. He heard Campagna say: "You're dead, dear friend, you're dead. You won't get up to the end of the street still walking."

Aiello was quaking with fear. "Can't we settle this?" he pleaded. "Give me fourteen days and I'll sell my stores, my house and everything and quit Chicago for good. Can't we settle it? Think of my wife and baby."

Campagna was unmoved. "You dirty rat! You've broken faith with us twice now. You started this. We'll finish it."

It was no idle threat. When Aiello was later found shot down on the street, 59 slugs, more than a pound of bullets, were dug out of his body.

At the height of the assassination scare against Capone, the gang boss made Campagna his main bodyguard. At night, the devoted little killer slept on a cot just outside Capone's bedroom door. Anyone going in would have to climb over Campagna's body.

In the 1930s and early 1940s, Campagna became a key figure in the mob's union rackets and extortion plots against Hollywood movie studios. Along with six others, Campagna was convicted of conspiracy to extort $1 million from studio executives and sentenced to 10 years. He served one-third of his sentence and was paroled to a firestorm of protest by Chicago newspapers. In later years Campagna played the role of a gentleman farmer on an 800-acre spread near Fowler, Ind. He died of a heart attack aboard a pleasure cruiser off Miami in 1955.

Capone, Alphonse "Scarface Al"

(1899–1947) gang leader

Al Capone was a mindless, brutal and obscure Brooklyn hood in his teens, but by the age of 26 he had become the most powerful crime boss of his day and could boast that he "owned" Chicago, that city of gangsters, during the Prohibition years.

At its zenith the Capone mob had probably upward of 1,000 members, most of them experienced gunmen, but this represented only a portion of Capone's overall empire. Capone often proclaimed, "I own the police," and it was true. Few estimates would place less than half the police on the mob's payroll in one way or another. Capone's hold on the politicians was probably greater. He had "in his pocket" aldermen, state's attorneys, mayors, legislators, governors and even congressmen. The Capone organization's domination of Chicago and such suburban areas as Cicero, Ill. was absolute. When Capone wanted a big vote in elections, he got out the vote; when he wanted to control the election returns, his gangsters intimidated and terrorized thousands of voters. The politicians he put in power were expected to act the way the Big Fellow desired. The mayor of Cicero once took an independent action. Capone caught him on the steps of City Hall and beat him to a pulp; a police officer standing nearby had to look elsewhere to avoid seeing the violence.

Capone was born in Brooklyn in 1899 and attended school through the sixth grade, when he beat up his teacher, got beaten by the principal and quit. After that, he learned his lessons in the streets, especially with the tough teenage James Street gang, run by an older criminal, Johnny Torrio, as a subsidiary of the notorious Five Points Gang, to which Capone eventually graduated. Among his closest friends, both in school and in the gang, was a kid who grew up to become a major crime boss, Lucky Luciano, and the two remained lifelong friends.

When he was in his late teens, Capone was hired by Torrio as a bouncer in a saloon-brothel he ran in Brooklyn. Capone picked up a huge scar on his left cheek in an altercation with a tough hood named Frank Galluccio, who slashed him with a knife in a dispute about a girl. Later, Capone would claim he got the wound serving with the "Lost Battalion" in France during World War I, but he was never in the army.

In 1920 Torrio, who had relocated in Chicago to help his uncle, Big Jim Colosimo, the city's leading whoremaster, ply his trade, summoned Capone to come and help him. What Torrio wanted to do was take advantage of Prohibition and gain control of the booze racket, an endeavor that promised profits in the millions. But he was being thwarted by Colosimo, who was so rich and content he saw no need to expand. Torrio soon decided Colosimo would have to be eliminated so that he could use Big Jim's organization for his criminal plans. He and Capone plotted Colosimo's murder and imported New York talent to do the job.

The Torrio-Capone combine was then on the move, taking over some mobs that bowed to their threats and going to war with those that failed to cooperate. Their biggest coup was the assassination in 1924 of Dion O'Banion, the head of the largely Irish North Side Gang, utilizing the talents of Frankie Yale of Brooklyn, the same man who had rubbed out Colosimo. However, the O'Banion killing resulted in all-out war with the rest of the North Siders. Torrio was badly shot in an ambush and hovered near death in a hospital for days. When he got out in February 1925, he told Capone, "Al, it's all yours," and retired back to Brooklyn with an estimated $30 million.

It was a sobering experience for the 26-year-old Capone, who found he now needed to use brains instead of muscle to run things. He had to become a top executive, bossing a firm employing more than 1,000 persons with a weekly payroll of over $300,000. He demonstrated he could do this as well as work with other ethnic groups, such as the Jews, the Irish, the Poles and the blacks. Capone appreciated any man provided he was a hustler, crook or killer, and he never discriminated against any of them because of their religion, race or national origin, being perhaps the underworld's first equal opportunity employer.

This mug shot of Al Capone was taken in 1929 in Philadelphia, where he allowed the police to arrest him in order to "take off some heat" brought on by the St. Valentine's Day Massacre.

Capone's secret of success was to limit his mob's activities mainly to rackets that enjoyed strong demand from the public: liquor, gambling and prostitution. Give the people what they want and you have to gain a measure of popularity. Al Capone was cheered when he went to the ball park. Herbert Hoover was not.

Capone surrounded himself with men in whom he could place his trust, a quality he in turn inspired in many of his underlings. He was even smart enough to hire Galluccio, the thug who had scarred him, as a bodyguard, an act that demonstrated to the underworld the Big Fellow's magnanimity. Still, he faced many assassination attempts, including an effort to poison his soup. In September 1926 the O'Banions sent an entire convoy of cars loaded with machine-gunners past Capone's Cicero hotel headquarters. They poured in 1,000 rounds, but Capone escaped injury.

One by one, Capone had his North Side enemies eliminated, and he did the same to others who resisted bending to his will. His most famous killing involved treachery within his own organization. Hop Toad Giunta and Capone's two most competent killers, John Scalise and Albert Anselmi, were showing signs of planning to go independent. Capone invited them to a banquet in their honor and, at the climax of the evening, produced an Indian club with which he bashed their brains in.

By this time, Capone started to look invincible, but he erred terribly when he ordered the St. Valentine's Day Massacre in an effort to kill Bugs Moran, the last major force among the old O'Banions. Seven men were machine-gunned to death by Capone hit men masquerading as police officers. Suddenly, the public had had enough of the savage bootleg wars. Washington began applying intense pressure, and while he could not be convicted of murder, Capone was nailed for income tax evasion and sentenced to the federal prison at Atlanta for 11 years.

He was transferred to Alcatraz in 1934 and within a few years his health began to deteriorate. When released in 1939, he was a helpless paretic, a condition generally attributed to the ravages of syphillis contracted in his early whorehouse days. Chances are he had also gone "stir crazy," a common fate among Alcatraz inmates.

Capone retired to his mansion in Miami Beach, no longer capable of running the Chicago mob. For several years he wavered between lucidity and mental inertia. He died on January 25, 1947.

Al Capone had left an imprint on America and the rest of the world. Even in the minds of foreigners, he was the "Chicago gangster" personified. His impact on Chicago was significant and long lasting. During his reign Capone ordered the extermination of more than 500 men, and an estimated 1,000 died in his bootleg wars. The pattern of violence he set and the organization he built did not disappear with either his imprisonment or death. It is still not dead.

See also: ANTHONY JOSEPH ACCARDO, JOSEPH AIELLO, LOUIS "TWO GUN" ALTERIE, ANSELMI AND SCALISE, LOUIS "LITTLE NEW YORK" CAMPAGNA, FRANK CAPONE, VINCENT "SCHEMER" DRUCCI, GENNA BROTHERS, MACHINE GUN JACK MCGURN, CHARLES DION "DEANIE" O'BANION, HYMIE WEISS.

Capone, Frank (1895–1924) brother of Al Capone

Had Frank (Salvatore) Capone, Al Capone's elder brother, survived until the latter's climb to the pinnacle of power, it might well be that he would have been just as famous—Frank Capone's killer instincts and savagery exceeded those of his brother. Despite Al's acknowledged ruthlessness, he was a man who would try to deal before he tried to kill. Frank Capone never exhibited such patience. "You never get no back talk from no corpse," he used to say, a sentiment made all the more ominous by his quiet, almost bankerlike demeanor.

Frank's labors on behalf of his mentor Johnny Torrio and his brother Al were generally employed in situations where persuasion had failed and force was called for. Such was the case in the 1924 city election in Cicero, Ill., where the Democratic Party had actually dared to mount a serious effort against the Torrio–Capone-backed regime of Joseph Z. Klenha. What ensued on April 1 was one of the most terror-filled elections in American history. Frank Capone showed his great ability as a political campaigner by leading an assault on election eve against the Democratic candidate for town clerk, William K. Pflaum, beseiging him in his office, roughing him up and finally destroying his office. At polling places during the balloting, a thug would sidle up to a voter waiting in line to cast his or her ballot and inquire as to the person's preferences. If the voter gave the wrong answer, the thug ripped the ballot from the person's hand and marked it properly. The thug then waited, fingering a revolver, until the voter dropped the ballot into the box. Voters who still protested were simply slugged and carried from the polling place to vote another day. When honest election officials and poll watchers objected, they too were slugged, kidnapped and held until the voting ended. Three men were shot dead, and another had his throat cut. A policeman was blackjacked. Michael Gavin, a Democratic campaign worker, was shot in both legs and carted off to be held prisoner in the basement of a mob-owned hotel in Chicago. Eight other balky Democrats kept him company and ministered to his wounds.

By late afternoon a group of honest citizens appealed to the courts for assistance and County Judge Edmund K. Jarecki swore in 70 Chicago policemen as deputy sheriffs. Over the next several hours officers and Capone's followers fought a series of battles. A police squad commanded by Detective Sgt. William Cusick pulled up in front of a polling place near the Hawthorne works of the Western Electric Co. where Al and Frank Capone, Charles Fischetti, a cousin, and Dave Hedlin were "campaigning" with drawn revolvers. In that era unmarked police cars were long limousines no different in appearance from the type gangsters used, and Al Capone, Fischetti and Hedlin hesitated at the sight of the vehicle, unsure whether its occupants were police officers or merely gangsters who supported the anti-Klenha ticket. Frank Capone exhibited no such inhibitions and immediately opened fire on an officer at virtually point-blank range. Frank missed and the officer and another policeman responded with double blasts from their shotguns, killing the elder Capone instantly. Al Capone fled the scene.

Frank Capone was given the biggest underworld funeral Chicago had seen up till then, even eclipsing that of Big Jim Colosimo a few years earlier. His coffin was silver-plated, satin-lined and surrounded by $20,000 worth of flowers. The *Chicago Tribune* called the affair fitting enough for a "distinguished statesman." In deference to the sad occasion, every saloon, gambling joint and whorehouse in Cicero closed down for two solid hours. But perhaps the crowning tribute to Frank Capone was the election returns. The entire Klenha slate was swept back into office by overwhelming margins.

Cardinella, Salvatore "Sam" (1880–1921)

murderer

One of the most terrifying and obese criminals in Chicago history and chief of a gang that even the beer barons of Prohibition were fearful of crossing, Sam Cardinella was the mastermind of an incredible plot of self-resuscitation. Known as Il Diavolo, or "the Devil," Cardinella was one of the city's most powerful Black Handers until police cracked down on that racket, whereupon he and his gang turned to banditry and violent crime. Il

Diavolo's top triggerman was Nicholas Viana, better known as the Choir Boy, an accomplished murderer at the age of 18. The gang committed 20 murders and well over 100 holdups before Cardinella, Viana and Frank Campione were captured and sentenced to be hanged. But the Cardinella story did not end there.

In his death cell at the Cook County Jail, Cardinella went on a hunger strike and lost 40 pounds. Only 11 minutes before Cardinella was slated to die, Lt. John Norton, who had apprehended him, received a telephone tip that Cardinella's friends "are going to revive him after the execution." Norton quickly gathered a squad of detectives and hurried to the prison, posting men at the rear entrances where the bodies were taken out. A hearse turned into the alley and stopped. The officers surrounded the vehicle and opened the back door. Inside were a doctor and a nurse, dressed in white.

"What does a dead man need with medical attention?" Norton wanted to know, but he got no answer. The hearse contained a rubber mattress filled with hot water and heated by pads attached to batteries. At the head of the bed was an oxygen tank. There was also a basket jammed with hot-water bottles and a shelf loaded with syringes and stimulants.

Rushing into the jail, Norton found Cardinella laid out on a slab and his relatives eagerly signing papers for possession of the body. Norton bluntly announced that the body would be held for 24 hours, and though Cardinella's relatives screamed in anger, they were powerless.

Later, medical men agreed Cardinella's neck had not been broken when the trap was sprung: his body had been too light. Death had resulted from choking. The doctors said that had sufficient heat been applied to the body quickly, he might have been revived.

Carpenter, Richard (1929–1956) murderer

The object of one of the greatest manhunts in American criminal history, Richard Carpenter was the real-life villain of Hollywood's *The Desperate Hours*, holding a Chicago family hostage and forcing them to hide him in a drama reported in headlines around the world after he was finally caught.

The Sunday supplements still carry stories of Carpenter as a prime example of a "mama's boy" turned killer. His probation report showed he was passionately fond of his mother and would always come to her as a child, sit on her lap and moan, "Mother, I'm terribly lonely."

In 1951 Carpenter had begun to make excursions into crime. He was finally arrested for pulling a gun on a taxi driver and robbing him of $8; he got a year in jail. On her visits to the prison, Carpenter's mother brought him cakes and other sweets, which he shared with nobody. He made no friends among his fellow prisoners. His cellmates tagged him Mama's Boy and savagely never let him forget it. When Carpenter was released, he vowed never to fool around with crime or guns again. He became a cabbie, earning about $80 a week. His streak of puritanism showed through when he refused any fare to a gambling joint or brothel. He remained his lone wolf self but occasionally would take his sisters and a girl cousin to a skating rink or the movies. While he couldn't skate, he didn't approve of the girls going out alone at night. Carpenter always bought clothes for the girls, although he neglected himself to the point of going around in tatters. In addition, he always kept his grandfather supplied with three cigars a day. Suddenly, his thin veneer of sanity cracked.

On December 4, 1953 Carpenter stole a car, which he later wrecked, and held up a grocery for $100. From that day on, he never returned to his home or saw his family. He ran up a string of more than 70 heists and became a cop killer in August 1955, gunning down a police detective who attempted to arrest him on a Chicago subway. Once, he was recognized and almost caught in a downtown movie theater by an off-duty policeman named Clarence Kerr, who happened to be there with his wife. When Kerr ordered Carpenter into the lobby and demanded identification, Carpenter faked a stumble and came up shooting, hitting Kerr in the chest and wounding him badly. Kerr was able to fire one shot off at the fleeing Carpenter, injuring him in the leg. Before passing out, Kerr gasped to his wife: "It was Carpenter—Carpenter—I know it was Carpenter."

The manhunt for Carpenter, pressed by Chicago police for more than a year, intensified, with the fugitive's picture splashed across television screens. While police cars wailed through the streets, Carpenter took refuge in the house of a truck driver and his family and threatened to kill them all unless they kept him hidden. But Carpenter was really not that much of a menace to his captives. He yearned for a family environment and ended up trusting the truck driver and his wife too much. They managed to elude his watch long enough to get out of the house and call the police. Within minutes 30 police cars surrounded the house. Carpenter was able to flee through a barrage of bullets and made it across the roof to another building, where he took refuge in a room. When police burst in on him, Carpenter tried unsuccessfully to pretend he was the real occupant of the room.

After his arrest, he said: "I'm sorry about one thing—I didn't do a single thing to make my mother and my sisters proud. It was a lousy life I led—but it is too late now. . . . I'll go to the chair, but I hope I can see my mother before I die."

Carpenter got his wish before dying in the electric chair on March 16, 1956.

Castellano, Paul (1915–1985) murdered "boss of bosses"

Whatever may be said of Paul Castellano, the head of the Gambino crime family, he must be acknowledged to have enjoyed "great press." This was never more obvious than at his death. When Castellano and his driver, Tommy Bilotti, were hit Mafia style in front of a steakhouse on New York's East Side on December 16, 1985, the news made headlines around the country. "Big Paul" Castellano was hailed as the Mafia's "boss of bosses," and "the most feared don in America." In fact, he was not the most feared don in America, although perhaps the most hated by other mafiosi, and he was never the so-called boss of bosses. That the 6-foot-2 Castellano actually believed he deserved the dubious distinction may explain why he was taken out more easily than any other crime boss.

Despite all the buildup given Castellano, he never had total control of the Gambino family, but rather only of what was accorded him by his enemies. Castellano had come to power only through his connection to the previous and much heralded and respected boss Carlo Gambino. Gambino was a true power within the Mafia and rightfully could have been heralded as the boss of bosses. But

Big Paul Castellano, head of the Gambino crime family, lies shot to death outside a Manhattan steak house in 1985. Never popular with his men, Castellano got his power in 1976 by edict of his dying brother-in-law, Carlo Gambini. His murder propelled John Gotti into Mafia leadership.

like Lucky Luciano decades earlier, Gambino opted for de facto power rather than an ephemeral moniker.

A sick man in his last years, Gambino settled on Castellano to succeed him, although he knew Paul was not the man for the job on the basis either of right or ability. What Castellano had going for him was blood; he was Carlo's cousin, and in addition the husband of Gambino's sister. Everyone in all the crime families expected that the mantle would be passed to Gambino's underboss Aniello Dellacroce, a tough, heartless killer who could prevent incursions into the family's operations.

Gambino, a master manipulator, knew that if Dellacroce fought for the top spot, Castellano would be destroyed. It is unclear whether Gambino knew that Dellacroce was already suffering from cancer (certainly Dellacroce's allies probably did not know). What Gambino did know was that killing Dellacroce would solve nothing. The Young Turks under John Gotti, followers of Dellacroce, had the power to destroy Castellano, and Dellacroce was the only man who could keep them in line. What Gambino had to do was make Dellacroce Castellano's life insurance policy. Gambino pulled that off by offering Dellacroce and his faction total control of the family's Manhattan activities as a sort of crime family within a crime family. It was an offer Dellacroce could not refuse.

Gambino sought further support for Castellano through his friendship with Funzi Tieri, who then headed the Genovese crime family. That group had been the number one family in the Mafia since the days of Luciano, Frank Costello and Vito Genovese, but Gambino had maneuvered his family to the pinnacle of power without alienating Tieri. Tieri promised Gambino he would not do anything to shake Castellano from power. He kept his word, but Tieri was a master criminal, and inevitably the Genovese family reasserted its top position among the mobs. In a sense Castellano presided over a decline of the Gambinos.

However, Tieri died in 1981 and lesser, and perhaps divided, leadership weakened the Genovese family and allowed the Gambino mobsters to regain rackets and territories that the Genovese could not maintain. Over the next few years Castellano actually did start thinking he was the boss of bosses.

But on December 2, Dellacroce died of the cancer wracking his body. Apparently Castellano did not realize how vulnerable he now was without the life insurance Gambino had provided him. One of the big knocks made against Castellano by other mobsters in the family was that he was weak, hesitant, didn't go for the kill when it was required. A smart Mafia boss would have moved instantly and started killing the competition. It was as though Castellano thought he was in some sort of corporate proxy fight. He thought he could name the none-too-bright Bilotti his underboss and then start breaking up and isolating the Gotti crew.

John Gotti had a different idea. Even before Dellacroce was buried, he or his representatives were meeting with other Mafia families in New York and elsewhere, getting approval for what had to be done. The Gottis were smart enough to offer other mobsters a "piece of Paul." It probably wasn't necessary, considering the contempt in which Castellano was held. All the mobs had been stunned when they learned that Castellano had allowed his 17-room mansion on Staten Island to be bugged by the FBI. And when the tapes were revealed it was learned that Castellano had talked disparagingly about all of them.

That was bad enough, but Castellano had blabbed about Mafia business with almost anyone who entered his home. He told Bilotti things that violated the mob's need-to-know code. He even told his maid (and mistress) things she wasn't to know. More important than that, it was clear that Castellano was even more of a menace, since he was under indictment on a number of racketeering counts. The boys had to worry if the 70-year-old Castellano could take prison and the knowledge he'd never enjoy his twilight years as a free man. Under such circumstances a weak boss like Big Paul could start talking.

Gotti moved with astonishing speed. Two weeks after Dellacroce died, Castellano came to Sparks Steak House on East 46th Street to meet three men and discuss family affairs and no doubt outline his future plans. At least one of the three men who was already there knew what was going to happen. As Castellano and Bilotti stepped out of their Lincoln limousine, neither of them armed, and not even accompanied by a backup car of armed gunmen for protection, three men wearing trenchcoats and fur hats approached, pulled out semiautomatic handguns and shot both men repeatedly in the face. One of the assassins stopped long enough to pump a coup de grâce into Castellano's head. The gunmen walked rapidly away, one talking into a walkie-talkie. They got into a waiting dark car that quickly disappeared.

John Gotti then was driven past the scene to make sure everything had gone as planned. It most certainly had, thanks to Castellano's absolute lack of any semblance of precaution. Apparently he thought as the boss of bosses he could walk on water. As it was, only his car blocked his body from ending up in the gutter.

The media promised their audience that the murder of the so-called boss of bosses was certain to trigger a family war as the Castellano forces wreaked their vengeance. There turned out to be no Castellano supporters. The transfer of power went smoothly, proving that in the Mafia at least, there was nothing like violence to promote peace.

Chapman, Gerald (1892 or 1893–1926) robber and murderer

The term "Public Enemy No. 1" was first coined by a newspaperman to describe Gerald Chapman, the most popular criminal in the country for a time in the 1920s. When his picture was flashed in movie newsreels, the audience responded with thunderous applause, a phenomenon not repeated until Franklin D. Roosevelt was perceived by moviegoers in the 1930s as the savior of the nation.

Even the *New York Times*, on April 7, 1923, editorialized under the heading "Something Almost Heroical":

> *It is getting to be rather difficult to keep in mind that fact that Gerald Chapman is a thoroughly bad man, whose right place is in jail. The difficulty arises from the fact that in his battle with the law he shows qualities—courage, persistence, ingenuity and skill—which it is impossible not to admire. The result is that unless one is careful one finds one's self hoping that he isn't caught, and, so great are the odds against him, that the struggle seems somehow unfair. . . . The temptation is strong to lament that such a man should make of his abilities and peculiarities such miserable employment as devoting them to theft. There must be some explanation of that, however, and the probability is that he is defective. But it does seem hard that his punishment for his crimes should be increased because of his attempts to evade it. That he hates imprisonment is only human, and that he takes desperate risks in his efforts to get out is rather to his credit than his discredit—from every standpoint except the safety of society.*

Thus did the *Times* come down on the side of law and order, but it was a close decision.

Gerald Chapman had that way about him. An accomplished criminal a dozen or so years older than Chapman, Dutch Anderson, similarly impressed with young Chapman when both were doing time in New York's Auburn Prison, taught him all he knew about committing crimes and was eventually to become his willing underling. When the pair got out within two months of each other, they teamed up as con men and made about $100,000 trimming suckers in Chicago with varied swindles. They returned to New York City to live the high life, with their hotel suite a parade ground for showgirls, whores and impressionable young things.

In 1921 they got together with an old Auburn crony, Charley Loeber, and robbed a mail truck in New York City in a daring escapade with Chapman jumping from a moving car onto the running board of the truck and, gun in hand, forcing the driver to stop. The trio made off with five sacks of registered mail containing $1,424,129 in cash and securities, the greatest mail theft up to that time.

Chapman and Anderson fenced the securities slowly while living the good life, but Loeber proved incapable of handling the fruits of such a big-time heist and was caught disposing of his loot. When he was nabbed, he implicated Chapman and Anderson, and unaware of any danger, they were easily captured. The pair had been on a jaunt upstate, robbing five banks just to stay in shape.

Taken to the main post office building for questioning, Chapman made his first electrifying attempt at an escape. In the midst of the interrogation of Anderson and himself, Chapman, in the middle of a yawn, leaped from his chair, said "Sorry, gentlemen", and dashed to a window, stepped over the sill and disappeared.

"He's jumped," someone yelled, and everyone rushed to the window. However, they did not see what they had expected on the ground 75 feet below. There was no spread-eagled body.

Gerald Chapman might have escaped had not a detective noticed a cleaning woman in a building across the street frantically pointing to one side. Chapman had stepped onto a ledge and wormed his way down to another open window. He was captured four offices away.

Both men were convicted and sentenced to 25 years in the Atlanta Penitentiary. Chapman refused to testify, but one of his lawyers, Grace F. Crampton, reported later:

> *Chapman's philosophy of life excused his crimes. He told me that he did not believe it as sinful to hold up a mail truck or rob a store as it was to speculate on Wall Street and probably steal money from widows and orphans and poorly paid teachers. "At least we do not take money from poor people," he said to me. "What we steal hurts nobody. Everything that is sent by mail or express is fully insured and in the end the sender loses nothing. The man who comes out the winner on Wall Street is respected, and he is envied for his yachts and cars and homes, while we are hunted and despised. I think I am the more honorable of the two."*

After seven months in Atlanta, Chapman escaped. He feigned illness by drinking a disinfectant, overpowered a guard and went out the window using bedsheets for a ladder. He was free only two days before being cornered by a posse and shot in the arm, hip and back. One bullet had penetrated his kidney. He was taken back to the prison hospital for a real reason this time. Yet, though it was feared he might die, Chapman escaped the same way six days later. The authorities were sure they would find his body shortly, but Chapman made a clean break.

Two months later, Dutch Anderson tunneled out of Atlanta, and the team was back in business as two of the most wanted men in the country. The *Times* was not the only publication having difficulty managing restraint in its admiration of Chapman. Meanwhile, Chapman, separated for security reasons from Anderson, made the mistake of teaming up with one Walter J. Shean, the black-sheep son of a wealthy hotel owner and a fledgling criminal. They attempted to hold up a department store in New Britain, Conn., on October 12, 1924, and in the process one of the bandits shot and killed a police officer. Shean was captured and, with some pride, proclaimed, "My pal was Gerald Chapman."

Finally, Chapman was caught in December in Muncie, Ind. and returned to federal prison under incredibly tight security. For a time the government refused to turn over Chapman to Connecticut for trial, fearing he would escape, but finally it relented. The trial was an event that had the country going haywire. Chapman fan clubs sprang up, and at least four or five bouquets arrived each day at the front door of the prison where he was kept during the trial.

It didn't help Chapman, nor did his claim that he had never been in New Britain and never even met Shean. He was found guilty and sentenced to death.

Meanwhile, Dutch Anderson was going off his rocker. Convinced that Chapman had been betrayed by a man named Ben Hance, who had once shielded the pair in Muncie, Anderson killed Hance and his wife. He then tried to assassinate Shean, but he was too well guarded and Anderson could not get near him. Anderson was finally recognized by a policeman in Muskegon, Mich. Both went for their guns at the same time, and each killed the other.

Chapman's execution was postponed a couple of times. In his death cell he whiled away the time writing epigrams ("The more we learn, the less we discover we know") and poetry (his favorite poet was Shelley). A poem of his, "Reward," was released by one of his lawyers, who said, "I do this because I don't want people to think Chapman was merely a bandit with nothing in his head." It read in part:

Comes peace at last! The drums have
beat disray,
No armistice of hours, but ever and ever
The slow dispersing legions of decay,
Under the muffled skies, tell all is over.
Returns the husbandman, returns
the lover,
To reap the quiet harvest of alway,
The bright-plumed stars those wide fields
may not cover
Though wings beat on forever and
a day. . . .

Chapman was hanged on April 6, 1926.

Cherokee Bill (1876–1896) holdup man and murderer

It was often said that the man Hanging Judge Isaac Parker most enjoyed sending to the gallows was Crawford Goldsby, a part-Cherokee, part-white, part-Mexican and part-black murderer better known as Cherokee Bill, who killed 13 men before his 20th birthday.

Goldsby came to live with a foster mother at Fort Gibson, Okla. when he was seven years old. The woman imbued the boy with the credo: "Stand up for your rights. Don't let anybody impose on you." When he was 18, he followed her advice. He shot a man who beat him up at a dance. The man lived, but Goldsby fled to Indian Territory and soon joined the outlaw band of Bill and Jim Cook. In June 1894 the Cooks and Goldsby shot their way out of a posse trap after Goldsby killed a member of the law party, Sequoyah Houston.

After that, the killings came fast, and Goldsby became known and hunted as Cherokee Bill. The young killer had a dozen notches on his gun before he was betrayed by a couple of supposed friends while he was paying a courting call on a young girl. The duo, Ike Rogers and Clint Scales, clubbed him unconscious and collected $1,300 in reward money. Cherokee Bill was speedily tried before Judge Parker for just one of his crimes and sentenced to be hanged. However, his lawyer succeeded in delaying the execution through several appeals. While the murderer was still being held in his prison cell, he somehow got hold of a gun and attempted to make an escape. The attempt failed, although Cherokee Bill did kill a prison guard, Lawrence Keating, the father of four children.

The escape effort roused Judge Parker to a fit of anger. He blamed the guard's death on the U.S. Supreme Court and told reporters that the High Court's obsession with the "flimsiest technicalities" was allowing the 60 "murderers" then in his Fort Smith jail to fight off their executions—Cherokee Bill among them. Parker brought the outlaw to trial for the guard's murder without waiting for the outcome of his appeal on the previous conviction. The judge found Cherokee Bill guilty of this second charge and sentenced him to death, but again the execution was forestalled by appeals. Finally, though, the first appeal went against the defendant, and on March 17, 1896, with Judge Parker watching the execution from his office window, Cherokee Bill mounted the gallows. Asked if he had any last words, the young murderer replied, "I came here to die, not to make a speech." Cherokee Bill paid for his 13 murders, but it appeared later that he was responsible for one more. Ike Rogers, one of the men who betrayed him, was murdered. The crime was believed to have been the work of Cherokee Bill's young brother, Clarence Goldsby, in an act of vengeance. If Clarence was the killer, he was never brought to justice.

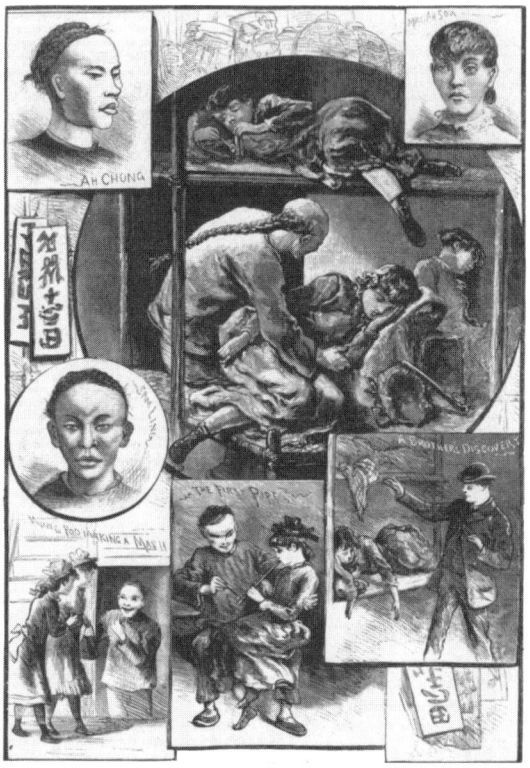

Scandal sheets of the 19th century constantly fanned public opinion against the Chinese by depicting their alleged corrupting influence on young white females.

Chinese riots

When the Chinese first arrived in this country in about 1850, they were greeted warmly, especially in San Francisco, where they worked for very low wages as household servants and menials. Within a year or two, as their numbers increased, the Chinese became one of the most hated ethnic groups because they allegedly took jobs away from "Americans," mostly other ethnics who had also come to America from foreign shores. The wanton killing of Chinese probably was even less hindered by legal sanctions than the slaughter of Indians or Mexican "greasers." The saying "not having a Chinaman's chance" had a very awesome meaning for a "chink," "heathen," "celestial," "coolie," "moon face" or "slant-eyes" meeting a white man with a gun. Riots became common, with particularly bloody ones occurring in Los Angeles, San Francisco, Denver, Seattle, Rock Springs, Wyo. and Pierce City, Idaho. Cities like Tacoma, Wash. expelled their entire Chinese populations. The main opposition to the Chinese was economic, since such employers as the Union Pacific preferred to hire Chinese because, besides being docile, they worked for low pay and were satisfied with a bowl of rice. However, their large numbers and their insistence on maintaining their own customs—an attitude not really different than those of all other ethnic groups—became an added irritant. Not surprisingly, the Chinese were unmoved by efforts to Christianize them, one missionary observing, "They were unable to distinguish between our mobs and our Christian workers and could not be expected to favor or tolerate our religion. They had no way of knowing that Christianity was a religion of love, not one of bowie knife, insult, and the worst oppression the world has yet seen." Henry Ward Beecher's comment was more sarcastic: "We have clubbed them, stoned them, burned their houses and murdered some of them; yet they refuse to be converted. I do not know any way, except to blow them up with nitroglycerin, if we are ever to get them to Heaven."

It would probably be impossible to try to estimate the hundreds or thousands of Chinese who were murdered by whites in this country during the 19th century since most newspapers did not regard the killing of a Chinese as newsworthy. Diaries of 49ers in California constantly refer in passing to the killing of a "chink" here or there. Practically no white man was ever convicted of killing a Chinese; the crude Texas judge Roy Bean once dismissed a case because he said he found no statutory restriction against the activity. Lawmen in general showed no inclination to ascertain the facts in the violent death of any Chinese. Perhaps the 19th-century attitude in the West is best summed up in a ballad still popular around the turn of the century:

Old John Martin Duffy was judge of the court
In a small mining town in the West;
Although he knew nothing about rules of the law,
At judging he was one of the best.

One night in the winter a murder occurred,
And the blacksmith was accused of the crime;
We caught him red-handed and give him three trials,
But the verdict was "guilty" each time.

Now he was the only good blacksmith we had
And we wanted to spare him his life,
So Duffy stood up in the court like a lord
And with these words he settled the strife:

"I move we dismiss him, he's needed in town";
Then he spoke out these words which have gained him renown:
"We've got two Chinese laundrymen, everyone knows;
Why not save the poor blacksmith and hang one of those?"

Eventually, anti-Chinese violence petered out, although not for any commendable reason. First, President Chester A. Arthur signed a bill suspending Chinese immigration. Second, the focus of bigotry shifted to newer immigrant groups, such as the Japanese.

LOS ANGELES

One of California's bloodiest and most barbaric mob actions occurred on October 4, 1871, when a huge group of whites—men, women and children—rampaged through Calle de los Negros, or "Nigger Alley," which had become the city's Chinatown. Ostensibly, the reason for the riot was to avenge the death of a white who had been killed in the cross fire of fighting between two rival Chinese gangs, or tongs. But it was clear that this was little more than a rationale for an explosion of racially motivated violence. On the day of the riot, hundreds of people charged through Nigger Alley smashing windows and battering down doors. Any Chinese seized was beaten or stabbed. When one Chinese man broke free of his tormentors and tried to run away, he was shot down in the street. Having thus tasted blood, the crowd grabbed another Chinese and hauled him through the streets to a corral, where they hanged him. Other victims were pulled over the cobblestoned streets with a rope around their necks until they died.

Perhaps the most shocking killing, one that drew international attention, was that of an elderly Chinese doctor named Gene Tong. When caught by the mob, he pleaded to be spared and offered several thousand dollars he was carrying in exchange for his life. The rioters just laughed and hanged him anyway. As the old man was choking to death, several women in the crowd stepped forward and ripped off his trousers to get at his money. Someone also severed his ring finger with a bowie knife when a diamond ring would not slip off readily.

The death toll in the 1871 massacre was placed at 20 to 25, with many more injured, and it was estimated that the rioters had robbed and looted every room, every strongbox, every trunk in all Chinatown. A grand jury investigation condemned the mob for "disgracing our city" and charged that the authorities had failed to perform their duty properly, but not one person was ever brought to trial. Not surprisingly therefore, a few years later, after the first initial shock and revulsion had passed, Anti-Coolie Clubs began to spring up in the city. Finally stung by charges of intolerance, the officials of Los Angeles did something: they changed the name of Nigger Alley to Los Angeles Street.

PIERCE CITY, IDAHO TERRITORY

Compared to some anti-Chinese massacres, the slaughter at Pierce City, Idaho Territory was, as one participant put it, "small potatoes." However, it is most illustrative of the brutal and inhuman attitude of whites toward Asians.

On September 10, 1885 the body of a white merchant, D. M. Frazier, was found "chopped to pieces in his own store." A vigilante mob was formed quickly and on no apparent evidence, deduced the crime had been committed by two Chinese merchants who were in competition with the victim. The Chinese partners were seized and tortured until each accused the other of committing the crime. The verdict was that both should be hanged, and as long as they were hanging them, the vigilantes thought it would be a good idea to get rid of three other undesirable Chinese—a gambler, a barber, described as "hard featured," and a "parasite," meaning a local camp prostitute. Cooler heads among the mob convinced the others that the five should be turned over to the law so that they could be tried formally before being hanged. That night when a half-dozen lawmen set out with the prisoners for the county seat, they were stopped by a large mob of masked men who abducted the five. It seems some discussion among the vigilantes had led to the conclusion that the three additional prisoners would most likely not be hanged for the murder and that perhaps the confessions extracted from the two merchants by torture might also be disallowed in a courtroom. Direct action would solve that problem, and all five were hanged, if somewhat inefficiently and slowly, from a pole placed between the forks of two pine trees. The incident triggered wholesale expulsions of Chinese from a number of Idaho towns with the tacit approval of high government officials.

When news of the lynchings spread, the Department of State received a protest from the Chinese government, but it was six months before the territorial governor E. A. Stevenson, arrived in Pierce City to launch an investigation. The "investigation" consisted solely of talking to anti-Chinese elements and announcing he had failed to discover the identities of any perpetrators of the lynchings. He did express regret at the hangings but added, "The Chinese hanged were the identical parties, who so cruelly, shockingly and brutally murdered without the least provocation (except jealousy) one of the best citizens of Idaho." The governor also insisted that deportation was the only solution to the Chinese problem, since "their low, filthy habits, their high-binder piratical societies, together with their low dens of infamy, prostitution and opium smoking, have disgusted our people."

After the Pierce City affair a prodeportation movement seemed to be gaining ground in Washington, but by this time a new wave of immigrants, this one from Japan, had started to arrive and hostility was shifted away from the Chinese to meet this new menace. Deportation of the Chinese was forgotten, and they went on to become one of the most law-abiding ethnic groups in America.

ROCK SPRINGS, WYOMING TERRITORY

As terrible as the slaughter was in the Los Angeles Chinese massacre of 1871, it did not compare with the mob riot in Rock Springs, Wyoming Territory in 1885.

When the main line of the Union Pacific was completed in 1869, many of the Chinese laborers settled in the railroad town of Rock Springs. In 1885 there were 500 Chinese in Rock Springs, the great majority working in the Union Pacific coal mines. In fact, the Chinese were the majority in the mines, and this led to friction as unemployment grew in the white community. When on September 2 a white miner and two Chinese got into an altercation underground, the fighting soon spread in the shaft among other miners, leaving one Chinese killed and three others severely injured. Word of the battle was passed above ground, and a heavily armed mob of white miners formed for the destruction of Chinatown. The Chinese had no reason to expect an attack and were easily routed from their dugouts and shacks. One white miner's diary recalled, "Bullets followed the fleeing Chinese and sixteen of them were killed brutally, while the other casualties met an even more horrible fate the same evening when some of the citizens satisfied their murderous instincts and inhumanly slew the few remaining Chinese for the money which their victims had hidden on their persons, after setting fire to the buildings to hide their crimes." The entire Chinatown section was burned to the ground and "the smell that arose from the smoking ruins was horribly suggestive of burning flesh." Overall, the death toll was put at 50, or 10 percent of the Chinese community.

The *Rock Springs Independent* put out an extra edition the following day and sided with the anti-Chinese forces. It especially complimented saloon operators for shutting down during the riot: "It cannot be said that a 'drunken mob' drove out the Chinamen. Everyone was sober, and we did not see a case of drunkness. All of the stores in town were closed, and men, women and children were out watching the hurried exit of John Chinaman and everyone seemed glad to see them on the wing."

Because of demands by the Union Pacific, federal troops were called in and took over the task of feeding the destitute Chinese wandering about the countryside. Many of the men involved in the massacre were identified; instead of being prosecuted, they were paid off by the railroad, given train tickets and "strongly advised" by the commander of the troops to leave the state. The federal troops remained on duty in Rock Springs for the next 13 years, finally departing at the start of the Spanish-American War in 1898.

Christie, Ned (1867?–1892) Indian outlaw

Along with the Apache Kid, Ned Christie, a full-blooded Cherokee, became one of the most wanted Indian outlaws in the West.

A bright youth, Christie served in the Cherokee tribal legislature, but in 1885 he became an outlaw in a big way. For some unknown reason, he killed Deputy U.S. Marshal Dan Maples and vanished into the Cookson Hills of the Oklahoma Indian Territory. In that area he functioned as a horse thief, rumrunner, bandit and murderer, although there is no doubt that, as was the case with the Apache Kid, just about any crime committed in the territory by a young Indian was pinned on him.

It took Hanging Judge Parker's deputies seven years to catch up with Ned, who was cornered by U.S. marshals Heck Thomas and Paden Tolbert in a log fort near Tahlequah on November 1, 1892. Finding Ned and flushing him out were two different matters, however, as the fort was close to impregnable. The marshals sent all the way to Kansas for an army cannon and then set about the task of blasting out the Indian outlaw with the aid of about 20 reinforcements. They pumped an estimated 2,000 bullets into the fortress that did no damage at all; the cannon proved even less helpful. The logs held firm and the cannon balls had the disconcerting habit of bouncing back at the besiegers. Twenty-four hours of battle had not added up to a day of glory for the law. Finally, the attackers used dynamite to breach the walls. Although shellshocked, the Indian came out fighting, riding hard and pumping away with his Winchester. With some 20 guns trained on him, Ned Christie was blasted off his mount, full of holes and dead.

Photograph of the lifeless body of Indian outlaw Ned Christie nailed up to an old door became the most popular pinup in the Oklahoma Territory during the 1890s.

The killing of Oklahoma's most wanted Indian desperado deserved special artistic commemoration. His body was allowed to harden somewhat into a pre–rigor mortis pose, propped up against an old door with his rifle cradled in his hands, and then his picture was taken. Ned Christie became the most popular pinup in Oklahoma during the 1890s.

Clark, Douglas (1959–) the "Sunset Slayer"
Perhaps the most infamous serial killer of recent years, Ted Bundy left his mark in the chronicles of serial killings in many ways, particularly as an inspiration to "copy-cat" criminals. It is apparent that a sometime factory worker named Douglas Daniel Clark—the "Sunset Slayer"—had been much impressed by Bundy's murder spree and sought to imitate it. His murders, often in company of his lover, Carol Mary Bundy (no relation of Ted Bundy), began in 1980 and were far more ghoulish than those of his role model.

Calling himself the "king of the one-night stands," he dated either women older than himself or young girls between ages 10 and 15. However, sexual liaisons, even kinky ones, hardly sated his desires, which ran to dark reflections on rape, mutilation, murder and necrophilia. In 1980, Clark met Carol Bundy, a vocational nurse in Burbank, who at age 37 was a half-dozen years older than he, and she became his willing accomplice in his gruesome activities. When their game turned deadly, Carol cruised the Sunset Strip looking for prostitutes—with a strong preference for blonds—for Clark to murder and then engage in depraved sexual acts. Clark and Carol committed about 10 known murders in this fashion; at times, the heads of their decapitated victims were stored in a refrigerator for later gory fun and games. In one case, Carol later confessed to making up one face with cosmetics, saying, "We had a lot of fun with her. I washed her up like a Barbie with makeup."

Typical of Clark's killings were those of two half sisters, 16-year-old Cynthia Chandler and 15-year-old Gina Narano, who vanished from a beach. They were later found on the side of the Ventura Freeway in Los Angeles, each shot in the head. Gleefully, Clark described to Carol how he had had forced sex with the girls before killing them.

Carol clearly had become a murder slave for Clark, a fairly common occurrence among female consorts of serial killers, but she was also responsible for his eventual capture. In the past, she had had a romantic attachment with an apartment house superintendent and part-time singer in country and western bars, John Robert Murray. On a date with Murray after her murderous involvement with Clark, a liquored-up Carol let too much slip out about Clark and their doings. Murray said he might well go to the police about it all, a prospect that threw Carol into a panic. On August 5, 1980 she set up a midnight rendezvous with Murray in his van near the bar where he was doing a gig. She shot him in the head. Murray's body turned up four days later with nine stab wounds and deep slashes across his buttocks. The head was missing, removed by Carol and Clark to prevent any ballistics identification.

Two days after the discovery of the corpse, Carol sank into a state of depression, crying out on her job to another nurse, "I can't take it anymore. I'm supposed to save lives, not take them." Her coworker reported her comments to the police, who arrested Carol and in a search of her home found shocking pictures involving Clark and young girls. Clark was arrested at his job, where police found a pistol that ballistics tests linked to five of the known victims of the Sunset Slayer.

According to Carol, Clark claimed he had killed at least 50 young girls both before and after meeting her and that he hoped to hit 100 before he inevitably was caught. At his trial, Clark tried to shift the Sunset Slayings to Carol and victim Murray, claiming it was they who were ardent fans of Ted Bundy. The jury believed otherwise. Clark was sentenced to death and joined the growing list of condemned prisoners waiting for years for execution with the restored California death penalty. Carol first claimed insanity but then admitted her part in some of the slayings, including that of John Murray, and she was sentenced to a total of 52 years in prison.

Cline, Alfred L. (1888–1948) bluebeard

One of the most successful criminals at marrying and murdering widows for their money was Alfred L. Cline, until the law cut off his career in California in 1945.

His modus operandi remained constant, and he is known to have killed eight unfortunate wives after he had convinced them to will their estates to him. Cline would take his brides on a lavish vacation and in some smart hotel get them to drink a glass of buttermilk that he had laced with a heavy amount of a sleep-producing drug. He would follow this up a few hours later with a fatal dose of the drug, but in the meantime he would call the house physician and inform him that "Mrs. Cline has had another heart attack." When he resummoned the doctor shortly thereafter, his wife would be dead, and the doctor, prepared for that event, would not be suspicious and would issue a death certificate, citing heart failure as the cause.

Eventually, many of the facts about Cline's crimes surfaced, but the law invariably foundered on one key element. Cline always had his wives' bodies cremated, a process that destroyed all evidence of the poison he had used. However, the authorities were able to prove that he had used forgery to get his hands on his wives' money, and for this he was sentenced to 126 years in prison. Cline died in California's Folsom Prison in 1948.

Cohen, Mickey (1913–1976) gangster

One of the most shot-at gangsters of the 1940s and 1950s, Mickey Cohen was the gambling czar of the West Coast, succeeding to that position after the underworld execution of Bugsy Siegel, Cohen's mentor, in 1947 by "persons unknown." Those unknown persons were members of the national syndicate. Cohen later did battle with them, especially the syndicate's Los Angeles representative, Jack Dragna, refusing to turn over a cut of the proceeds from his bookmaking operations despite a series of attempts on his life.

Cohen lived in a mansion surrounded with an electrified fence and spotlights. On two occasions his home was dynamited. While he survived both times, he bemoaned the loss of much of his 200-suit wardrobe in one of the blasts.

Noted for his colorful and fiery comments, Cohen told television interviewer Mike Wallace, "I have killed no man that in the first place didn't deserve killing by the standards of our way of life." When asked to name the California politicians who had once protected his gambling interests, he refused, stating, "that is not my way of life."

Cohen wasn't any more communicative when he appeared before the Kefauver Committee's hearings on organized crime in 1950. When asked by Sen. Charles Tobey, "Is is not a fact that you live extravagantly . . . surrounded by violence?" Cohen responded

"Whadda ya mean, 'surrounded by violence'? People are shooting at *me*."

When pressed on how he had obtained a $35,000 loan without putting up collateral from a Hollywood banker, Mickey quipped, "I guess he just likes me."

In 1958 Cohen, ever the publicity hound, gave the newspapers love letters written by actress Lana Turner to Johnny Stompanato, her gangster lover and a former Cohen bodyguard who was stabbed to death by Turner's teenage daughter. What upset Mickey was the fact that he had been stuck with the bill for Stompanato's funeral.

The Internal Revenue Service nailed Cohen twice for income tax violations. He served four years the first time and did 10 years of a 15-year term the second time. Released in 1972, he announced his intention to go straight. Cohen didn't have too much choice in the matter since he was partly paralyzed as the result of a head injury inflicted by a fellow convict in the federal penitentiary at Atlanta in 1963. In 1974 Cohen attracted attention by campaigning for prison reform and, later, by stating he had been in touch with people who knew the whereabouts of kidnap victim Patricia Hearst.

Cohen died of natural causes in 1976.

Coll, Vincent "Mad Dog" (1909–1932)

gangster and murderer

Alternately known as Mad Dog and the Mad Mick, Vincent Coll stands as the best remembered of the so-called baby-faced killers of the 1930s. On another level, he was typical of the latter-day Irish gangsters who resisted the growth of organized crime, fighting a bloody war for an independent existence.

Some have described Coll as at least half-demented, with no regard for human life. Others have said he had no regard for even his own life, exhibiting a death wish as he invaded the far stronger gangland empires of Dutch Schultz, Legs Diamond and Owney Madden. With mindless nerve, he even accepted a commission to assassinate Lucky Luciano, Vito Genovese, Frank Costello and Joe Adonis. He was hired by Salvatore Maranzano, then the Mafia's "boss of bosses," who wished to rid himself of the Young Turks he knew were plotting against him. Maranzano wanted the killings done by a non-Italian so that he could insist he was above the bloodshed. Coll drew a $25,000 advance and was on his way to Maranzano's office, where a trap was being laid for Luciano and Genovese. Luciano learned of the plot and had Maranzano killed first. When Coll got there, he found he had lost his murder contract, but being ahead $25,000, he walked off content.

Vince Coll emerged from the Irish ghetto of New York's Hell's Kitchen, where criminal activity was an accepted mode of behavior. In his early twenties, he and his brother Peter hired out as rumrunners to Dutch Schultz at $150 a week each. As he told his brother, the job was merely a way of learning the ropes before they either started up a bootleg empire of their own or simply took over the Dutchman's. Within a short time, Coll was demanding a cut of the action from Schultz, a proposal that was angrily rejected. The Coll brothers then started laying the groundwork for their own organization. As the fate of Vincent Barelli, a Schultz hood, and Mary Smith, Barelli's girlfriend, proved, Vince Coll was prepared to use gratuitous violence to accomplish his goal. The Coll brothers and Mary's brother, Carmine, had attended the same Hell's Kitchen grade school, and on the basis of this connection, Mary got Barelli to attend a meeting with the plotting brothers. When Barelli refused to desert Schultz, Coll shot him and Mary.

Schultz was unaware of the scheming and still regarded the Coll brothers as being in his stable. After Vince was arrested for violating the Sullivan Law aginst carrying weapons, Schultz put up $10,000 bail. He became duly incensed when Coll promptly jumped bail; as a moral lesson, the beer baron had Peter Coll murdered. This launched the bitter Coll-Schultz war, in which at least 20 gunmen were killed. An exact count was impossible since the Castellammarese War for control of the New York Mafia was raging at the same time and the police had difficulty figuring out which corpse resulted from which feud.

Even though he had less firepower, Coll held his own against the Schultz forces. Constantly pressed for cash, he raised it in desperate fashion by kidnapping mobster kingpins attached to the Legs Diamond and Owney Madden gangs and collecting huge ransoms for their freedom. Thus, Coll was soon being hunted by a large portion of the New York underworld. In July 1932 Coll won his sobriquet of Mad Dog when he tried to gun down several Schultz gangsters on East 107th Street. Riding by them in a car, Coll cut loose a machine-gun blast that missed the gangsters but hit five small children, aged five to seven, leaving them writhing on the ground, some shot as many as five times. Five-year-old Michael Vengalli died, most of his stomach blown away.

The public was indignant, and orders went out to the police to bring in Mad Dog Coll dead or alive. Realizing he would be caught sooner or later, Coll kidnapped yet another Owney Madden aide and collected $30,000 in ransom. He used this money to hire the top lawyer of the day, Samuel Leibowitz, to defend him. Remarkably, Coll was acquitted of the murder charge after the masterful Leibowitz somehow seemed to make the eyewitnesses, rather than his client, the defendants. The Mad Dog was back on the streets.

Later, the underworld put a $50,000 reward out for the trigger-happy youth. Schultz gunners almost cornered Coll on four occasions but he fought his way to safety each time. Then one day late in 1932, Coll was in a drug store telephone booth talking to Owney Madden, threatening to kill him unless he was given money. Madden kept talking to him while the call was traced. Coll was still in the phone booth when a black automobile pulled up outside the drug store. One man stood outside on the street and another just inside the door. A third with something bulging under his overcoat strode toward the phone booth. Coll saw him as the man leveled a tommy gun at him. In his cramped position Coll was unable to react as the man squeezed the trigger.

At the autopsy 15 steel-jacketed bullets were removed from Coll's face, chest and stomach.

See also: OWNEY "THE KILLER" MADDEN, SALVATORE MARANZANO.

Colonel Plug (?–1820?) river pirate

With Bully Wilson, Col. Plug was one of the two most important pirates who preyed on boat traffic along the Ohio and Mississippi Rivers. A bewhiskered giant whose real name was Fluger, Col. Plug boasted he had been a colonel in the American Revolution. Plug's modus operandi was to hide aboard a flatboat that was tied up for the night. When it got going in the morning, he would dig out the caulking between the planks and bore holes in the bottom. Col. Plug would time his work so that the boat would be scuttled opposite his hideout. His gang would row out to the flatboat in skiffs, supposedly coming to the rescue. The only person to be rescued would be Col. Plug, of course, along with the cargo; the crew and passengers would be left to drown, or, if they resisted, to be shot. Col. Plug was active for many years until, according to the legend, he bored too many holes one day and the boat he was sabotaging went to the bottom before Plug could climb out of the hold. At least, so the story was told in pirate circles, presumably accurate since suddenly Col. Plug ceased to be a scourge of the rivers.

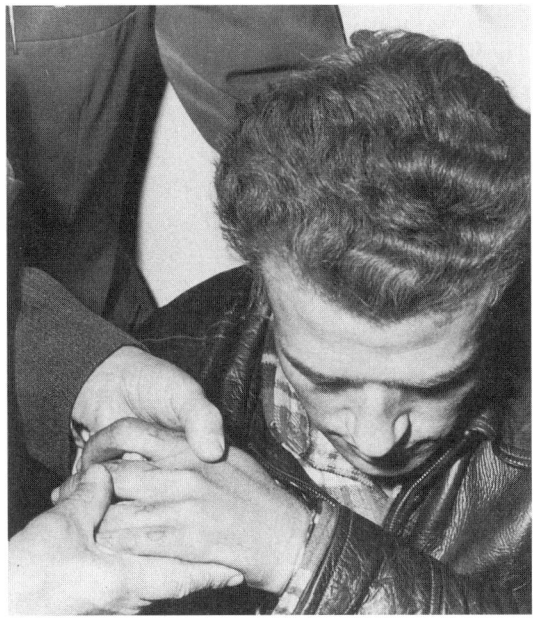

Police officers hold up left hand of mass murderer Billy Cook to show "Hard Luck" tattoo across his fingers.

Cook, William (1929–1952) mass murderer

Few mass murderers have ever gone on a worse bloodletting spree than the one 21-year-old Billy Cook launched on December 30, 1950. On that day, Cook, posing as a hitchhiker, forced a motorist at gunpoint to get into the trunk of his own car and then drove off. Over the next two weeks Cook went on a senseless killing rampage. He kidnapped nearly a dozen people, including a deputy sheriff; murdered six in cold blood, including three children; attempted other killings; and generally terrorized the Southwest border area.

A hell raiser as a child, Cook was in and out of reform schools. He sported a tattooed letter between the knuckle and first joint of each finger of each hand, and when he held his hands together, the letters spelled H-A-R-D-L-U-C-K, an obvious form of self-pity that in retrospect psychologists said fostered a feeling of persecution. He clearly turned this feeling outward, even shrieking to his lawyer in the San Quentin death house, "I hate them; I hate their guts—everybody!"

Cook exhibited that feeling from the moment he kidnapped his first victim, a motorist, near Lubbock, Tex. Luckily for the motorist, he was able to force open the trunk and escaped on a small road. Far less lucky was the family of Carl Mosser. Mosser, his wife, Thelma, and their three small children were on a motor trip from Illinois to New Mexico when they picked up the killer. Cook soon produced a gun and forced Mosser to drive on. Following the gunman's mercurial directions, they went to Carlsbad, N.M., to El Paso, to Houston. After a time, Cook shot and killed all five of them and, for good measure, the family dog. He dumped their bodies in an abandoned mine shaft just outside Joplin, Mo.

Eventually, the Mossers' car was found abandoned near Tulsa, Okla. The car was a complete shambles, the upholstery blood-soaked and ripped open by bullets. Then their bodies were discovered. But Cook left something in the car besides bullets, a receipt for a gun he had bought. The killer's identity was learned and a massive manhunt was launched. Cook headed for California and there kidnapped a deputy sheriff who had almost captured him. He forced the deputy to drive him around while he bragged about killing the Mosser family.

After a 40-mile ride in the deputy's car, Cook ordered the lawman to stop. "Out," he ordered his prisoner. Then he forced the deputy to lie down in a gully and tied his hands behind him. "I won't bother to tie your feet because I'm going to put a bullet through your head anyway," Cook said.

The mass murderer was just having his joke. He drove off as the officer waited for the shot that would kill him. A short time later, Cook stopped another motorist, Robert Dewey, whom he did kill. With the alarm for him covering the western half of the country, Cook headed into Mexico, kidnapping two other men. In the little town of Santa Rosalía, 400 miles below the border, Cook, with his hostages in tow, was recognized by the police chief. The officer simply walked up to Cook, snatched a gun from the killer's belt and placed him under arrest. Cook was rushed back to the border and turned over to FBI agents. On December 12, 1952 he died in the gas chamber at San Quentin for the Dewey murder.

Coppola, Michael "Trigger Mike"

(1904–1966) syndicate gangster

Trigger Mike Coppola was successful in the Luciano-Genovese crime family because he was a raging sadist and thus an excellent enforcer.

Mafioso Mike Coppola and his first wife in happier moments, before he allegedly had her killed in the hospital where she had given birth to a baby daughter. She could, it was said, link Coppola to a murder.

When Vito Genovese fled a possible murder rap and Luciano was sent to prison in the 1930s, Coppola ran much of the crime family's rackets, including the lush artichoke racket, levying an underworld tribute on the vegetable no Italian family wanted to do without, and a goodly portion of the Harlem numbers racket. He was said to net something around $1 million a year. An oft-told underworld tale concerns the time Coppola woke up in the middle of the night remembering he had left a package in the freezer of one of his favorite night spots. A hurried phone call brought the package to his door and he spent the rest of the night thawing out $219,000 of mob money, which he had to dispense in the morning.

There is considerable evidence that Coppola would do anything and kill anybody to advance his fortunes or protect himself. His first wife, according to the subsequent testimony of his second wife, Ann, happened to overhear her husband discussing with another gangster the impending murder of a Republican political worker, Joseph Scottoriggio. She was called to testify against her husband in the case, but her appearance was postponed because of her impending pregnancy. She gave birth to a baby daughter and conveniently died afterward in her hospital bed. Coppola's second wife later charged that Trigger Mike had her killed to prevent her from talking.

Ann Coppola's marriage to Trigger Mike was a nightmare highlighted by mental and physical abuse. At their honeymoon party Coppola took a shot at her for the entertainment of the guests. In 1960 Ann discovered her husband was giving drugs to her teenage daughter by a prior marriage. She filed for divorce and testified in an income tax case against Coppola, who sent strongarm men to kidnap and beat her up. She was found badly mauled on an isolated beach, recovered and continued to testify against him. Finally, Trigger Mike gave in and pleaded guilty; he was sent to Atlanta Penitentiary.

Ann Coppola, who had squirreled away something like $250,000 of Trigger Mike's underworld money, fled to Europe to escape the mob's hit men. In Rome in 1962 Ann Coppola stopped running. She wrote a last letter to Internal Revenue, addressing certain portions of it to Attorney General Robert F. Kennedy. She penned a farewell to Trigger Mike as well, saying: "Mike Coppola, someday, somehow, a person or God or the law shall catch up with you, you yellow-bellied bastard. You are the lowest and biggest coward I have had the misfortune to meet." Then she wrote in lipstick on the wall above her hotel bed: "I have always suffered, I am going to kill myself. Forget me." She took a dozen sleeping pills and lapsed quietly into death.

Trigger Mike was released from prison the following year and died in 1966 of natural causes.

Corll, Dean (1940–1973) mass murderer

Many people who knew Dean Corll of Houston, Tex., thought of him as a friendly sort of guy, but there was another Dean Corll, a homosexual murderer of at least 27 young boys in that city's "crime of the century" during the early 1970s. Corll used two teenage boys, Elmer Wayne Henley and David Brooks, to steer young victims to him. They would get the victim drunk and then Corll would take over.

The victim would revive to find himself stripped naked, gagged and spread-eagled on a plywood plank. His legs and arms would be secured by handcuffs and nylon ropes. A radio would be going full blast and there would be plastic sheeting on the floor to take care of the blood. Sometimes Corll would kill his victim in as little as 10 minutes, but other times he'd stretch it out for as long as 24 hours or even more. On occasions, perversely, he would suddenly cut the boy loose and explain, laughing, that he was just kidding, seeing if he could scare the youth. But for the murder victims, there was a wooden "body box" on hand in which the slain boys were transported to a city boat shed, a Gulf Coast beach or a wooded area in East Texas for disposal.

On August 7, 1973, 17-year-old Henley shot and killed Corll in self-defense because of fear the sadistic murderer intended to turn on him and Brooks. The police investigation soon implicated Henley and Brooks in the murderous reign of terror, and the pair admitted they had been paid from $5 to $10 for each adolescent boy they had recruited for Corll. For their parts in the crimes, Brooks, convicted on one count, got life imprisonment and Henley, convicted on nine counts, got a total of 594 years. By then the Houston police had recovered somewhat from the criticism heaped on them when the murders were discovered. In most cases, when the victims were reported missing to the police, worried relatives had been informed they had probably run off and "joined those hippies in California."

Henley, who was not charged in the Corll killing, won a new trial in 1979 but was convicted for a second time.

Corona, Juan (1934–) mass murderer

A Mexican labor contractor who had started out as a migrant fruit picker, Juan Corona was convicted of the murder of 25 migrant workers in 1970-71, becoming labeled as the greatest captured mass killer in California history. (There is speculation that the uncaptured "Zodiac Killer" may have killed almost twice as many people.)

All Corona's victims were transient laborers between the ages of 40 and 68. They had been mutilated, usually with a machete, and buried in peach orchards and along a river bank in Yuba County. Unfortunately for Corona, some of his bank deposit slips and receipts had apparently been found buried with some of the victims, leading the authorities directly to him.

Bloodstained weapons and clothing were found in his home, including two butcher's knives, a machete, a pistol, a jacket and some shorts. The most sensational evidence, however, was what the prosecution called Corona's "death list," a ledger containing the names of many of the victims with a date after them.

In January 1973 Corona was found guilty and sentenced to 25 consecutive life terms, a somewhat meaningless exercise in overkill since he technically would become eligible for parole in 1980. Later that year he was attacked in his prison cell and stabbed 32 times, causing him to lose the sight of one eye. In 1978 a new trial was ordered for Corona on the grounds that his lawyer had failed to provide him with an adequate defense by not presenting what the appeals court called an "obvious" insanity plea. The court emphasized it did not doubt the correctness of the guilty verdict, but it insisted Corona was entitled to an insanity defense. Corona was sent to a mental facility for observation to see if he could eventually be put on trial again. In the early 1980s he was still there and was found guilty again.

Courtright, Longhair Jim (1845?–1887)
western lawman and murderer

A prime example of a lawman gone bad, Jim Courtright, variously reported as being born in Iowa or Illinois between 1845 and 1848, was a popular two-gun sheriff in Fort Worth, Tex., but after two years on the job, he was fired in 1878 for drinking. Courtright bounced around to a few other jobs as a lawman, but his brooding nature was such that these rarely lasted for long. Eventually, he drifted into a job as a guard for the American Mining Co., in whose employ he killed two would-be robbers in 1883. News of this exploit reached the attention of a New Mexico rancher named Logan, who had been Courtright's old Civil War commander. Logan offered him a job as a ranch foreman, but Courtright's real assignment would be to rid Logan's range of squatters. He got off to a fast start by promptly shooting two unarmed nesters. Because there had been witnesses, Courtright was forced to flee. He was arrested in Fort Worth and held for extradition. Courtright knew the jail routine well, and after being smuggled a pair of pistols, he escaped, fleeing to South America. After three years he returned to face trial, but by that time the witnesses against him had scattered, and he was easily acquitted. Returning to Fort Worth, he set up the T.I.C. Commercial Detective Agency. Finding little demand for his services, Courtright used the agency as a guise to demand protection money from the town's various gambling halls and saloons. For this ploy to be successful, a 100 percent record of collection was necessary; it was Courtright's misfortune that an emporium called the White Elephant Saloon was run by a pint-sized gambler named Luke Short, one of the West's grand masters of the six-gun. On February 8, 1887 Courtright sent a messenger into the White Elephant demanding that Short step outside. Short did, and moments later, Courtright called out, "Don't try to pull a gun on me." Courtright clearly was laying the legal basis for a claim that he was acting in self-defense. The matter was academic, however. Courtright started to draw one gun, but Short shot his thumb off as he tried to trip back the hammer. This was not a trick shot; Short's aim was slightly off on his first blast. As Courtright went to pull his other gun, Short was on target with three more shots, two in the chest and one in the forehead.

Crowley, Francis "Two Gun" (1911–1931)

murderer

Francis "Two Gun" Crowley was perhaps the nearest thing America produced to a 20th-century counterpart of Billy the Kid. The only differences were that Crowley lived two years less and the Kid was never involved in as fierce a gun battle as Crowley was. In a short but violent criminal career, Crowley engineered a bank robbery, shot down a storekeeper in one of several holdups, was involved in the murder of Virginia Banner, a dance hall hostess who had turned down his partner-in-crime, and killed Frederick Hirsch, a policeman who had asked him for identification in a deserted spot near North Merrick, Long Island.

By then the newspapers had labeled the sallow-faced 19-year-old Two Gun Crowley, a reputation he would enhance in the most savage gun battle in the history of New York City. On May 7, 1931, in what was termed the "siege on West 90th Street," Crowley traded bullets with 300 police attackers from his hideout room, while his 16-year-old girlfriend, Helen Walsh, and his partner, Rudolph Duringer, cowered under a bed. The police poured more than 700 bullets into the room, blasting away brick and mortar from the building's facade. In response, Crowley raced from window to window firing back and throwing tear gas cannisters lobbed into his room back to the street, where they overcame a number of his besiegers. Fifteen thousand persons jammed against police barricades, often seeming about to press through the barriers into the "no-man's-land" where the battle raged. More leaned out of neighboring windows, using pillows as armrests. It was violent Dodge City transferred to a Depression-weary Manhattan, an event to be savored. Finally, Crowley, shot four times and weakened by tear gas, was overwhelmed by a police assault squad that smashed through his door.

At his trial Crowley lived up to his press notices with an air of bravado, bantering with reporters, officers and the judge. He smirked when sentenced to the electric chair. In Sing Sing, Crowley maintained that attitude for a while. He fashioned a club out of a tightly wrapped magazine bound with wire from his cot and tried to slug a guard and escape from the death house. He set fire to his cell. He took off his clothes, stuffed the toilet with them and flooded the cell. Warden Lewis E. Lawes ordered Crowley be kept naked. Still, the youth looked for violence. He placed grains of sugar on the floor, and whenever a fly settled there, he would kill it and laugh.

Then slowly, Crowley changed. A starling flew into the cell, and Crowley didn't kill it. He fed it, and each day the bird returned. "The prisoner had tamed the bird," Lawes noted. "But more surprising was the fact that the tiny bird tamed the bandit." The warden allowed Crowley all his former privileges, and they talked for hours. Lawes saw Crowley for what he was, a pathetic youth with a mental age of 10, born illegitimately and deserted by his mother. The only mother he had ever known was a woman who took him from a foundling home. He had had to work since the age of 12.

Shortly before he was to be executed, a press syndicate offered him $5,000 for his signature on a series of articles already written that purported to tell his life story. Crowley rejected the deal, telling Lawes, "If mother [meaning his foster mother] had that five grand when I was a kid, maybe things would have been different."

A few hours before he died, Crowley pointed to a large water bug running around his cell floor. "See that?" he said to Lawes. "I was about to kill it. Several times I wanted to crush it. It's a dirty looking thing. But then I decided to give it a chance and let it live." Lawes doubted if Crowley even grasped the significance of his remark.

He went to his death without the braggadocio of the newspaper-bred Two Gun Crowley. "Give my love to mother," he called out to Lawes as the hood went over his head.

Dahmer, Jeffrey (1960–1994)
the underinvestigated killer

In February 1992, 31-year-old Jeffrey L. Dahmer was convicted of the murder of 15 young men and boys (plus another one in a later prosecution), most of them killed right in his apartment. Far from being on the alert for a serial killer, the Milwaukee police did nothing to catch Dahmer early on—and actually were subjected to national outrage as being virtually guilty themselves of ignorant complicity *before* the fact!

In one case, a Dahmer victim escaped naked and bloodied from the killer's apartment and raced screaming down the street. Three police officers who "investigated" simply decided the matter was no more than a quarrel between gay lovers and turned the victim back over to Dahmer without so much as checking out his apartment. Dahmer took his victim in tow and after terrorizing him for a few hours, he got around to butchering him. It would be charged that if the victim had been white, rather than a member of a minority—in this case, a Laotian—the police would have been more competent in the investigation.

Jeffrey Dahmer, killer of 16 young men and boys, was actually caught once by Milwaukee police but was inexplicably let go. (Reuters/Corbis-Bettmann)

Meanwhile Dahmer went on luring victims to his home, drugging them to perform primitive lobotomies by drilling holes in their heads in an effort to make them into zombie-like sex slaves. Dahmer also engaged in frightful practices of cannibalism and necrophilia, descriptions of which are best left to medical texts.

On July 22, 1991 two police officers stopped a black man running with a set of handcuffs around one wrist. The man, near hysteria, told them a white man with a big knife was saying he was going to cut out his heart. The officers went to Dahmer's home and asked to enter. Dahmer, having consumed a large amount of beer, did not object, and the officers found a knife under a bed in the two-room apartment. In a dresser drawer there were scores of photographs of homosexual acts and other pictures of apparently dead male bodies and body parts. Opening the refrigerator, the police found a human head. (It became a bit of talk radio black humor that this find made the police somewhat suspicious.)

Dahmer was taken into custody, and detectives and technicians took over a frightening search of the premises. Body parts turned up in drawers, coolers, closets, boxes and a large plastic drum. Checking missing persons reports, authorities were able to determine the identities of the victims, ranging in age from late teens to 30 years old. The victims were mostly black but some were white, Hispanic, Laotian and American Indian.

Since Wisconsin had no death penalty, Dahmer was given 15 life sentences, plus one more for a fatal beating of an 18-year-old in Ohio. Only technically was Dahmer spared execution. He and another prisoner, Jesse Anderson, a wife killer, were attacked by prisoners while they were cleaning a washroom and shower area in Columbia Correctional Center in Portage. Both were killed with a metal club wielded by Christopher Searver, who was doing life for robbery-murder.

Even in death, Dahmer did not escape a bizarre circumstance: Shackles were kept on him during his autopsy as though there was some fear that he might rise from the dead to kill again. His brain was preserved for forensic study.

Daniels, Murl (1924–1949) mass murderer

With another parolee, Murl Daniels committed a series of senseless murders in Ohio in 1948, making him the quarry in what came to be labeled the "greatest manhunt in Ohio history."

Both Daniels, a psychopath, and his partner, John Coulter West, had done time at the Mansfield Reformatory, where, said Daniels, they had formed a compact that they would return someday to "take care" of one or more of the guards who had mistreated them. At the time, Daniels was serving a one-to-25-year term for a stickup and West, a feeble-minded man, was doing a one-to-seven-year stretch for stealing tires off a truck. Some critics of the American justice and penal systems have said that Daniels never should have been paroled, while others have insisted that the state was negligent in permitting an inmate such as West to mingle with a dangerous psychopath like Daniels.

When the two were paroled, they teamed up to commit stickups throughout the Midwest, finally killing a tavern owner during a robbery. They continued to rove the Midwest, committing several more holdups before they remembered their compact about killing some of their former guards. They headed for Mansfield, especially determined to kill a guard named Harris. But they were unable to locate him. They then decided to get Harris' address from his superior, John Elmer Niebel, who was in charge of the reformatory farm. They awakened Niebel about midnight and decided they would have to hold him and his wife and daughter until after they had killed Harris. They took the three of them to a cornfield outside of town and ordered them to take off their clothes, in order to make it more difficult for them to give an alarm if they worked themselves loose from their bindings, but then the pair realized that they had neglected to bring any rope with them. So instead, they shot and killed all three and fled to Cleveland. When they were identified as the killers an intensive manhunt was mounted. Daniels and West raced around the state, killing a farmer to get his car and later a truck driver for his truck.

They almost made it out of the state with the truck, a haulaway carrying new Studebaker cars. They were waved through a number of police roadblocks until one sheriff realized that the truck was headed back toward the auto plant instead away from it. The two were ordered to stop, and West started shooting, hitting a guard before he himself was killed. Daniels surrendered meekly and went to the electric chair on January 3, 1949.

The Boston Strangler, Albert DeSalvo, dances with a senior citizen in a 1972 prison affair sponsored by a volunteer community agency "trying to show how both these neglected groups of people [senior citizens and prisoners] can help each other." DeSalvo was stabbed to death the following year by one or more of his fellow inmates.

DeSalvo, Albert H. (1933–1973)

Boston Strangler

Between June 1962 and January 1964, a mass murderer who became known as the Boston Strangler killed 13 women in Boston, Mass. He used various devices to talk his way into the homes of women living alone and then sexually assaulted and strangled them. The first murder, that of 55-year-old divorcée Anna Slesers in June 1962, was typical. She was found sprawled on the floor of her apartment, strangled with the cord from her own housecoat. In some of the other cases, there was a hint of a robbery attempt, but police concluded this was merely a blind to cover up the clear sexual motivations of the murderer.

As the murders continued, a hysteria developed among Boston women, and many would never open a door to a stranger's knock. While the police pressed their hunt and brought in numerous suspects, the crimes continued up to January 1964, when they suddenly stopped without explanation. Then in October the Strangler struck again, molesting a young woman in her home after gaining entrance by pretending to be a detective. But although he threatened her with a knife, he left without killing her. The victim was able to identify her attacker as Albert DeSalvo, who had been released from prison in April 1962 after serving time for indecent assault. When his photograph appeared in the papers, scores of women reported to police that he was the man who had assaulted them.

There still was no direct proof that DeSalvo was the Boston Strangler until he made a confession, relating scores of details no one but the murderer could have known.

After his incarceration for life, a weird interest in the quotations of the Boston Strangler continued. Some, in letters by DeSalvo, were auctioned off, while others were recorded by reporters who had managed to have themselves confined in cells near him. Two sample quotes:

"Ha, they even know me in the Soviet Union."

"Boston people are sexpots, they all love sex. . . . Most broads are just waiting to get so-called raped."

Copies of a paperback about him, which DeSalvo attempted to slip to female visitors at the institution where he was confined for a time, were inscribed with the dedication, "Can't wait to get my hands around your throat."

Apparently, some of his fellow inmates at the Walpole State Prison, where he was confined in 1973, had somewhat similar feelings about him. He was found dead in his cell, stabbed 16 times by an unidentified convict or convicts.

Diamond, Jack "Legs" (1896–1931) racketeer and murderer

Two things often said about Jack "Legs" Diamond, one of the most notorious gangsters of the 1920s, were that "the only woman who ever loved him was his mother and she died when he was a kid" and "the bullet hasn't been made that can kill Legs Diamond." Both were inaccurate. Although he was a brutal killer, quite a few women loved Legs, especially his wife, Alice, and his showgirl mistress, Kiki Roberts. While he was indeed called the Clay Pigeon of the Underworld, he was the ultimate proof that no one can live forever with bullets constantly being fired at him.

Legs' main problem in life was that almost everyone in the underworld hated him. He was a double-crosser, a chiseler, a man totally incapable of keeping his word. At various times, he fought with most of the leading criminals in New York, thinking nothing of continually increasing his roster of enemies.

Legs started out as a sneak thief in his early teens, heisting packages off the backs of delivery trucks and outracing pursuers, thus gaining his nickname. In the early 1920s Legs had moved up to work for Little Augie Orgen, the top labor racketeer in the city, after he arranged the death of Nathan Kaplan, better known as Kid Dropper. Little Augie turned over to Diamond his smaller bootlegging enterprises. It appears that Augie was the last important gangster Diamond was loyal to. He acted as his bodyguard and even took some bullets in his arm and leg when Little Augie was shot down on a Lower East Side street in 1927. That loyalty did not extend to seeking vengeance for the death of his boss, however, even though Diamond had recognized the killers—Louis Lepke and Gurrah Shapiro. When he got out of the hospital, he made peace with them. They got what they wanted—the labor rackets—and Diamond took over the rest of Little Augie's bootleg business and his narcotics trade.

Suddenly, Legs Diamond was a big-timer, a sport on Broadway. He even opened his own joint, the Hotsy Totsy Club, a second-floor bistro on Broadway in the 50s. The club provided Diamond with a cover, and he often invited underworld rivals to peace meetings there. Many of the overly trusting gangsters were murdered in a back room. In 1929 Diamond committed a murder that really demonstrated his recklessness and total lack of conscience. He and his lieutenant, Charles Entratta, murdered a hoodlum named Red Cassidy right at the bar in front of a number of employees and patrons. Diamond and Entratta were forced to flee. Then from hiding, they decided to eliminate the law's case against them. Four witnesses who had seen the killing were in turn murdered, three customers and the club bartender. Four other persons, including the hat-check girl, simply disappeared and were never heard from again. Apparently, Diamond and Entratta had no fear that the missing witnesses might suddenly turn up again because the two resurfaced, confident the police no longer had a case against them.

However, Legs' forced retirement caused complications. The notorious Dutch Schultz had moved in on Diamond's rackets while he was gone, and what the Dutchman took, he seldom gave back. It led to a full-scale war between the two. Schultz was never a popular figure with the rest of the underworld, but no one complained about his efforts to kill Diamond.

Legs Diamond, in pinstripes, was considered "unkillable" by the underworld and "unconvictable" by the law. The theory proved to be half true.

There were many who were convinced that Diamond couldn't be killed. It had always been that way. In October 1924 some unknown gunmen had peppered his head with birdshot and put a bullet in his heel. Diamond then drove himself to Mt. Sinai Hospital and had his wounds taken care of. The second near miss was the attack on Little Augie. Diamond had lost so much blood from wounds in his arm and leg that he was not expected to survive. The war with Schultz added to his battle injuries. Shortly after he killed a couple of Schultz's men in

October 1930, Legs was curled up in a cozy suite with showgirl Kiki Roberts when gunmen broke in and pumped five bullets into him. Kiki was unhurt.

Legs was rushed to a hospital and, to the amazement of doctors, survived. In April 1931 Diamond was ambushed as he left a roadside inn. He got a bullet in the lung, another in the back, a third in the liver and a fourth in the arm. Once again, surgeons gave up on him, but again he recovered.

By this time, Diamond himself was convinced he couldn't be killed. He let it be known that once he was all better, he intended to take a bigger slice of the action in Manhattan. Legs indicated he was not satisfied with what he had gotten when criminal mastermind Arnold Rothstein was murdered and his empire divided. He served notice on Joey Fay that he wanted more of the nightclub rackets and on Waxey Gordon that he deserved more of the bootlegging and moonshining business.

All of this made it rather difficult to determine whose troops paid him a fatal visit on December 18, 1931. Diamond was hiding away in a room in Albany, N.Y. that only a few confederates knew about. He was sound asleep when two gunmen slipped into the room. One held him by the ears and the other shot him three times in the head. This time Diamond was absolutely dead.

See also: DUTCH SCHULTZ.

Dillinger, John Herbert (1903–1934)

public enemy

John Dillinger was the consummate public enemy, certainly the "superstar" gangster of the 1930s. But what is really amazing is that he achieved this status in a criminal career that spanned a mere 11 months, from September 1933 to July 1934. Dillinger and his mob—he actually was not the leader but merely a member among equals of the first so-called Dillinger mob—robbed between 10 and 20 banks. They also plundered three police arsenals, engaged in three spectacular jail breaks and fought their way out of police traps, murdering 10 men and wounding seven others in the process. This last fact was never considered very important by the public, just as Missourians did not hold such indiscretions against Jesse James a half-century earlier.

Dillinger captured the public's imagination with his style and verve; he displayed dash and derring-do in a spectacular but apocryphal "wooden gun" jail escape, had a casual impudence toward authority and often displayed a form of chivalry during robberies, especially flirting with older women bystanders, that turned him into a Depression-day Robin Hood. After all, he just robbed banks, not people, and on occasion told depositors to hang on to their money, that all the gang wanted was the bank's money. Undoubtedly, Dillinger was smart enough to understand such behavior stood him well with the public and could conceivably help him out of a tight spot someday.

Dillinger was a master bank robber. His gang's jobs were all well planned and timed to precision. During his nine-year stretch in prison for attempting to rob a grocer, he had learned the meticulous "Baron Lamm method" of bank robbery, named after a former Prussian army officer turned American criminal, which called for careful casing of a bank beforehand, pretested and timed getaway routes, and the like. Dillinger followed the technique to the utmost detail but added his own daring touches. The day before one

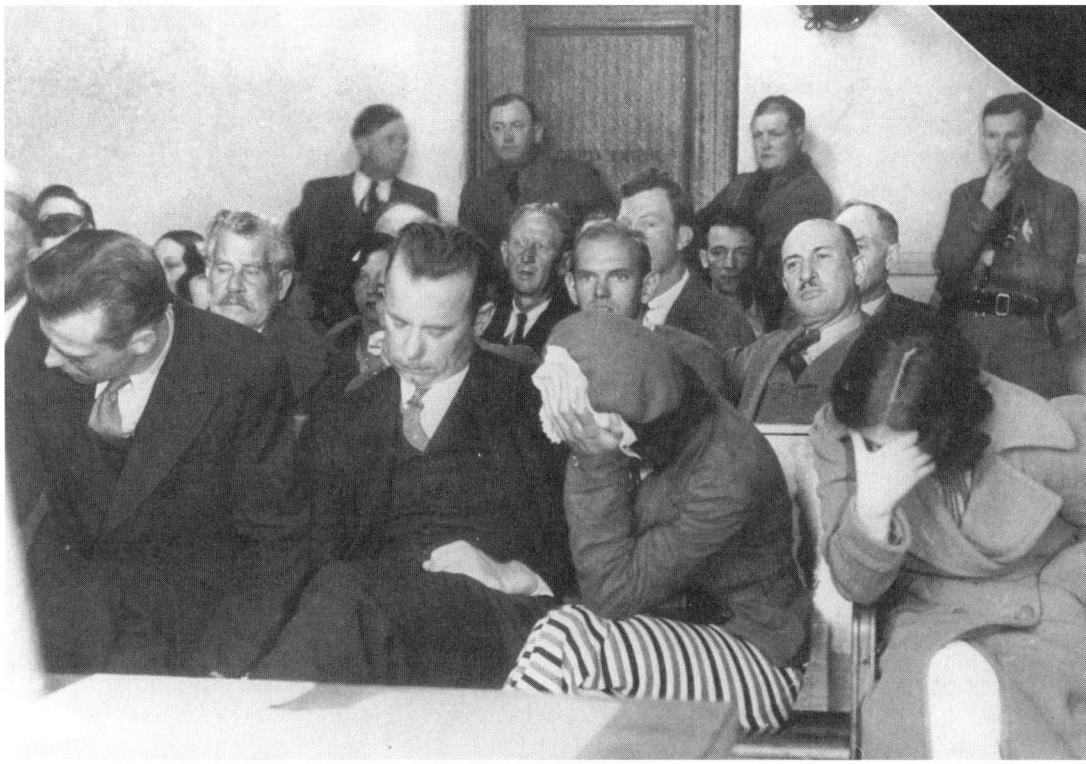

John Dillinger (second from left) is photographed at arraignment in Arizona, the last time he would be taken alive.

robbery, two of his men cased a bank posing as journalists and were taken on a grand tour of the institution by its chief officer. During another caper the townsfolk thought they were witnessing a rehearsal for the filming of a movie; a "movie director"—reputedly Homer Van Meter, the daring clown of the gang—had visited the scene the day before to publicize the event.

The product of an unhappy home life—John's mother died when he was three and his father subsequently remarried—young Dillinger became a juvenile delinquent. As a member of a youth gang called the Dirty Dozen, he was charged with stealing coal from the Pennsylvania Railroad's gondolas to sell to residents of his Indianapolis neighborhood; he was in the sixth grade at the time.

So far as the record shows, Dillinger did not get involved in serious crime until 1924, following a stint in the navy from which he just "walked away." That year he and an older, more seasoned criminal, Ed Singleton, attempted to rob a grocer whom they knew carried the day's receipts on him. The two men accosted their victim, B. F. Morgan, on a darkened street, and Dillinger, armed with a .32, struck him on the head with a bolt wrapped in a handkerchief. The grocer stayed erect and struggled, and Dillinger's gun went off. The hapless robbers then fled.

Apprehended quickly, Dillinger drew a sentence of 10 to 20 years, although he had been assured by the local prosecutor that as a first offender, he would be treated lightly if he pleaded guilty. Dillinger's accomplice, 10 years older, was brought before a different judge and drew a far shorter sentence; he was released after doing two years. Dillinger ended up serving nine and the experience embittered him.

In 1934 Indiana governor Paul V. McNutt's secretary, Wayne Coy, would observe: "There does not seem to me to be any escape from the fact that the State of Indiana made John Dillinger the Public Enemy that he is today. The Indiana constitution provides that our penal code shall be reformative and not vindictive. . . . Instead of reforming the prisoner, the penal institutions provided him with an education in crime."

Doing time first in the Indiana State Reformatory at Pendleton and then in the state prison at Michigan City, Dillinger came in contact with criminals who became his mentors and later his accomplices, among them accomplished bank robbers like Harry Pierpont, John Hamilton, Homer Van Meter, Far Charley Makley, Russell Clark and Walter Dietrich. Despite his youth and relative inexperience, Dillinger was accepted as a member of this clique of hardened criminals because of his personal trustworthiness and willingness to help other prisoners. These were qualities much respected by men behind bars, even causing Pierpont, the group's nominal leader, to overlook a failing in Dillinger that he tolerated in no other associate—having an "old lady" prison lover.

Several members of the Pierpont clique had unsuccessfully attempted to break out of the prison, leading most of them to conclude their only chance for escape was a scheme based on having aid from outside and making the proper payoffs inside. Dillinger, soon to be paroled, was designated the "outside man." As such, he would have to raise a lot of money and fast, and the group, which included a number of "jugmarkers" (men who had knowledge of good banks to be robbed), told him how to go about it. Pierpont and others also supplied him with names of trustworthy accomplices to use on various capers. Dillinger's duties were to get enough money to make the proper payoffs, buy guns, obtain getaway cars and clothes, and find a hideout for the escapees. With only limited experience but a vast amount of criminal knowledge, Dillinger emerged from prison to become the greatest public enemy in the history of American crime.

He was released in May 1933, after a petition bearing the signatures of almost 200 residents of his adopted hometown of Mooresville, Ind., including that of his grocer victim, was presented to the governor. Dillinger immediately set about committing robberies to raise the funds needed for the mass escape. Many of his capers were pulled with criminals little more experienced than he was and were badly bungled, often clearing less than $100. But Dillinger kept trying for bigger scores and finally pulled off a bank robbery that netted $10,600, no small sum for a bank in a Depression-racked area, and then a payroll heist that yielded more than $24,000. He now had enough funds to spring the Pierpont group, being totally unmindful at the time that Capt. Matt Leach of the Indiana State Police had identified him as the busy holdup artist. Leach had an alarm out for Dillinger and had just missed catching him on a number of occasions.

Meanwhile, Dillinger gave a large part of the escape money to Mary Kinder, a 22-year-old woman whose brother was one of the convicts slated to be in on the escape and who would become Pierpont's mistress. The complete story about the Michigan City breakout of 10 convicts was never fully revealed. Payoffs were made, that much is certain. In addition, Dillinger traveled to Chicago, where through an intermediary he bribed the foreman of a thread-making firm to conceal several guns in a barrel of thread destined for the prison's shirt shop. The barrel was marked with a red X so that the escapees would recognize it.

On September 26, 1933 Pierpont and nine others took several hostages and made their way out of the prison, a feat that resulted in all sorts of political recriminations in Indiana. The new McNutt administration contended that holdover Republican guards or some who had been dismissed must have been involved, but the former Republican governor, Harry Leslie, blamed the breakout on the 69 new guards appointed by the Democrats. It mattered little to the Pierpont bunch. They were free. It mattered less to Dillinger. He had in the meantime been captured in Dayton, Ohio while visiting one of several new girlfriends.

The Pierpont bunch were stunned when they learned from Mary Kinder that Dillinger had been arrested. There was no question of what they were going to do about it. Dillinger had kept his word and freed them, and now they were going to free him. They planned a raid on the jail in Lima, Ohio, where Dillinger was being held. Dillinger had been informed of the escape plot in advance and asked that another of his girlfriends, Evelyn "Billie" Frechette, a half Indian in her mid-twenties, be waiting for him when he got out.

The grateful Pierpont would deny Dillinger nothing. Billie, the wife of a bank robber then in Leavenworth, was brought to an apartment in Cincinnati to await Dillinger's release. On October 12, Columbus Day, Pierpont, Makley and Clark broke into the Lima Jail, mortally wounded Sheriff Jess Sarber and freed Dillinger. On the way out of the jail, Dillinger paused to look at the dying sheriff, who had treated him kindly and whom Dillinger had developed an affection for, and said sharply to Pierpont, "Did you have to do that?"

Pierpont shrugged. He might not have taken such a rebuke from another man, but he genuinely liked and respected Dillinger.

The "Dillinger mob" was now ready for action, although at the time, it should have been called the "Pierpont mob." Dubbing it the Dillinger mob was the idea of lawman Matt Leach, who thought he might produce friction between the pair by making Dillinger into a greater criminal than he was. However, Leach's ploy failed. Nothing would come between Dillinger and Pierpont, and in fact, the latter wanted Dillinger to assume a more active leadership. He quickly grasped that Dillinger inspired confidence, trust and loyalty, vital qualities in a criminal organization, and could bring peace between feuding gangsters.

The mob pulled off a string of somewhere between 10 to 20 bank robberies; the number could not be determined because the gangsters never confessed which ones they had perpetrated and which were falsely attributed to them. This first so-called Dillinger mob functioned until January 1934, by which time the gang, after going to Florida for a rest, had moved to Tucson, Ariz. Several members were captured there by police work that was partly brilliant, partly pure luck and partly a result of tips from persons who recognized some of the gang from detective magazine pictures.

Dillinger was caught with Billie Frechette. Pierpont, Makley and Clark were taken with Mary Kinder and another woman. The three men were shipped to Ohio to be charged with the murder of Sheriff Sarber. Dillinger was flown to Chicago, where that city's entire "Dillinger Squad," 40 officers permanently assigned to the job of capturing him, and 85 other policemen met the plane. A 13-car convoy then took America's most famous prisoner to an "escape-proof" jail in Crown Point, Ind.

It was here that Dillinger was to electrify the nation with his famous "wooden gun" escape. According to the first version of the story, he used a knife to whittle a wooden gun out of the top of a washboard, colored it with shoe polish and used it to escape. But how did America's number one criminal get hold of a knife in jail? All right, change that to a razor blade. Both versions were sheer nonsense. Dillinger's wooden gun was a real one. The true story behind his escape from the Crown Point Jail was that his lawyer, an incredible rogue named Louis Piquett, had met with a prominent Indiana judge on the grounds of the Century of Progress in Chicago and handed over an envelope containing several thousand of dollars. In return, the judge agreed to smuggle a gun into the jail. Dillinger used the gun to capture and lock up several guards and then made his way to the warden's office, where he grabbed two machine guns.

He gave one of the machine guns to a black prisoner, 35-year-old Herbert Youngblood, and together they locked up several more officers; snatched the car of a lady sheriff, Mrs. Lillian Holley, from the jail parking lot; and made good their escape, taking two hostages with them. Dillinger later released the two hostages, giving one, an auto mechanic, $4 for his troubles.

Naturally, the supposed wooden gun escape made headlines. Sometime later, however, a secret investigation conducted by the Hargrave Secret Service of Chicago on orders of Gov. McNutt turned up the true story about the gun. McNutt and Attorney General Philip Lutz, Jr. decided not to reveal the information because they quite properly didn't want Dillinger to know that certain informants whom he might trust again in the future had talked to private detectives. By the time Dillinger was killed, the judge too had died, and the findings about the gun never were made public.

Meanwhile, Dillinger basked in the glory of the wooden gun story and sought to perpetuate it. In a letter to his sister, he told her not to worry about him and that he was "having a lot of fun." Concerning the gun, he added:

> *. . . [the reports] I had a real forty five Thats just a lot of hooey to cover up because they don't like to admit that I locked eight Deputys and a dozen trustys up with my wooden gun before I got my hands on the two machine guns. I showed everyone the wooden gun after I got a hold of the machine guns and you should have seen* thire *faces. Ha! Ha! Ha! Pulling that off was worth ten years of my life. Ha! Ha!*

Dillinger's intention obviously was to cover up the fact that a real gun had been smuggled to him and to satisfy his ego. It was not the only time he had done that. Dillinger had often tormented his chief pursuer, Matt Leach, with phone calls and letters. And on one occasion he supposedly sent a book entitled *How to Be a Detective* to the excitable Leach. When he was captured in Arizona, Dillinger had been asked if he had in fact sent the book. He replied, "I was there when it was sent." That too was sheer nonsense. The book had been sent to Leach as a practical joke by Jack Cejnar, the bureau chief of the International News Service in Indianapolis.

After their escape Dillinger and Youngblood immediately separated. Thirteen days later, on March 16, 1934, Youngblood was mortally wounded in a gun battle with lawmen in Port Huron, Mich. As evidence of the loyalty Dillinger inspired in men, the dying Youngblood falsely told police that Dillinger had been with him the day before.

Immediately, Dillinger put together the real Dillinger mob, including among others Van Meter, jugmarker Eddie Green, Hamilton, Tommy Carroll and a newcomer, a short, violent-tempered punk named Lester Gillis, better known as Baby Face Nelson. It took considerable skill on Dillinger's part to keep Nelson and Van Meter, and occasionally some of the others, from shooting at one another. Dillinger undoubtedly disliked Nelson but he needed him. Nelson was the sort who would never desert his post in a robbery, and Dillinger had to commit several robberies fast. He had to get money to provide a legal defense for Pierpont, Makley and Clark, who were to be tried for murdering Sheriff Sarber.

Dillinger sent the money, but it did little good. All three were convicted: Clark got life and the other two were sentenced to the electric chair.

Time was running out for Dillinger as well. The same month as his breakout from the Crown Point Jail, he barely escaped in a barrage of machine-gun fire during a confrontation with FBI agents in St. Paul. Dillinger was wounded in the leg, but Billie Frechette drove him to safety. The next month, April 1934, Dillinger and the rest of the mob were hiding out at Little Bohemia Lodge, a closed summer resort about 50 miles north of Rhinelander, Wis., when the FBI closed in. Warned by barking dogs, Dillinger and his men escaped. Baby Face Nelson killed Special Agent W. Carter Baum and wounded another agent and a local police officer. The FBI wound up capturing only three of the mob's women, who were found hiding in the basement. They also managed to shoot two innocent bystanders, a salesman and a Civilian Conservation Corps (CCC) cook, and kill another young CCC worker, all of whom they thought were escaping gangsters.

It was a debacle for the FBI and, in a sense, another laurel for Dillinger. Will Rogers got into the act, writing, "Well, they had Dillinger surrounded and was all ready to shoot him when he come out, but another bunch of folks come out ahead, so they just shot them instead. Dillinger is going to accidentally get with some innocent bystanders some time, then he will get shot."

Dillinger and Van Meter both submitted to plastic surgery to alter their faces and fingerprints. Neither job was overly effective. Ironically, Dillinger "died" on the operating cot. Given a general anesthetic, he swallowed his tongue and stopped breathing. One of the panicky outlaw doctors managed to pull out his tongue with a forceps and applied artificial respiration, and Dillinger started breathing again.

By this time Hamilton had died of wounds received in a shoot-out with pursuing officers, and while Dillinger was recovering from the plastic surgery, Tommy Carroll was killed near Waterloo, Iowa. The mob was falling apart, and Dillinger could only think of making a few big scores and then fleeing to Mexico.

Still, Dillinger's facial surgery gave him enough confidence to venture openly in the streets. Using the identity of Jimmy Lawrence, he took up with a 26-year-old Chicago waitress named Polly Hamilton. Polly shared rooms with a friend, Anna Sage, whose real name was Ana Cumpanis. Sage had come to America from Romania just after the war and had operated whorehouses in Gary, Ind., and East Chicago, Ill. She had twice been convicted of operating a disorderly house but had won pardons from Indiana governor Leslie. Recently, however, Sage had been convicted a third time and Gov. McNutt had refused her request for a pardon. The Immigration Bureau was seeking to deport her as an undesirable alien.

Dillinger felt safe with Polly Hamilton and Anna Sage; he had never had trouble with women betraying him. It is doubtful that Hamilton knew his true identity, but Anna Sage soon discovered it. Dillinger felt comfortable talking to her. She was 42, an older woman and perhaps even a mother figure for him. Sage listened to his stories and ramblings and perhaps would not have informed on him merely because there was a $10,000 reward for his capture. But through a police contact in East Chicago, she made a deal with the FBI to betray Dillinger in exchange for a promise that the deportation proceedings against her would be dropped and the reward money would be given to her. Melvin Purvis, agent in charge of the Chicago office of the FBI, agreed to help with those matters as far as possible.

On July 22, 1934 Dillinger took the two women to a Chicago movie. Earlier in the day Sage had called the FBI to tell them about Dillinger's plans, but at that time she did not know which of two movies they would attend. The FBI staked out both and waited. As planned, Sage dressed in red so that the FBI men would recognize her. The agents at the Biograph Theater saw Dillinger and the two women enter. FBI inspector Sam Cowley, in charge of the nationwide hunt for Dillinger, telephoned J. Edgar Hoover and the decision was not to try to take Dillinger inside the movie house but to wait until he came out. When Dillinger and the women walked out of the theater, Purvis lit a cigar, the signal that identified Dillinger. Then he called on Dillinger to halt. The gangster looked about suddenly, and he saw that his female companions had vanished. In that brief instant he must have realized he had been betrayed by a woman. He pulled a Colt automatic from his right pants pocket and sprinted for the alley at the side of the movie house. Three FBI agents fired. They wounded two women passing, but they also shot Dillinger. One bullet went through his left side, another tore through his stooped back and came out his right eye. Dillinger fell dead.

Within a few months the second Dillinger mob was completely wiped out. Eddie Green was shot by the FBI. A month after Dillinger died, Homer Van Meter was also killed in an alley, this one in St. Paul, after being betrayed by friends. In November, Baby Face Nelson killed two FBI agents but died himself of wounds received in the gun battle. Meanwhile, Pierpont and Makley attempted to escape from the death house at the Ohio State Prison in Columbus by imitating Dillinger's mythical wooden gun ruse. With guns carved out of soap, they succeeded in overpowering one guard and were trying to batter their way out through the door leading from the death house when a riot squad opened fire. Makley was killed and Pierpont wounded. A month later, Pierpont died in the electric chair.

See also: GEORGE "BABY FACE" NELSON.

Dolan, Dandy Johnny (c. 1850–1876)

gangster and murderer

One of the most imaginative and brutal gangsters of the 19th century, Dandy Johnny Dolan probably qualified as the Thomas Edison of the underworld. A renowned member of the Whyos, a gang that dominated crime in New York during the decades following the Civil War, Dolan came up with a host of innovative methods to maim and kill, his prize invention being a great advance in the technique of gouging out eyes. Dolan produced an apparatus, made of copper and worn on the thumb, that could do the gruesome job with dispatch. It served the Whyos well both in criminal endeavors and in battles with other gangs. Dolan also designed special fighting boots for himself with sections of a sharp ax blade imbedded in the soles. A simple stomping of a downed enemy produced an ending both gory and mortal.

Dolan's downfall came when James H. Noe, a brush manufacturer, caught him in the process of robbing his factory. The gangster managed to get away by using his terrible eye gouger on Noe and then beating his victim to death with an iron bar. Later, Dolan proudly displayed eyes to admiring members of the Whyos. The police did not catch Dolan with the eyes, but they did find him in possession of Noe's cane, which had a metal handle carved in the likeness of a monkey, as well as his watch and chain. This evidence was enough to doom Dolan, and he was hanged on April 21, 1876.

Driscoll, Danny (?1860–1888)

gang leader and murderer

The last great New York ruffian gang of the 19th century was the Whyos, captained jointly in their heyday by Danny Lyons and Danny Driscoll. In the 1880s Lyons and Driscoll reportedly mandated that a potential member of the gang had to kill at least one man. It is perhaps fitting that this brutal pair were themselves hanged within eight months of each other.

Driscoll went first. In 1887 he and tough Five Points gangster Johnny McCarthy became involved in a shooting dispute over whom a young prostitute, Breezy Garrity, was working for. Breezy made the mistake of standing around to see who the winner would be, presumably to hand over to him her recent receipts. In the fusillade one of Driscoll's stray shots struck and killed her. It was clearly a case of unintentional homicide, and by most measures of justice Driscoll should have escaped with something less than the ultimate penalty. However, the authorities had been after Driscoll for years on suspicion of several murders and were not going to allow a golden opportunity such as this to slip away because of legal niceties. The prosecution hardly had to remind the jurors of the many atrocities committed by the Whyos, since everyone living in New York ventured out in constant fear of these gangsters. Driscoll, screaming outrage and frame-up, was sentenced to death, and on January 23, 1888 he was hanged in the Tombs.

See also: DANNY LYONS.

Drucci, Vincent "Schemer" (1895–1927)

bootlegger and murderer

One of the chief lieutenants in Dion O'Banion's North Side Gang during the 1920s,

Drucci took charge of the Chicago outfit after O'Banion and his successor, Hymie Weiss, were assassinated by the Capone forces.

In one sense, Drucci was Capone's toughest rival in that opposing gang, because he was, as Capone put it, "a bedbug." The Schemer had earned his nickname because of his imaginative but totally off-the-wall ideas for robbing banks and kidnapping millionaires. He was also a tough kill. In a street duel with ambushing Capone gunners, he traded shot for shot with them while giggling and dancing a jig to avoid the bullets that sprayed the pavement around him. When a police car appeared on the scene, the Capone gunmen sped off in their car, but the Schemer had not had enough. Despite a slight leg wound, he hopped on the running board of a passing car, poked his gun at the motorist's head and yelled, "Follow that goddamn car." Police had to drag him off the car. When questioned, Drucci claimed it was not an underworld battle but a stickup. "They wanted my roll," he said, flashing a wad of $13,500.

With Drucci at the head of the O'Banion gang, Capone had to beef up protection for himself, since the Schemer was capable of any wild plot to get at him. According to one unconfirmed story, Drucci actually cornered Capone alone in a Turkish bath and almost strangled him to death before the gang leader's bodyguards showed up. The Schemer escaped stark naked, hopped in his car and drove off.

Frustrated in his efforts to get Big Al, Drucci decided to hurt him as best he could. A few weeks later, he had Theodore "the Greek" Anton, the owner of a popular restaurant over a Capone headquarters, the Hawthorne Smoke Shop, kidnapped. Anton was an honest man who idolized Capone for what he considered the gangster's tenderheartedness, such as his practice of buying all a newsboy's papers for $20 and sending him home. Capone was eating in the restaurant when Anton was snatched by lurking O'Banionites. He understood what it meant and sat in a booth the rest of the evening crying inconsolably.

Anton's body was found in quicklime. He had been tortured and then shot.

Capone vowed to kill Drucci, but the next several murder attempts were made by the Schemer. As a matter of fact, the Capone gang never did get Drucci. He was arrested on April 5, 1927 for perpetrating some election day violence against reformers seeking to supplant the William Hale Thompson machine. Put in a squad car, Drucci got enraged because a detective, Dan Healy, had dared lay a hand on him. He screamed, "I'll get you for this!" and tried to wrestle the detective's gun away. The officer pulled his hand free and pumped four quick shots into Drucci's body.

The O'Banionites wanted Healy charged with murder. "Murder?" asked Chief of Detectives William Schoemaker. "We're having a medal struck for Healy."

The North Siders gave Drucci a marvelous funeral. He lay in state a day and a night in a $10,000 casket of aluminum and silver at the undertaking establishment of Assistant State's Attorney John A. Sbarbaro. The walls of the room were hidden by masses of flowers; the dominant floral design was a throne of white and purple blooms with the inscription "Our Pal." After Drucci was buried, his blond wife declared proudly, "A cop bumped him off like a dog, but we gave him a king's funeral."

See also: CHARLES DION "DEANIE" O'BANION, HYMIE WEISS.

Durrant, William Henry Theodore

(1872–1898) murderer

William "Theo" Durrant, who became famous in this country and Europe as the Demon in the Belfry for the murder of two young women in San Francisco in 1895, was as close to a real-life Jekyll and Hyde as America ever produced.

At 23 Theo was an excellent student in his senior class of Cooper Medical College and a dedicated member of the Emanuel Baptist Church, functioning as assistant Sunday school superintendent, Sunday usher, church librarian and secretary of the young people's Christian Endeavor Society. Whenever there were repairs to be made on the church, Theo could be counted on to offer his services. Several times a week, in his less sane moments, Theo patronized the notorious brothels on Commercial Street, regarded as far more degenerate than those elsewhere in the city. Theo's custom was to bring with him a sack or small crate containing a chicken or pigeon; during the high point of the evening's debauch, he would slit the bird's throat and let the blood trickle over himself. The only hint of Theo's other life was some gossip that he had attempted to kiss girls at church socials.

On April 3, 1895 Theo was seen entering the church with 18-year-old Blanche Lamont, a high school student who often spoke of becoming a teacher. Inside the church Theo excused himself, saying he had a chore to perform. He returned a moment later, stripped naked. When the girl resisted him, Durrant killed her in a frenzy, strangling her and mutilating her body. He then dragged the body up to the belfry and hid it. Two hours later, he calmly appeared at a Christian Endeavor meeting.

The Demon in the Belfry is depicted carrying a beautiful victim to his hiding place in the bell tower.

Theo was questioned when Blanche was reported missing, but he earnestly informed the police that it was his theory that white slavers might have kidnapped her and installed her in a brothel somewhere in San Francisco or perhaps shipped her to some faraway locality. Nothing much would have developed from the investigation had not Theo struck again that same month, killing 20-year-old Minnie Williams in the church after some naked trysts. Minnie, unlike Blanche, had responded to Theo's bizarre wooing, but he murdered her just as well. He slashed the body with a knife and left it hidden behind a door in the blood-spattered church library, where it was found the next day. The theory was that Theo might have told her about Blanche's murder, and Minnie responded by saying she was going to the police.

Again, Theo had been seen with a young woman who later disappeared or was murdered, but he denied any knowledge of the crime. However, police found Minnie's purse hidden in a suit pocket in his closet, and they finally trekked up to the belfry and found Blanche Lamont's body as well.

Theo's trial was a spectacle, perhaps the first to receive sensational "sob-sister" coverage. William Randolph Hearst's *Examiner* printed a front-page sketch of Theo's hands so that its readers could recognize the "hands of murder." A "sweet pea girl" appeared at each session of the court and offered Theo a bouquet of flowers. This was either a defense tactic or a newspaper trick to generate reader interest. In all, 125 witnesses testified, including Theo himself, who thought he had convinced the jury with his denials of guilt. He was nonetheless found guilty on the first ballot. Appeals delayed the execution for almost three years until January 7, 1898, when Durrant was hanged.

On the scaffold, Theo told the hangman, "Don't put that rope on, my boy, until I talk." The sheriff merely waved to the hangman to continue his work, and Theo was hanged without further ado. The newspapers were somewhat peeved at being deprived of some final words from the fiendish killer, but they were able to report one final macabre incident.

Theo's mother and father had apparently reveled in their notoriety during the trial. After the hanging they called for their son's body. While waiting in a prison anteroom, the couple was offered some food by the warden. When the body arrived, with Theo's face contorted in a hideous grimace, they sat eating not 5 feet from the open coffin. Hearst's newspaper reported that at one point Mother Durrant said, "Papa, I'd like some more of that roast."

Eastman, Monk (1873–1920) great gang leader
There are those authorities on crime who consider Monk Eastman the greatest gangster this country ever produced. Historian Herbert Asbury called him "the prince of gangsters" and "as brave a thug as ever shot an enemy in the back."

Eastman was the boss of the last great primarily Jewish street gang in New York City, able to field 1,200 to 1,500 vicious gangsters on short notice. The Eastmans wiped out the remnants of the brutal Whyos, a truly murderous collection of thugs, near the end of the 19th century and were always ready to do battle with Paul Kelly's notorious gangsters, the great Italian Five Points Gang. After the turn of the century, the Five Pointers boasted on their roster such future devotees of mayhem and violence as Johnny Torrio, Al Capone, Lucky Luciano and Frankie Yale. Yet, in comparison to Eastman's crew they were choir boys.

In appearance, Eastman looked precisely the way a gangster should—squat, massive, bullet-headed, with a busted nose and a pair of cauliflower ears. And his behavior was worse than his appearance. He deserted his home area in the Williamsburg section of Brooklyn, where his respectable Jewish restaurateur father had set up a pet store for him, and headed for the crime-ridden fleshpots of lower Manhattan. He was to become a legend.

One of the most famous turn-of-the-century gang leaders, Monk Eastman once clubbed a hapless bar patron because "I had 49 nicks in me stick, an' I wanted to make it an even 50."

In the early 1890s Eastman became a bouncer at a rough dance hall, New Irving

Hall, where a girl might well get raped by a number of the boys if not by her date. Eastman patrolled his domain with a huge bludgeon, a blackjack in his hip pocket and brass knuckles on each hand. He was always proud of the fact that during the six months of his reign no less than 50 men required the attention of surgeons and that jocular ambulance drivers referred to the accident ward of Bellevue Hospital as the Eastman Pavilion. Eastman kept close count of the victims he clubbed and notched each assault on his club. One night an inoffensive little man was sitting at the bar drinking beer when Eastman walked up to him and cracked his scalp open with a mighty swipe. When asked why he'd done so, he replied, "Well, I had 49 nicks in me stick, an' I wanted to make it an even 50."

If that seemed a bit antisocial, at least Monk could pride himself on his near-Victorian treatment of women. He never once struck a woman with his club, no matter how trying she became. At most, he simply blackened her eyes with his hammy fist. "I only gave her a little poke," he would exclaim. "Just enough to put a shanty on her glimmer. But I always takes off me knucks first."

With behavior such as that, Monk Eastman became a legend on the East Side, and other young bloods took to imitating him in speech and manner. Of course, from such personal magnetism great leaders are born, and Eastman soon gathered around him a band of hoodlums eager to do his bidding. It didn't take long before he told them to go forth, beat up some citizens and bring back some money.

From then on, Eastman's gang grew rapidly. He and his men took over much of the crime on the Lower East Side, engaging in robberies, burglaries, assault, muggings and murder for pay. Eastman seized control of many of the gambling dens and houses of prostitution, and even individual streetwalkers and hoodlums had to pay him for the privilege of operating in his turf. Although a crude savage, Eastman was smart enough to ingratiate himself with Tammany Hall and, in exchange for protection and a regular stipend, handled any chore required. On election day he furnished the largest contingent of voters, his own men, who voted early and often, and then blackjacked any honest citizen who was considering voting against Eastman's patrons. Whenever Eastman or his men got in trouble, Tammany Hall lawyers appeared in court for them. Bail was posted and promptly forfeited until the case was expunged from the records.

As rich and powerful as he became, Eastman could never resist doing violence himself, sometimes even personally carrying out a blackjacking commission. "I like to beat up a guy once in a while," he used to say. "It keeps me hand in."

In one confrontation with the hated Five Pointers, Eastman was shot twice in the stomach and left for dead, but he climbed to his feet and staggered to Gouverneur Hospital, plugging a gaping wound with his fingers. Eastman hovered near death but, in keeping with underworld tradition, would not name his assailant. When he got out, Eastman personally shot the Five Pointer and dumped his body in the gutter.

In time, the Eastmans appeared to be winning the war with the Five Pointers and also routing the forces of another major gang leader, Humpty Jackson, but in 1904 Eastman caused his own downfall by holding up an expensively dressed young man who had overimbibed. It was a robbery Eastman did not have to commit but could not resist. Unfortunately for the gangster, the victim was a scion of wealth whose family had hired a Pinkerton to follow him for his protection. Seeing Eastman accost the young man, the detective opened fire on him, and the gangster fled right into the arms of a policeman, who knocked him out before recognizing him.

If Eastman expected aid from Tammany, he was sadly disappointed. In view of the rising spirit of reform, the political bosses were happy for the chance to be rid of him. The great gangster was shipped off in ignominy to do 10 years in Sing Sing. When he was released, he found his power was gone. The Eastmans had factionalized a dozen ways, as the times would no longer support great street gangs. Eastman could not understand what had happened. But World War I proved to be a godsend for him, and he went off to fight. When he returned, he was awarded a pardon by Gov. Al Smith, who signed an executive order restoring him to full citizenship.

In December 1920 Eastman was shot dead by a corrupt Prohibition agent with whom he was running a penny-ante bootlegging and dope-selling operation.

Espinosa brothers murderers

In 1861 three Mexican brothers and some other kin invaded Colorado with the announced purpose of killing 600 Americans. This vendetta, they said, was to make up—at the rate of 100 to one—for the loss of life suffered by the Espinosa family during the Mexican War. By mid-1863 the three brothers, Felipe, Julián and Victorio, had managed to dispatch 26 Americans. Their typical victims were freighters, prospectors, sawmill workers or soldiers whom they had caught alone. While vengeance was supposedly the first order of the day, the Espinosas saw to it that their victims were also worth robbing; their soldier-victims, for instance, had generally been waylaid right after payday.

With 574 victims to go, Felipe Espinosa, the leader and most audacious member of the family, sent a message to the territorial governor, offering to quit the murderous campaign if the Espinosas were given a land grant of 5,000 acres and made captains in the Colorado Volunteers. Such an offer was hardly likely to be accepted, as Felipe most certainly knew, and probably represented a bold attempt to put the best possible face on the criminal acts. The governor responded by placing a reward of $2,500 on Felipe's head.

The killings went on and terror gripped the territory. Groups of vigilante miners rode hell-for-leather around the countryside trying to corner the Espinosas and hanged more than one suspect, even some who quite clearly were not Mexicans. Finally, however, they did catch Victorio Espinosa in the Fairplay–California Gulch area and strung him up. Later they staged a drunken celebration because they mistakenly believed their victim was Felipe, without whom the Espinosas were thought to be incapable of continuing their murderous activities.

When the terror did not end, it was obvious Felipe was still alive. He continued to elude posses of miners and army patrols. Finally, the army commissioned a storied scout named Tom Tobin to bring in the Espinosas with the aid of a 15-soldier detail. Late in 1863, Tobin successfully tracked down the remaining two Espinosa brothers, but at the last moment he slipped away from the troopers because he did not want to share the reward money with them. Tobin cornered Felipe and Julián Espinosa at Indian Creek and shot them dead before they could return his fire. He cut off their heads as proof he had gotten the right men and returned to Fort Garland to claim his reward. However, because of a shortage of cash in the territorial coffers, Tobin was given only $1,500 and some buckskins.

For several years pickled "Espinosa heads" were exhibited around the West. Long after, in 1955, Kit Carson III labeled these exhibits, some still around, as fakes. Carson said Tom Tobin, his maternal grandfather, had always insisted the heads had been buried behind Fort Garland and never removed.

Farrington brothers outlaws

It has been estimated that at least 25 young Missourians turned to a life of crime when they saw the public adulation that was lavished on the James brothers. Two of these were the Farrington brothers, Levi and Hilary. Like the James boys, they were ex-Confederate guerrillas who had taken part in Quantrill's bloody raid on Lawrence, Kan. Later, they rode under George Todd. These two bearded, hardly literate giants witnessed what "ole Jesse and Frank were adoin" and saw no reason they couldn't do the same. They, however, lacked the flair of the James brothers, being nothing more than brutish killers, and never basked in the hero worship accorded to Jesse and Frank. Nonetheless, they were skillful riders and gunmen and their crimes cut a wide swath from Missouri and Tennessee down into Mississippi.

In 1870 they teamed up with another bloody pair, William Barton and William Taylor; flagged down the Mobile and Ohio flyer at Union City; and robbed the express car of $20,000. As they continued their depredations and recruited new members to their gang, Pinkertons and express company detectives picked up their trail and finally cornered the gang in a hideout deep in the canebreaks at Lester's Landing in Mississippi. The raiders, headed by William Pinkerton, the son of the founder of the agency, and Pat O'Connell, considered the best express company detective of the time, captured five gang members after a gunfight but then discovered the Farringtons had pulled out two hours earlier. Weeks later, Pinkerton and O'Connell cornered Hilary Farrington in a farmhouse in Verona, Mo. and captured him after a daylong gun battle. Extraditing him to Union City, Tenn., his captors placed Hilary aboard the sternwheeler Illinois. When he attempted a nighttime escape, he fell overboard in a battle with William Pinkerton and was crushed to death by the vessel's stern paddle.

In 1871 Levi Farrington was taken by the Pinkertons during a hand-to-hand battle in the town square in Farmingdale, Ill. Crowds gathered, but unlike the admiration people showed for the James boys, they wanted to string Levi up. The Pinkertons held off the mob at gunpoint and got their prisoner back to Union City. They could have saved themselves the trip, however. A large band of nightriders seized Levi Farrington from the sheriff and hanged him from a tree near the main gate of the Union City cemetery.

Fish, Albert (1870–1936) mass murderer and cannibal

A harmless-looking house painter in New York City, Albert Fish was a degenerate who admitted molesting more than 400 children over a span of 20 years. Fish, labeled by the press as the "inhuman monster," was described by one shocked psychiatrist as a man of "unparalleled perversity. There was no known perversion that he did not practice and practice frequently."

Fish had a personal and married life that was odd, to say the least. He enjoyed sticking needles into himself, spanking himself with a nail-studded paddle or having children beat him until he bled. He appreciated children because of their innocence and because, as he once put it, "They don't tell." Certainly, the 15 to 17 children he murdered never told.

He got married when he was 28. It lasted for about 20 years before his wife ran off with a half-wit. She returned about a year later and asked to move back in with her lover. Fish said she could stay but her lover could not. Later, he discovered his wife had hidden her lover in the attic. He kicked him out and again told his wife she could stay, but she went off with her lover and Fish never saw her again. Fish had six children. They were aware their father was a bit peculiar, but he was kind to them and never beat them. The children had seen him use his nailed paddle on himself, but they assumed he must be sane, if somewhat eccentric, since they knew he had been under psychiatric observation a number of times and had always been discharged by the doctors.

His occupation as a house painter allowed him to move from town to town and gave him access to cellars and deserted buildings. By his own count, he committed offenses in at least 23 states. He had some close calls. In St. Louis Fish had almost been caught with a small boy he had been torturing for days but escaped just in time. There were narrow squeaks in Virginia and in Delaware and several in New York. Children disappeared with a kindly old man never to be seen again; others were found brutally mutilated. He was questioned several times but was never a serious suspect.

At a very minimum, he killed and ate at least 15 children. His last such victim apparently was a 12-year-old New York City girl, Grace Budd, whom he lured from her parents in 1928 by telling them he was bringing her to a party a friend was giving for a daughter. He cut up her body and cooked the parts in a stew with onions and carrots. It took him nine days to eat most of her. He buried what was left. It was six years before he was caught for that crime. The police were baffled by the case, but Fish could not resist writing Mrs. Budd to tell her what he'd done. He didn't sign the letter, but the police readily traced him. Fish acted as though he had been waiting for them for a long time. He immediately confessed and led them to a spot in White Plains where they found the girl's bones. He also confessed to a number of additional cannibal murders.

Fish's trial consisted of a long parade of psychiatric specialists. Only Dr. Frederic Wertham and two other defense experts insisted he was insane. Fish was judged guilty and sane enough to die in the electric chair. The prospect excited Fish. "What a thrill that will be if I have to die in the electric chair," he said with a broad smile. "It will be the supreme thrill. The only one I haven't tried." When he did go to the chair on January 16, 1936, he was described by the press as being positively joyful. He even helped adjust the electrodes when he was being strapped down.

The newspapers had one more ghoulish report for their readers. The first massive jolt of electricity failed to kill Fish. The theory was that the 400 plus needles he had inserted into his body over the years had apparently caused a short circuit. A second potent jolt was needed to complete the job.

Fisher, John King (1854–1884) gunman and lawman

John King Fisher was one of the 19th century's controversial gunmen for whom Texas was famous or infamous, becoming a popular hero to some and a callous murderer to others. Fisher once shot a man in the head because he wanted to see if a bullet would bounce off his bald pate. Perhaps his mean streak was best illustrated by the sign he erected at a crossroads when he established his own spread in southern Texas: "This is King Fisher's Road—Take the other one." The sign became something of a landmark and was considered no idle threat. In 1878 Fisher said he was responsible for killing seven men in gunfights, not counting Mexicans.

Fisher's first scrape with the law occurred in 1870, when at the age of 16 he drew a two-year term for robbery but served only four months. Gaining a pardon, he worked as a cowboy for a few years and then started his own spread, which became headquarters for an unsavory crew of rustlers, killers and deadbeats. He formed an alliance with Mexican rustlers, but after a dispute on a division of the spoils, he pistol-whipped one, shot a second as he went for his gun and then gunned down two others who were just sitting on a fence. During Fisher's "ranching" days he reputedly formed a partnership with an *insurrecto* named Porfirio Díaz, who later became president-dictator of Mexico, whereby Díaz delivered stolen Mexican cattle to Fisher and received Fisher's rustled American beef. On both sides of the border there were stock buyers who were not particularly mindful of brands if they were from the other country.

Fisher frequently was arrested on murder charges and was subject to considerable Texas Ranger harassment, but he was inevitably found not guilty or the charges were dismissed for lack of evidence. Then King Fisher made a sudden transformation: he got religion and in 1881 became a lawman, appointed deputy sheriff of Uvalde County. There were those who insisted he backslid a bit now and then, but in 1883 he made plans to run for sheriff the following year. In March 1884 Fisher went to Austin, the state capital, on official business and ran into an old gunman buddy, the crazed Ben Thompson. The pair rode together to San Antonio, where they entered the Vaudeville Variety Theater, a gambling hall whose proprietor, Jack Harris, Thompson had murdered some two years previously.

Thompson and Fisher had a drink at the bar and then repaired to a box upstairs to watch the variety show. They were joined in the box by bouncer Jacob Coy and two of Harris' former partners, Billy Simms and Joe Foster. Thompson made several nasty remarks about the Harris killing and then playfully jammed his six-gun into Foster's mouth, whereupon bouncer Coy moved in and seized the cylinder. There was a moment of tense silence, and Fisher made a remark about leaving before things got out of hand. Suddenly, there was a blaze of fire and

Thompson was dead, with nine slugs in him. King Fisher went down in a hail of 13 bullets.

Some suggested that but for his chance meeting with Thompson, the reformed King Fisher would have lived out a full life as a respected rancher and lawman. Not everyone was sorry about Fisher's demise. A woman whose son Fisher had killed came to the Uvalde cemetery on every anniversary of her son's death, set a brush fire atop Fisher's grave and danced "with devilish glee" around it.

Flores, Juan (1835–1857) outlaw and murderer

Unlike Joaquin Murieta, there was nothing fictional about Juan Flores, one of California's most spectacular and bloodthirsty villains. He was no more than a minor rustler and horse thief when he was put away in San Quentin in 1856. If he had served out his term, he probably would have remained a smalltimer, but Flores and a number of other prisoners escaped. Their method of escape made Flores a well-known figure, held in awe by both the public and other outlaws.

Flores viewed the walls of San Quentin and decided escape that way was difficult and dangerous, if not impossible. But he soon found a weak spot in the prison's security. When the opportunity came, Flores and a group of followers stormed aboard a provision ship tied up at the prison wharf, took control of the vessel and managed to sail off, erratically, but successfully in the end.

The fugitives were unsophisticated, to put it kindly, since they seriously debated sailing their stolen vessel to Australia to "take over the country." Instead, the winds and tides settled the matter, and they landed farther down the California coast. Because of his new fame, Flores, now an outlaw leader, had little trouble recruiting a gang of 50 guns within a few days, including a fairly noted badman named Andrés Fontes. From their hideout in the hills around San Juan Capistrano, the gang terrorized the area south of Los Angeles. They held up stagecoaches and mining supply wagons and invaded small towns to loot stores. Flores also led the gang in kidnapping or waylaying travelers and holding them for ransom. When a German settler wouldn't or couldn't meet his ransom demands, Flores paraded him into the plaza at San Juan Capistrano and summarily shot him to death as a warning to future victims to be more cooperative.

A posse headed by Sheriff James R. Barton went out after Flores in January 1857 and only three members of the posse came back alive. Sheriff Barton was not among them, having been gunned down by Fontes. Since the outlaw attacked Americans and Mexicans alike, he was soon hunted by posses of both nationalities. Led by Don Andrés Pico, a 50-man Mexican-American posse armed with lances routed the gang in one encounter, killing and capturing several of its members, but both Flores and Fontes escaped. On February 1 Flores was finally run to ground by a 40-man posse headed by a Doc Gentry. Held prisoner in a ranch house, Flores broke free but, unarmed, was easily recaptured two days later. He was brought back to Los Angeles, and on February 14, by what was described as a "popular vote," the 22-year-old outlaw was sentenced to hang, the penalty being exacted forthwith. Fontes made it back to Mexico but soon died there in a gunfight.

Gacy, John Wayne (1942–1994) mass murderer
Charged with 33 killings, more than any other mass murderer in American history, John Gacy was a building contractor who lived in a neat three-bedroom brick-fronted house in Knollwood Park Township, Ill., a Chicago suburb. During the period from 1972 to 1978, Gacy, who was in his thirties, murdered 33 boys and young men whom he had lured to his home with the promise of a job. After having sexual relations with them, he killed them and disposed of their bodies in a variety of ways.

Gacy was arrested in December 1978, when authorities traced a missing youth, 15-year-old Robert Piest, to his home. Twice-married, twice-divorced, he had come under suspicion after police learned that he had once served 18 months in an Iowa prison for sodomy with a teenage boy. By the time the killer was apprehended, however, young Piest was dead. Under questioning, following the discovery of three skeletons on his property, Gacy made a rambling statement. He had strangled the Piest boy and tossed his body in the Des Plaines River. Police began searching for victims and found three bodies in his garage, fished four out of the river and discovered 28 buried beneath the crawl space under his house. Of these, he was charged with a total of 33 deaths. It was clear that Gacy himself didn't know the exact count.

At his trial in March 1980, the chief issue was whether Gacy was a cold-blooded murderer who planned the killings or a mentally unbalanced man who lacked the capacity for understanding his actions. He was convicted and, on March 13, 1980, sentenced to the electric chair. At the time, the last execution in Illinois had occurred in 1962. He was finally executed in 1994.

Galante, Carmine (1910–1979)
murdered mafioso
After the death of Vito Genovese in 1969, Carmine Galante was considered to be the most ruthless and brutal of Mafia leaders. It could only be guessed how many murders he had committed during a life of crime that dated back to 1921. He was known to have carried out many killings for Genovese,

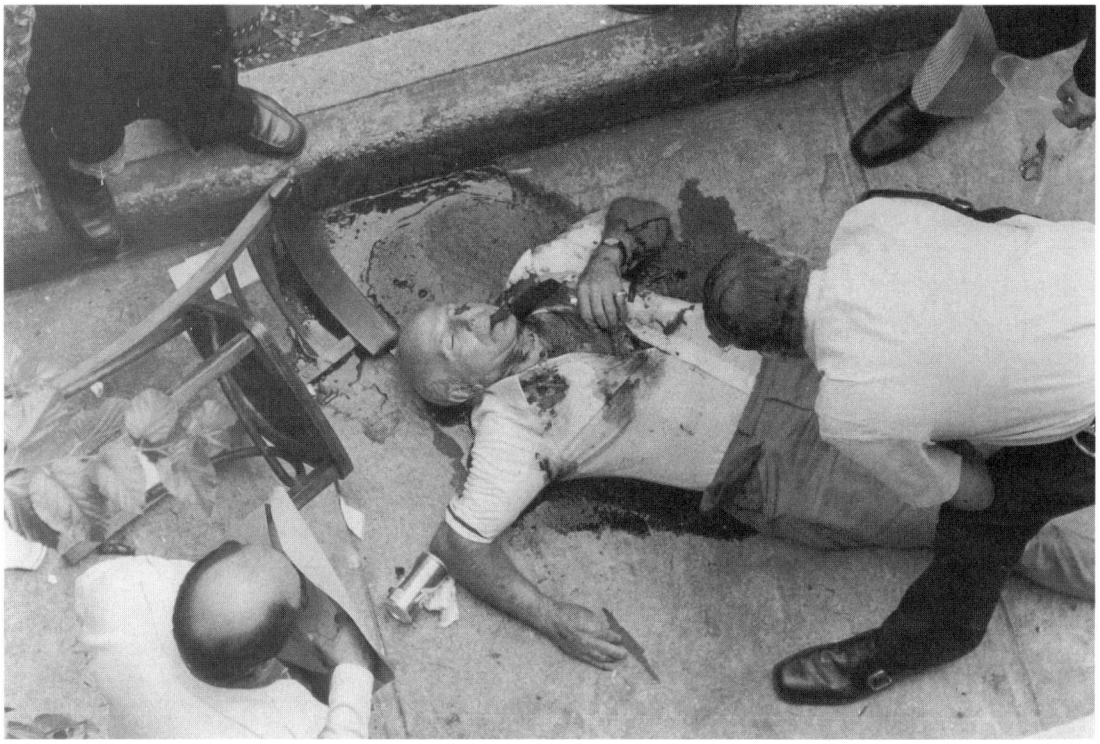

The assassination of mafioso Carmine Galante in the garden of a Brooklyn restaurant in 1979 was said to have solved the underworld's "Cigar" problem.

including the 1943 murder of radical journalist Carlo Tresca in New York. (Genovese was in Italy at the time and seeking to curry favor with Benito Mussolini, who was enraged by Tresca's antifascist activities.) Galante eventually became an underboss in the Joe Bananas family, specializing in narcotics trade.

He was finally sent to prison for 20 years on a narcotics charge. While serving time, he plotted to seize power from the other Mafia families in New York upon his release and was considered fearsome and capable enough to have done so. Even from prison, he ran the Bananas family, in which he had ascended to power in 1974, issuing orders to an estimated 200 members, among them many of the top gunners in the country.

The Bananas family had been nothing but grief for the other crime families in New York and elsewhere in the country. In 1964 its retired head, Joe Bananas, had plotted to eliminate virtually the entire governing board of the Mafia and take over. After waging a bloody five-year war, he gave up. Now, it appeared certain Galante would make the same try. Galante talked less than Bananas, believing the best policy was kill, kill, kill. Freed in 1979, he was gathering strength and making demands backed up with threats.

According to the underworld grapevine, a number of crime leaders held a meeting in

Boca Raton, Fla. to decide the "Cigar" problem (Galante was noted for always having a large cigar in his mouth). Mob leaders not present were consulted about whether or not to issue a contract on him. Those said to have been involved included such big shots as Jerry Catena, Santo Trafficante, Phil Rastelli and Frank Tieri. Even the retired Joe Bananas was consulted and okayed the contract on Galante.

On July 12, 1979 Galante had just finished the main course of a meal in the outdoor rear area of an Italian restaurant in Brooklyn. His cigar was in his mouth and he held a glass of wine in his right hand. Three masked men suddenly came through the indoor restaurant into the courtyard.

"Get him, Sal!" one of the masked men said and a hood with a double-barreled shotgun stepped forward and fired two blasts into the gangster. Galante died with his cigar still in his mouth.

A joke that made the rounds in the underworld asked, What's the first thing Galante would do if he could come back to earth alive? Answer: Have dessert.

See also: VITO GENOVESE.

Gallo, Crazy Joe (1929–1972) Brooklyn Mafia leader

Joseph Gallo was nicknamed Crazy Joe by rival Mafia figures who considered him "flaky" and hard to deal with. Crazy was all that and mean besides, but at the same time he was among the most perceptive of the new breed of underworld leaders. In the 1960s Crazy Joe recognized the changing tides in the underworld, the steady shift in power from Italian to black and sought to reach an accommodation with the emerging power structure, much in the fashion that Meyer Lansky had recognized the decline of Jewish gangsterism in the 1920s and allied with the Italian Mafia, under which he continued to prosper. In prison, Crazy Joe befriended black criminals. He attempted to break down convict color lines by having a black barber cut his hair; he became friends with Leroy "Nicky" Barnes and tutored him on taking over control of the drug racket in New York's Harlem and then far beyond; he sent released black prisoners to work. In all this, Crazy Joe realized nothing was permanent in crime. Years before, he had questioned the stranglehold the older underworld element had on various activities. "Who gave Louisiana to Frank Costello?" he once demanded in a conversation taped by law enforcement officials.

Crazy Joe started his criminal career at the age of 17, accumulating such charges as assault, burglary and kidnapping. He moved up rapidly in the Carlo Gambino family and was believed to be the chief gunman in the murder of Albert Anastasia in 1957. Gallo went to war against the Profaci family, a war that took more than a dozen lives, because he felt the Gallos were entitled to a bigger slice of the rackets in Brooklyn. After Profaci died and Joe Colombo, Sr. became head of the Profaci family, the war continued. When Colombo was shot and "vegetabled," to use Gallo's term, the murderer turned out to be a black man, Jerome A. Johnson. Gallo was immediately brought in for questioning because of his ability to recruit black troops whenever he needed them. But nothing could be proved against him and he was released.

On April 7, 1972 Crazy Joe left the safe confines of his Brooklyn territory and went to Umberto's Clam House in New York's Little Italy to celebrate his 43rd birthday. It seemed safe. There was always a tacit agreement within the Mafia that no rubouts would take place in Little Italy. In Crazy Joe's case, however, an exception was made. The Gallo party was seated at two tables when a man walked in with a .38-caliber pistol in his hand. Women screamed and customers hit the floor as the killer opened up on Gallo. Gallo's two bodyguards fired back. In all, some 20 shots were fired before the assassin fled. Mortally wounded, Gallo staggered out the front door and collapsed and died in the middle of the street—one block from police headquarters.

Gein, Edward (1906–1984) murderer

Few murderers in the 20th century have evoked such horror as Ed Gein, a Wisconsin farmer, did in the 1950s. Indeed his career inspired the movie *Psycho*. Gein worked the family farm at Plainfield, Wis. with his brother Henry and his elderly mother, who always insisted that her two boys never marry. His mother died in 1945, and brother Henry followed her within a year, leaving Ed alone on his farm with his strange fantasies. Gein developed a strong interest in female anatomy and, greatly affected by Christine Jorgensen's successful transsexual operation, apparently wanted to change his sex. He developed a morbid need to acquire women's bodies in order to study the anatomical structure of female organs, and to satisfy that desire, he took to digging up female corpses from their graves.

To aid in this secret task, Gein recruited a lame-witted old farmer, assuring him that their ghoulish activities would advance the cause of science. The old man helped Gein bring the corpses to a shed next to his farmhouse. Here, Gein skinned the bodies and sometimes even donned the skin and walked around his house so clad for hours. He also kept parts of the bodies as trophies, mounting the heads, hearts, livers and sex organs. When the doting farmer was committed to an old-age home, Gein was faced with the task of gathering the corpses on his own—or finding some easier way to collect bodies than exhuming them from all those graves. Some time in the early 1950s, he apparently decided it would be simpler to kill fresh victims rather than go through all the trouble of digging graves

Later, Gein would helpfully try to name his victims, but he suffered from a lack of memory on the subject and could recall only two for certain. In 1954 Gein walked into a bar run by 51-year-old Mary Hogan in Pine Grove and, seeing her alone, pulled out a pistol and shot her in the head. He piled her body on a sled and took her home. Subsequently, he accumulated some other bodies, although after his arrest he couldn't remember if he had killed them or dug them up. In November 1957 he killed Mrs. Bernice Worden, the operator of a hardware store in Plainfield. Ironically, the night before the murder Gein had mentioned to Mrs. Worden's son, who happened to be a deputy sheriff, that he would have to buy some antifreeze. The following evening the deputy went to his mother's store and found her missing. There was some blood on the floor and a half-written receipt for a purchase of antifreeze, and the cash register was gone.

Mrs. Worden's son remembered his conversation with Gein, and the latter's farm was searched. There the authorities found all sorts of grim relics, including bracelets made of human skin, a sewn-up skull fashioned into a soup bowl and dozens of other gruesome remains from at least 15 bodies. Gein admitted the grave robbings and the murders but was most upset when accused of robbing the cash register from his last victim's store. "I'm no robber," he said indignantly. "I took the money and the register only because I wanted to see how the machine worked."

Gein was committed for life to an institution for the criminally insane. For some years the Gein farmhouse was regarded as a place of horror until finally the local people burned it to the ground.

Genna brothers Prohibition-era Chicago family gang

The Genna brothers, known as the Terrible Gennas, were the first Chicago gang to jump into moonshining in a big way with the advent of Prohibition. Most of the brothers had been Black Hand extortionists preying on the residents of the city's Little Italy section, but in 1919 they realized there was more money putting people to work producing illegal alcohol, and they turned Little Italy into one large cottage moonshining industry.

The brothers Genna—Bloody Angelo, Tony the Gentleman, Mike the Devil, Pete, Sam and Jim—had come to Chicago from Sicily in 1910. Five of them were typical Sicilian killers—haughty, vicious, treacherous, murderous and devoutly religious. They carried their crucifixes in the same pocket with their pistols. The "different" Genna was Tony the Gentleman, or, as he was sometimes called, Tony the Aristocrat. He studied architecture, constructed model tenements for poor Italian immigrants, was a leading patron of the opera and lived elegantly in a downtown hotel. Tony had strong personal convictions against killing and never did a job himself, although he attended all family councils at which rubouts were planned. When Johnny Torrio and Al Capone were setting up their operation, the two feared the Gennas more than any other gang because they commanded the most savage set of killers. Among them were Sam "Smoots" Amatuna, the gangland dandy who loved music almost as much as he loved committing murder; Giuseppe "the Cavalier" Nerone, a university graduate and mathematics teacher turned gunman; and the celebrated murder duo John Scalise and Albert Anselmi, who introduced the practice of rubbing bullets with garlic in the hope of inducing gangrene should the victim survive the initial gunshot wound.

Combined with the Gennas' constant application of deadly force was their ability to corrupt the police. In 1925 a confession by their office manager indicated the brothers had on their payroll five police captains and some 400 uniformed officers, mostly from the Maxwell Street station, as well as many plainclothesmen from headquarters and the state attorney's office. The Gennas' booze-making operation grossed $350,000 a month, and the six brothers netted a clear monthly profit of $150,000. When Johnny Torrio brought most of the gangs together under one umbrella, the Gennas were the hardest to control. Ever devious, they constantly flooded other gangs' areas with their cheap booze, underselling them with terrible rotgut. A three-way competition soon developed among the Gennas, the North Side O'Banions and the Torrio-Capone mob.

Eventually the Gennas started getting picked off one by one, especially after Anselmi and Scalise deserted their banner to join the Capone forces.

Bloody Angelo Genna fell victim on May 25, 1925 to North Side gangsters who had followed his roadster through Chicago streets. When Angelo first became aware of them, he picked up speed. But in his desperate haste to get away, he smashed into a lamppost and was pinned behind the wheel, unable to do anything but watch as the pursuing black sedan glided to a stop by him and three shotguns blasted him apart.

Mike Genna vowed vengeance on the O'Banions who had done the job. The following month he and Anselmi and Scalise were out hunting for North Siders. What Mike Genna didn't known was that he was being taken for a ride by the pair, who had secretly defected to Capone. The three got caught in a gunfight with police. Anselmi and Scalise killed two officers, wounded a third and fled, leaving a wounded Genna to be captured by police. As Mike Genna was being placed on a stretcher, he cut loose a powerful kick with his good leg and knocked out one of the attendants. "Take that, you dirty son of a bitch," he snarled. He died two hours later.

Tony the Gentleman, the real brains of the Terrible Gennas, realizing that Anselmi and Scalise had deserted, knew he was next. Just as he was about to leave the city, he arranged for a final meeting with his supporter Nerone on a darkened street corner. He did not know that Nerone also had defected. When Tony Genna emerged from his car, Nerone grasped his hand in a steel-like handshake. Just then one or two gunmen stepped out of the darkness and filled Tony with bullets. Tony the Gentleman lingered for days before dying.

The power of the Gennas was now broken. The three surviving brothers fled, Sam and Pete to hideouts outside Chicago and Jim all the way back to Sicily. In Palermo, Jim Genna got two years for stealing the jewels that adorned the statue of the Madonna di Trapani.

Eventually, the three brothers came back to Chicago but avoided the rackets. They ran an olive oil and cheese importing firm, finishing out their days in relative obscurity.

See also: ANSELMI AND SCALISE, ALPHONSE "SCARFACE AL" CAPONE.

Genovese, Vito (1897–1969) Mafia chieftain

Vito "Don Vito" Genovese was probably the most awesome of the Mafia dons. He is credited with being the moving force that put the Mafia in the narcotics business, a shift some others, such as Frank Costello and, despite the contentions of federal narcotics investigators, Lucky Luciano, strongly opposed. Genovese, who started out in the shadow of Luciano in the early 1920s, rose to the top of the syndicate crime empire by killing off his many rivals. He is known to have ordered the deaths of Willie Moretti in 1951, Steve Franse in 1953 and Albert Anastasia in 1957. He was the obvious mastermind behind the attempt on the life of Frank Costello, which eventually led to the latter's retirement.

Genovese was always a cunning criminal. Faced with a murder charge in 1937, he fled to Italy, where he ingratiated himself with Benito Mussolini despite the fascist leader's ruthless campaign to wipe out the Italian Mafia. Genovese became the chief drug supplier for Mussolini's foreign minister and son-in-law, Count Ciano. During the war, to further gain Mussolini's favor, Genovese ordered the execution of Il Duce's longtime nemesis, radical editor Carlo Tresca, in New York City, a hit carried out by a Genovese underling, Carmine Galante.

In 1944, with the Mussolini regime crumbling, Genovese turned up as an interpreter for the army's intelligence service. Due to his energetic and diligent efforts, a number of black market operatives were caught in southern Italy. However, the military's pleasure with Genovese's performance vanished when it was discovered that as he unearthed the black marketeers and put them out of business, he simply took over their rackets.

Genovese returned to the United States after the war, when the witnesses to the murder charge against him had been dealt with. He took control of the Luciano family and, with his mentor now in exile, set about making himself the dominant figure in the American underworld. To do that, he had to gain dominance over the five New York crime families, eliminate Frank Costello and lessen the influence of Meyer Lansky, all the while paying lip service to Luciano.

It took Genovese almost a decade to solidify his position to the point that he could attempt this takeover, in the process gaining needed revenues from the narcotics trade. By 1957 he was ready to move. He first ordered the execution of Costello, whose importance in the underworld had diminished as a result of the Kefauver hearings. The plot failed and Costello was only slightly wounded. A few months later, however, another of his assassination orders was spectacularly successful. Albert Anastasia was shot to death as he sat in a barber's chair in a New York hotel. At the time, Anastasia was Costello's most important ally, and without him the fabled Prime Minister of the Underworld appeared helpless.

Later that year Genovese sought to solidify his new power by calling the famed Apalachin Conference in upstate New York. That meeting ended in a fiasco when the state police raided it and took dozens of leading Mafia dons into custody. Genovese was not perceptive enough to realize the meeting had been sabotaged by enemies far smarter and craftier than he, including Costello, Lansky, Luciano and Carlo Gambino, the heir to the Anastasia crime family. Gambino and Lansky had cooperated with Genovese in the elimination of Anastasia for their own reasons—Gambino to gain new power for himself and Lansky to eliminate the pressure the kill-crazy Anastasia was putting on him for a share of his vast Cuban gambling profits.

In these four, Genovese was facing the top double-dealers of the underworld. They understood better than Genovese that war between the two camps would be senseless, leading only to trouble for all. Instead, they plotted to eliminate Genovese by cunning and treachery. They decided to set him up for a federal drug bust, but the narcotics agents who were tipped off muffed the opportunity and Genovese slipped away. The underworld conspirators then arranged a trap that even allowed for the government's ineptitude. The four pitched in a $100,000 kitty and paid a minor Puerto Rican dope pusher named Nelson Cantellops to implicate Genovese in a deal. Although it was not logical that an unimportant street pusher like Cantellops would have the type of inside information to put away a power like Genovese, the government gladly accepted his testimony and convicted Genovese. In 1959 he was sentenced to the Atlanta Penitentiary for 15 years. According to underworld informer Joe Valachi, Genovese continued to direct the activities of his crime family from behind bars, but there is no doubt his influence lessened. Unquestionably, his effort to become the top boss of the underworld had been a disaster.

It was said that Genovese and Costello, sent to the Atlanta Penitentiary on tax charges, later held a tearful reconciliation in prison. If so, Genovese didn't understand the role Costello had played in his downfall; the facts of the plot were not revealed until Luciano broke his silence on the matter shortly before he died in 1962. When Genovese died in 1969, still a federal prisoner on a trumped-up charge, he was proof that mere brawn would never be enough to take over organized crime in America.

See also: ALBERT ANASTASIA, CARMINE GALANTE.

Giancana, Sam "Momo" (1908–1975)

syndicate leader

Considered by many to have been the most ruthless Mafia killer in the country, Sam "Momo" Giancana was for years the crime boss of Chicago and was suspected of involvement in various CIA plots to assassinate Cuban premier Fidel Castro.

Giancana's arrest record dated back to 1925, when he was a gun runner for Al Capone. Unlike other crime bosses, whose arrest records were usually short, Giancana was a "doer," with more than 70 arrests for everything from assault and bookmaking to bombing and suspicion of murder. He served prison sentences for auto theft, operation of an illegal still and burglary. During World War II he was asked by the draft board how he made his living; Giancana replied: "Me? I steal." He was rejected for service as "a constitutional psychopath."

According to well-publicized charges, Giancana was recruited in 1960 by the U.S. Central Intelligence Agency to "hit" Fidel Castro. Some say Giancana deliberately botched the assignment because he still had hopes of rebuilding the Mafia's gambling business in Cuba. In 1975 the Giancana-CIA connection talk was so widespread that the crime boss was about to be summoned before a Senate investigating committee. Before Giancana could appear, gunmen entered his fortresslike home in Chicago's Oak Park suburb and put seven bullets in him. CIA director William Colby announced forthwith, "We had nothing to do with it." Newsmen contacting unofficial spokesmen for the syndicate got the same response from that source.

See also: ANTHONY JOSEPH ACCARDO, FIORE "FIFI" BUCCIERI.

Gilmore, Gary Mark (1940–1977)

murderer

In 1977 Gary Gilmore, age 36, became the first man to be executed in the United States in about a decade. His death followed the reinstatement of the death penalty, which had been outlawed in 1972, under constitutional limits set by the Supreme Court.

Gilmore had been convicted of murdering a Utah gas station attendant and a motel clerk in July 1976. His case attracted worldwide attention not only because his execution would mark the return of capital punishment but also because he disparaged groups and individuals opposed to capital punishment who tried to block his execution. One stay was granted by the Supreme Court on the request of Gilmore's mother. The High Court ruled that the state of Utah was required to prove the prisoner, who had twice attempted suicide in his cell, had been of sound mind when he waived his right to appeal his death sentence. In its final decision, however, the Supreme Court ruled five to four that Utah's capital punishment law was constitutionally sound.

While a last-minute effort was made to get the High Court to prevent his execution, Gilmore went to his death on January 17, 1977 before a firing squad in the Utah State Prison at Point of the Mountain. The condemned man spent his last hours with his family and attorneys and showed little tension until he learned that a federal judge had granted a restraining order delaying the execution. However, a few hours later, a federal appeals court reversed that order.

Meanwhile, as lawyers again petitioned the Supreme Court to halt the proceedings, Gilmore was removed from his cell to a warehouse on the prison grounds. He was strapped in a chair on a raised platform, and a black paper target with a white circle was pinned to his T-shirt directly over his heart. Asked by the warden if he had anything more to say, Gilmore responded, "Let's do it." At 8:07 A.M. five men armed with .30-caliber rifles fired from a cubicle 10 yards in front of Gilmore. One of the rifles contained a blank cartridge and each of the other four had a real bullet. All four bullets pierced Gilmore's heart, but he lived a full two minutes after the shooting.

The final Supreme Court ruling against Gilmore had been handed down at 8:04, just three minutes prior to the shooting. Prison officials later admitted the execution had taken place before they had received word of the verdict on the appeal to the Supreme Court.

Gilmore's life and execution were scrutinized in detail in a best-selling book, *Executioner's Song,* by novelist Norman Mailer.

Glatman, Harvey Murray (1928–1959)

rapist and murderer

By masquerading as a detective magazine photographer, Harvey Glatman, a particularly sadistic California murderer in the 1950s, got three young women to pose for the usual "bound-and-gagged" stuff and, after sexually abusing them and taking many pictures, strangled them to death. Glatman was the classic example of a mama's boy turned killer. He had previously done time in New York State for a string of "phantom bandit" attacks on lone women and been imprisoned in Colorado for aggravated assaults on women. After each run-in with the law, Glatman fell back on his aged mother, who paid for his psychiatric treatment for five years. In 1957 his mother gave him the money to attend a television repairman's school in Los Angeles and supplied him with funds to open a TV repair shop.

Glatman's murder victims were two young photographic models and an attractive lonely hearts club divorcée. On separate occasions he had succeeded in convincing 19-year-old model Judy Dull and 24-year-old model Ruth Rita Mercado that he was a photographer on assignment for a detective magazine. With his third victim, divorcée Shirley Bridgeport, he simply made a date. In each case, after gaining their confidence, he then lured the women to his home, pulled out a gun and tied them up. After sexually assaulting his victims, he took lewd pictures of them. Later, he drove each of the three women into the desert, where he inflicted additional perversities on them for many more hours before finally killing them.

"I used the same five-foot length of sash cord for all three," he later said, almost gloatingly. "I kept it in my car with the gun. . . . I made them lie on their stomachs. Then I tied their ankles together, looped the end of the cord about their necks and pulled until they were dead."

Two other women almost suffered the same fate. One escaped when she grew suspicious of Glatman's actions. The other, 28-year-old Lorraine Vigil, offered desperate resistance when he pointed a gun at her and tried to tie her up on the shoulder of the Santa Ana Freeway. Although shot in the leg, she managed to pull the gun from Glatman's hand and had it pointed at him when a highway patrolman arrived on the scene.

Glatman eagerly described his murderous acts and seemed to bear no remorse for them. His main concern was keeping his 69-year-old mother from attending his trial. "It would have been too hard on her," he said after his conviction. He refused to cooperate with lawyers trying to appeal his case, announcing in San Quentin's death row that he wanted to die. "It's better this way," he said. "I knew this is the way it would be." Glatman was executed in the gas chamber on August 18, 1959, undoubtedly pleased that a number of publications had engaged in spirited, if unseemly, bidding to publish the photographs he had taken of his victims.

Gohl, Billy (1860?–1928) mass murderer

Billy Gohl undoubtedly belongs somewhere near the top of any list of the most deadly American mass murderers, having killed a minimum of 40 men and almost certainly many more.

Gohl was always mysterious about himself. He turned up in the spring of 1903 in Aberdeen, Wash. as a delegate of the Sailors' Union of the Pacific. Nobody among Aberdeen's 12,000 inhabitants knew him, and he seems to have told differing tales of his labor and maritime past, although that was not unusual in a wide-open town like Aberdeen. He was a squat, bull-necked man with a shaven head and an almost angelic-looking face. But everyone realized that Billy Gohl was a man who could take care of himself and that earned him respect in the Sailors' Union.

As a union official, Gohl performed all sorts of chores for seamen. The union office was generally the first stop for sailors from schooners and four-riggers arriving in port. The seamen would check with Gohl for mail and would leave their valuables with him when they went carousing. Since this would often be their first shore leave in months, their pay generally came to rather large sums. Union delegates always kept the money in the safe until the sailors called for it. Billy Gohl just kept it.

Gohl's technique was to murder a seaman as soon as he showed up, before he had time to make friends. He would look out the window to see if anyone had seen the man enter the union office; if not, and if the sailor had turned in enough cash or other valuables to make the effort worthwhile, Gohl would simply take a gun from his desk drawer and shoot the man through the head. From there on, Gohl had everything down to a science.

He cleaned the gun, searched the corpse for additional money and stripped the body of all identification. Gohl's office was on the second floor of a building whose rear extended out over the Wishkah River, which fed into Gray's Harbor. Supported by stilts, the house had a trapdoor with a chute leading to the water. Down the chute went the corpse to be carried away by the rapid river current. If and when the body bobbed to the surface, it would be miles out in the harbor.

After 1903 Aberdeen began to be known by sailors as a "port of missing men," but no one thought to attribute that sad turn of events to Billy Gohl. Between 1909 and 1912 a total of 41 "floaters" were fished out of the water. Most were believed to be merchant seamen, and the most upset man in town was invariably Billy Gohl, demanding the law do something. He was finally trapped when one of his victims was traced to his office and no further. Gohl had shot the man as soon as he entered his office. When he searched the body, he found a gold watch with the name August Schleuter of Hamburg, Germany engraved on it. Gohl decided it would be too incriminating to keep and returned it to the body. When the corpse drifted ashore, Gohl identified Schleuter as one of his men. It took the law weeks to find out the truth, which as good as convicted Gohl. It turned out the victim really was a Danish seaman named Fred Nielssen. He had bought a watch in Hamburg, and the name of the watchmaker was August Schleuter.

In 1913 Gohl was convicted of two murders but only laughed when asked to make a complete roster of his victims. He avoided execution because the year before, the state of Washington had eliminated capital punishment. Gohl's mass murder spree was used as an argument for its restoration, even though he had committed his murders while the death penalty had been in effect. In 1914 the death penalty was restored. Gohl died in prison in 1928.

Gotti, John (1940–) imprisoned godfather and former "Teflon Don"

Certainly the most storied and important "godfather" in American organized crime in the 1980s and 1990s, John Gotti could well have become the "boss of bosses," even though that is nothing more than a mythical title bestowed by the media and some prosecutors. Gotti was cut from the old mold, a type not seen in New York Mafia circles since the demise of the vicious Albert Anastasia, the "Lord High Executioner" of Murder, Inc., and the mobster Gotti most admired.

Mob boss John Gotti in a victory pose after beating a case during his "Teflon Don" period.

On one occasion Gotti was overheard chastising an underling for failing to return his phone calls. "Follow orders," he snarled, "or I'll blow up your house." The mobster, thoroughly terrified, swore it would not happen again. "You bet it won't," Gotti responded, "I got to make an example of somebody. Don't let it be you." Veteran officers agreed that if they shut their eyes and heard the words, they would have been sure it was the ghost of Albert Anastasia talking.

By 1985 Gotti was considered the top capo, or lieutenant, in the Gambino crime family, the most powerful Mafia outfit in the country. He bossed a number of lucrative rackets, including those at John F. Kennedy Airport as well as other Gambino operations in much of the New York metropolitan area. Additionally he was the favorite of underboss Aniello Dellacroce, an aging but brutal mafioso. As much as Dellacroce admired

Gotti, boss Paul Castellano hated—and feared—him.

Gotti moved up the mob ladder in 1972 when the nephew of Carlo Gambino was kidnapped by Irish gangsters who demanded a $350,000 ransom. When part of the ransom was paid, the kidnappers killed the Gambino kin. The FBI grabbed two suspects but not the third one, James McBratney, on whom Gambino put out a contract. Gotti was part of a mob execution squad that caught up with McBratney in a Staten Island bar. Gotti was convicted of his part in the job and drew a seven-year prison sentence. When he got out Gotti was embraced by Gambino, who moved him steadily up the crime family ladder. In about 1978 or 1979 Gotti became a capo and top associate of Dellacroce. Like many others in the family Gotti felt Dellacroce should succeed the dying Gambino, but the latter wanted his kin, Castellano, to succeed him.

Dellacroce kept Gotti in line in this period, since he, Dellacroce, knew he was dying of cancer. He urged Gotti to be patient, a characteristic which was not Gotti's strong suit. And neither was gentility. He was once quoted complaining to another mafioso: "Can you beat this—they're telling me I'm too tough for the job. Can you imagine what our thing [Cosa Nostra] is coming to?"

When Dellacroce died in early December 1985, there was no stopping Gotti. Two weeks later Paul Castellano was murdered outside a Manhattan steakhouse on Gotti's orders, Gotti audaciously riding past the murder scene to make sure everything had gone off without a hitch. Normally, the killing of a boss has severe ramifications, but not in this case. Castellano was under indictment and faced a likely long prison sentence as he approached age 70. Many in the crime family were not sure that "Big Paul" could take it. It was thought likely that Castellano might crack and flip for the government. That was one of the lines Gotti used on members of the family as well as other crime families. No one had any problems with Castellano being erased.

Gotti was in, now the godfather of the most powerful crime family in the country, or what had been so until Castellano's misrule had weakened it to the extent that the Genovese crime family was at least its equal or even its superior.

Gotti became known as the "Dapper Don." As one police veteran stated, "He [operated] in style, brutal perhaps, but suave. Gotti looks like a movie star. He wears hand-tailored clothes, drives a big black Lincoln and likes good restaurants."

In 1986 Gotti became the target of federal prosecutors on charges that could take him out of action. But Gotti probably marked a new trend in the Mafia—back to younger bosses, as was common in the 1920s and '30s. In recent years the mobs were concerned about the older dons taking heat. If even one talked, the damage would be enormous. A 20-year prison term wasn't too bad if young leaders got out in seven with good behavior. Everyone knew Gotti was tough enough to take it. Not that Gotti couldn't exhibit coolness. When entering a federal courtroom he insisted on a female radio reporter entering before him. "I was brought up to hold doors open for ladies," he said.

He had a different disposition in family "business," ordering murder after murder without a qualm.

The government clearly had Gotti dead to rights on some major criminal charges, yet three times in a row, Gotti beat the rap, perhaps not always without certain dishonest means. But in any event, the media now had a new nickname for him. He was the "Teflon Don," against whom charges bounced harmlessly off.

Finally the FBI built a solid case against Gotti, involving some 100 hours of incriminating tapes in which Gotti spoke openly about many murders and sundry criminal activities. The game now involved the RICO statutes, which meant if convicted Gotti was gone for good. Even better for the FBI they were able to "flip" Sammy "the Bull" Gravano, Gotti's underboss, a criminal as vicious as Gotti himself. In fact, Gravano had to get on the witness stand and admit to having committed 19 murders. In the deal Gravano made with the government, Gravano "walked" while Gotti was convicted in 1992 and sentenced to life without parole.

For a time Gotti sought to continue to run the family through his son John Gotti, Jr., but that went awry when the younger Gotti was indicted on other charges. Still Gotti appeared to have an influence on his crime family, even though he was probably now hated as much as Castellano had been. From the mobsters' viewpoint, the main charge against Gotti could be summed up in one word—stupidity.

Even the boys in the mob could count. In the brief time before Gotti was tucked away in jail, the membership of the family seemed to have dropped from 250 wise guys to about 150 (not counting the associates and wise guy wanna-bes who numbered at least 10 times as many). With Gotti in charge, the family had gained a reputation for dapperness (by Gotti's decree), but the boss's imposing presence on the TV nightly news exposed many capos and soldiers to scrutiny by law enforcement officials. Gotti insisted his top guys constantly show up at the mob's Ravenite headquarters on Mulberry Street, even though the FBI had the area blanketed with FBI cameras. The appearance of these mobsters proved an incredible boon to law enforcement, allowing them to be identified. Many of the wise guys knew that quiet discretion was the correct call, but who was going to contradict Gotti? Failure to show up brought the certain guarantee of a Gotti hit sentence on them.

Clearly all the Gambinos hated Sammy the Bull for ratting, but they privately acknowledged Gravano's charge that the boss's arrogance had done much to bring down not only himself but major portions of the organization.

Law enforcement officials generally believed that Gotti's attitude would eventually make him and his son less imposing figures in the Gambino family, which some federal officials had pronounced doomed. By the very late 1990s, however, it was conceded by much of the media and a number of prosecutors that the Gambino family was still a power. Indeed, crime would probably march on with or without the Gotti influence.

See also: PAUL CASTELLANO, SAMMY "THE BULL" GRAVANO.

Graham, John Gilbert (1932–1957)

mass murderer

John Graham was a typical, if awesome, example of the plane saboteurs most active in the 1950s and 1960s who placed bombs on airliners to collect the insurance on a single passenger. He thought nothing of the fact that he had to kill 43 other persons because he wanted to murder his mother, Mrs. Daisy King of Denver, Colo.

On November 1, 1955 Graham placed a time bomb made with 25 sticks of dynamite in his mother's luggage before she boarded a DC-6B at Stapleton Airport. The plane was aloft only 10 minutes before it crashed in flames. When traces of a bomb device were found, suspicion soon focused on young Graham because he had attracted so much attention to himself in the terminal before flight time buying insurance policies on his mother's life from a vending machine. He had nervously spoiled a number of them and kept buying more, finally salvaging $37,500 worth.

When the FBI found material used to make bombs in his home, Graham confessed the plane sabotage. Public speculation as to how anyone would kill in such a manner and take the lives of so many innocents brought a simple explanation from a psychologist: "People actually have very few restraints concerning a person they have no intimate knowledge of. A mine disaster that claims 120 lives doesn't really impress many people. But should a neighbor fall from a ladder and die, the effect on these same people is tremendous."

Certainly, Graham showed no remorse about all his victims, being more concerned about his mother. Mrs. King had been going to visit her daughter in Alaska and, planning to go hunting, she had carried a box of shotgun shells on board the plane. Graham laughed, "Can't you just see Mother when all those shells began to go off in the plane?"

At his trial Graham, found sane but resentful of his mother's neglect when he was a child, recanted his confession but was convicted by the overwhelming evidence. He refused to take any steps to appeal his death sentence and went silently to the gas chamber on January 11, 1957.

Gravano, Sammy "the Bull" (1945–)

highest-ranking Mafia informer

Without doubt, he was the most important Mafia bigwig to turn informer in the entire history of the battle against organized crime in America. Federal prosecutors were never able to bring down John Gotti, the boss of the powerful Gambino crime family, until his underboss, Salvatore Gravano, better known as Sammy "the Bull,""flipped" and testified against Gotti, dubbed by the media as the "Teflon Don" for his ability to beat rap after rap.

This time the Feds could be said to have Gotti with "the meat in his mouth," doomed by 100 hours of taped conversations he conducted. Later criticism was raised that the prosecutors needlessly let Gravano "walk." Experts found that prosecutors were "tape-shy," since cases had previously been lost even though there were plenty of tapes for the government to use. In those cases Gotti's lawyers tore into the tapes, saying they were misleading and just plain "garbage." Jurors seemed to agree.

Faced with that reality the government decided Gravano was vital to their case. The Bull—so named for his compact muscular body and thick bovine neck—had witnessed the events Gotti talked about so damningly and was able to provide personal corroboration that prosecutors were never able to come up with before. That hardly meant that Gravano put a "human face" on the case. More accurately what made the Bull so fascinating to the authorities, the media and the public was his very unwholesomeness. Without a qualm or real note of regret, Gravano confessed to 19 murders, and a reading of his testimony made a number of observers conclude that in some cases Gravano pushed the killings on Gotti rather than the reverse.

Gravano enumerated his 19 murders stretching from 1970 to some two decades later. Still the prosecution had to have him on the stand, immunity for him a small price to pay for tying Gotti to the curbside murder of Paul Castellano, the head of the Gambinos whom Gotti had to eliminate to achieve power.

Gotti went to prison for life with no parole, and he was to be only one of dozens of mobsters to end up in prison, as were corrupt union officials, having been convicted of racketeering. So too fell a crooked cop who supplied information to Gotti and a corrupt juror who aided the Gotti cause in a previous prosecution.

Since it was true that Gravano very easily would have been convicted without testimony from Gotti on the basis of the taped conversations and gotten at least 50 years, some have argued that obviously Gotti could have been convicted without Gravano's testimony. Gravano made it clear he felt Gotti's "big mouth" on the tapes was what had doomed him. The fact was that Gravano probably knew he was in a top-dog position because the prosecutors knew this was their last chance to get Gotti on all the charges under the RICO law. If they lost the case, Gotti could never be charged again on any of that evidence.

That meant, some legal experts say, Gravano actually was in a position to dictate the terms of his own treatment. In 1985 he drew a five-year sentence, but since he had been held for five years, mostly for his own protection, he went free.

Gravano at first went into the witness protection program. He was supposed to crawl into the most remote cave and stay there, fingers firmly crossed and hoping the mob wouldn't find him. That was not the Bull's way. He left the program and increasingly appeared in the open. In 1999 he was living in Phoenix, Ariz., having popped up on television to promote his 1997 biography, *Underboss*. He also returned to the construction business, which is where he operated during his crime days, and even talked to a local newspaper as long as it did not reveal his new name.

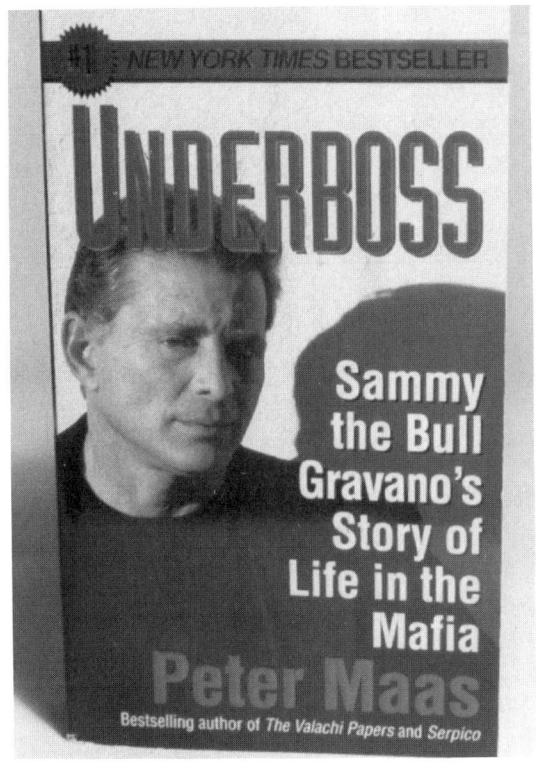

Mafia turncoat Sammy "the Bull" Gravano achieved best-seller status with his account of his life in the Mafia. (Author's collection)

Apparently, Gravano concluded the Gambinos were not about to go after him. True, family members all hated him, but secretly many agreed that Gotti was the one who had caused their woes, starting by his insistence that all his capos and other underlings appear regularly at the gang's Manhattan headquarters, the Ravenite. This allowed the FBI years of surveillance that eventually identified them.

As for Gotti himself, it became a fair bet he would not order the Bull's murder, if he still maintained the power to do so. Gotti had come down with cancer, which might in time allow him his freedom. The killing of the Bull would certainly "queer" that hope.

About the only ones really after Gravano were the kin of several of the Bull's hits. They launched a legal campaign to deprive him of any financial rewards from his book and they filed a $25 million suit against him. Despite his dark past, Gravano was making no deals and not giving up any of his money, rumored to include funds he got for his many "legitimate" businesses.

Apparently he felt secure in what the *New York Times* called his "all-American sun-belt future."

Even more amazing was another act of daring. Some newsmen have been trying to confirm that Sammy the Bull turned up in 1998 or 1999 walking around the New York's Howard Beach section, the heart of Gotti country. True or not, Sammy the Bull seemed to have a way about him.

See also: PAUL CASTELLANO, JOHN GOTTI.

Green River Killer the one that got away

Quite possibly the most prolific unidentified serial killer is the "Green River Killer," so called because the 49 victims attributed to him or her were dumped in or near Washington State's Green River. The victims started appearing on January 21, 1982, when 16-year-old Leann Wilcox of Tacoma was found strangled 8 miles from Seattle. Then in the fall of 1984, the parade of corpses abruptly stopped. There have been no further attributable Green River killings since then, but a law enforcement Green River Task Force remained in place to find the killer. That goal was not achieved, but over the next several years the force solved seven unrelated murders and three rapes. In what some observers thought a bizarre development, serial killer Ted Bundy was used as an adviser to the task force. Bundy was himself facing conviction and the death penalty. In point of fact Bundy contributed little to the investigation and clearly was motivated by a desire to postpone his own death sentence.

Why did the Green River Killer stop? Some have speculated that he or she died or was in prison or a mental institution, his or her Green River crimes not suspected by authorities. Another theory held by some experts was that the killer had simply left the area. These experts noted that in 1985, a series of murders started in San Diego, Cal. that seemed related to the Green River cases. The number of murders attributed to the unknown San Diego serial killer ranged from 10 to perhaps 18 by a recent count. This would raise the combined toll to anywhere from 59 to 67.

Gunness, Belle (1859–?) murderess

It would be difficult to estimate whether Belle Gunness or Jane Toppan holds the record as America's greatest murderess. The latter did not keep score, and the former just plain never told. The best estimate on Belle Gunness was given by Roy L'Amphere, a Canadian farmhand who became her on-and-off lover. He said she killed at least 49 persons—42 would-be husbands, two legal husbands, a young girl left in her care, three of her own children and an unknown saloon wench she'd hired as a servant and whose body she used as a stand-in corpse for herself.

Belle turned up in La Porte, Ind. at the age of 42 as the Widow Sorenson from Chicago. She was not the friendly sort and kept neighbors off her property with a high-wire fence. All the local folks seemed to know about her was that she slaughtered hogs for a living. Actually, she also carried on another very profitable slaughtering business, that of killing off would-be suitors. She would place advertisements in matrimonial magazines announcing she was seeking a husband with two fine attributes. He had to be "kind and willing to help pay off a mortgage." The first man to answer an ad was an amiable Norwegian named Peter Gunness. Belle married him, insured him and then he died. One of Belle's children told a schoolmate that her mother had killed her father. "She hit him with a cleaver." But Belle explained her unfortunate husband had met his end when a meat grinder toppled off a shelf. Naturally, the widow Gunness was believed, children being given to overactive imaginations.

After that, Belle never bothered going to the trouble of marrying her mail-order suitors. She'd have them bring their money with them, and if they didn't have enough, she'd send them back home for more. Then she murdered them and buried them within a day or two on her farm. Once, according to L'Amphere, Belle got $20,000 from a victim, but in most other cases it was around the $1,000 mark. In all, it was estimated she collected well over $100,000 from 1901 until 1908, when her murder spree ended. It probably ceased because a relative or two of the murdered men began writing in an effort to locate their missing relatives. Belle must have concluded it was only a matter of time before the law would close in on her.

On April 28, 1908 the Gunness farmhouse burned to the ground. Inside were found the bodies of Belle's three children, aged 11, nine and five, and Belle herself. Well, it could have been Belle except the woman was shorter and weighed about 150 pounds while Belle was a good 250, at least. And to top it off, the head was missing. The head, of course, would have contained teeth that could have been traced. Belle was known to wear a false plate anchored to a tooth, and this was found in the ashes. The obvious conclusion was that Belle had even ripped out her anchor tooth and plate to deceive the law. No one was fooled, but that didn't do much good. Belle Gunness had disappeared. It was soon proven that mass murder had taken place on the Gunness farm. All or parts of the bodies of at least 14 different men were dug up before the law stopped looking. It would have been virtually impossible to unearth completely 40 acres of farmland. And there was already more than enough evidence to convict Belle, if she were ever found. She was not. Over the years various bulky ladies from coast to coast would be identified as Belle Gunness and then cleared with the law's apologies.

L'Amphere was sent to prison in 1909 for his part in the activities of the Lady Bluebeard of La Porte. He died there two years later after revealing all he knew about Belle's murderous activities. He said Belle was supposed to get in touch with him after she had settled elsewhere but she never did. About the only legacy Belle Gunness left was a bit of bad poetry written about her. The last stanza went:

There's red upon the Hoosier moon
For Belle was strong and full of doom;
And think of all them Norska men
Who'll never see St. Paul again.

Gyp the Blood (1889–1914) gangster and killer
One of the most vicious gangsters in New York during the early 1900s, Gyp the Blood (real name Harry Horrowitz) worked on commission for Big Jack Zelig as a slugger, bomber and killer. He filled in slow periods as a mugger and, at times, as a bouncer in East Side dance halls, gaining the reputation as the best bouncer since Monk Eastman, which was high praise indeed. Having enormous strength, he boasted he could break a man's back by bending him across his knee, and he lived up to the claim a number of times. Once, he won a $2 bet by seizing an unfortunate stranger and cracking his spine in three places. Gyp the Blood truly loved violence; Gyp's explanation for his eagerness to take on bombing assignments was, "I likes to hear de noise."

When the violence business got a bit slow, Gyp the Blood formed his own gang, the Lenox Avenuers, who engaged in muggings, burglaries and stickups around 125th Street. Gyp the Blood and three of his underlings, Whitey Lewis, Dago Frank and Lefty Louie, murdered gambler Herman Rosenthal on July 16, 1912 because he had begun revealing to District Attorney Charles S. Whitman the tie-ins between gamblers and the police. All four were apprehended despite a police slowdown on the investigation. Gyp the Blood, in an effort to save himself, said they had been hired to do the killing by Big Jack Zelig at the behest of Lt. Charles E. Becker. Zelig then talked about Becker, and although Big Jack was assassinated before he could testify in court, Becker was convicted and executed. Gyp the Blood and his three henchmen went to the electric chair on April 13, 1914.

See also: CHARLES E. BECKER, BIG JACK ZELIG.

Hahn, Anna (1906–1938) mass poisoner

The first woman electrocuted in the state of Ohio, Anna Hahn specialized in being a companion to well-off elderly men who had no relatives, providing them with tender loving care and a little arsenic. After each one died, she either produced a will naming her the beneficiary or simply looted her victim's bank accounts before moving on to brighten up the last days of another old gentleman. Exactly how many men she killed is not known. Anna was not cooperative on the subject, and the authorities stopped exhuming bodies after they found five loaded with arsenic.

Anna Hahn arrived in Cincinnati from her native Fussen, Germany in 1927, married a young telegraph operator named Philip Hahn and opened a bakery in the "Over the Rhine" German district. Then Anna's husband became afflicted with a strange illness and finally was taken to a hospital, where he recovered, by his mother over Anna's protests. In retrospect, it seemed likely that her husband was suffering from something he ate, but in any event, Anna Hahn took the opportunity to move in with a septuagenarian burgher named Ernest Koch, who seemed remarkably vigorous despite his age. Under Anna's ministrations that condition did not continue for long. On May 6, 1932 a much weakened Koch died. When his will was probated, Anna was bequeathed his house.

Anna's next victim was Albert Palmer, an aged and ailing railroad retiree who lasted almost no time at all. Anna avoided the embarrassing coincidence of twice being named heir to an old man's estate by simply borrowing Palmer's money before he died. She insisted on giving him an IOU for the money, but after he expired, she simply tore up the note and no one was the wiser. Anna then sold the Hahn house and moved to another part of the city.

Next on her list was a man named Jacob Wagner, who left an estate of $17,000 to his "niece" Anna. She earned another $15,000 taking care of one George Gsellman for a few months until his demise. One who escaped her deadly attention was a man named George Heiss. As he revealed after Anna's arrest, Heiss became suspicious when flies sipping the beer she brought him kept flipping over and dying. He demanded that Anna share his stein, and when she refused, he ordered her from his house.

Not quite as careful was Anna's last victim, George Obendoerfer. Anna lured him to Colorado with a story about a ranch she had there. Obendoerfer never made it to the ranch however, expiring in a Denver hotel. In the meantime Anna had gained possession of his bankbook and looted it of $5,000. But when it came time to pay for Obendoerfer's burial, she refused, claiming she had just met him on a train and had pretended to be his wife at his suggestion. Police became suspicious when they discovered the bank transfer, and an autopsy was performed, revealing lethal amounts of arsenic in the dead man's viscera. Upon her return to Cincinnati, Anna was arrested. The bodies of four other of Anna's old gentlemen were exhumed and post mortems confirmed the presence of arsenic in each case.

After a sensation-packed trial a jury of 11 women and one man convicted Anna with no recommendation of mercy. She exhibited iron nerve until shortly before her execution on June 20, 1938. But when strapped into the electric chair, Anna broke and screamed hysterically. She regained her composure with the help of a prison chaplain. As she removed her hand from his, Anna said, "You might be killed, too, Father."

Hansen, Robert (1940–) Alaskan serial killer

It could be said that Robert Hansen came out of Iowa to open up Alaska for serial killing. This was facilitated by the immense size of the state and the fact that Hansen had his own private Piper Super Cub bush plane. By his own admission he killed 17 women and consulted his aviation chart to pick out likely burial spots in forsaken areas of snow and ice.

Hansen came to Alaska at the age of 20 with a brand new wife and, following his father's profession, obtained work as a baker. He prospered at his trade and soon had his own business. His marriage, however, ended in six months, but he remarried six years later. His new wife had no idea of the degree to which her husband was mad. By the early 1970s he was making his mark as an outdoorsman and pilot-hunter who stalked Dahl sheep, wolves and bears with a rifle and bow and arrow.

Hansen began to send his wife and children to visit relations in Iowa and also on a European vacation. By 1973 Hansen was killing women in earnest. Over the next decade, he committed 17 murders and more than 30 rapes. His usual targets were prostitutes, exotic dancers and those he lured through singles ads. Some he took into his Anchorage home, pulled a rifle on them and marched into his trophy room. His usual practice in such cases was to have sex with his captives and then kill them, consult his charts and fly off with the body to be dumped where it was hardly likely to be found. Others he forced into the plane at gunpoint and then threatened with death if they did not do as he said. Many did, and he returned them to town with a warning that if they said anything about what happened he would have them prosecuted as prostitutes through connections he had with the police.

The key to the women's survival was to obey his every whim, and if they did not displease him they might be spared. Unfortunately Hansen's displeasure was easily aroused. The slightest resistance or a request for payment was, as far as Hansen was concerned, a capital offense. If a woman was particularly offensive to him, he would turn her loose in the wilderness and stalk her with rifle or bow and arrow. There were no survivors in that sporting game.

No suspicions fell on Hansen, and indeed it appeared the authorities had no idea a serial killer was in their midst for six to seven years. Discovery of a couple of bodies, one in a gravel pit near Seward and another in a shallow grave along the Knik River where hunters made the grim find, caused authorities to begin to suspect the worst.

Hansen was not unmasked until 1983 when a 17-year-old captive broke free as he was taking her to his plane hangar. She cried for help with a handcuff still dangling from one wrist. Hansen quickly confessed his killing spree and on a flying tour of the wilderness pointed out the spots where he had buried his victims. Eleven bodies were recovered in this manner. Some of the women were never identified, and Hansen had no idea what their names were. It was assumed that several were among the women listed as missing in police files.

Hansen was prosecuted for four murders, which resulted in his receiving a life with 461 additional years sentence.

Hardin, John Wesley (1853–1895) gunfighter and murderer

John Wesley Hardin was one of the dedicated gunfighters of the West who delighted in showing a gun full of notches. In his case the boast was deserved. By his own count Wes Hardin killed 44 men. Some historians credit him with 40, and even the most skeptical will grant him 34 or 35.

Hardin started killing in his native Texas in 1868 at the age of 15. He shot a black who had taken his new citizenship rights too seriously, a not unpopular crime of that era. Then he gunned down three Yankee soldiers who came after him for the shooting. Hardin went on the run and received the ready assistance of most folks who knew him. By 1871, at about 18 years of age, he was a trail cowboy driving cattle from Texas to Kansas, and his murder toll stood at about a dozen, give or take a corpse or two. Many of his victims had died in face-to-face confrontations, but Wes was certainly not fussy about putting a slug in a man's back. Around Abilene he knocked off another eight or so and for a time escaped the wrath of Marshal Wild Bill Hickok, who clearly wanted no trouble with this fast-drawing young hellion.

When Hardin killed a man in his hotel, however, Hickok came after him. Hardin later claimed the man had tried to knife him because he had made some big gambling winnings the night before. The other version was that Hardin had shot him because his snoring in the next room had disturbed the gunfighter's sleep. Fleeing out a second-story window in his long johns, Hardin avoided being arrested by Hickok. On the trail he trapped three members of a posse sent out by Hickok, and in a rare gallant gesture, Hardin refrained from killing them. Instead, he made them strip off their pants and sent them back toward Abilene in that condition. Through the years Hardin supported himself mostly by gambling and only occasionally by punching cattle. A man who was especially fast on the draw had a way of facing down an opponent in a disputed hand. If a man got into a lone game of poker with a young feller who he later learned was the notorious Wes Hardin and was then informed that a straight beat a flush, why that was an unarguable proposition as long as Hardin had his gun.

And Hardin always did, and did something about it if anyone tried to take it away from him. In his memoirs he wrote of an incident in Willis, Tex.: "Some fellows tried to arrest me for carrying a pistol. They got the contents of it instead."

In 1874 Wes Hardin celebrated his 21st birthday by shooting Deputy Sheriff Charley Webb of Brown County between the eyes. By now his murder toll stood somewhere between 35 or 36 and 44. Hardin himself was no authority on the matter, preferring to ignore some of his back-shooting escapades. With a $4,000 price on his head, the gunfighter decided to head for points east. He moved through Louisiana to Alabama and into Florida. He gambled and drank but avoided killing anyone, so as not to mark his trail. Despite his care, Hardin was captured by Texas Rangers aboard a train at Pensacola Junction on August 23, 1877.

Back in Texas, Hardin got only 25 years instead of the death sentence, a fact that produced a bitter protest from a condemned gunman, William P. Longley. He had only killed half as many men as Hardin—at most—and he was due to be hanged. Where was the justice in that, Longley demanded in a death cell letter to the governor. The governor didn't bother to respond, and Longley was hanged, while Hardin went to prison.

Hardin studied law behind bars, and when he was released in 1894 with a full pardon, he set up a law office. However, he did most of his lawyering in saloons and at the gaming tables. In El Paso he gained the enmity of a nasty old lawman, John Selman, who was a sterling advocate of the principle that one shot in the back was worth more than two up front. On August 19, 1895 Hardin was standing at the bar, being his loud and boisterous self, when Constable Selman walked in and put a bullet in the back of his head. Selman was acquitted, claiming self-defense. He said it had been a fair fight since Hardin had seen him in the mirror. They might not have bought that one even in Texas had not Wes Hardin been the notorious character he was.

Further reading: *The Life of John Wesley Hardin* by John Wesley Hardin.

Harpe brothers 18th-century highwaymen

For more than 50 years during the latter part of the 18th century, the Natchez Trace, which was little more than a narrow path from Natchez to Nashville, was probably the most crime-infested area in America.

Among the bandits who roamed the Trace and the Wilderness Road were two brothers, Micajah and Wiley Harpe, better known as Big and Little Harpe. There is no accurate record of how many men, women and children the Harpes butchered in the 1790s, but it was well up in the scores. In 1799 a large posse of frontiersmen cornered the Harpes in the Ohio wilds. Little Harpe escaped, but Big Harpe was shot from his horse and, while still alive, had his head cut off by a man whose wife and children he had slaughtered; Big Harpe was 31 at the time. After his escape Little Harpe, two years his brother's junior, joined up with the bandit gang of Samuel Mason, a strange character who had turned to outlawry in middle age after being a soldier and justice of the peace in Kentucky. Mason would boastfully carve on a tree at the scene of one of his many murders, "Done by Mason of the Woods."

Late in 1803 Little Harpe, now going under the name of Setton, and Sam Mays, another member of the Mason gang, axed their chieftain's head off. They packed it in clay and went to Natchez to claim a reward. Unfortunately, while waiting for their money, they were accused of stealing horses, and Setton was identified as Little Harpe. Little Harpe and Mays were hanged at Greenville, Miss. on February 8, 1804. Their heads were cut off, and Harpe's head was stuck on a pole and displayed on the Trace to the north of the town. May's head was placed on view to the south of town, a warning to other outlaws that the murderous days of the Natchez Trace were coming to a close.

See also: SAM MASON.

Harrison, Lester (1923–) serial killer with unusual bid for freedom

Lester Harrison had a long history of killing and a habit based on his obvious insanity, of never being convicted for his most gruesome murders. While confined in a state hospital in 1951, Harrison killed another inmate but was deemed incompetent to stand trial. Two decades later Harrison was found competent for trial on robbery counts and was given a term of 18 months. He served less than that when he was subjected to psychiatric evaluations.

When he was released, he was not even suspected of beating a woman to death in Chicago's Park in 1970. And immediately after his being put back on the streets, a number of women were murdered, subjected to nightmarish sexual abuse in the process. In one case, Harrison gnawed his victim's body. In August 1973 Harrison stabbed to death a 28-year-old woman in a park restroom. The victim's husband observed Harrison running from the women's bathroom, gave chase and apprehended him without knowing his wife had been killed.

Harrison then confessed to at least four murders, although authorities were sure he had committed many more in the area. He was found competent to stand trial, but the defense succeeded in delaying trial for five years and Harrison was subjected to several psychiatric examinations.

A jury acquitted Harrison by virtue of insanity, but authorities then resorted to a special and seldom invoked measure by which Harrison could be found in a hearing to be "sexually dangerous" and subject to confinement as long as he remained a menace.

It was hard to dispute an affirmative verdict, which resulted, and Harrison was put away. That proved to be but the prelude to a bizarre occurrence eight years later. By that time Harrison's health had deteriorated to the extent that at age 62 he was now a quadriplegic. Lawyers taking Harrison's case insisted he should be released since he was barely able to move at all and thus unlikely to do harm to others. The state attorney's office fought the claim, a representative stating that if Harrison "were able to get his hands on any woman that woman would be in danger of being killed. If he could use one arm, he would use it to try to beat somebody to death."

Testimony from guards at Belleville State Hospital where Harrison was being held indicated that Harrison could raise his arms. More important testimony was given that he became what was euphemistically referred to as "visibly aroused" when nurses he liked entered the room.

The case failed to become a matter of some special legal interpretation when the petition for the patient's release was withdrawn.

Harvey, Donald (1952–) medical serial killer
While any attempt to catalog the full extent of nurse's aide Donald Harvey's brutality results in a mind-boggling numbers game, there is little doubt that he was easily the most lethal medical serial killer of the 20th century.

At 18 Harvey became an orderly at a hospital in London, Ky. in May 1970. He stayed on the job 10 months and later confessed to killing about 12 patients. He would reveal he had smothered two with pillows and hooked another 10 to virtually empty oxygen tanks because he wanted to "ease their suffering." He left the job after being arrested for burglary and got away with only a small fine from a judge who recommended he get psychiatric treatment. Instead, Harvey joined the air force but was discharged ahead of time for unstated reasons. He was committed a couple of times to a Veteran's Administration medical center suffering from mental disorders, which may have included a suicide attempt. He got a number of electroshock treatments but was released with no obvious improvement.

Despite this, he served as a nurse's aide in two hospitals at the same time in Lexington. After holding clerical jobs at another hospital, he then moved on to the Cincinnati V.A. Medical Center, holding nursing positions, including that of an autopsy assistant. In that job he sometimes smuggled out tissue samples to take home to "study."

He did not ignore his "mercy murders" and disposed of some 15 patients by his former methods as well as by poison. Now that he was playing God, Harvey took to putting people who weren't hospitalized out of their misery, apparently deciding that anyone who annoyed him was clearly in misery. Angered by a neighbor, he gave her hepatitis serum to drink. By the heroic efforts of doctors the woman was saved.

In July 1985 Harvey was forced to resign his job after he was found leaving work with hypodermic needles and other medical gear as well as a cocaine spoon. In February 1986 he turned up as a part-time nurse's aide in another Cincinnati hospital and was soon promoted to full time. During a period of just over a year, 23 patients fell victim to his murderous rampage. Some had their life support system disconnected or were injected with mixtures of cyanide, arsenic and a petroleum-based cleanser.

In addition, he poisoned his live-in lover, Carl Hoeweler, after a dispute and then nursed him back to health. Harvey also poisoned Carl's parents; Hoeweler's mother died.

But 23 murders in a hospital were too many to get away with. Patient John Powell was given an autopsy and found to have lethal doses of cyanide in his body. Charged with murder in the case, Harvey pleaded not guilty by reason of insanity. Over the next few months Harvey confessed to a total of 33 murders. Harvey kept adding victims to his list until it climbed to 52. Subjected to a number of psychiatric examinations, Harvey nonetheless was found to be sane and competent although a compulsive killer.

In August 1987 Harvey pleaded guilty to 25 counts of aggravated murder and sundry other charges. He was given four consecutive life sentences with no eligibility for parole for 80 years. Kentucky tacked on nine counts of murder in November. That got him eight more life terms plus 20 years. In February the following year he got three more homicide convictions as well as convictions on other charges. It was said that Harvey was impressed that he had surpassed John Wayne Gacy in total murders committed.

Hatcher, Charles (1929–1984) serial child killer
When serial child killer Charles Hatcher was brought to justice in the early 1980s and started making wholesale confessions, there was at least one fortunate consequence. Melvin Reynolds, serving a life sentence for the sex murder of four-year-old Eric Christgen, was freed when Hatcher was discovered to have been the actual murderer.

From 1969 onward Hatcher confessed to some 16 child murders, the first being that of 12-year-old William Freeman, who vanished in Antioch, Calif., in August of 1969. Ironically the day after the Freeman murder, Hatcher was charged in a child molestation case in San Francisco. In the aftermath of the Freeman disappearance Hatcher was later convicted in California and several Midwest states several times in cases involving sexual assaults and kidnappings of children. What the law was unaware of was that there were intervening murders of children.

Early in 1982 Hatcher was committed to a state mental institution for the abduction of a young boy. After psychiatrists studied Hatcher for two months they sent him free. Then on July 29 the nude, violated body of 11-year-old Michelle Steele turned up on a bank by the Missouri River outside St. Louis. Hatcher was taken into custody the following day when he attempted to check in at the St. Joseph State Hospital. It was in this period that Hatcher began confessing to his cross-country child murders, which proved eminently verifiable. Using a rough map drawn by Hatcher, searchers found the body of James Churchill on the grounds of an army arsenal near Davenport, Iowa.

Hatcher was at first tried only for the Christgen killing for which Reynolds had previously been convicted. He was given a life sentence with no parole for a minimum of 50 years. In 1984, tried and convicted for the Steele killing in Missouri, Hatcher asked for the death penalty, but the jury declined, recommending life. Four days after that sentence was imposed, Hatcher was found hanged in his prison cell. Prison authorities in Jefferson City were satisfied that the child killer had committed suicide and that it was not a case of murder.

But why had Hatcher killed himself? Remorse? A desire to avoid a life sentence that he regarded as worse than execution? Or was there recognition on his part that he faced years of torment from fellow inmates in an institution where child killers can be subjected to extreme violence at any moment?

Heirens, William (1929–) murderer
Beginning at the age of nine, William Heirens committed hundreds of thefts, most often slipping into women's bedrooms and stealing their underthings, which he would later fondle in his room. He dressed in women's clothing and stared at pictures of Nazi leaders for hours. At the age of 13 he was arrested on a charge of carrying a loaded pistol. In his home police found an impressive arsenal of weapons. Heirens was sent to private corrections home. Since he was an above-average student, he was enrolled in Chicago University at the age of 16. But he continued to commit burglaries.

In March 1945 he disturbed a sleeping woman, Mrs. Josephine Ross, slit her throat and stabbed her several times. Three months later, another victim saw him, but he merely knocked her out. In October he killed Frances Brown, shooting her twice and stabbing her. Her body was draped over the tub in the bathroom; the top part of her pajamas was around her neck and a long breadknife was stuck in her neck just below the left ear.

Young Heirens knew he was being overwhelmed by madness. On the wall of Miss Brown's living room, he scrawled in bright red lipstick: "For heavens sake catch me before I kill more I cannot control myself."

Unfortunately, the police did not catch William Heirens until after he committed his most shocking crime, kidnapping six-year-old Suzanne Degnan from her home and slaughtering her in January 1946. He dismembered the body and scattered the parts in Chicago sewers.

While his killings were gory almost beyond description, he had always cleaned the blood off his victim's body. Both Miss Brown and Mrs. Ross had been washed clean. The parts of the child, which were found inside bags, had also been immaculately washed.

Heirens was caught the following June 26 by a caretaker and a tenant in an apartment complex he was trying to enter. For a time he denied the killings, insisting they had been done by one George Murman, who psychiatrists discovered was his alter ego. Even when Heirens made a full confession, he seemed less remorseful about the murders than the fact that his school grades were only average. "I should have been a 'B' level student," he said, "but my grades slipped due to my messing around and cutting up."

Judged insane, Heirens was sentenced to three consecutive life terms with a provision that he never be paroled.

Helm, Boone (1824–1864) killer and vigilante victim

The tales told about Boone Helm describe him as one of the grisliest and most depraved killers ever to set foot on the Western scene. Among his multitude of crimes, he once killed a companion as they crossed the mountains in deep snow and then ate his flesh. When drunk he could be coaxed to talk about it and he would freely admit the act. "You don't think I was damned fool enough to starve to death, do you?" he would snarl. While the vigilantes of the 1860s would later receive considerable criticism for being "excessive" in their hanging, there was never a harsh word said about their elimination of Helm.

A vacant-faced Missourian who somehow inspired fear just by the way he could look at a person, Helm committed his first murder at the age of 27, stabbing a man to death in a drunken dispute. Deserting his wife and young daughter, Helm fled to Indian Territory in the vicinity of what is now Oklahoma, where he was captured and returned to Missouri. His trial was postponed three times because of the difficulty of finding material witnesses. Helm claimed he had acted in self-defense and wondered out loud how the witnesses against him would feel when he was acquitted. The three main witnesses apparently gave some thought to this prospect and finally decided that they hadn't seen a thing.

Deserting his family a second time, Helm next turned up in Oregon, where, despite an unsavory record of violence, he was hired by Elijah Burton to guide a small party through the mountains to Salt Lake City. The trek was disastrous, as Helm was anything but a competent guide. Along the way, members of the group dropped out to await warmer weather, but Burton himself pressed on with Helm, not realizing he would be killed and eaten by his scout. When Helm arrived in Salt Lake City, he looked rather well fed. He did not remain there long enough for firm suspicion to be established against him, however. After killing a gambler in a particularly brutal fashion, he was driven out of town.

Nothing was heard from Helm until he turned up in San Francisco, where he slaughtered a customer in a brothel parlor who had insisted he should be served before Helm. The eager lover was hacked to death with a variety of hatchet and bowie knife blows, causing the establishment's madam to complain that her parlor looked like a butcher shop. Helm committed his next murder in Idaho and then drifted into Canada, where the law became suspicious of him after he had gone trapping with a man named Angus McPherson and returned alone with a rich load of furs. However, since nobody could be found, the authorities were forced to release him. Helm was then escorted to the Montana border.

In Montana he joined up with Henry Plummer's murderous gang of road agent killers known as the Innocents. Helm became one of Sheriff Plummer's deadliest gunmen and was probably responsible for a dozen slayings. When the vigilantes finally rode against the Innocents, one of their main targets was, of course, Helm. Captured on the morning of January 14, 1864, he was hanged along with four others that same afternoon. Helm had never shown any pity for his victims and showed none for himself. "I have looked at death in all forms and I am not afraid to die," he said. He scorned those of his companions who pleaded for mercy. As George Lane swung from the gallows, he commented, "There's one gone to hell." When Jack Gallagher strangled to death, he called out: "Kick away, old fellow. My turn next. I'll be in hell with you in a minute!"

Hicks, Jeffrey Joe (1959–) sex murderer and prison snitch

Much is made that imprisoned sex murderers, especially those whose victims are children, are among the most hated by other inmates. Compounding that hatred, however, is a genuine fear that such a vulnerable prisoner could be forced by his keepers to turn snitch. In Hicks' case it was not illogical that he should be suspected of snitching on an elaborate escape plan worked out by his cellmate. According to the plan Hicks and the cellmate were to be rescued from Leavenworth Penitentiary by a helicopter pilot who would swoop down in the prison yard and pick up the two of them. Negotiations were said to be going on for hiring a pilot when suddenly prison officials swept down on the pair.

As punishment for having conceived the plot—which obviously never got off the ground—the cellmate was sent to the federal penitentiary in Marion, Ill., where he would be locked up in an individual cell 23 hours a day and denied virtually all privileges. Hicks was moved to an isolation cell in Leavenworth for a time. The thought of many inmates was that Hicks had snitched.

Still no retribution was taken on Hicks since it was not absolutely certain that he had snitched—or had a reason to snitch. Hicks had been an inmate in a Michigan state prison when suddenly he was transferred to Leavenworth. In general there were only two reasons for that to have happened: he was a problem prisoner Michigan could not control or he was in personal danger.

The truth surfaced when a prisoner came across an issue of *Inside Detective* that reported on the case of a sexual sadist who had snatched a 13-year-old boy off his bicycle in Green Oak Township, Mich., in October 1986 and driven away in his jeep. The boy's naked body was found in the woods a few days later. He had been molested and strangled. The magazine referred to other kidnappings and molestations to which he had subjected other young boys.

Hicks was sentenced to life plus 65 to 100 years and was serving his time in state prison. It was obvious to Leavenworth convicts that Hicks had to be transferred to Leavenworth for his own protection, and according to accepted criminal protocol, such a prisoner is accepted only when it is made clear to him that in return for "sanctuary," he must turn informer. Naturally in such cases prison authorities deny any such deal has taken place.

In Hicks' case the harassment became so intense that it was only a matter of time before he would be murdered. He disappeared from Leavenworth, undoubtedly transferred to a much lower-security federal prison in another state where he could hope no one would learn of his past so that he might live to serve his sentence without constant fear.

"Hillside Strangler" duo Bianchi and Buono

In addition to being more adept than other serial killers, the so-called Hillside Strangler eluded apprehension for some time due to the fact that the law enforcement authorities were not suspecting two perpetrators of the crimes. The Strangler's modus operandi was readily recognizable: it started out in imitation of that of Caryl Chessman, California's notorious "Red Light Bandit" of the 1940s. Chessman would approach parked couples in lonely spots, flashing a red light resembling that on a police car. He robbed the drivers and sometimes took off with their female companions and forced them to perform sexual acts with him.

Chessman never killed his victims, but the Hillside Strangler murdered at least 10 women, starting in 1977. What prevented the police from catching him sooner was, again, the fact that the Hillside Strangler was not one man but two—cousins Kenneth Bianchi, born in 1952, and Angelo Buono, Jr., born in 1935. At times, the cousins killed together. They first planned their murder rampage after a long drinking bout in which they speculated how it would feel to kill someone. (This statement may be giving them the benefit of the doubt. It is still not clear whether one or both had previously committed murders on their own.) Both decided that Chessman's method of pretending to be a law officer was the perfect way to grab women.

Their technique was to stop women motorists or streetwalkers, flash badges, demand identification, and force them into their car, supposedly an undercover police vehicle. The women were invariably raped, sodomized, then strangled to death. Most of the bodies were left in spots where they were certain to be found. The bodies were generally washed clean—apparently at Buono's suggestion—so as to leave no clues for the police to follow.

After a while, Bianchi decided a change of scene was called for, and he moved to the state of Washington, where, in Bellingham, he found work as a security guard. Eventually, he was linked to the murder of two young women who had been lured by him to investigate a nonexistent house-sitting job. A search of Bianchi's home turned up evidence tying him to the killings, and cooperation with California authorities linked him to at least five Hillside Strangler slayings. Fearful of a possible death penalty in Washington State, Bianchi offered to identify his cousin as the "real" Hillside Strangler. Based on Bianchi's evidence, Buono was convicted in 1983 of nine murders. Despite Buono's care in always fixing up the death scene after one of the pair's murders—he always cleaned his home after Bianchi left so that no fingerprints of any victims were found—a meticulous scientific search turned up a single eyelash from one of the murder victims. Also, some strands of fiber from a chair in Buono's home were discovered on one body.

One witness in the Buono trial was 27-year-old Catherine Lorre, who identified the two cousins as the men who had stopped her on a Hollywood street in the late 1970s and demanded identification. She had produced her driver's license, next to which was a picture of herself as a little girl sitting on the lap of her proud father, actor Peter Lorre. Bianchi testified that he decided not to ensnare her, for fear that murdering the daughter of a celebrity might put too much heat on the homicidal partners.

Buono was sentenced to nine terms of life imprisonment without parole, while Bianchi was returned to Washington to a life sentence with no possibility of parole before 2005.

Like several other serial murderers, the Hillside Strangler—or at least Bianchi—maintained a romantic liaison with a woman drawn to him because of his crimes as Carol Bundy was to Douglas Clark. While Bianchi was in California prior to Buono's trial, a 23-year-old poet and aspiring playwright named Veronica Lynn Compton sought Bianchi's opinion of her new play about a female serial killer. Correspondence and conversations followed, which reveal how close Veronica's tastes came to serial killing. Bianchi then concocted a plan to spring him from his own guilty verdict in the Bellingham murders by having Veronica strangle a woman and leave specimens of Bianchi's semen at the scene to convince authorities that the real killer was still at large.

Compton visited Bianchi in prison and got from him a book in which he had hidden part of a rubber glove containing his semen. Compton went to Bellingham and attempted a murder but botched the job. She was convicted and was sent to prison with no hope of parole before 1994. For a time, she continued to correspond with Bianchi, but finally her ardor for him cooled, and she shifted to corresponding with Douglas Clark, then in San Quentin waiting execution as the Sunset Slayer. A typical ghoulish passage in one letter to Clark read: "Our humor is unusual. I wonder why others don't see the necrophilic aspects of existence as we do."

In 1988 Compton escaped from prison and disappeared.

See also: DOUGLAS CLARK.

Hoch, Johann (1855–1906) mass murderer

In 1905 Chicago police inspector labeled a Chicago packinghouse employee named Johann Hoch "the greatest mass murderer in the history of the United States." No accurate list of victims could ever be compiled, so the claim cannot be verified statistically, but Hoch's record was certainly formidable in many respects. From about 1890 until 1905 it was estimated that he married bigamously as many as 55 women. The lucky ones he robbed of all their possessions and deserted; the unlucky ones he not only robbed but poisoned as well. While the more sensationalist newspapers placed his murder toll at about 25, diligent police work determined the number to be about 15. He was convicted of only one homicide, however, that of his next-to-last known bride, 46-year-old Marie Walcker, the owner of a small candy shop. His other 14 unfortunate spouses all died rather quickly after exchanging vows with him. All their bodies were found to contain traces of arsenic, but virtually all embalming fluid at the time contained some arsenic, and Hoch always saw to it that each of his dearly departed was very heavily embalmed.

Hoch located his victims by simply advertising in German-language newspapers. The ad that attracted Mrs. Walcker read:

> *WIDOWER, quiet and home-loving, with comfortable income and well-furnished house wishes acquaintance of congenial widow without children. Object, matrimony. Write Box B-103.*

Mrs. Walcker did write and within days became Mrs. Hoch. She managed to live only a month following the wedding, taken mysteriously ill shortly after she'd transferred all her life savings to her husband. In keeping with Hoch's record of the most marriages in the shortest period of time, he promptly married his widow's sister four days later. He did not kill her, but instead took her money and ran. Unaware of his intentions, Hoch's new wife reported him missing. In the ensuing police hunt, Hoch's picture appeared in newspapers around the country, and woman after woman came forward to say he, under the name of Hoch or various other aliases, was her husband as well. Other persons came forward to identify Hoch as the short-term husband of a departed member of their family. Hoch was finally located in New York City as he was popping his favorite question to the landlady of a boardinghouse.

By this time, authorities were convinced they had a monstrous mass murderer on their hands. The newspapers named him Stockyard Bluebeard, a reference to his sometime work in Chicago packinghouses. Arsenic traces were found in a number of Hoch's dead wives, and he was returned to Chicago to be tried for Marie Walcker's death. It was a prudent choice, the one case in which Hoch could not use his pat defense that the traces of arsenic in the dead body came from the embalming fluid. By this time science had made advances in the undertaking field, and the newest embalming agents contained no arsenic. The undertaker who'd embalmed Marie Walcker had switched to one of the new fluids just two weeks before. That fact and the testimony of several of Hoch's wives about how he had absconded with their money—one told of him stealing off in the night, even taking the gold bridgework she had left in a water glass beside her bed—sealed the verdict against the defendant. He was hanged on February 23, 1906 before 100 witnesses at the Cook County Jail.

Forty-nine years later, some very old human bones were found in the wall of a cottage where Hoch had lived. The police had searched the premises at the time hoping to find evidence of additional killings by Hoch but had discovered nothing.

Holmes, H. H. (1858–1896) mass murderer

His real name was Herman Webster Mudgett, but he became infamous as H. H. Holmes—probably the greatest mass killer in American history. At various times, he admitted killing anywhere from 20 to 27 persons, being a master of inconsistency, and undoubtedly he murdered many more. Some wild-eyed biographers credit him with killing

200 women in his "murder castle" in Chicago during the 1890s, while a more reasonable count would fall somewhere between 40 and 100.

If there was any question about his arithmetic, there was none about his dedication. Holmes killed with a bizarre fervor to make the last possible cent out of his victims, mostly marriage-starved women whom he murdered for their money. He kept a keen eye out for newspaper ads requesting skeletons, and when he found such an ad, he would scrape his latest victim's bones clean and sell the skeleton to an interested medical student or institution.

As a medical school student, Herman Mudgett had always shown the greatest interest in bodies, more so in those of women than those of men. However, he lost interest in his studies of female anatomy and in time, despite a marriage before he was 20 and a second bigamous one before he was 30, became adept at such additional careers as horse thieving, forging and swindling. He finally went into murder in a big way. With the proceeds from his various crimes, he built a massive "hotel" in 1892 at Sixty-third and Wallace, in anticipation of the Columbian Exposition the following year.

The first floor consisted of stores and the second and third floors of about 100 rooms. Holmes used several as his office and his living quarters. The remaining rooms were for guests, many of whom were never seen alive again. A newspaper subsequently described one of the rooms as an "asphyxiation chamber" with "no light—with gas connections." The room had no windows; the door was equipped with stout bolts; and the walls were padded with asbestos. All Holmes had to do was get a victim in the room and turn on the gas. Most of the rooms featured these gas connections and certain ones had false-bottom floors, which covered small airless chambers. Some of the rooms were lined with iron plates and some had blowtorchlike appliances. Various rooms had chutes that carried human cargo to the basement. Here, Holmes maintained a crematory, complete with vats of corrosive acid and quicklime pits. The pits later yielded up bone and skull fragments of many women he had held prisoner and killed. All the "prison" rooms had an alarm that buzzed in Holmes' quarters if a victim attempted to break out. The evidence indicated that he kept many of the women prisoners for months before he decided to dispose of them.

Holmes obtained most of his victims through ads offering good jobs in a big city or through offers of marriage. If the offer was for a job, he would describe several in detail, and a young woman on her first visit would select the one she wanted. Holmes then sent her home to pack her things and withdraw all her money from the bank since she would need the money to get set up. He would require that the woman not reveal his name to anyone and he would not tell her where the job was until she returned with her money, claiming he had business competitors who were trying to steal his clients. When the woman returned and Holmes was satisfied she had revealed nothing about him, he would take her prisoner. If he was not satisfied, he would say the job had been canceled and send her away. Those whom he offered to marry got the same sort of line. If they came back with less than all their worldly goods, Holmes would use various types of torture apparatuses to make them reveal the whereabouts of their remaining valuables. He then would imprison the women while he went to get their property.

Amazingly, Holmes was able to keep his wholesale murder operation secret for four years. His trouble started when he got involved in an insurance swindle with a shady character named Benjamin F. Pitzel. To pull it off, they both traveled around the country, and in the process Holmes was arrested in St. Louis. He revealed part of the insurance scam to a cell mate, a notorious bank robber named Marion Hedgepeth. Holmes offered Hedgepeth money to put him in touch with a good lawyer. Hedgepeth obliged and Holmes got out, promptly forgetting to pay Hedgepeth. He went to Philadelphia and met up with Pitzel. The two had a falling out, and Holmes killed his partner in crime. About this time, Hedgepeth decided his former cell mate had stiffed him and told the authorities what he knew. Holmes was captured and the Pitzel murder discovered. When Chicago police searched his "hotel," the results were awesome.

Before he was hanged in Philadelphia on May 7, 1896, for the Pitzel murder, since that city refused to surrender him to Chicago for his more gruesome deeds, Holmes made a number of confessions concerning the women he had killed. He accepted an offer of $5,000 from a Chicago newspaper for his story and then perversely concocted a death list that included several women who were still alive and omitted others who had been identified among his victims.

Horn, Tom (1860–1903) hired killer

In recent years there have been efforts by some writers and even by Hollywood—in a 1980 movie—to "rehabilitate" Tom Horn, probably the most callous hired gun and bushwacker the Old West ever saw. Much is made of Horn's early years and his heroism as an army scout under the celebrated Al Sieber and as a lawman and cowboy. Some of the more unquestioning also applaud his four years as a Pinkerton, although during that period he can only be described as a roving gun for the agency, with a toll of victims reputedly amounting to 17. Horn quit the Pinkertons, announcing he "had no more stomach for it." Agency apologists said that indicated he found the job too boring; others thought it meant Horn felt he was underpaid for the work. Immediately thereafter, he offered his lethal services to Wyoming cattlemen. There was no one Tom Horn wouldn't kill for $500. "Killing men is my specialty," he once remarked. "I look at it as a business proposition and I think I have a corner on the market."

Born in Missouri in 1860, he left home at about age 13, after an altercation with his father, and headed west. A tough, headstrong youth, he is believed to have had a row with Billy the Kid and slapped his face. No one was ever to accuse Horn of lacking guts. At 15 he was a stagecoach driver and from 1875 to 1886 he worked off and on for Al Sieber, chief army scout at the San Carlos Indian Reservation. It was Horn who arranged the final surrender of Geronimo to Gen. Nelson Miles in 1886. After that, he became a deputy sheriff in the Arizona Territory.

By the time he went to work for the Pinkertons, he had quite a reputation, one that only worsened while he served in the agency. He ached with the desire for big money, but his only real talent was his skill with guns. The law paid peanuts, the Pinks somewhat more. The real money lay in working directly for the big cattlemen, settling old scores for them and eliminating small ranchers and rustlers (in Cheyenne's cattle baron circles the two terms were used interchangeably). Members of the Wyoming Cattlemen's Association bid high for Horn's services and Horn gloried in their attentions. He smoked their cigars, drank their liquor, backslapped with them and murdered for them.

Horn was a tidy butcher and regarded his assassinations as works of art. Testimony at his later trial would reveal how even in a driving rain, he waited for hours chewing on cuds of raw bacon, to get the one sure shot at a victim. After the kill he always left behind his trademark, a small rock under the victim's head, so that there could be no argument over who had carried out the assignment.

Horn once even offered his deadly services to Gov. W. A. Richards of Wyoming. The governor, who owned a large ranch in the Big Horn country, was fearful of having the gunman seen at his office in the state capital, so he used the premises of the state Board of Livestock Commissioners. Another big stockman, William Irvine, who took part in the meeting, later recollected:

> *The Governor was quite nervous, so was I, Horn perfectly cool; told the Governor he would either drive every rustler out of the Big Horn County, or take no pay other than $350 advanced to buy two horses and a pack outfit; that when he had finished the job to the Governor's satisfaction he should receive $5,000 because, he said in conclusion, "Whenever everything else fails, I have a system which never does." He placed no limit on the number of men to be gotten rid of.*

Irvine said the governor clearly got cold feet when Horn matter-of-factly made his murder proposition. The killer saw this immediately and tactfully ended the discussion by saying: "I presume that is about all you wanted to know, Sir. I shall be glad to hear from you at any time I can be of service."

Horn's murder dealing became so well known that rustlers and other desperadoes often cleared out of an area when he appeared on the scene. But the small rancher, his entire life tied up in his meager holdings, could not. And if a big cattleman said a small rancher was rustling his cattle, that was good enough for Horn.

Because of his powerful connections, Horn was considered immune from the law. But in 1901 he murdered a 14-year-old boy, Willie Nickell, from ambush. Hired to shoot the boy's sheepman father, Horn mistook the youth for the father in the early dawn light. The case remained unsolved until Joe Lefors, a deputy U.S. marshal who led the famous posse that chased Butch Cassidy and the Sundance Kid, took over the investigation. He wormed his way into Horn's confidence, and when the latter was drinking heavily, he got him to boast of his killings, including the Nickell affair, while hidden witnesses and a stenographer listened.

Horn was thrown in jail. When he sobered up, he insisted he had merely been telling tall tales and accused the stenographer of adding statements he had not made. Horn had brilliant legal talent defending him at his trial, with some $5,000 donated to his defense fund by an unknown "admirer." However, the case against him was overwhelming and he was sentenced to hang.

While he awaited execution, people wondered if Horn would start naming all his powerful employers, and it appears that employers wondered too. In August 1903 someone smuggled a pistol to him, and he escaped with another prisoner. He was quickly recaptured, however, and spent much of the rest of his time hurriedly penning his memoirs, leaving out, of course, all references to his murderous "range detecting." With the streets of Cheyenne patrolled by militiamen, Tom Horn was hanged on November 20, 1903, his lips still sealed.

A Wyoming cattleman was to recall, "He died without 'squealing,' to the great relief of many very respectable citizens of the West."

In recent years some effort has been made to discredit the Lefors testimony. Dean Krakel, Horn's chief biographer and author of *The Saga of Tom Horn,* insists the Horn confession was a frame-up and would be inadmissible in modern courts and that Horn was innocent of the Nickell shooting.

Jackson, Mary Jane "Bricktop" (1836–?)
female ruffian and murderess

Nicknamed Bricktop because of her flaming red hair, Mary Jane Jackson was reputedly the most vicious street criminal, male or female, New Orleans has ever produced. Any number of the Live Oak gangsters, the city's toughest gang, backed off from confrontations with her. In about a decade of battling, Bricktop Jackson never lost a fight, killed four men and sent at least two dozen more to the hospital, from which many emerged permanently maimed. When she took up living with a notorious criminal named John Miller, the pair became known as New Orleans' toughest couple.

Born on Girod Street in 1836, Bricktop, a husky, well-endowed girl, became a prostitute at age 13. The next year she attained a measure of security when a saloon keeper took her as his mistress. When he tired of her after three years and threw her out, she charged into his saloon and gave him a fearsome beating, sending him to the hospital minus an ear and most of his nose. Bricktop then entered a Dauphine Street whorehouse, where, while she gained a following with the customers, she terrified the other girls. She was turned out of the Dauphine Street establishment and subsequently, several other brothels. Bricktop was headed for the dance halls of New Orleans' toughest thoroughfare, Gallatin Street, and got a job with the redoubtable Archie Murphy in his notorious Dance-House. Nothing was considered too rough for Murphy's place, but Bricktop Jackson proved the exception to the rule. She had to be forcibly evicted from there as well as many other tough dance houses, whose owners had foolishly thought they could control her. Bricktop finally became a freelance prostitute and street mugger. In 1856 she killed her first man and in 1857 her second; one had called her a "whore" and gotten clubbed to death for the insult, and the other, Long Charley, had been cut down with Bricktop's made-to-order knife following an argument over which way he would fall if stabbed (the nearly 7-foot-tall Charley was reported to have fallen forward when Bricktop tested her hypothesis).

One of Bricktop's more famous murders occurred on November 7, 1859, when she visited a beer garden with two other vicious vixens, America Williams and Ellen Collins. A man at the next table, Laurent Fleury, objected to Bricktop's language and told her to shut up. Bricktop cursed even more and threatened to cut Fleury's heart out. Fleury, who had not recognized the scourge of Gallatin Street, slapped her. In a second the three women were all over him, and the luckless Fleury disappeared in a mass of flailing hands, swirling skirts and flashing knives. Joe Seidensahl, the owner of the beer garden, tried to come to his rescue but was driven back, severely cut up. A Seidensahl employee shot at the women from a second-floor window, but they drove him off with a barrage of bricks. By the time the police arrived, they found Fleury dead and his pants pocket cut out. The pocket, with money still inside, was found tucked under Bricktop's skirt. She was locked up in Parish Prison but eventually freed when an autopsy failed to show the victim's cause of death. Bricktop's lawyer contended he had died of heart disease.

It was in Parish Prison that Bricktop Jackson met a man who was, for the time, the love of her life, a jailer and ex-criminal named John Miller. The pair became a colorful item, even by Gallatin Street standards. Miller had lost an arm in a previous escapade and now walked about with a chain and iron ball attached to his stump, which made an awesome weapon. The couple supported themselves by close teamwork based on their respective skills. Bricktop would start up a romance with a stranger in a French Quarter dive and repair to the back streets with him. The man would end up with a very sore skull, no recollection of what happened and empty pockets.

The romance between Bricktop and Miller was marred by a dispute over who was the master of their nest. One day in 1861 Miller came home and decided to bullwhip Bricktop into subservience. She snatched the whip away from him, however, and gave him a bloody beating. He lashed out with his iron ball but she seized the chain in midair and began dragging him around the room. Miller pulled out a knife and slashed at Bricktop, who bit the knife free, grabbed it and then stabbed her lover five times. It was a fatal end to their relationship and one that caused Bricktop to be sent to prison for 10 years. She was released after only nine months when Gen. George F. Shepley, the military governor of the state, practically emptied the penitentiary with blanket pardons. Upon her release, Bricktop Jackson disappeared from New Orleans, a loss that went totally unlamented by honest and dishonest citizens alike.

Judd, Winnie Ruth (1909–1993) murderess

Winnie Judd was called the Tiger Woman by a devoted press, which kept her supplied with clippings for 40 years after her conviction in the trunk murders of two young women in Phoenix, Ariz.

Winnie had been friendly with 27-year-old Agnes LeRoi, a nurse who worked at the same medical clinic as herself, and Hedvig Samuelson, with whom Agnes shared an apartment, and often stayed with them. On October 16, 1931, screams were heard coming from the apartment. The next day Winnie showed up for work but Agnes did not. On October 18 Winnie went by train to Los Angeles with a large trunk and a small one. Upon her arrival she asked a baggage room employee to help her load them in her car. The employee noticed a dark red fluid dripping from a corner of one of them and demanded to know what was inside, suspecting the trunks might contain contraband deer meat. Winnie said the keys were in the car and went to get them. She drove off, but the baggage clerk managed to write down her license number.

When authorities opened the trunks, they found the body of Agnes LeRoi in the large one and most of the dismembered body of Hedvig in the smaller one. She had been cut up to make her fit. An alarm went out for Winnie, who finally surrendered five days later after an appeal from her Los Angeles husband, from whom she had been separated for some time.

The public was enthralled by the trunk murderess, but it was difficult to tell whether people were more taken by the grisliness of the crime or letters that Winnie had written but never sent to her husband, which revealed strange heterosexual, bisexual and homosexual activities that were common at the LeRoi-Samuelson apartment.

Winnie insisted she had killed in self-defense after Hedvig pulled out a gun and shot her in the hand following a bitter argument. She said she had struggled for the gun, managed to wrest it from Hedvig and in the ensuing melee shot both women. At her trial the prosecution made the point that no one had noticed the gun wound in Winnie's hand until two days after the killings.

Winnie was found guilty and sentenced to hang. Pressure around the country built up for Winnie to be spared the death penalty in light of her claims of self-defense and her lawyer's insistence that she was mentally ill. Thirty state legislators and 34 priests and ministers signed a petition, and thousands of letters poured in on her behalf, including from Mrs. Eleanor Roosevelt.

Winnie Ruth Judd (center), the trunk murderess, being returned to prison after one of her many escapes.

The governor granted her a stay and a sanity hearing 72 hours before her scheduled execution. At the hearing the Tiger Woman put on a show that delighted the newspapers. She clapped, laughed and yelled at the jury. She got up once and told her husband she was "going out the window." Winnie's mother testified that she herself was feeble-minded and that her daughter had "been more or less insane all her life." Her father produced a family tree that traced insanity back 125 years to Scotland. Winnie emphasized the point by ripping at her hair and trying to pull off her clothes. She finally had to be removed from the hearing room and ultimately was judged insane and sentenced to life imprisonment in the state mental institution.

When she arrived at the institution Winnie no longer acted crazy. She was quiet, helpful and plotting. She fashioned a dummy of herself, put it in her bed and escaped. She was found some days later, and it was discovered that strangers had helped her on a number of occasions.

Winnie was brought back and tightly confined. It did no good. Over the years she escaped seven times, each time sparking headlines. One of her escapes lasted six years. It got so that in newsrooms on dull news days an editor would say, "Well, maybe Winnie Ruth Judd will escape again." One of the more sensational crime publications warned its readers, "When you read this story, the country's cleverest maniac may be at large again, perhaps walking down your street, or sitting next to you!"

In 1969, after one of her long-term escapes, attorney Melvin Belli fought Winnie's extradition from California to Arizona, but Gov. Ronald Reagan ordered her returned. Doctors then ruled Winnie was perfectly sane and she was sent to prison. In 1971 Winnie won a parole. She was then in her 60s and no one seemed to be upset about the Tiger Woman being on the loose, possibly because she had had so much free time before.

Keene, John (?–1865) murderer

Had there been a 10 Most Wanted List during the Civil War, John Keene most likely would have made both the Union and Confederate rosters, each for a different set of crimes.

Keene's early background is unknown, but before the outbreak of hostilities he was working in Memphis, Tenn. Immediately after Fort Sumter, he joined the Confederate Navy and was assigned to a ram. Hardly the material with which wars are won, Keene's first hostile action was directed against his own captain, whom he brained with a marlinespike.

Viewing his act as a sort of informal resignation, Keene went on the run. While being hunted by the Southern authorities, Keene allegedly killed a man or two along the way. He eventually made his way back to Memphis, which at the time was in the hands of the Union. This circumstance provided Keene with a new lease on life, but in almost no time, he killed a man named Dolan and was again forced to flee. Changing his name to Bob Black, Keene organized a gang of highway robbers and terrorized the Tennessee countryside, with Union troops in constant pursuit.

Finally captured by Union forces, Keene broke out of the guardroom and headed north. For a while, Keene-Black ran a saloon in St. Paul, Minn. which was little more than a cover for fencing and other criminal activities. When the law closed in on him, he took the only escape path open to him—west. Not surprisingly, he fell in with the wrong sort of people, got in trouble in Salt Lake City and had to make for Montana. There he had a minor association with those notorious outlaws the Innocents, but the Montana Vigilantes soon ordered him out of the territory.

Instead of leaving Montana directly, he headed for Helena, where a short time later he spotted a former acquaintance named Harry Slater sleeping off a jug or two outside a saloon. Back in Salt Lake City, Slater had made it clear that he disliked Keene and intended to do something about it. Keene, a man who always believed in seizing an opportunity, shot the sleeping Slater dead. He was apprehended for the crime and brought before a miners court, which dispensed justice with lightning rapidity. They gave him an hour's grace and then hanged him high from a giant pine.

Kemper, Edmund Emil, III (1948–)

California's "Coed Killer"

In 1972 and 1973, 25-year-old Edmund Kemper, a 280-pound, six-foot-nine giant, terrorized Santa Cruz County, Calif., particularly female students at the Santa Cruz campus of the University of California. Kemper killed six women, decapitating them and performing sex acts that could not be fully reported in the newspapers.

Kemper had an earlier history of murder. In 1964, at the age of 16, he was living with his grandparents when he started wondering what it would be like to shoot his grandmother. So he did. Then he shot his grandfather and called his mother to inform her that both her parents were dead. Judged insane, Kemper was confined at the Atacadero State Hospital. In 1969 the medical board at the institution found him "fully recovered," and he was released over the strenuous objection of the prosecuting attorney in his case.

Apparently free of antisocial tendencies, Kemper expended considerable effort to have the record of his earlier murder sealed and convinced four psychiatric specialists to support him in court. During his last two psychiatric interviews, the head of his most recent victim was in the trunk of his car parked just outside the psychiatrist's office.

Because Kemper's mother worked for the university, Kemper was able to obtain a school parking sticker, which allayed any suspicions of hitchhiking coeds when he offered them a ride. Kemper always kept large cellophane bags in his car so that if he killed and dismembered a girl, the upholstery would not be stained. He safely delivered many more girls than he actually killed, making certain not to harm any who had been seen getting into his car. Kemper generally decapitated the victims with a power saw and kept some of the bodies in his room for a day or two before disposing of them.

On April 20, 1973 Kemper bludgeoned his mother to death as she slept and dismembered her body, severing her hands and throwing them into the garbage disposal. He shoved the headless torso into a closet and then invited over a woman neighbor, his mother's best friend, and strangled her also. He threw her body in with his mother's and went to a local bar called the Jury Room, where he often drank with a number of off-duty police officers. After a time, Kemper got in his car and drove off. Three days later, in Pueblo, Colo., he called Santa Cruz police, who still knew nothing of the murders, and gave himself up, warning he might kill more unless he was taken.

Convicted of eight counts of first-degree murder, Kemper was asked what he considered to be a fit punishment. He replied, "Death by torture." He was sentenced to life imprisonment and first became eligible for parole in 1980.

Lake, Leonard (1946–1985), **and Ng, Charles Chitat** (1961–) serial killer duo

It is understood in law enforcement circles that when a serial killer links up with a like-minded individual, the horror of their predations becomes especially gruesome, each killer feeding off the other's pathological behavior. This was especially true in the case of Leonard Lake and Charles Chitat Ng.

Lake was a veteran who served for two years in Vietnam as a marine spotter for air strikes and returned to the States to what had previously been a rather bizarre lifestyle. At a young age he was bent on photographing nude girls, which soon degenerated into an obsession for pornography. He frequently spoke of the joys of collecting sex "slaves," and apparently he did so during his military service, which might explain why, following his two-year stint in Vietnam, he underwent two years of psychiatric therapy at Camp Pendleton for unspecified mental problems.

Lake was discharged in 1971 and proceeded to participate in a strange series of activities. He became known to others as a gun buff, "survivalist," and sex freak with a passion for making bondage films. He spoke constantly of impending war and acknowledged keeping a cyanide capsule with him so that he could commit suicide if he was ever taken by the enemy; this proved not to be an idle comment. Lake also spent some time in offbeat communal groups, including one that was engaged in collecting unicorns, or, rather, surgically altered young goats, that they could worship. Lake liked the group but in the end was kicked out for being too strange for the other members.

Charles Ng, born of wealthy parents from Hong Kong, was seemingly always in trouble. Sent off to England by his exasperated parents, he attended Oxford for a time until his family disowned him for unspecified reasons. Ng headed for the United States and contacted Lake through an ad the latter had apparently placed in a soldier-of-fortune–type publication. This occurred after Ng had joined the marines and was confined to prison at Leavenworth. The pair corresponded while Ng was still confined. Lake liked what he knew about Ng. He was looking for someone who could help him with his future murderous plans.

When they got together in 1984 the pair went on a monumental kidnap-murder spree, much of which occurred at a cinderblock bunker that Lake constructed on two-and-one-half acres of woodland near Wilseyville, California, in Calaveras County. Lake lived in a wooden cabin, and his neighbors actually helped him build his bunker, which he alleged was to be fortified solely in preparation for a potential foreign invasion.

Lake and Ng stockpiled a huge store of illegal weapons and stolen video equipment that could presumably warn them of a surprise attack. The bunker, they said, could survive a nuclear holocaust. Actually it was set up to hold prisoners, both men and women, until the duo got around to killing them.

How many victims did the pair dispatch? No one will ever know the exact tally. The authorities dug up about a dozen complete or partial skeletons in the woods near the bunker, but eventually they retrieved 50 shopping bags of broken human bones as well as infant teeth. It proved to be a nightmare to try to identify all of these ghoulish remains. Eventually police felt that Lake and Ng were responsible for the disappearance of at least 25 people.

Authorities found a considerable number of videotapes and diaries that indicated some of the frightening practices that were carried out in the bunker. Some would qualify as "snuff tapes," involving sadistic rapes of several women who were then murdered—to accommodate new victims.

Lake left written entries in various diaries of his opinion of the women and how they were to be converted to sex slaves, which he thought would be a vital need if there were to be a nuclear holocaust. He wrote, "God meant women for cooking, cleaning house and sex. And when they are not in use, they should be locked up." Even before he started imprisoning women, he recorded his plans. The female captives were to be brainwashed in order to submit to sexual servitude. Their babies, husbands or boyfriends were also to be held captive and threatened with death if the women did not comply. If the women showed any hesitation of submitting to complete depersonalization their families would be killed. (In actuality, killing of the families of female victims was carried out immediately without the women knowing. Ng was known to have killed two babies in such a manner.) One tape records a woman being forced to undress while pleading for her baby to be returned to her. Her pleas produced only laughter. The baby had undoubtedly been killed, and the woman would suffer the same fate.

In a short time Lake and Ng dispatched a dozen victims, some of them neighbors, without arousing suspicion. One neighbor who got suspicious was Brenda O'Connor, who lived in a nearby cabin. She told friends she saw Lake in the woods burying what she thought was a woman's body. Rather than inform the police, her husband invited a Guardian Angel named Robin Stapely to move in with the couple and their infant son. That proved no impediment to Lake and Ng. In May 1985 all four disappeared (Brenda ended up in a snuff videotape).

Another family that came to a frightful end was Harvey and Deborah Dubs. Dubs was a San Francisco photographer who disappeared in 1984 with his wife and infant son. Dubs' equipment ended up being used for some of the snuff tapes, including one of Deborah Dubs.

Almost anyone coming in contact with the serial killer duo could end up dead. In November 1984 a car dealer named Paul Cosner left his San Francisco home saying he was going to sell his car to "a weird guy." Weird-guy Lake ended up with Cosner's car and Cosner ended up among the permanently missing.

A stranger fate awaited 23-year-old Mike Carroll, who had done time with Ng in Leavenworth and had come west to join him. Carroll sought to ingratiate himself with Ng and Lake by offering to dress up in "fruity" clothes and lure homosexuals whom the pair could rob and kill. The duo liked the idea and the trio carried out a few such killings, but Lake and Ng tired of the routine and pulled the plug on the operation by dispatching Mike Carroll.

That left the matter of 18-year-old Kathleen Allen, who had become Carroll's girlfriend. Lake got her to quit her job in a supermarket and go to Carroll who had supposedly been shot and wounded near Lake Tahoe. Actually Carroll was no longer in this world and Kathleen ended up as yet another snuff-tape "actress."

Other victims had only the most tenuous connection to their murderers. One, a 25-year-old man, simply made the mistake of offering to help Ng move some furniture. For that act of kindness he ended up dead.

By contrast, at least six girls who had been taped by the duo were released rather than killed. However, none of them ever went to the authorities, so terrified were they of the cruel pair.

As a matter of fact, none of their murders led to Lake and Ng's exposure, but rather an almost silly burglary of a south San Francisco lumberyard. Ng grabbed the loot and flipped it into a car that Lake was driving. He was observed and Lake was apprehended, although Ng got away. Unfortunately for Lake the car he was driving was the one taken from Paul Cosner, who was a missing person. Inevitably, Lake realized, police would check out his cabin and discover the bunker and its gruesome secrets.

Brought in for questioning, Lake realized this was the "enemy attack" he had long awaited. He asked for a glass of water, slipped his cyanide capsule in his mouth and lapsed into a coma, dying four days later. Now the Lake-Ng atrocities were discovered and the hunt was on for Charles Ng. Ng had flown to Chicago and made it into Canada. He was arrested in Calgary, Alberta. Ng fought being returned to the United States but in 1989 the courts ruled he could be extradited to California. It was not until mid-1999 that Ng was convicted of a number of murders that prosecutors could prove he had committed, that of six men, three women and two baby boys. He was sentenced to death.

Lucas, Henry Lee (1936–)

Baron Munchhausen of serial killings

In the 1980s the American public and media were in a frenzy over serial killings due to the increasingly brutal confessions of a weak-minded drifter named Henry Lee Lucas. Born to dysfunctional parents in 1936 and subjected to considerable family abuse, Lucas led an early life of lawbreaking spent in prisons and mental institutions. Upon his latest release in 1975 Lucas roamed the country carrying out robberies and the like and, at least according to his later claims, wholesale murders.

In 1980 Lucas hooked up with another drifter named Ottis Toole and the pair went around the nation on a robbery and burglary spree. Each told the other of the weird murders they had allegedly committed. In retrospect the claims seemed to be a sort of bizarre one-upmanship.

In 1983, Toole created a nationwide sensation when he confessed to the kidnap-murder of six-year-old Adam Walsh in 1981. His confessions were at first embraced by law officials, with the obligatory declaration that Toole had offered details no one else could have. But within a few weeks, all charges against Toole were dropped, an obvious indication that Toole had become regarded as a "full mooner."

In the meantime, Lucas, being held on a weapons charge and suspicion of murder, went Toole many times better. With incredible perversity he started making confession after confession. He said he personally knocked off 69 men and women and with the aid of Toole some 20 or so others. In later statements to Texas Rangers Lucas kept raising the total as though it was some sort of macabre auction. The law wanted details; Lucas gave them hair-raising details. He said he engaged in mass torture and willy-nilly slaughters all around, and claimed he crucified some unfortunate victims and "filleted" others. Lucas boasted, "If I wanted a victim, I'd just go get one. I had nothing but pure hatred."

Law agencies around the country were overjoyed and started "clearing the books" on grisly crimes by the score. It seemed Lucas had made it a habit to travel about visiting murder scenes and the like and later picked up vibes when the reaction of police indicated he was around the area when a corpse had been found. Ever-obliging, Lucas pleaded guilty to killing an 80-year-old woman in a robbery in Texas and he was sentenced to 75 years.

When Toole recanted his killing of Adam Walsh, the law continued its acceptance of Lucas' claims. In late 1983 police from 19 states decided his confessions had solved 210 slayings. Later it was estimated Lucas' death toll was definitely at least 100. Of course, during that time Lucas just kept confessing more and more murders. Would they like 250 . . . 300 . . . 400? Soon Lucas topped the 500 mark and then he said he was responsible for at least 600 murders—and worldwide at that, including Spain and Japan. And, oh yes, he had delivered poison to the People's Temple cultists in Guyana.

Then reporter Hugh Aynesworth wrote a series of articles in the *Dallas Times-Herald* blasting Lucas' confessions as "a massive hoax." Previously, it would be fair to say Aynesworth had been a believer, having signed a book contract to write Lucas' biography in 1984. In February 1985 Aynesworth did an interview in *Penthouse* magazine. Later Lucas got around to denying the killings and had supplied alibis that Aynesworth could check that indicated Lucas was clearly elsewhere at the time.

Predictably, Lucas then recanted his recantations, claiming he had been drugged and forced to lie.

While there were police agencies still clinging to Lucas' confessions, most observers had had enough, and his statements had taken on a comic quality unworthy of much newspaper space.

In an interesting climax to the Lucas saga, he was sentenced to be executed for one murder in Texas. However, in that generally unforgiving state, the sentence of weak-minded Henry Lee Lucas was reduced to life imprisonment, indicating some further possible uneasiness about him.

Perhaps more significantly it is obvious that the murders had indeed occurred (except for some people Lucas said he had killed who turned out to be alive) and, if Lucas hadn't done them, a legion of murderers had got away with their crimes.

Overall, it could be said that the Lucas saga had been ghoulish fun while it lasted.

Luetgert, Adolph Louis (1848–1911)

murderer

Few murders have ever shocked the citizens of Chicago as much as the gruesome killing in 1897 of Louisa Luetgert by her husband, Adolph, the owner of a leading sausage-making business.

Luetgert had emigrated from his native Germany in the 1870s and, over the years, had acquired three distinctions: he made just about the best German sausages in the city; he was a man of enormous appetite and considerable girth, weighing about 250 pounds, and he had sexual appetites that equalled or exceeded his culinary one, having three regular mistresses at the time of his wife's demise and a bed installed at his plant for his many trysts.

Luetgert was relatively happy except for one thing: his hefty wife, Louisa. She annoyed him, so much so that he often felt, as he told one of his lovers, "I could take her and crush her." Actually, as the police were to surmise in 1897, he probably stabbed her to death with a huge knife. That much is conjecture because almost nothing of Louisa's body was ever found. After Adolph killed her, he did something that was to damage the sale of sausage meat in Chicago for a long time. He melted her body down in a vat at his meat plant and made her part of his sausages.

Louisa turned up missing on May 1, 1897. Adolph told her relatives that he had hired private detectives to find her and that he would not go to the police because, as a prominent businessman, he could not afford to have any scandal. Eventually, his wife's relatives went to the police, who in turn searched Adolph's sausage factory. After several searches the police emptied one of many steam vats and found some pieces of bone, some teeth and two gold rings, one a wedding band with the initials "L. L." engraved on it. Both rings belonged to Louisa Luetgert. Although Adolph insisted the bone fragments were animal, analysis identified them as human. The wedding ring was even more damning because the sausage maker's wife suffered from swollen joints in some of her fingers and had been unable to remove the ring for years. However, as the police theorized, she could have been melted out of it.

Luetgert's trial was sensational, although most unsavory. The evidence against him was formidable, especially when one mistress after another took the stand to testify against him. Convicted, Luetgert was sentenced to life at Joliet Prison, where he died in 1911.

Lupo the Wolf (1870?–1944) Black Hander and murderer

From the 1890s until 1920, Ignazio Saietta, better known as Ignazio Lupo, or Lupo the Wolf, was the most important Black Hander in New York City. The Black Hand was not an organized society but a mixed bag of amateur and professional extortionists who terrorized various Italian communities throughout the United States, threatening victims with death unless they paid to stay alive. The victims would receive letters demanding money and at the bottom of the letter there would usually be the outline of a hand that had been dipped in black ink, a sign sure to produce icy terror. Lupo the Wolf fostered and perfected the Black Hand technique, promoting himself into the embodiment of evil in the Italian section of Harlem.

Lupo came from Sicily as a grown man and soon won a reputation as one of the most desperate and bloodthirsty criminals in the history of American crimes. His followers knew they had to kill without questioning his authority, so terrified were they of him. It was the custom in Italian Harlem for a resident to cross himself on the mere mention of Lupo's name and extend his fingers to ward off the spells of this evil creature. Many of Lupo's killings took place in the infamous Murder Stable at 323 East 107th Street, where eventually the bodies of some 60 murder victims were found. Some of these were individuals who had refused to meet Lupo's Black Hand demands, but more were victims of murder-for-pay jobs done for other gangs, secret societies or private individuals who had contracted with Lupo for an old-country vendetta killing.

Included among the victims were gang members who had strayed, such as the 18-year-old stepson of Giuseppi Morello, Lupo's chief ally. The youth was tortured and slaughtered because he was suspected of having betrayed the gang's counterfeiting activities. Using fear and intimidation, Lupo continued to operate through the first two decades of the 20th century seemingly immune to arrest for his various murders and extortions. Finally, in 1920 Secret Service agents caught him in a counterfeiting plot in which dollars were forged in Sicily and then smuggled into this country.

Lupo the Wolf was sent to prison for 30 years. Released in the late 1930s, he emerged to find much of the criminal world altered. Black Hand operations had long since ceased because of the increased sophistication of the Italian community whose members now would go to the law if pushed. There was no longer any room for Lupo in other rackets. Mafia racketeers had joined in an organized crime confederation that used murder only as a last resort and in accordance with sound business procedures. Clearly, Lupo the Wolf, with his crude methods, did not belong, and he was so informed. Terror and murder as he practiced them would only cause serious legal and political problems for the organization and simply would not be tolerated. Lupo took the warning to heart and went into retirement until his death in 1944.

Lyons, Danny (1860–1888) murderer

A leading member of the Whyos, easily the most murderous gang in New York City during the late 19th century, handsome Danny Lyons was available to do any job at a price. He would blacken both eyes of a victim for a $4 fee, break his leg for $19, shoot him in the leg for $25 or "do the big job" for $100 and up. A strutting rooster, he kept three women in prostitution on the streets: Lizzie the Dove, Bunty Kate and Gentle Maggie. When they failed to bring in the revenues that Lyons felt were necessary to maintain him properly, he recruited a fourth, Kitty McGown. But Kitty already had a lover, Joseph Quinn, who vowed to get Lyons for stealing his inamorata and meal ticket. The two prowled lower New York for months and on July 5, 1887 their paths finally crossed. They blazed away at each other, and Quinn dropped with a bullet in his heart.

Lyons went into hiding but was caught some months later and hanged on August 21, 1888. In underworld circles there was much denunciation of the execution for what was considered a bum rap. The story was that Quinn had shot first, and Lyons had merely acted in self-defense. Certainly, the authorities had been hoping to get a noose around Lyons' neck and such a God-sent opportunity was not to be lost because of a quibble over who had shot first.

Kitty McGown and Bunty Kate immediately found themselves new protectors, but Lizzie the Dove and Gentle Maggie put on widow's black and canceled all business engagements while they went into mourning. One night toasting their departed lover in a Bowery dive, they got into a heated argument over which of them he had loved more and whose sadness was greater. Gentle Maggie won the argument by plunging a cheese knife into Lizzie the Dove's throat. As she lay dying, Lizzie told her rival, "[I will] meet you in hell and there scratch your eyes out."

See also: DANNY DRISCOLL.

McGurn, Machine Gun Jack (1904–1936)
hit man

Machine Gun Jack McGurn was the kind of subject Hollywood embraced for its gangster movies of the 1930s. James De Mora was 19 when his father was murdered in Chicago's Little Italy. Legend has it that the son soaked his hands in his father's blood and vowed vengeance. He started practicing to take his revenge by shooting birds off telephone wires with a Daisy repeating rifle.

Meanwhile, he tried boxing, becoming a reasonably good welterweight, under the name of Jack McGurn. When it was apparent he didn't have the stuff of a top-notch fighter, McGurn's manager dropped him, and he went back to hunting his father's killers, whose identities were, in fact, hardly a dark secret. McGurn's father had been an alcohol cooker for the vicious Genna gang, which controlled illegal booze production in Little Italy. When he made the mistake of supplying alcohol to the competition, he was killed. Young McGurn could hardly expect to learn which Genna gunman had done the job, so he decided to kill any and all Genna men. The best way to do that was to join the Capone outfit, which sooner or later would have to make war on the Gennas.

McGurn became one of Capone's most reliable hit men, exceedingly proficient with a machine gun, hence he was called Machine Gun McGurn. The police supposedly attributed 28 killings to McGurn, including about six of the Genna gang. In the hand of each of these, McGurn had placed a nickel to show his contempt for the dead men, lousy nickel-and-dimers. His devotion to killing for Capone knew no limits. He is said to have personally held the heads of Albert Anselmi, John Scalise and Hop Toad Giunta as Al Capone battered their brains out with an Indian club at a famous party thrown in their honor. He also is generally believed to have been one of the machine gunners and certainly one of the chief planners of the St. Valentine Day's Massacre. But charges against him had to be dropped when Louise Rolfe, a showgirl, insisted he had been with her at the time of the massacre, thus winning her fame as the Blonde Alibi. Later, the police were able to prove the story was false and charged McGurn with perjury, but he beat that rap by marrying Louise Rolfe, who, as his wife, could not be forced to testify against him.

McGurn was a great nightclub crawler. With the shoulders of his suit heavily padded and his hair pomaded, he did his best to look like Rudolph Valentino. He so prospered in his criminal endeavors that he soon owned a number of Loop nightclubs. One of his entertainers was a young comer named Joe E. Lewis, who eventually deserted him to work in a rival club. A week later, Lewis was waylaid by three of McGurn's men. Two of them pistol-whipped him while the third worked him over with a knife, carving up his face and slashing his throat and tongue. Somehow Lewis survived. He had to learn to talk all over again, and it was 10 years before he once more rose to the top of his profession.

After Al Capone was convicted of income tax evasion, McGurn went into a slow decline. By 1936 things had really gotten tough for him. He was being edged aside by other Capone gang members and his nightclubs had folded because of the Depression. On February 13, the eve of the anniversary of the St. Valentine's Day Massacre, McGurn was in a bowling alley with two other men when three gunmen entered. The trio drew their guns, as did the two men with McGurn. All five turned their weapons on him and opened fire. In his right hand they pressed a nickel, perhaps indicating McGurn's killing was an act of revenge for his earlier slayings of Genna gang members. On the other hand, the fact that the murder occurred on the night before the anniversary of the massacre may mean it was the work of Bugs Moran and remnants of the O'Banion gang. Then again, both touches could have been deliberately staged by the Capone mob to cover their tracks. In any event, neither the police nor the public seemed too concerned about who had been responsible.

McKinney Touch sadistic trademark

A Western term that for the most part became extinct when the frontier tamed down, the McKinney Touch was named after James McKinney, who won fame from Leadville, Colo. to California's San Joaquin Valley as, for want of a better description, a mad buttocks mutilator.

Born in Illinois in 1861, McKinney is officially credited with killing his first man in Leadville. In a display of gratuitious sadism, he then shot off the nipples of his victim's girlfriend. Moving westward, he introduced the McKinney Touch when he deliberately decorated a cancan dancer's rump with bullet ridges. In California he whittled off a bit of a schoolteacher's ear and knifed two lawmen, the last offense earning him seven years in San Quentin. Within a short time after he got out, McKinney had refined his trademark to the point that folks started calling it the McKinney Touch. On December 13, 1901 McKinney shot and killed a man named Sears. When a lawman hearing the shooting bounded out of an outhouse gun in hand, McKinney sent him scurrying with two shots that grazed his rump. Amazingly, McKinney was held blameless in these shootings: it was ruled he had acted in self-defense when Sears tried to kill him and that he had taken due care not to maim the officer when he came at him without first ascertaining the facts.

That was the last time the McKinney Touch was considered a mere prank. After he killed a man named William Linn and wounded two lawmen, McKinney fled California with a posse hot on his heels. He crossed into Mexico but soon returned to California and killed two prospectors. The law knew the killings were McKinney's work because of where the two had been shot. Finally, on April 18, McKinney was cornered in a Chinese opium den in Bakersfield, Calif. City Marshal Jess Packard and five deputies stormed the den. When the smoke cleared, McKinney, Marshal Packard and Deputy Marshal William Tibbett, the father of Lawrence Tibbett, the future Metropolitan Opera star, lay dead.

Madden, Owney "the Killer" (1892–1964)

bootlegger and murderer

The transformation of Owney "the Killer" Madden from a vicious young thug, who was called "that little banty rooster out of hell," into a sleek, dapper sophisticate of crime was truly remarkable. During the early 1900s Madden was known as a heartless, mindless murderer. He killed his first victim at the age of 17 and had done in five by the time he reached 23. During the 1920s and 1930s he was one of the top bootleggers and gang leaders in New York, a debonair character who was still capable of murder—but with a certain flair.

Owney came to New York from his native Liverpool, England when he was 11 and soon enrolled in one of the major gangs of the day, the Gophers. He ran up a total of 44 arrests in his youthful escapades without ever doing any time in prison. In the process he became accomplished with a slung shot, a blackjack, brass knuckles and his favorite weapon, a piece of lead pipe wrapped in a newspaper. Because of his callousness and daring, Madden quickly gained the nickname the Killer and advanced to the leadership of the gang. In that exalted position he raked in an estimated $200 a day for the robberies, labor beatings, killings and intergang attacks

A stone killer in his youth, Owney Madden left the New York rackets to become the crime king and good ole boy of Hot Springs, Arkansas, which he ran as a sort of cooling-off spot for organized crime big shots.

he planned. By the time he was 20, he was receiving extortion money from scores of merchants eager to pay "bomb insurance" to avoid having their storefronts blown out.

The police charged but couldn't prove that Madden had killed his first man, an Italian, for no other reason but to celebrate his rise to power in the Gophers. Some of his homicides, on the other hand, resulted from affairs of the heart. When he learned in 1910 that an innocuous clerk named William Henshaw had asked one of his girls for a date, Madden followed him onto a trolley car at Ninth Avenue and West 16th Street and shot him in front of a dozen other passengers. Before departing the trolley, he paused to toll the bell for his victim. Henshaw lived long enough to identify Madden, who was captured after a chase across several roof tops in Hell's Kitchen. He was not convicted of the murder, however, since all the witnesses thought it wise to vanish.

In November 1912 a youthful Owney the Killer almost had his career cut short during a confrontation in a dance hall with 11 gunmen from the rival Hudson Dusters. When he tried to outdraw and outshoot the bunch of them, he ended up with five bullets in his body. Rushed to the hospital, Madden refused to tell the police who had shot him. "It's nobody's business but mine," he said.

By the time he got out of the hospital, his men had knocked off six of his assailants. However, Owney the Killer had other pressing problems to deal with. Little Patsy Doyle had moved to take over the Gophers, spreading the false word that Owney was crippled for life. Little Patsy was motivated by more than blind ambition; the Killer had appropriated his woman, Freda Horner, and made Patsy a laughingstock. Little Patsy played tough, shooting up a number of Madden loyalists. In due course, Owney ended Little Patsy's bid for power and his entire insurrection by filling him with bullets. For this offense Madden was imprisoned in Sing Sing from 1915 to 1923.

By the time Owney the Killer got out of prison, he had undergone a sort of metamorphosis. He had attained a measure of finesse and respectability. Owney went into rumrunning and into the coal and laundry rackets, proving such a dependable crook that Tammany's Jimmy Hines stood behind him. Owney the Killer moved in the top criminal circles with such ascending powers of the 1920s as Lucky Luciano, Dutch Schultz, Frank Costello, Waxey Gordon, Longy Zwillman, Louis Lepke and the Bug and Meyer team of Bugsy Siegel and Meyer Lansky. Despite his rise in status, Madden had not lost his instinct for violence. When Mad Dog Coll was running around Manhattan kidnapping and murdering top criminals, it was Owney who kept him talking on the telephone one day until gunmen arrived to cut off the Mad Dog's connection.

In the 1930s Madden moved into the world of sports, promoting the dimwitted Primo Carnera into the heavyweight boxing championship. Carnera ended up stone broke, but Madden was said to have made a million, taking a 100 percent cut of the Italian fighter's earnings.

Owney was picked up in 1932 for a parole violation, but after a short stay in prison he was back on the town. The police kept the heat on him with all sorts of minor arrests until in the mid-1930s he decided to retire. If 20 years earlier a veteran cop had been asked what young punk would most assuredly end up on a slab in the morgue, more than likely he would have picked Owney the Killer. Instead, Madden retired to the good life in

Hot Springs, Ark., a famous underworld "cooling-off" spot where his protection by the local law was to become legendary. The local cops performed heroic work keeping him from being annoyed by pesky journalists. If they didn't, Owney warned them, he would have them transferred and broken. By the time he died in 1964, Owney the Killer had almost achieved the stature of a southern gentleman.

See also: VINCENT "MAD DOG" COLL.

Manson, Charles (1934–) murder cult leader

The highly publicized leader of a "family," or self-aggrandizing cult, Charles Manson burst on the California scene in shocking style, even in a state long thought inured to bizarre bloodletting. On August 9, 1969 Charles "Tex" Watson and three female accomplices, Patricia Krenwinkel, Susan Atkins and Leslie Van Houten, entered the Beverly Hills estate of film director Roman Polanski, who was away at the time, and murdered his pregnant wife, actress Sharon Tate, and four others—Abigail Folger, heiress to the Folger coffee fortune; Voyteck Frykowski, a Polish writer and producer, who was living with Folger; Jay Sebring, a hairstylist; and 18-year-old Steven Earl Parent. The five were shot, stabbed and clubbed to death, with Sharon Tate begging to be allowed to live for the sake of her unborn baby. The killers used the

Charles Manson (right) and two of his female cultists, Patricia Krenwinkel (left) and Leslie Van Houten, were in a jovial mood at a court appearance after their arrest. All were convicted of murder.

victims' blood to scrawl crazed slogans and words like "Pig" and "War" on the walls. During the slaughter Watson kept screaming, "I am the devil and I have come to do the devil's work!"

Two nights later, the shocking process was repeated at the home of Leno and Rosemary La Bianca; they were butchered and the same sort of bloody messages were scrawled all over their home.

The murderers were soon traced back to the Manson family. Manson, at 34, had done time in several prisons and reform schools for such charges as procuring and forgery. After his last release from prison, he had set up a sort of commune for a cult of shiftless hippies and drifters at the Spahn Ranch outside Los Angeles, once a filming location for Hollywood studios. At the ranch the cult practiced free love, experimented with drugs and conducted pseudo-religious ceremonies built around Manson as a Christlike figure. When Manson ordered guerrilla tactics, his followers practiced guerrilla tactics, and when he told them to kill, they killed.

After their capture none of the actual killers or Manson, who had directed them, showed any sign of remorse over the horrifying crimes. At their trial—during which a number of Manson's shaved-head female followers kept daily vigil outside the courthouse—the prosecutor called Manson "one of the most evil, satanic men who ever walked the face of the earth." For a time the three women defendants offered to admit their guilt if Manson was declared innocent. Manson waved off their offer, telling the court: "I have done my best to get along in your world, and now you want to kill me. I say to myself, 'Ha, I'm already dead, have been all my life . . . I don't care anything about any of you.'"

All were found guilty and sentenced to die, but they were spared the death penalty because of the Supreme Court ruling outlawing capital punishment and were given life instead. They have been eligible for parole since 1978. In 1980 Manson was turned down on his third annual application for parole. The parole board advised him to train for a trade as part of his rehabilitation, but Manson said: "I'll stay here forever. I'm too old. I can't do too much. I like to sit around, smoke grass, read the Bible now and then."

Maranzano, Salvatore (1868–1931)

Mafia "boss of bosses"

For four months in 1931, Salvatore Maranzano was probably the most important criminal boss in the United States, even more important than Al Capone, whom Maranzano put on a list of mobsters to be eliminated in order to solidify his authority throughout the entire country. Maranzano founded what came to be known as the Cosa Nostra.

Maranzano was a "Mustache Pete," an old-line Mafia leader who held to the criminal society's traditions of "honor" and "respect" for the gang boss and bloody feuds with foes of decades past. Nevertheless, he had modern ideas about crime and wanted to institutionalize it in America—with himself on top. If he had survived 1931, organized crime in America today would operate much differently.

Maranzano had come to the United States late in his criminal career, around 1918, but he had been an established mafioso in Sicily (he had fled because of a murder charge and because the older Mustache Petes resented his new ideas and probably would have killed him if he had stayed). His magnetism quickly made him a gang power and he surrounded himself with gangsters from his hometown in Sicily, Castellammare del Golfo. College-trained and originally a candidate for the priesthood, he was a far cry from the standard mafiosi. Within a few years he had grown so powerful he was becoming a threat to the acknowledged Mafia boss of New York, Giuseppe "Joe the Boss" Masseria.

Masseria was a glutton, both in personal habits and in the way he ran criminal affairs, demanding enormous tribute from his subchiefs. Maranzano shrewdly used the resentment this produced to lure many leading gangsters away from Joe the Boss. But he could not bring in the biggest prize, a rising young mobster named Lucky Luciano, a brilliant strategist whose reorganization of much of Joe the Boss' empire resulted in greatly increased profits.

When Maranzano seemed to be getting too strong, Joe the Boss declared war on him. The police, having no way of separating gang war killings from other underworld executions, never knew how many men died in what was called the Castellammarese War; the toll between 1928 and 1930 may well have been 50. Because he could field probably 200 more gunmen than his foe, Joe the Boss did not take the threat seriously at first. But Maranzano kept winning defections by promising Masseria men a better share of the loot if they joined him.

While Maranzano and Masseria fought their two-sided war, a third side was developing. Luciano had been cultivating the younger gangsters within the Maranzano forces, telling them an entirely new crime setup, one that would really bring in big money. He had developed contacts with the Jewish gangs that would lead to the formation of a new crime syndicate and end the Mafia's internecine struggles as well as its battles with other ethnic groups involved in crime. Luciano, through Frank Costello, had also established rapport with the New York police, sending $10,000 a week directly to police headquarters (the sum was doubled in the late 1920s), and he could thus supply better protection than either Joe the Boss or Maranzano.

For a time Luciano had hung back waiting to see which of the two leaders would eliminate the other. When a stalemate developed, he decided to help matters along by getting rid of Joe the Boss, who would be easier to kill since he trusted Luciano. On April 15, 1931 Luciano and Masseria had lunch in a Coney Island restaurant. About 3:30 P.M. Luciano went to the men's room. Just then four assassins stepped up to Masseria and fired a fusillade of 20 shots at him, hitting him six times. Joe the Boss lay dead.

Luciano had handed the crown to Maranzano. Now, he bided his time to allow Maranzano to think he was secure. As a supposed act of gratitude, Maranzano gave Luciano the number two position in his new organization. In a memorable conclave he summoned 500 gangsters to a meeting in the Bronx and outlined his great new scheme for crime. The New York Mafia would be divided into five major crime families, with a boss, a sub-boss, lieutenants and soldiers. Above them all would be a "boss of bosses"—Salvatore Maranzano. He called this new organization La Cosa Nostra, which meant nothing more than "Our Thing." Years later, the phrase "Cosa Nostra" would be used to get J. Edgar Hoover out of a bad hole of his own making. For decades Hoover had insisted there was no such thing as organized crime and no Mafia. Oh yes, he was able to announce, there was a Cosa Nostra.

While Maranzano was constructing his new empire, he was aware that not all those under him were loyalists. He knew better than to trust the ambitious Luciano, who was too worldly and was setting up a partially non-Italian power base. Maranzano composed a death list that, when carried out, would guarantee his rule. On that list were Luciano, Costello, Vito Genovese, Joe Adonis, Willie Moretti, Dutch Schultz and the "fat guy" in Chicago, Al Capone, who was friendly with Luciano.

It would be a prodigious undertaking to eliminate them all, and Maranzano realized it would be dangerous to trust other Italians with the task—whomever he picked might be a secret ally of Luciano. So, he decided to have the job handled by a non-Italian. He enlisted the notorious young killer Vince "Mad Dog" Coll and arranged for him to come to his office in the Grand Central building at a time when Luciano and Genovese would be present. Coll was to kill them and then get as many of the others on the list as possible before the murders became known. Maranzano gave Coll $25,000 as a down payment and promised him another $25,000 upon successful completion of the assignment.

The boss of bosses then invited Luciano and Genovese to a meeting in his office. Unaware of how many gunmen Luciano had won over to his cause, Maranzano made the mistake of trusting a gangster named Tommy Lucchese, who had been a secret friend of Luciano for years and his chief spy in the Maranzano organization. Lucchese learned of the murder plot and warned Luciano. On the day set for the meeting, Lucchese innocently dropped into Maranzano's office a few minutes before Luciano and Genovese were due. Just then four men walked in flashing badges and announced they had some questions to ask. The four were Jewish gangsters Luciano had borrowed for the plot because they were unknown to Maranzano and his bodyguards. On the other hand, since the gunmen did not know Maranzano, Lucchese was there to ensure they got the right man.

The phony officers lined the bodyguards up against the wall and disarmed them. Then two went into Maranzano's office and shot him to death. The assassins charged out, as did the bodyguards after ascertaining their boss was dead. On the way down the emergency stairs, one of them ran into Mad Dog Coll coming to keep his murder appointment. Appraised of the new situation, Coll exited whistling. He had $25,000 and nothing to do for it.

The death of Maranzano meant a new deal for crime in America. The forces of Luciano, Meyer Lansky and Dutch Schultz would form a national crime syndicate. Over the years Schultz would be killed by the others, but the apparatus was there to stay.

See also: VINCENT "MAD DOG" COLL.

Mason, Sam (c. 1755–1803) highwayman and murderer

A brawling river man who for a time had been one of George Rogers Clark's rangers, Sam Mason was the greatest terror of the Mississippi, beginning in 1800. He collected a large gang of cutthroats, who seldom let a robbery victim live to tell about it. Mason would often leave his trademark at the scene of the crime, carving on a tree, "Done by Mason of the Woods."

Like the Harpe brothers, a pair of brutal killers of the same era, Mason often killed indiscriminately. But he might turn around and let his next hapless victim go with no more than a boot in the pants. The governors of both the Louisiana and the Mississippi territories put him at the head of the list of wanted men. Mason was captured early in 1803 but escaped before he was identified.

Meanwhile, a bearded man named Setton joined the Mason gang and took part in a number of forays and killings. Mason did not know it, but Setton was the much-sought Little Harpe, whose older brother, Big Harpe, had been captured by the law and executed earlier that year. There was a handsome reward out for Mason and Harpe-Setton had designs on it. One day in late 1803, Harpe, with the aid of another gang member named Sam Mays, waited until Mason was separated from the rest of his men and then tomahawked him to death. Harpe and Mays took Mason's severed head to Natchez to claim their reward. Unfortunately, Little Harpe was recognized and they, like their victim, ended up with their heads cut off.

See also: HARPE BROTHERS.

Masseria, Giuseppe "Joe the Boss"

(c. 1880–1931) Mafia leader

Joe the Boss Masseria was the undisputed boss of the New York Mafia in the 1920s, a rank he achieved by knocking off a number of rivals for the throne. Masseria had come from Sicily in the early years of the 20th century with solid Mafia connections. He soon teamed up with Lupo the Wolf, often regarded as the cruelest mafioso in the country and the owner of the infamous Murder Stable in East Harlem where his foes or victims were hung on meat hooks.

Masseria looked like a round little cherub except for his cold eyes, which betrayed a fearsomeness that made him a worthy partner of Lupo. When the pair made extortion demands of Italian immigrants, their victims paid whether they could afford to or not. In 1920 Lupo went to prison on a counterfeiting charge and Masseria fell heir to his operations, the most important of which, with the onset of Prohibition, was control of the liquor stills and wine-making vats that were common in many Italian households.

The revenues from bootleg booze made Masseria richer than any Mafia leader before him, and he moved quickly to consolidate his power. Whenever any leader appeared to be gaining strength, Joe the Boss had him killed. He too was the subject of numerous assassination attempts. Once, two gunmen sent by his archrival, Umberto Valenti, shot at him as he left his Manhattan apartment on Second Avenue. Joe the Boss darted into a millinery shop, trailed by the gunners, whose bullets shattered windows and mirrors and hit Masseria's straw hat twice. But they missed the Italian gangster, who thereby gained the mystique of being able to dodge bullets.

In due course, Joe the Boss announced he wanted to make peace with Valenti and asked for a conference to discuss terms. The pair met in an Italian restaurant on East 12th Street and Masseria pledged his loyalty to his new "brother." As they left the restaurant, Masseria draped his arm over Valenti's shoulders. On the sidewalk Joe the Boss suddenly moved away and Valenti was cut down by a hail of bullets.

Masseria ruled supreme for several years until he received a challenge, the most serious of all, from Salvatore Maranzano, who wanted to be the "boss of bosses." Masseria was upset by the effrontery—after all, he was

Joe the Boss. Soon, war broke out and bodies littered the streets in all the boroughs of New York.

Masseria felt secure. He had twice as many gunners as Maranzano had and some very able assistants as well. His top aide was Lucky Luciano, and among others were Joe Adonis, Frank Costello, Carlo Gambino, Willie Moretti and Albert Anastasia. And under them was a host of savage killers. Masseria especially liked Anastasia, who shared his own instincts for solving matters by murder, but he had to admit Luciano was his most cunning assistant, a brilliant planner and organizer. All these young hoods had one problem: they kept telling him the gang had to abandon the ways of the old country and make deals with other ethnic gangsters, like the Irish and the Jews. Luciano insisted everyone could make more money if they cooperated, and he and Adonis were working their bootleg rackets with the Bug and Meyer gang—Bugsy Siegel and Meyer Lansky. Joe the Boss did not trust Siegel and Lansky, and he bridled at working with Dutch Schultz, even if he had converted to Catholicism. Moreover, he disliked the fact that Costello was paying off all the politicians. It was all right to bribe an official now and then when needed, but one should not "sleep with them" all the time. The politicians would eventually corrupt you, Masseria felt, even though Luciano insisted it was the other way around.

Joe the Boss didn't realize that these younger mafiosi hated him as intently as they hated Maranzano. They looked forward to the day when they would be rid of all the "Mustache Petes," as they disdainfully called old country mafiosi. They even had secret contacts within the Maranzano organization, especially with Tommy Lucchese and Tom Gagliano, intended to stop the senseless killings between the groups so that everyone could just concentrate on making money.

Luciano counseled the others to bide their time until either Masseria killed Maranzano or vice versa, but by 1931 both leaders were still around and others were doing the dying. That year Luciano decided something had to be done. Since it would be easier to kill someone who trusted him rather than one who did not, he decided Joe the Boss would have to die first. On April 15, 1931 Luciano suggested to Masseria that they drive out to Coney Island for lunch. Joe the Boss agreed and they dined at a favorite underworld haunt, Nuova Villa Tammaro, owned by Gerardo Scarpato, an acquaintance of a number of gangsters. During lunch Joe the Boss gorged himself, and after the rest of the diners cleared out, he and Luciano played pinochle while owner Scarpato went for a walk along the beach.

About 3:30 P.M. Luciano went to the toilet. As soon as he left, four men came marching through the door. They were Vito Genovese, Joe Adonis, Albert Anastasia and Bugsy Siegel, loaned especially for the operation by Meyer Lansky, who was destined to become Luciano's closest associate. All pulled out guns and fired at Masseria. Six bullets hit home, and the reign of Joe the Boss came to an abrupt end.

In newspaper reports of the sensational assassination, Luciano told the police he had heard the shooting and, as soon as he had dried his hands, went out to see what was going on. Actually, Luciano's recollection was not accurately reported, possibly a form of self-censorship by the press. What he told the police was: "I was in the can taking a leak. I always take a long leak."

In any case, the first significant step in the Luciano-Lansky plan to establish a new national crime syndicate had been completed.

See also: SALVATORE MARANZANO.

Meldrum, Robert (1865–?) hired killer

Famed, not entirely accurately, as a "hired killer who never was caught," Robert Meldrum was, next to Tom Horn, probably the most notorious gunman employed by what Westerners called "the interests," generally meaning ranchers and mine operators who wanted troublesome nesters and activists neutralized. As was common in such matters, the case or cases against Meldrum were always shrouded in mystery and controversy. When he arrived in Baggs, Wyo. in 1899, Meldrum had the reputation of a paid killer. According to local tales, he was a New Yorker, the son of a British army officer. The following year Meldrum was appointed town marshal of Dixon, Wyo., quite possibly based on his supposed ability to handle troublemakers. During the course of his duties there, he won fame for killing Noah Wilkinson, a Texas outlaw with a price on his head.

In 1901 Meldrum quit being a lawman in favor of more lucrative work as a guard at the Smuggler Union Mine in Telluride, Colo., which was having strike troubles. Shortly after Meldrum's appearance, a number of the strikers were assassinated, and it was suspected that Meldrum had done the killings. He also had dealings with Tom Horn, another paid killer of the interests. A popular notion was that Meldrum helped Horn with a number of range assassinations. When Horn was hanged for his crimes in November 1903, there was speculation that his silence had saved Meldrum from a similar fate.

Over the next four years Meldrum had two brushes with the law: once, in 1904, when he killed a miner, apparently for the offense of smuggling whiskey into the workings in violation of company rules; and again, in 1908, when he killed another miner, a man named Lambert, who was considered a troublemaker. The first matter did not even reach the indictment stage and the second resulted in a not-guilty verdict. In 1910 Meldrum, back in Baggs, committed a "personal" killing shooting down John "Chick" Bowen because of the attention Bowen was paying to Meldrum's common-law wife. The personal nature of the killing did not prevent a number of ranchers from raising Meldrum's $18,000 bail, which he promptly jumped. Six years elapsed before Meldrum surrendered to stand trial, and there was considerable speculation that his friends among the ranchers and mine operators had made a deal for him. That theory seems to have been borne out by Meldrum's relatively light sentence of five to seven years for a reduced charge of manslaughter. After serving only three months, he was paroled into the custody of an obliging rancher.

Following that experience Meldrum's gunslinging days appeared at an end, as much due to the general taming of the area as to his own advancing years. For a time he ran a saddler's business in Walcott, Wyo., but he was still known as a man with a violent temper and one to stay clear of. Meldrum's business burned down in 1929; some said the fire was the result of one of his rages and others claimed it was the work of enemies. Shortly thereafter, Meldrum disappeared from sight.

Mullin, Herbert (1947–) mass murderer
Voted most likely to succeed by his 1965 high school class, young Herbert Mullin went on to become a college dropout, dope addict and all-round weirdo. Late in 1972 he went on a four-month murder spree, during which he killed at least 10 persons because he somehow believed this would prevent a major earthquake popularly, if not scientifically, predicted to happen in early 1973. According to his later confession, Mullin said that he had been telepathically "ordered" to kill and that only human sacrifices could prevent the impending tragedy. He stated, "I'm a scapegoat person made to carry the guilt feelings of others. . . . Every day people die. There's a steady flow of death in order to keep the coast free of cataclysmic earthquakes and the earth in orbit."

Declared legally sane, Mullin was found guilty of murdering three women, one man and six boys in the Santa Cruz Mountains of northern California and was sentenced to life imprisonment. He was not tried for three additional murders to which he confessed, including that of a Catholic priest in Los Gatos, Calif., whom he had stabbed to death, he said, after having second thoughts about a confession he had made to him.

Murder, Inc. syndicate's professional hit squad
Murder, Inc., a gang of professional killers who carried out homicides on assignment in the 1930s, was hardly a new criminal idea. Professional killer gangs existed in the American underworld in the 19th century and murders were committed for pay, with prices generally ranging from $100 down to $5 and even $2. But the Brooklyn "troop" of killers, dubbed by the press Murder, Inc., was an elitist outfit. Not available for hire by outsiders, they were solely at the disposal of the emerging national crime syndicate formed primarily by Lucky Luciano and Meyer Lansky, an ethnic conglomerate composed of "Young Turk" mafiosi and the great Jewish and, to a lesser extent, Irish gangs that blossomed in the Prohibition era. The purpose of the new syndicate, especially after Repeal, was to divide up such criminal activities as gambling, loansharking, labor racketeering, prostitution and narcotics in some sort of acceptable and orderly fashion. Of course, what was acceptable to one gang was not necessarily acceptable to others and thus there developed a need for an enforcement arm to put muscle in the national board's edicts.

Murder, Inc. killed only for business reasons and was never to be used against political figures or reporters—Meyer Lansky and Moe Dalitz, then the criminal power in Cleveland, were most insistent on this point—because of the public stir and "heat" such assassinations caused.

A whole new vocabulary was developed by the troop of killers. The assassins accepted "contracts" to "hit" "bums." Perhaps the most significant term was "bums," meaning marked victims. Psychiatrists could see in this a rationalization for the killers' crimes, one that allowed them to regard victims as subhumans deserving of dying. Thus, a Murder, Inc. killer could, as happened, go directly from a cold-blooded killing to the bedside of a dying grandparent and weep real tears over the sad event.

Operating commanders of the troop were Albert Anastasia, its so-called Lord High Executioner, and Louis Lepke, the nation's number one labor racketeer and a member of the crime cartel's national board. However, none of the estimated 400 to 500 murders committed by the outfit was ever allowed to proceed without the concurrence, or at least the absence of any negative votes, of other top executives, especially Luciano, Lansky, Joe Adonis and Frank Costello. Bugsy Siegel probably best summarized the top gangsters' attitude toward Murder, Inc. as merely a necessary business device when he told construction executive Del Webb he had nothing to fear from the mob because "we only kill each other."

Directly below Anastasia and Lepke were a number of lieutenants, such as Louis Capone (no relation to Chicago's Al), Mendy Weiss and Abe "Kid Twist" Reles. Instructions on a specific contract generally were only given to one underling, who then passed the word on, so that no legal proof of the top men's involvement could be found. Some of the quaint killers of the mob included Vito "Chicken Head" Gurino, who sharpened his shooting skills by blasting off the heads of chickens; Frank "the Dasher" Abbandando; Happy Maione, who wore a permanent scowl; Buggsy Goldstein; Blue Jaw Magoon; and, the most notorious of all, Pittsburgh Phil Strauss. Pittsburgh Phil was the troop's most prolific and resourceful killer and was named in 58 murder investigations around the country. His actual kill toll was most likely about twice that figure. The boys would hang around a certain 24-hour candy store in the Brownsville section of Brooklyn called Midnight Rose's, awaiting assignments, and then hit the trail for wherever in the country their victim happened to be. More often than not, the assigned killer had never before met the "bum," creating a difficult situation for the police. Murder by a stranger with no personal motive presents a puzzle that is seldom solved.

Probably the most famous victim of Murder, Inc. was top gang lord Dutch Schultz, himself a founding member of the crime syndicate. In 1935 Schultz had become the chief target of special prosecutor Thomas E. Dewey and responded with a demand to the national board that Dewey be hit. This was in direct defiance of the founding rules that no politicians were to be murdered. When Schultz' demand was rejected, he stormed away, vowing to handle the job himself. Immediately, a contract was voted on Schultz to prevent him from carrying out his desperate and dangerous-for-business plot.

In 1940 Murder, Inc. came apart when a number of lesser mob members were picked up on suspicion of various murders. Abe Reles got the idea that somebody would talk and implicate him, so he started singing first. He eventually gave details of some 200 killings in which he had either participated or had knowledge of. In the ensuing investigation several top killers went to the electric chair, including Pittsburgh Phil, Mendy Weiss, Louis Capone, Happy Maione and Frank Abbandando. Also executed was Lepke, the only top-level syndicate leader to suffer that fate.

In November 1941 Reles was still doing his canary act and was considered the key witness in a case against Bugsy Siegel and Albert Anastasia, but before he could testify, he "went out the window" of a Coney Island hotel, where he was being held under police protection. Whether Reles' death was suicide, accident or murder has never been established, although in his later years Luciano insisted that he gave the orders from his prison cell to kill Reles before he doomed Siegel and Anastasia and that money was paid to certain members of the New York

Police Department to make sure "the canary who could sing couldn't fly."

Of course, Murder, Inc. did not end with the breakup of the Brooklyn troop. The syndicate has kept right on ordering contracts and having them filled.

See also: FRANK "THE DASHER" ABBANDANDO, ALBERT ANASTASIA, LOUIS "LEPKE" BUCHALTER, PITTSBURGH PHIL, ABE RELES, DUTCH SCHULTZ.

Murrel, John A. (1794–?) mass murderer

Murrel has often been described as the most extraordinary criminal America has ever produced. Certainly, as a wholesale murderer, not even H. H. Holmes or Murder, Inc.'s Pittsburgh Phil was a match for him, even taking into account their highest estimated kill totals. Murrel may have killed over 500 victims.

With his brother, Murrel owned a very profitable plantation in Tennessee, which he used as a cover for his activities. Murrel found he could make it more profitable by stealing slaves, whom he would then resell. If he couldn't make a fast sale on a slave or if he had stolen the same slave so often that another sale might be dangerous, he would have the slave murdered. Murrel became known as a rich, if eccentric, visitor to the gambling dens and bordellos of New Orleans. Actually, he would be on scouting missions looking for money-ladened travelers who would be leaving the city along the Natchez Trace. When they left, Murrel left and only Murrel would be seen again. His technique for getting rid of a victim was to disembowel him, fill his stomach cavity with sand and stones and sink his body in a creek or river.

But even Murrel's estimated 500 killings were minor compared to what he had in mind. He concocted an incredible scheme, probably the most grandiose ever developed by a criminal mind. It called for fomenting a slave rebellion; while the authorities would be battling to quell it, Murrel and 500 underworld confederates would sack New Orleans, Nashville, Memphis, Natchez and a number of other cities. He actually planned to establish an underworld empire in the captured cities and become the supreme ruler, with New Orleans as the capital. The trouble with the scheme was that it involved too many people and too many mouths. The slaves had to be drilled for their uprising and some were overheard discussing the plot. Various criminals were also overheard discussing their part in the bizarre operation. Then a man named Virgil Stewart, whom Murrel thought he had convinced to join his "army," defected and talked to authorities. Following Stewart's disclosures, Murrel was taken into custody. By this time it was too late to stop the uprising, which was scheduled for July 4, 1835, but without Murrel's leadership the campaign foundered. Authorities easily contained outbreaks in the criminal districts of Nashville, Memphis and Natchez. In Tennessee about 20 slaves and 10 white men were hanged for their part in the conspiracy.

After the grandiose plan collapsed, Murrel sulked in prison under a 10-year sentence. He served his term, but by the time of his release, he had degenerated to the level of an imbecile. When last seen, he was a derelict in the Gut, the red-light district of Memphis.

Nelson, Earle Leonard (1892–1928)
mass murderer

For almost a year and a half, Earle Leonard Nelson terrorized the nation with a series of vicious rape-murders. His official murder toll between February 1926 and June 1927 stands, by most counts, at 20.

Born in 1892 in Philadelphia, Nelson was orphaned at an early age and raised by an aunt. He suffered a head injury in a childhood accident that would cause him intense pain from time to time. As a teenager, he exhibited a streak of meanness and violence usually directed at children or women. At other times, he became a Bible fanatic, spending hours either reading the Bible alone in his room or loudly lecturing others with long quotations from it. His aunt would point to his devout character whenever one of his more antisocial peccadilloes got him in trouble with the law. Nonetheless, in 1918 he was placed in a home for mental defectives after raping a young Philadelphia girl. Nelson promptly escaped but was soon caught and placed on a state prison farm. He escaped from there but was captured again and this time was sent to the state penitentiary, from which he quickly escaped yet again.

That was the last time the law would have him in its hands for nine years. In 1919, under the alias of Roger Wilson, he married a young schoolteacher. Life for Mrs. Wilson was a horror; Nelson lectured her constantly from the Bible and accused her of consorting with other men. She finally had to be hospitalized because of a nervous breakdown. Nelson visited her in the hospital and had to be ejected from the building when he was caught trying to rape her in her bed. Thereafter nothing was heard from or of him for seven years. Considering his prior record and his bloody record afterward, if he was entirely law-abiding during that time, it would have been one of the greatest self-rehabilitative efforts in the annals of crime.

On February 20, 1926 Nelson entered a San Francisco rooming house in search of lodgings. As the landlady, Mrs. Clara Newman, ushered him up the stairs to the third floor, a murderous urge overcame Nelson. He strangled the woman with her own pearl necklace before they even entered a room. Then he dragged her body into an empty room, raped the dead woman and left. Over the next few months Nelson strangled, killed and raped three other landladies in the San Francisco-Oakland area. By now the police had a description of the killer as a short, blue-eyed, dark-complexioned man. But they didn't catch him.

Nelson moved on to Portland, Ore., where in two days he killed two more landladies. A few weeks later, he killed another landlady. Then he went back to San Francisco for his next murder, after which he returned to Portland and killed again. Nelson moved toward the East Coast, killing more women all the way to Philadelphia. By June 1927 authorities all over the country were hunting for the man who had definitely murdered 20 landladies and was strongly suspected of having killed two others.

Feeling the pressure of the police hunt, Nelson fled into Canada and took lodging in a rooming house in Winnipeg. His landlady remembered him as a very devout gentleman who always carried a Bible. Nelson did not kill his landlady, realizing that would only open up his trail again, but the blood urge in him could not be stilled. Within a few days of his arrival in Winnipeg, the city was rocked by two murders. One was of a teenaged girl living in the same house as Nelson. In another section of town, the raped and strangled body of Mrs. Emily Paterson was found by her husband.

Nelson had killed them both, but this time he left a trail that could be followed. He had stolen a number of items from the Paterson home and left some of them at a second-hand clothing dealer where he purchased a change of clothes. A description of the killer led to his capture within four miles of the border, which he was preparing to recross to evade pursuit.

Although the vast majority of Nelson's crimes were committed in the United States, he was tried, sentenced to death and, on January 13, 1928, hanged in Canada. On the gallows the man whose aunt had predicted he would grow up to become a minister turned biblical one final time. "I am innocent," he said. "I stand innocent before God and man. I forgive those who have wronged me and ask forgiveness of those I have injured. God have mercy!"

Nelson, George "Baby Face" (1908–1934)

public enemy

None of the "public enemies" of the 1930s more thoroughly deserved the description "mad dog" than did George "Baby Face" Nelson. All the gangsters of the 1930s, Dillinger, the Barkers, Pretty Boy Floyd and others, killed to escape capture, but Nelson was addicted to violence, much as were Bonnie and Clyde. Even the latter were a bit more restrained, frequently turning from murderous to maudlin because of a potential victim's white hair. Nelson was vulnerable to no such sentimentalism, as demonstrated by his approach to bank robbery, which was to come through the door shooting and then simply force the lucky survivors to hand over the loot. Once when Dillinger henchman Homer Van Meter, a believer in a slightly more thoughtful approach, laughed sarcastically at Nelson's ideas on a robbery, only the quick intervention of John Dillinger prevented Baby Face from punishing such disdain with a submachine gun.

Chicago-born Lester J. Gillis, a name he discarded as too "sissy," preferred to be known as Big George Nelson, a ludicrous

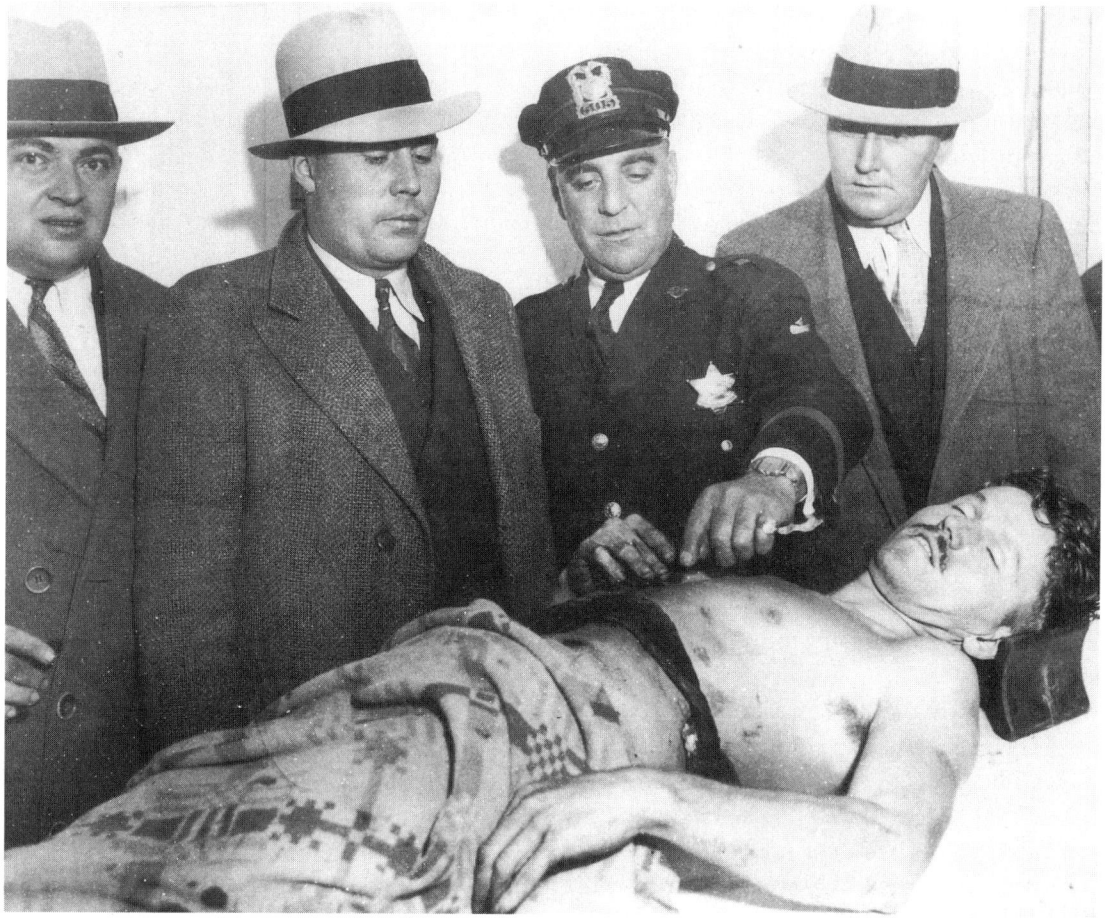

Photo shows Baby Face Nelson's bullet-riddled corpse on an undertaker's slab in Niles Center, a suburb of Chicago.

sobriquet considering his five-foot five-inch stature. Behind his back he was called Baby Face Nelson. He started his criminal career in 1922, when he was sent to a home for boys after being arrested for auto theft. Paroled in April 1924, he was in and out of custody thereafter for parole violations and other crimes. By 1929 Nelson was working for the Capone mob as a goon in the union field. Apparently he took the work too earnestly and was dismissed as unreliable because he sometimes killed when he was only supposed to injure.

Nelson was caught pulling a bank job in 1931 and got one year to life. He escaped from a prison guard in 1932 while being escorted back to the penitentiary from Wheaton, Ill., where he had been tried for another bank robbery charge. Now accepted as a "big-timer," something he always wanted, Nelson hooked up with the Dillinger mob. Dillinger was not overly fond of Nelson and his quick temper and even quicker trigger finger, but when several of his gang, including Harry Pierpont, Russell Clark and Charlie Makley, were clapped behind bars, he was forced to make do. Inevitably, Dillinger's capers became bloodier after the arrival of Nelson, who often needlessly shot down bank guards and bystanders.

As his victim toll mounted, Nelson grew to resent the fact that Dillinger got more notoriety than he got and that the latter had a bigger price on his head. He did all he could to change that. In the famous shootout at the Little Bohemia Resort in northern Wisconsin in April 1934, Nelson separated from the rest of the Dillinger gang and shot it out at close quarters with FBI agents, killing Special Agent W. Carter Baum and escaping in an FBI Ford.

Later, Nelson rejoined Dillinger and they pulled several more capers. By now, Dillinger wanted no more of Baby Face but was so "hot" himself that he had no chance of recruiting new help. On the night of July 2, 1934 Dillinger was shot dead by FBI men outside a Chicago movie house. Thereafter, Nelson, who had not been with Dillinger that night, became Public Enemy No. 1. His reign, however, was destined to be short.

Just as Dillinger fell, so did other members of the gang. Tommy Carroll was killed in a gunfight in Iowa and in separate incidents in St. Paul, Minn., G-men caught up with Eddie Green and police gunned down Homer Van Meter. The only support Nelson had left was his wife, Helen, and his longtime faithful sidekick, John Paul Chase. Still, the insane Nelson decided to become the greatest criminal the country had ever known, one who would make the public forget about the fabled Dillinger. He started organizing a gang with the intention of robbing every day for a month straight.

That grandiose scheme never came to fruition, however. On November 27, 1934 two FBI agents, Sam Cowley, who played a key role in catching Dillinger, and Herman E. Hollis, came upon Nelson, his wife and Chase in a stalled car near Barrington, Ill. Hollis, armed with a shotgun, crouched behind an FBI car while Cowley rolled into a nearby ditch with a submachine gun. Nelson opened up with his trusty submachine gun while Chase started firing an automatic rifle. As the wild gunfight began, Helen Nelson ran for cover and several highway construction workers hugged the ground.

Finally, Nelson grew impatient with the standoff, stood up erect and announced, "I'm going down there and get those sons of bitches."

He strode forward, his weapon spewing bullets.

"It was just like Jimmy Cagney," one of the workers later recalled. "I never seen nothing like it. That fellow just came right a'coming at them two lawmen and they must of hit him plenty, but nothing was gonna stop that fellow."

From his place in the ditch, Cowley fired desperately as Nelson advanced. The gangster took a bullet in the side but came plodding on. He sprayed the ditch with bullets, cutting Cowley almost in half, even as he absorbed more lead himself. Then Nelson turned his fire on Hollis. The agent dropped his empty shotgun and ran for cover behind a telegraph pole, where he drew his pistol. Hollis scored several hits on Baby Face before being fatally shot in the head.

Nelson walked to the FBI car, got in and backed it up to his wife and Chase, who loaded their arsenal inside. "You'll have to drive," Nelson told Chase. "I've been hit."

He had been hit—17 times.

The next day Nelson's body, stripped nude to prevent quick identification, was found in a ditch some 20 miles away. He got the same mawkish coverage from the press that Dillinger had received. An interview with Helen Nelson, who had surrendered two days later, read in part:

> *'Baby Face' Nelson died in the arms of his wife with a smile on his lips, but with tears in his eyes for his two young children.*
>
> *Those were the high-lights of a thrilling story told by Nelson's pretty widow, in which she gave a heart-broken account of his death at the hands of federal agents.*

Such journalistic excess greatly upset the FBI's J. Edgar Hoover, but he could revel in the knowledge that the last important member of the Dillinger gang had been eliminated. Chase was captured a short time later in California and sent to prison for life.

See also: JOHN DILLINGER.

O'Banion, Charles Dion "Deanie"

(1892–1924) gang leader

Of all the Prohibition-era Chicago gangsters, Dion O'Banion is credited with the greatest number of remarkable traits. Indeed, he may have been the most pious killer in that city of gangsters, carrying his rosary with him on murder assignments. He was a cheerful swashbuckler who was never without a carnation in his buttonhole and three pistols tucked away in special pockets of his expensive made-to-order suits. Although labeled by Chief of Police Morgan Collins as "Chicago's archcriminal" and declared the murderer of at least 25 men, a figure that may have been underestimated by 35, O'Banion, at the pinnacle of his power, was celebrated by the Democrats, who reveled in his ability to get out votes until he switched to the Republicans for more money. A contemporary joke asked, "Who'll carry the Forty-second and Forty-third wards?" The answer was, "O'Banion, in his pistol pocket."

The more cynical members of the city's press corps saw O'Banion as a man of humor. One of his funnier stunts, at least from Dion's viewpoint, was his shotgun challenge. The gangster would fill a shotgun with hard-packed clay and then wager an unsuspecting victim that he could not hit the side of a barn some 30 feet away. Naturally, the challenge would be accepted and O'Banion would load the weapon, hand the gun to the sucker and move far away. When the man pulled the trigger, the backfire would cause him to lose an arm or an eye or perhaps most of his face. The gang boss would still be laughing about it the next day.

O'Banion, the son of a Chicago plasterer, grew up in a section of Chicago's North Side known as Little Hell. He was an altar boy and a choir boy at Holy Name Cathedral, but outside the church he learned the law of the street jungle in a tenement district jammed with unruly saloons and whorehouses. Thanks to his voice, trained in church, he launched on a career as a singing waiter in a number of tough dives, including McGovern's Cabaret at Clark and Erie. While bringing tears to the customers' eyes with sentimental ballads of the old country,

Dion O'Banion and his bride on their wedding day. Deanie was a devoted husband and churchgoer as well as a bootlegger and murderer.

he would pick their pockets. After hours, young Deanie was a street mugger. While pursuing this trade one night, the 16-year-old met a youthful Lou Greenberg, who was destined to become the multimillionaire owner of the Seneca Hotel on Chicago's Gold Coast, when both sprang out of the shadows to crack the skull of the same victim. A moment of suspense followed as each of the attackers tried to decide who would get the proceeds of the mugging. With the wisdom of Solomon, they divided the loot evenly and formed an alliance for the rest of the night, sharing the revenues from additional skull rappings of unsuspecting revelers.

The O'Banion-Greenberg combine continued for several months until Deanie was convicted of robbery in 1909 and was sent to Bridewell Prison for three months. In 1911 Deanie was arrested for carrying concealed weapons (a set of brass knuckles, a revolver, a sheath knife and a leather blackjack) and sent away for another three months. It was the last sentence O'Banion ever served, although he was arrested often thereafter. He learned how to work the fix, Chicago style, and spent the required funds to pay off police officers, prosecutors and judges.

Quickly, O'Banion progressed from street mugging and robbery to slugging newspaper dealers for Maxie Annenberg, Moe Annenberg's brother, when Maxie was circulation manager for the *Chicago Tribune*. After learning the techniques of this brutal trade, O'Banion abandoned the *Tribune* for a higher-paying position with the Hearst papers. At the same time, he became adept at safecracking, picking up that art from the top man of the era, Charlie "the Ox" Reiser. He got caught cracking safes a few times, but he was so prized by his newspaper employers that on at least one occasion an executive of Hearst's *American* put up $5,000 bail to secure his release on a safecracking charge.

By the time Prohibition arrived, O'Banion had formed an impressive gang on the North Side, including such stalwarts as Bugs Moran, Frank Gusenberg, Two-Gun Louis Alterie, Dapper Dan McCarthy, Hymie Weiss and Schemer Drucci (the only Italian O'Banion ever liked and vice versa). The O'Banions, who were primarily Irish, ran the 42nd Ward and soon formed an alliance with the Jewish gangsters of the old 20th Ward, especially those attached to Nails Morton. Morton's demise in a riding accident resulted in the O'Banions' execution of the horse that had thrown him.

Seeing the profits Prohibition promised even before the law went into effect, O'Banion began hijacking booze while its distribution and sale was still legal. At first, O'Banion saw no great economic rewards in making his own booze. "Let Johnny Torrio make the stuff," he was quoted. "I'll steal what I want of it." However, as soon as he realized that thievery would never be enough to take care of the demand in the North Side, he started buying up some of the area's best breweries and distilleries.

As O'Banion started making his own liquor instead of stealing Torrio's, a major irritant between the North Siders and the Torrio-Capone mob was removed. As aggressively as the Italian gangsters sought to take over Prohibition rackets in Chicago and much of the surrounding suburbs, they were very content not to tangle with the North Siders, who were known, justifiably, as fierce killers. O'Banion could have continued operating in peace, even though his refusal to allow any bordellos on the North Side angered the Torrio-Capone combine and cut the Chicago underworld's revenues by millions of dollars annually. O'Banion was too pious to allow the sale of bodies, although he had no qualms about filling them with bullets.

While he tolerated a wide variety of other ethnics within his own gang, O'Banion bore an unabiding hatred for Sicilians. He robbed and murdered bootleg liquor deliverers employed by the Terrible Gennas, a brutal family of Sicilians who organized moonshining as a cottage industry in Little Italy and worked closely with Torrio. O'Banion listened to and often agreed with Torrio's appeals for peace and tranquility to allow all elements of the underworld to make their profits without harassment, only to resume hijacking the supplies of the other gangs almost immediately thereafter.

The final affront to the Torrio-Capone forces came when O'Banion, announcing his retirement from the rackets, sold an illegal brewery to Torrio for $500,000. Literally just minutes after the transaction was completed, federal agents swooped down on the brewery, closed it and seized Torrio for violation of Prohibition laws. Torrio, who later received a nine-month sentence, was out the $500,000, which O'Banion refused to return even after it was learned that he had received advance warning of the raid. When Hymie Weiss advised O'Banion to make peace with Torrio and Capone and the Gennas, O'Banion, with huge contempt, rejoined, "Oh, to hell with them Sicilians."

The phrase made war inevitable, although Mike Merlo, an important Italian political figure and head of Unione Siciliana, prevailed for a time in his efforts to achieve a peaceful solution. However, when Merlo died a natural death on November 8, 1924, no one else was capable of maintaining peace among the various factions—the Italians, the Jews, the Irish, the Poles, the Greeks, the blacks—reaping profits from Prohibition. O'Banion did not understand how rapidly his opponents would strike.

Deanie ran a florist shop on North State Street, directly opposite the cathedral where he had once been an altar boy as well as a choir boy, partly because he wanted a legitimate front and partly because he genuinely loved flowers and found he could make a small fortune supplying them for many gangland funerals.

Merlo's death supposedly cast a pall over underworld activities and O'Banion busied himself supplying wreaths for the funeral, some of his creations selling for hundreds or thousands of dollars. On the night of November 9, O'Banion received a telephone order to prepare a special wreath for the following morning. The next morning three men, all apparently unknown to O'Banion, entered the flower shop. "Hello, boys," Deanie said. "You from Mike Merlo's?"

The man in the middle, decked out in an expensive overcoat and fedora, nodded and grasped O'Banion's hand in a firm handshake, so firm that O'Banion could not pull free. Immediately, the man's two companions pulled out pistols and pumped several bullets into the Irish gangster. The last shot, through the left cheek, was fatal. O'Banion was given one of the grandest underworld funerals in Chicago's history.

The O'Banion murder was never officially solved, although the killers were identified as two Capone gunmen named Albert Anselmi and John Scalise and the man with the firm handshake as Frankie Yale, imported specially for the job by Torrio and Capone.

The Torrio-Capone combine fought many bloody battles with the remaining O'Banions until the new leaders, first Weiss and then Drucci, came to violent ends. However, in the process Johnny Torrio was badly wounded and retired back to Brooklyn. The O'Banion gang's last leader, Bugs Moran, saw his power broken by the Capone-ordered St. Valentine's Day Massacre in 1929. The North Siders were finished and Chicago belonged to Big Al.

The O'Banion assassination marked the beginning of the great Chicago gang wars of the 1920s and led to the eventual dominance of the Windy City by Al Capone. But the real importance of O'Banion's death was that it and the resulting battles came to be viewed by the Chicago underworld as senseless bloodletting which prevented the formation of a national crime syndicate in which all factions—Italians, Irish, Jews—could achieve enormous profits.

See also: LOUIS "TWO GUN" ALTERIE, ANSELMI AND SCALISE, ALPHONSE "SCARFACE AL" CAPONE, VINCENT "SCHEMER" DRUCCI, CHARLES "THE OX" REISER, HYMIE WEISS.

Oklahoma City bombing

It was in many respects a bomb blast heard in every corner of the country, so devastating were its results. On April 19, 1995, the explosive fashioned into a truck bomb in a Ryder truck literally vertically sheared off half of the Alfred P. Murrah Federal Building in Oklahoma City, Okla. The death toll was horrendous, numbering 150 men and women and 19 children. Hundreds more were wounded. Rescue workers did all they could. In one case a rescuer trying to save a woman yelled to a companion to turn off a dripping faucet. It was not water, but blood.

Who could have caused such a horror? The instant response by many Americans was that it could only have been the work of foreign terrorists. But it was to turn out to be a homegrown conspiracy, carried out by two and probably not more than three men. Descriptions of the man with the rented Ryder truck quickly made 27-year-old Timothy McVeigh the lead suspect. McVeigh was described as a minor right-wing protester known for his militant criticisms of government actions against terrorists and heavily armed cultists such as the Branch Davidian cult in Waco who were attacked by government agents with the resulting death of more than 67 men, women and children of the group.

Actually McVeigh was taken into custody less than an hour and a half after the devastating explosion in Oklahoma City, although he was not recognized as having any connection with the bombing. He was picked up by a state trooper, Charles Hangar, driving a dirty yellow car outside Billings, Oklahoma. He was charged with carrying a concealed gun and a six-inch knife. Two days later, just as he was about to be released on $500 bond, Trooper Hangar recognized a composite sketch of the Oklahoma City bombing suspect, had him kept in custody for federal authorities.

Charged with the bombing, McVeigh admitted nothing but was outspoken in his rage toward the government for the raid on the Branch Davidian compound in Waco. McVeigh was described as a model teenager from a good family in Lockport, New York, near Buffalo. He joined the army and was awarded a Bronze Star in the Gulf War. In the hours following the bombing, McVeigh's army buddy, Terry Nichols, was seen dusting his lawn in Herrington, Kansas, with ammonium nitrate fertilizer, the same substance that was used to make the deadly bomb. Authorities declared he was not interested in taking care of the lawn but rather seeking to destroy evidence. Nichols was charged in the case as well, although he had not been in Oklahoma City at the time.

The two men were tried separately. One graphic account apparently reflecting McVeigh's mindset was printed in a Texas newspaper, which said that when he was asked by one of the lawyers defending him why he had not bombed the federal building at night so that the death toll would have been vastly reduced, McVeigh dismissed the idea, saying, "That would not have gotten the point across to the government. We needed a body count to make our point."

Both defendants were found guilty, and McVeigh was sentenced to death. When the judge passed sentence on him, McVeigh quoted a dissenting opinion by the late U.S. Supreme Court justice Louis Brandeis: "Our government is the potent, the omnipotent teacher. For good or for ill, it teaches the whole people by its example." McVeigh added, "That's all I have to say." McVeigh was executed by lethal injection on June 11, 2001, in Terre Haute, Indiana.

For his part in carrying out the bomb plot, Terry Nichols drew a life sentence. Many relatives of the victims of the bombing express anger that Nichols has not been given the death sentence also.

Outlaw Exterminators, Inc.

western bounty hunters

Five hard-riding, fast-shooting bounty hunters, dubbed Outlaw Exterminators, Inc. by the press because they never brought 'em back alive, contributed greatly to clearing the Arizona Territory of badmen in the 1870s and 1880s.

Clay Calhoun and Floyd Davis were deputy sheriffs, but the other three members of the group were part-timers—Ben Slack and Dick Hunter, cattlemen, and Fred Beeber, a bartender—who laid aside their mundane jobs whenever the prospects of a nice reward thundered across the mesa. Since rewards at the time were paid on a "dead or alive" basis, the Exterminators decided "dead" was easier and just as profitable.

The band's prize catch was probably bad John Allman, so-called Cavalry Killer who went on an orgy of murder in the Arizona Territory in 1877. When Clay Calhoun brought in Allman, the body contained four bullet holes: one in the groin, stomach, chest and mouth. The holes were in such a perfect line that Calhoun's story about a shoot-out was almost certainly a fabrication. More likely, the bounty hunter had killed Allman while the outlaw was asleep. But like the dozen-odd other victims of the Exterminators, Allman was not exactly popular and nobody worried much about such details. Despite numerous gunfights and the fact that they made a lot of enemies, the Exterminators lived out full lives, the last survivor, Clay Calhoun, dying on November 21, 1948, at the age of 97.

See also: JOHN ALLMAN.

Packer, Alfred (1842–1907) cannibal

The person who became famous in Colorado as The Man Who Ate Democrats made his first recorded appearance on the Western scene as a prospector in southwestern Colorado; he was in his mid-twenties at the time. In 1873 Alfred Packer guided a party of 20 men from Salt Lake into the rugged San Juan Mountains. Described as a "tall man, with long, dark curling hair, dark mustache and goatee, deep set dark grey eyes," Packer had a reputation of knowing Colorado as well as any man. Thus, it was surprising that, having brought the party to Chief Ouray's camp on the Uncompahgre, near the Los Pinos Indian Agency, Packer rejected the chief's advice against pushing on through the heavy snows. Because they offered to pay him well, Packer continued the trek with five men, Israel Swan, Frank Miller, Shannon Bell, George Noon (or Moon) and a man named Humphrey.

Some weeks later, Packer staggered back to Los Pinos, claiming his five companions had abandoned him when he became footsore and snowblind. Suspicion, however, buzzed around Packer. He was found in possession of a Wells Fargo draft belonging to one of his companions as well as the gun and skinning knife of another member of the party. He seemed to have money enough to spend freely at the bar. Perhaps the most damning comment reported came from Chief Ouray, who looked at Packer and grunted, "You too damn fat."

Months later, search parties turned up the bodies of the five missing men. Four had had their skulls crushed, apparently while they slept, and the fifth appeared to have been shot after a struggle. Four of the skeletons had been totally stripped of flesh and the other was partially so. According to one of several stories that Packer then told, 60-year-old Swan had been the first to die of starvation when the party ran out of food, and the others had eaten him to stay alive. Next, Shannon Bell, Packer related, killed Humphrey to replenish the group's food supply. Then Miller was murdered, and a few days later, Bell shot Noon. When Noon was finished, Bell tried to kill Packer, but the latter got him first. Packer said he carved off strips of Bell's flesh to provide him with enough food to make it back to the agency.

Packer was found guilty of murder and sentenced to 40 years at hard labor. So awesome was his crime that he became a legend celebrated in story and song as The Man Who Ate Democrats, an accolade given him by the judge who leaned down from the bench and cried, "Packer, you depraved Republican son of a bitch, there were only five Democrats in Hinsdale County, and you ate them all!"

Packer served 17 years before being released. He died in 1907 at the age of 65.

Panzram, Carl (1891–1930) mass murderer

Among America's most vicious mass murderers, Carl Panzram was a study in hatred and violence, a self-confessed killer of 21 persons and sodomizer of at least 1,000.

Panzram's first arrest came at the age of eight, when he was charged with being drunk and disorderly in his native Minnesota. Many of his early years were spent in correctional facilities, where the brutal treatment he received almost guaranteed that his vicious instincts would blossom. By the time he completed a term in Fort Leavenworth Prison in 1910, he said, "All the good that may have been in me had been kicked and beaten out of me long before." Thereafter, Panzram spent his life robbing, sodomizing and killing his victims. He did time in various institutions and frequently escaped.

Panzram said, "I don't believe in man, God nor devil. I hate the whole damned human race including myself." Many of his crimes were done in revenge for the treatment he had received behind bars. At the Montana State Training School he had been beaten on the bare back, legs and buttocks with a baseball bat; at Leavenworth Prison he had been chained across the chest and by the arms and left dangling for hours; at the Oregon State Prison he had been chained naked to a wall and given the water hose treatment with such force that his eyes blackened, his genitals swelled enormously and his body welted all over. Also at Oregon he had been tortured with the "humming bird," which involved placing an inmate in a steel bathtub filled with water, chaining him hand and foot and rubbing him down with a sponge electrified by a battery.

If such treatment was intended to reform Panzram, it failed miserably. Each time he got free, he robbed, sodomized and murdered.

Finally in 1928 Panzram was sentenced to Leavenworth for burglary and murder, whereupon he announced, "I'll kill the first man who bothers me." On June 20, 1929 Panzram bashed in the skull of the prison laundry foreman. Sentenced to death for the murder, he was incensed when the Society for the Abolishment of Capital Punishment sought a commutation for him, citing as one of its arguments Panzram's previous mistreatment. Panzram wrote to President Herbert Hoover insisting on his "constitutional rights" to be hanged. As for the reformers, he said, "I wish you all had one neck, and I had my hands on it. . . . I believe the only way to reform people is to kill them."

On September 5, 1930 Panzram went to the gallows. When the hangman asked him if he had anything to say, he replied: "Yes, hurry it up, you Hoosier bastard! I could hang a dozen men while you're fooling around!" He spat twice at his executioner before the trap was pulled.

Piper, Thomas W. (1849–1876) mass murderer
In the 1870s, about 90 years before the Boston Strangler began his rampage, a mass murderer terrorized the city of Boston with a series of sex-related murders.

He committed four brutal murders and raped a number of young girls. The first victim was a girl named Bridget Landregan, who was attacked as she passed some bushes lining a snow-covered road on the night of December 5, 1873. The killer had clubbed her to death and was about to attack her body when a passerby happened along. The murderer, with black cloak flowing, fled. Later that same night, apparently the same assailant beat another girl bloody and raped her before being frightened off. Again, he was described as a black, batlike figure with a flowing cape. At the time, Boston Chief of Police Savage remarked to the press, "It was unseemly queer that only the nicest and most modest young ladies seem to get themselves raped."

When this fiend in black later killed two other girls, one in her own bedroom, the police and the public knew they had a real crime wave on their hands. As hysteria gripped the city, Chief Savage issued an order that all lone men seen wearing cloaks about the streets after dark were to be stopped and questioned, and for the following season opera cloaks fell out of fashion among the young blades of the town.

It was only after the killing of yet a fourth victim, a five-year-old girl named Mabel Hood Young, that the strange killer was found. His identity was a terrible shock to proper Bostonians. Little Mabel was murdered in the tower of the old Warren Avenue Baptist Church, and the murderer, 26-year-old Thomas W. Piper, the church sexton, had been seen taking her there. After the girl's body was discovered, Piper was arrested and soon confessed not only Mabel's murder but the previous murders as well.

Piper was tried and convicted only for the murder of little Mabel and sentenced to hang; he had in the meantime retracted all his confessions. Before he died, Piper once more admitted his crimes to Chief Savage, who asked him to commit them to paper. "I'll be hanged if I will," Piper snapped. Then he was hanged. There was no doubt Piper was the mass murderer, for the brutal killings by a man in a black cape ceased after his execution. In due course, opera cloaks returned to favor.

Pittsburgh Phil (1908–1941) Murder, Inc.'s top hit man
Probably the most prolific and certainly the most cold-blooded professional hit man this country has ever seen, Harry Strauss, better known as Pittsburgh Phil, was the top killer of the national crime syndicate's enforcement arm, Murder, Inc. So far as is known, Strauss was never in Pittsburgh in his life, having been born and bred in Brooklyn; he just liked the sound of the name. He also liked committing murder; he often volunteered for murder contracts, as Brooklyn District Attorney William O'Dwyer once said, "sometimes just for the lust to kill."

"Like a ballplayer, that's me," he once told a friend, explaining his enthusiasm. "I figure I get seasoning doing these jobs. Somebody from one of the big mobs spots me. Then, up to the big leagues."

And that's just what happened. He made it into the Murder, Inc., and it got so that whenever a call came in from one of the out-of-town mobs for someone to fill a special "contract," Phil was almost always the one requested. Phil would pack his briefcase with a shirt, a change of socks, underwear, a gun, a knife, a length of rope and an ice pick—he was an artist at a multitude of murdering methods—hop a plane or train to his port of call, pull the job and catch the next connection back to New York. More often than not, Phil didn't even know the name of the person he had killed, and generally it didn't matter to him. It was the killing that counted. If, by chance, he was curious about or particularly proud of a job, he would buy an out-of-town paper when he got back to New York and read all about it.

When the Murder, Inc. story broke wide open in 1940, O'Dwyer's staff had concrete evidence linking Phil to 28 killings. In addition, an equal number of murders had been positively identified as Phil's work by law enforcement officials from Connecticut to California. And those were just the known killings. A present-day crime historian gives serious credence to an estimate that Phil killed at least 500 persons from the late 1920s until 1940. The figure is sheer nonsense, but there seems little doubt his total kills probably exceeded 100. This is an incredible figure, especially considering the next two most active killers in the "troop" —Kid Twist Reles and Happy (so-called because of his surly expression) Maione, probably did no more than 30 apiece.

Phil was the dandy of the troop. His love affair with Evelyn Mittleman, a Brooklyn beauty who was to be dubbed the Kiss of Death Girl, was one of the underworld's more touching affairs, climaxed by Phil's eradication of a rival for her affection. Tall, lean and handsome, Phil was a fashion plate. He wore the best suits $60 could buy—$60 in Depression times—and became known to the police and his colleagues alike as the Beau Brummel of the Underworld. Phil and his dandy dress, in fact, were what led to Police Commissioner Lewis J. Valentine's famous "muss them up" orders against hoodlums. One day the commissioner had come over to Brooklyn to look at a lineup and blew his top when he saw Phil standing against the white wall radiant in a well-fitting Chesterfield, pearl-gray fedora, blue shirt with tie to match, blue striped suit and gleaming black shoes. "Look at him!" the commissioner raged. "He's the best dressed man in the room and he's never worked a day in his life!"

The commissioner was wrong about that. Phil was working very hard. In fact, he had the Brooklyn police toiling over one of his murders at that moment. The victim was George Rudnick, whom labor extortionist Louis Lepke had suspected of being an informer.

After getting a contract to hit Rudnick, Phil and a few of his confederates snatched the suspected stoolie one afternoon as he walked along Livonia Avenue. It was a short drive to the execution chamber, a garage at Atlantic Avenue and Eastern Parkway. A few hours later, Rudnick's body turned up in a stolen car on the other side of the borough.

Deputy Chief Medical Examiner Dr. Edward Marten's autopsy report detailed Phil's savagery.

This was a male adult, somewhat undernourished; approximate weight 140 pounds; six feet in height. There were 63 stab wounds on the body. On the neck, I counted 13 stab wounds, between the jaw and collarbone. On the right chest, there were 50 separate circular wounds. He had a laceration on the frontal region of the head. The wound gaped, and disclosed the bone underneath. His face was intensely cyanic, or blue. The tongue pro-

truded. At the level of the larynx was a grooving, white and depressed, about the width of the ordinary clothesline. When the heart was laid open, the entire wall was found to be penetrated by stab wounds. My conclusion was the cause of death was multiple stab wounds, and also . . . asphyxia due to strangulation.

When the Purple Gang in Detroit marked a local gangster, Harry Millman, for death, they found him hard to kill; one attempt failed, and Millman thereafter was on his guard. Outside talent was needed and Pittsburgh Phil was one of two killers sent from Brooklyn. Millman was in a crowded restaurant eating dinner one evening when two men walked in, fired 12 slugs into him, wounding five other diners in the process, and paraded out. Sweet, direct and simple was the way Pittsburgh Phil liked it.

Phil could, at times, carry out a job with a touch of poetic irony. Walter Sage ran the syndicate's coin machine racket in the Catskills until he became what the mob called a trolley car conductor, shortchanging the organization on its profits. Phil ice-picked him 32 times. He got rid of the body by lashing it to a pinball machine and dumping it in a lake. Phil was very proud of that touch. "It's a symbol," he asserted proudly.

A week later, however, the grisly package rose to the surface because of buoyancy from gases in the decomposing body. As Phil learned, perforations made with a small weapon, like an ice pick, are virtually sealed by blood pumping from a still-beating heart. "How about that," Phil philosophized. "With this bum, you gotta be a doctor, or he floats."

So far as is known, Phil failed on only one job. Traveling to Florida to fill a contract, he followed his intended victim into a movie theater, where the man sat down in the last row. Rather than use a gun, which would attract attention, Phil secured the fire ax kept in a glass case. However, by the time he'd gotten the ax, his intended victim had moved ahead several rows. Angered, Phil walked out. As he complained later to the troop, "Just when I get him set up, the bum turns out to be a goddamn chair hopper."

Usually, though, he could get the job done regardless of any obstacles. In another Florida hit assignment, the victim was a Mafia old-timer who couldn't speak a word of English. That didn't faze Phil at all. Conversing with the man in sign language, Phil showed him his briefcase of weapons and led him to believe he'd come to kill someone else and wanted advice. The old-timer picked a rope and showed the hit man a dark street where the killing could be done safely. Phil strangled him there and went home.

How long Phil would have gone on with his killing had Kid Twist Reles not turned stoolie is something awesome to contemplate. Today, it seems incredible he could have operated for a decade without getting caught. Reles talked because he figured the law was closing in and if he didn't, someone else in the troop would and he would get the chair.

Reles later horrified a Brooklyn jury with a description of how Phil had killed one Puggy Feinstein. Puggy was decoyed to Abe Reles' house, where Phil was hiding behind the door, his trusty ice pick in hand. When Puggy walked in, Phil threw him on the couch and went to work with the pick. Puggy, fighting for his life, managed to bite Phil's finger. Enraged by such foul play, Phil yelled: "Give me the rope. I'll fix this dirty bum."

Reles then described Phil's mastery of the art of rope murder.

> *I give Phil one end of the rope, and I hold the other end. Puggy is kicking and fighting. He is forcing his head down, so we can't get the rope under his throat. Buggsy [Buggsy Goldstein, another of the murder troop] holds his head up, so we can put the rope under. Then me and Phil exchange ends . . . cross them, so we make a knot . . . a twist. Then we cross them once more. Then we rope around his throat again, to make two loops.*
>
> *Buggsy gets Puggy by the feet, and me and Phil get him by the head. We put him down on the floor. He is kicking. Phil starts finishing tying him up . . . [and] gets his feet tied up with the back of his neck. He ties him up like a little ball. His head is pushed down on his chest. His knees are folded up against his chest. His hands are in between. The rope is around his neck and under his feet. If he moves the rope will tighten up around his throat more.*

And so Puggy Feinstein died with Phil kicking him for biting his finger. "Maybe I am getting lockjaw from being bit," Phil yelled defensively.

Later, they dumped Puggy's body in a vacant lot and set it ablaze. But even after the boys adjourned to Sheepshead Bay for a seafood dinner, Phil was unhappy about his finger and barely finished his lobster.

The break in the Murder, Inc. case came when a few minor hoods were arrested and started talking. Phil, Reles, Maione and Goldstein were picked up on suspicion and the word went out that one or the other was "ratting." None had, but Reles decided to tell all, and when he did, Murder, Inc. was smashed. Big shots like Louis Lepke, Mendy Weiss and Louis Capone were to die in the electric chair before Reles' trilling came to a sudden end when he "went out the window" of a Brooklyn hotel while under police guard. Pittsburgh Phil was also doomed. He and Buggsy Goldstein were indicted for the Puggy Feinstein murder.

The authorities secured five more murder indictments and, if necessary, were ready to try him on those as well. It wasn't. Since he had no real defense, Phil did the next best thing: he feigned insanity. He refused to shave or change his clothes. When put on the witness stand and asked to give his name, he merely licked his lips. Sent back to the defendant's chair, he spent most of the rest of the trial nibbling on the leather strap of a lawyer's briefcase. It was a great act. The newspapers loved it. The jury didn't. They found him guilty.

Phil kept up his crazy act in the death house in the hope of winning a commutation. It wasn't until his last day that he gave up the act, combed his hair and became his old swaggering self. He said goodbye to Evelyn, the Kiss of Death Girl. On June 12, 1941 Buggsy Goldstein went to the chair. Moments later, at 11:06 P.M., Phil followed him. The best enforcer the syndicate ever had was dead.

Only later was it revealed that prior to his trial Phil had offered to turn state's evidence if he was allowed to talk to Reles first. The request was rejected. The authorities had no intention of letting Phil get in the same room with informer Reles. It was a wise precaution. As Phil said on his last day in the death house, he really had no intention of singing. "I just wanted to sink my tooth into his jugular vein. I didn't worry about the chair, if I could just tear his throat out first."

No one doubted he would have tried to.

See also: MURDER, INC.; ABE RELES.

Rees, Melvin David (1933–1961)
mass murderer

In the late 1950s Melvin David Rees, a professional musician, terrorized Maryland and Virginia with a total of nine murders, most accompanied by sexual assault on his women victims.

In June 1957 near Annapolis, Md., Rees drove alongside a car bearing an army sergeant and his girl, Margaret Harold, and forced their car off the roadside. When Rees tried to caress the woman, she resisted and he shot her. The sergeant bolted and, after running about a mile, reached a farmhouse, from which he called the police. They found Margaret Harold's body and the car, but no trace of the deadly marauder, whom the sergeant had described as tall and thin-faced. Nearby, the police found the basement walls of an unoccupied cinderblock building literally papered with pornographic photographs. They theorized that the murderer might have been using the basement building as his hideaway.

The Harold murder was still unsolved in January 1959 when a 29-year-old truck driver, Carroll Jackson, driving his wife and two young children home after a stay with relatives, was forced by another car to the side of a road near Fredericksburg, Va. The driver ordered the family at gunpoint to climb into the trunk of his car and drove off with them. Two months later, the body of Carroll Jackson was discovered in some underbrush. There was a bullet in his head. The Jacksons' 18-month-old girl was found suffocated under her father's body. A few weeks after that discovery, the bodies of Mrs. Jackson and her four-year-old daughter were found near the scene of Margaret Harold's death. The child had died of a fractured skull while Mrs. Jackson had been strangled, after having been repeatedly raped.

A massive manhunt followed, based on the description given in the Harold killing. Finally, the widespread publicity produced information from a Norfolk, Va. man who said he suspected a young musician named Melvin David Rees had committed the murders because of things Rees had said to him. Rees was arrested in West Memphis, Ark., where he was working as a piano salesman.

He denied the charges but was identified by the army sergeant in the Margaret Harold case. When investigators searched the home of Rees' parents near Washington, D.C., they turned up the murder gun and long, written accounts of his treatment of Mrs. Jackson before he murdered her. He had killed the woman in a most brutal fashion. Other evidence linked Rees—now known in the press as the Sex Beast—to four other murder victims not originally connected with the Harold and Jackson cases. Marie Shomettee, 16, and Ann Ryan, 14, both of whom had been sexually assaulted and murdered near College Park, Md., and Shelby Jean Venable, 16, and Mary Elizabeth Fellers, 18, whose naked bodies had been found floating in Maryland rivers.

For his Maryland crimes Rees got a life sentence, but he was then tried in Virginia for the Jackson family killings, found guilty and executed in 1961.

Reiser, Charles "the Ox" (1878–1921)

safecracker and killer

Charlie "the Ox" Reiser led a Jekyll-and-Hyde existence. Under the name of Shopes he was known as a reliable family man and a friendly landlord. Yet the underworld and the police regarded him as the premier safecracker in America during the early 20th century. He was also a brutal killer and indoctrinated many of the notorious Chicago gangsters of the 1920s into the ways of big-time crime, among them Dion O'Banion, Bugs Moran, Hymie Weiss and John Mahoney.

The Ox, a mountain of a man, could single-handedly shove a safe from one end of a room to the other. He was a brilliant "peterman," or handler of nitroglycerine. Reiser first ran afoul of the law in Chicago in 1903, when he was charged with safecracking. Out on bail, he killed the witnesses against him, and the case was dropped. In 1905 he was arrested again. The witness disappeared and there was no case. He beat another rap in 1907 and then was convicted of assault with a deadly weapon and did 30 days. In 1909 police from Seattle, Wash., apprehended him on a charge of burglary and murder. Thereafter all the witnesses died, and Reiser returned to Chicago.

During World War I he became friends with O'Banion and used that deadly Irishman and a number of his pals in several safecrackings. All this time, Reiser was living a double life under the name of Shopes and pouring his ill-earned money into real estate, becoming the owner of a large apartment building. He was known to tenants as a prince of a landlord; while he expected his rent, he did not hound a man if he got a little behind. He was considered to be a fine husband to his second wife. His first wife had not fared so well. Reiser boasted to his underworld acquaintances that when the woman had threatened to get the law after him, he promptly beat her to death. The coroner's jury thought she had died of asphyxiation.

Clarence White, who aided the Ox in the cracking of a Standard Oil Co. safe, was invited by the police to come in for questioning. White said he would but first telephoned the Ox, who rushed right over to White's apartment and shot him through the heart, making it look like a suicide. This intelligence came from another errant gang member, John Mahoney, who turned informer after being caught cracking safes on his own. Mahoney provided considerable evidence against Reiser, all of which proved useless when Mahoney was murdered in April 1921.

On October 10, 1921 the Ox entered the premises of a cold storage firm, planning to bust open its safe after first killing the watchman. He shot the watchman but took two bullets himself, one through the lung. Reiser was hospitalized and charged with murder. He became the subject of some bizarre newspaper stories, in which reporters informed their readers that if Reiser was convicted, his property would be confiscated and turned over to some of his past robbery victims. Although untrue, the stories may in some way have contributed to Reiser's death. His wife, who found the prospect of his property being confiscated rather souring, showed up at his hospital room and was admitted even though the police guard stationed outside the room had been instructed to let no one enter. A few moments later, there was "a rattle of shots." Mrs. Reiser-Shopes tearfully related that her husband had committed suicide. One thing was certain: the Ox was very dead, with 10 bullets in him.

Understandably, the police found the death suspicious, especially since Reiser had had both his right hand and his left arm broken in the storage firm robbery, making use of a gun rather difficult. Murder charges were brought against the widow, but Chicago being Chicago, a coroner's jury ruled Reiser's death a suicide after all. Reiser's estate of over $100,000 went to his wife.

See also: CHARLES DION "DEANIE" O'BANION.

Reles, Abe (1907–1941) Murder, Inc. killer and informer

What was so amazing about the criminal career of Abe Reles, better known as Kid Twist within Murder, Inc., was how long he remained out of serious trouble despite the fact that he personally took part in at least 30 murders. Until the Kid started "singing," the law did not even know about Murder, Inc., the enforcement arm of the national crime syndicate that committed an estimated 400 to 500 murders during roughly the decade of the 1930s. Once Reles went into what was called the most famous "canary act in underworld history," goggle-eyed investigators cleared up no less than 49 murders in Brooklyn alone, some of which they hadn't even known about. Reles was in a position to know. He was a second-rung leader of Murder, Inc., ranking just below the top leaders of the extermination "troop": Louis Lepke and Albert Anastasia. As an underworld stoolpigeon, he was much more highly placed than Joe Valachi, for instance.

Reles' police rap sheet in 1940 listed 42 arrests over 16 years, including many charges of assault, robbery, burglary, possession of narcotics, disorderly conduct and murder (only six). He had done six minor stretches but had never once talked to the authorities. However, when he was picked up in 1940, along with a number of other major and minor members of Murder, Inc., on a homicide charge, he feared someone else would talk. The Kid decided to save his own skin by talking first.

Reles revealed that he and other members of the troop, such as Pittsburgh Phil, Happy Maione, Dasher Abbandando, Chicken Head Gurino and Buggsy Goldstein, were given assassination assignments not only in New York but elsewhere around the country, at times not even knowing the identities of their victims. He made a deal with the prosecutors that he would walk away clear from any murder he had participated in provided

Informer Abe Reles jumped, fell or was pitched out a sixth-floor window of a Coney Island hotel.

he furnished them with all the details including the names of his accomplices, an easy task for the Kid since he had the most phenomenal memory of any informer prior to John Dean.

It was Reles' testimony that doomed Abbandando and Maione for the brutal killing of a loan shark named Whitey Rudnick. They had stabbed him more than 60 times, cracked open his skull and then, just to be sure, strangled him. With a perfectly straight face, Kid Twist said Rudnick had deserved his fate: he had been a stoolpigeon.

Reles gave chilling testimony against Pittsburgh Phil, who also took part in Rudnick's murder plus perhaps 100 others, and Buggsy Goldstein that sent them to the chair for the vicious garroting of a minor gambler named Puggy Feinstein. He provided key information about Charlie Workman, accused of murdering Dutch Schultz, so that when Workman heard all the testimony against him, he switched to a plea of guilty to get a life sentence instead of the electric chair.

The Kid's testimony helped build a successful case against the great crime boss Louis Lepke as well as underlings Mendy Weiss and Louis Capone, who were accused of murdering a garment industry foe named Joseph Rosen, even though Reles was no longer around to testify by the time of their trial.

Reles appeared at a number of trials for more than a year, during which time he was kept under protective custody in the sixth-floor wing of the Half Moon Hotel in the Coney Island section of Brooklyn. Then, in the early morning hours of November 12, 1941, despite the fact that he was always guarded by six officers and never left alone in a room even while he slept, Reles jumped, fell or was tossed out the window to his death. Several sheets tied together were found, and the police theorized that Reles had climbed out the window to escape; to climb down one floor in order to play a prank on his guards; or to commit suicide, although the sheets were hardly necessary for that option. One problem with all the police theories was that the Kid's body had landed a good 20 feet away from the wall of the hotel building.

Twenty years later, an ailing Lucky Luciano, the chief founder of the national crime syndicate in the early 1930s, stated that Frank Costello had arranged for Reles' demise and that $50,000 had been distributed within the police department to have Reles sent out the window. The murder had been necessary because at the time the Kid was about to give information that would have doomed two leading underworld leaders: Albert Anastasia and Bugsy Siegel. Subsequently, William O'Dwyer, then Brooklyn district attorney and later mayor of New York City, received much criticism for failing to proceed with the prosecution of Anastasia in what was described as a "perfect case" based on Kid Twist's testimony. O'Dwyer claimed that case "went out the window" along with informer Reles.

In 1945 a Brooklyn grand jury charged that there had been "negligence, incompetence and flagrant irresponsibility" in O'Dwyer's handling of the Anastasia prosecution. The jury stated O'Dwyer was

> *in possession of competent legal evidence that Anastasia was guilty of first degree murder and other vicious crimes. The proof admittedly was sufficient to warrant Anastasia's indictment and conviction, but Anastasia was neither prosecuted, indicted nor convicted . . . . The consistent and complete failure to prosecute the overlord of organized crime . . . is so revolting that we cannot permit these disclosures to be filed away in the same manner the evidence against Anastasia was heretofore "put in the files."*

Other ugly rumors swirled around Reles' death, including the charge by Ed Reid, a prize-winning reporter for the *Brooklyn Eagle,* that "Reles served several purposes besides being a fount of information about gang activities. Some of the information he gave out was used by unscrupulous persons connected with law enforcement in Brooklyn—to shake down gangsters."

In any event, Reles did not live long enough to fulfill his potential as a stoolpigeon. While Murder, Inc., or at least its Brooklyn branch, was destroyed, the crime syndicate continued in business.

See also: LOUIS "LEPKE" BUCHALTER; MURDER, INC.; PITTSBURGH PHIL.

ripper gangs serial killers acting in concert

Among serial killers, so-called ripper gangs are considered by many law officials to be the most frightening. Because they operate in a group, one member can frequently egg his companions into more and more terrifying acts. Probably the most hideous ripper gang of the 1980s was one in the Chicago area, headed by Robin Gecht, a terror who was to be called the Midwest's Charles Manson. While the gang's victims were often disfigured before or after they were killed, the term "ripper" seems to have gained its meaning in part from the way women victims were "ripped" off the street. In some cases the victim was ripped right out of her shoes and driven away in a van to a gruesome fate, the only clue to her disappearance was the shoes left in a mall parking lot or at the side of a highway where she might be waiting to be picked up by a friend or relative.

The shoe routine was also the mark of another ripper gang, led by Lawrence Sigmund Bittaker and Roy Lewis Norris, operating in California. Besides luring young girls into their new silver GMC van with promises of drugs or job offers, the boys simply maced their intended victims or ripped them out of their shoes and sped away in their van, called their "Murder Mack."

The Murder Mack's radio blared loudly to cover the victim's screams as they drove into the mountains to complete their crimes at leisure.

The Gecht rippers in Chicago were more brazen, not hesitating to rip women right off North Lake Shore Drive along Lake Michigan. One such victim was Rosemarie Ann Beck, abducted, tortured and left to die in a building along the Drive. Most of his followers were of more limited intelligence than Robin Gecht, who some said dominated his gang with his eyes and hypnotic ways. He was 28 years old in 1981, five to seven years or so older than most of his followers. As the mutilated bodies of some of their victims started turning up, newspaper speculation ran rampant, but one sure thing was that there seemed no way to conduct an accurate body count. The full extent of Gecht's predations was never really determined, and the media had to be satisfied by reporting a near-endless string of "cannibal murders," a description that was not inaccurate.

The rippers' last attempted kill involved a female hauled into the gang's van, stuffed with drugs and then mutilated and dumped still alive from the vehicle. She survived and identified some of the abductors while still in the hospital. One by one the rippers were picked up by police. Several of them broke and talked. Soon a trail led to Gecht. Gecht was found mentally competent to stand trial in March 1983 and in September he confessed in court to murder. One identified victim of the gang was 42-year-old Carole Pappas, the wife of the Chicago Cubs' pitcher. However, her remains were never found.

Robin Gecht was convicted and sentenced to 120 years in prison. Other members of the gang got life sentences, and one, Andrew Kokoraleis, drew a death sentence.

Schmid, Charles Howard (1942–)
mass murderer

Often called the Pied Piper of Tucson, Charles Schmid was 22 years old in 1964 when he led a weird clique of admiring young people on forays of rape and bizarre behavior, ending in a series of meaningless murders.

Even in his high school days Schmid behaved strangely. Only five feet three inches, he padded his cowboy boots to make him taller, dyed his red hair black, wore cosmetics and designed a phony mole on his face to make him look meaner. He told wild tales that somehow made him very popular, attracting a number of girls who prostituted themselves to provide him with money. One girl went to work in his parents' nursing home and faithfully deposited most of her week's pay in Schmid's bank account.

Schmid rented a cottage on the outskirts of Tucson, bought a beat-up car and became a fixture of the Speedway Boulevard area, a strip that attracted race-happy motorcyclists, souped-up car enthusiasts and rock-and-roll music lovers. On May 31, 1964 Schmid was drinking with two young friends, Mary French and John Saunders, when he announced he felt like killing a girl. "I want to do it tonight," he said. "I think I can get away with it!"

Mary French invited 15-year-old Alleen Rowe to join them late that night and they went for a drive in Schmid's car. After stopping in the desert, Mary stayed in the car while Schmid and Saunders took the girl to a secluded spot. Schmid raped her and then casually told Saunders to "hit her over the head with a rock." Saunders started to obey but the horrified girl ran off. After catching up with her, Schmid knocked her to the ground and smashed her skull in with a rock. They buried the girl in a shallow grave and went off to do some more drinking.

In August 1965 a girlfriend of Schmid's, 17-year-old Gretchen Fritz, disappeared with her 13-year-old sister, Wendy. Like Alleen Rowe, the Fritz girls were listed as runaways by the police, but a short while later, Schmid boasted to a friend, Richard Bruns, that he had strangled both sisters and thrown their bodies into a ditch. Since Bruns refused to believe the story, Schmid showed him the corpses.

Bruns kept silent about the matter for a while until he got it into his head that Schmid was going to kill his, Bruns', girlfriend. He started having nightmares about Schmid and finally went to the police. Schmid was arrested on November 11, 1965, as were French and Saunders. The latter two turned state's evidence against their bizarre hero. Schmid got 55 years for the rape-murder of Alleen Rowe and the death sentence for the slayings of the Fritz girls. French got four to five years and Saunders life imprisonment for their parts in the Rowe crime. When the Supreme Court abolished capital punishment, Schmid was resentenced to two terms of life imprisonment.

On November 11, 1972 Schmid escaped from the Arizona State Prison along with another triple murderer, Raymond Hudgens. The pair held four hostages on a ranch near Tempe, Ariz., and then separated. Both were recaptured within a few days and returned to prison.

Schultz, Dutch (1902–1935) underworld leader

Among the great underworld leaders spawned by Prohibition, Dutch Schultz was one of the flakiest, probably the cheapest and often the most cold-blooded. In the end, he had to be executed by his fellow gangsters because he threatened the status quo established between organized crime and the law. Born Arthur Flegenheimer in the Bronx, New York City, he tended bar and had only a minor criminal record until the mid-1920s, when he formed a gang and took over much of the beer trade in the Bronx. Tough, aggressive and probably keener in his appreciation of potential sources of illicit revenues than even Lucky Luciano, he was the first to see the fortune to be made out of the numbers racket in Harlem. He moved in on the independent black operators there and, using force and violence, turned them into his agents in a new multimillion dollar racket. Through a mathematical genius named Otto "Abbadabba" Berman, he figured out a way to fix the numbers game so that the smallest possible payout was made when someone hit.

Few other gangsters, including most of his own men, either liked or respected him, but they feared him. Schultz was a miser who paid his gangsters as little as he could get away with, and he would almost fly into a rage whenever he was asked for a raise. The only man in the organization he paid really well was Abbadabba, who got $10,000 a week, though only after he threatened to take his mathematical skills elsewhere.

Schultz never spent more than $35 for a suit or $2 for a shirt. "Personally," he once told an interviewer, "I think only queers wear silk shirts. I never bought one in my life. A guy's a sucker to spend fifteen or twenty dollars on a shirt. Hell, a guy can get a good one for two bucks!"

Lucky Luciano once said of him: "Dutch was the cheapest guy I ever knew. The guy had a couple of million bucks and he dressed like a pig, and he worried about spending two cents for a newspaper. That was his big spending, buying the papers so's he could read about himself."

Schultz was somewhat of an expert on newspapers. He admitted that he took the name of Dutch Schultz because "it was short enough to fit in the headlines. If I'd kept the name of Flegenheimer, nobody would have heard of me." Once, he raged at Meyer Berger, the star crime reporter of *The New*

York Times, because Berger had described him as a "pushover for a blonde."

Actually, only one offense truly enraged Schultz. His famous "mouthpiece" Dixie Davis, later said of him: "You can insult Arthur's girl, spit in his face, push him around—and he'll laugh. But don't steal a dollar from his accounts. If you do, you're dead."

Among those who did and died for it was the murderous Jack "Legs" Diamond, who became known as the underworld's clay pigeon in his wars with various gangsters, especially Schultz. When Diamond expired in an upstate New York hotel room with several bullets in his head, Schultz was quoted as saying, "Just another punk caught with his hands in my pockets." Vincent "Mad Dog" Coll, a former underling with a fiery temper and raging ambitions, also challenged Schultz. Coll staged wholesale raids on Schultz' beer drops and policy joints, and while he matched the Dutchman at killing, he was forced into hiding by the Schultz organization's superior firepower. On February 8, 1932 he ventured forth to use a telephone booth and was gunned down by Schultz' machine gunners.

After that, no one really wanted to take on Schultz. He would fight to the last man and had powerful political protection, mainly through Jimmy Hines, the Tammany boss who would later go to prison for his protection of the Schultz forces. Although Luciano, Meyer Lansky and the other founders of the national crime syndicate dealt the Dutchman in, considering him too powerful to leave out, they secretly sought to get rid of Schultz because they considered him too erratic and because they wanted to take over his lucrative beer and policy rackets. While Schultz was awaiting trial after being indicted on tax charges, Luciano and his associates moved quickly to take over his rackets through the cooperation of Schultz' top aide, Bo Weinberg. Amazingly, Schultz beat the case against him and returned to reclaim his domain. Rather than fight him, the syndicate leaders gave back large chunks they had gobbled up, explaining they had been simply minding the Dutchman's holdings in his absence. Schultz was almost forgiving, but not toward Weinberg. Shortly thereafter, Weinberg became a permanent missing person. According to one underworld report, Schultz personally put a bullet in his head, but in another version Weinberg was fitted with a "cement overcoat" and dropped—still alive—into the Hudson River. Either story could be true.

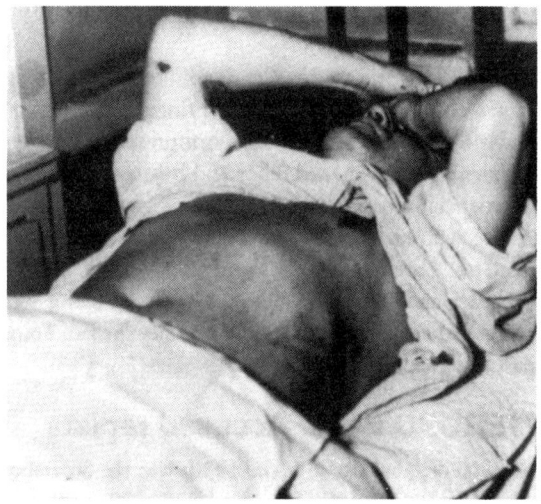

Dutch Schultz lingered for two days after being shot, but he did not name his killers. Instead he talked mostly gibberish, including some mysterious mumblings about all the money he had hidden.

Schultz' demise came about because of his desire to get rid of special prosecutor Thomas E. Dewey, whom Gov. Herbert Lehman had appointed in 1935 to investigate racketeering and vice. When Dewey started cracking down on the mobs, particularly on Schultz and his gang, the Dutchman, seeing his revenues decline, went before the national board of the syndicate to demand that Dewey be assassinated. The proposal was quickly turned down by Luciano, Lansky, Louis Lepke, Costello and others, who were convinced it would bring an avalanche of police pressure on the entire underworld.

Undeterred by the strong vote against him, Schultz stormed out of the meeting, defiantly declaring: "I still say he ought to be hit. And if nobody else is gonna do it, I'm gonna hit him myself."

When the syndicate learned Schultz was really going ahead with the plot and had even picked a murder site, they quickly put out a contract on him.

On October 23, 1935 Schultz, Abbadabba Berman and two bodyguards, Abe Landau and Lulu Rosenkrantz were in a favorite hangout, the Palace Chop House and Tavern in Newark, N. J. Schultz left his three henchmen sitting at a table in the back and went into the men's room. While he was in there, two gunmen entered the Palace. One of the two burst into the men's room and shot to death a man standing at a urinal, not realizing the victim was Schultz. He then charged at the table where Berman and the two bodyguards were seated and, with two guns blazing, killed them all. Only at that point did the gunmen discover that Schultz was not among the three. However, when they checked the men's room, they found Schultz was the man who had been shot simply to ensure that the pair were not surprised from behind. The gunman who had done all the shooting lifted a considerable amount of cash from Schultz' pockets and then fled.

Schultz lingered in a hospital for two days before dying. Eventually, one of his killers was identified as Charles "the Bug" Workman. He was tried and sentenced to 23 years for the crime.

Siegel, Benjamin "Bugsy" (1906–1947)

syndicate leader

"We only kill each other," the notorious Benjamin "Bugsy" Siegel once told construction tycoon Del Webb. Whether or not Webb took this assurance on the mores of syndicate gangsterism at full value is not known, but Siegel's own life and death certainly gives his statement some credence. Bugsy Siegel was simultaneously the most colorful, the most charming and the most fiery-tempered of all syndicate killers. As the saying went, he charmed the pants and panties off Hollywood, while at the same time functioning as a mob killer. It was an incredible act right up to the moment he got his head blown open by three 30.30 caliber bullets from a hit man's rifle.

Bugsy grew up on the crime-ridden Lower East Side and formed an early alliance with a runty little youth four years his senior, Meyer Lansky, already a criminal genius in his teens. By 1920 the Bug and Meyer Gang was running gambling games, stealing cars and getting into bootlegging. On occasion the gang hijacked booze shipments from other outfits until Lansky and Siegel realized it was a lot easier to hire out their gunmen as protectors for these shipments. They soon began working with rising young Italian gangsters such as Lucky Luciano, Joe Adonis, Frank Costello and Tommy Lucchese. The gang provided much of the muscle and, in Lansky's case, the brains for Luciano's big push to topple the old "Mustache Petes" of the

Mafia: Giuseppe "Joe the Boss" Masseria and Salvatore Maranzano.

The emerging national crime syndicate assigned Siegel to carry out numerous murders aimed at gaining control of the important avenues of crime. He was so enthused about killing, he was called "Bugsy," but not in his presence. Face to face, he was just plain Ben.

Bugsy was sent to California to consolidate the syndicate's West Coast operations. There, in his quieter moments, he was a genuinely suave, entertaining sort, hobnobbing with Hollywood celebrities and becoming close friends with such personalities as Jean Harlow, George Raft, Clark Cable, Gary Cooper, Wendy Barrie, Cary Grant and many others, some of whom invested their money in his enterprises. Siegel sometimes left his "class" friends at a party to go on a murder mission, which he did one night in 1939 when he, Frankie Carbo, later the underworld's boss of boxing, and Murder, Inc. wheelman Allie Tannenbaum assassinated an errant criminal named Harry Greenberg, better known as Big Greenie.

Big Greenie had had the death sentence passed on him by the syndicate board in New York. When Greenie fled to Los Angeles, it was decided to "let Ben handle it." Siegel was happy to, doing the job personally, although he was only supposed to arrange matters. Los Angeles County Deputy District Attorney Arthur Veitch later explained why Siegel had to lend a hand personally: "In gangster parlance Siegel is what is known as a 'cowboy.' This is the way the boys have of describing a man who is not satisfied to frame a murder but actually has to be in on the kill in person."

Others would say Siegel's craziness explained his bizarre actions. For example, there was the time he and one of his mistresses, Countess Dorothy diFrasso, trekked to Italy to sell Benito Mussolini a revolutionary explosive device. While staying on the diFrasso estate, Siegel met top Nazi officials Hermann Goering and Joseph Goebbels. According to underworld legend, Bugsy took an instant dislike to the pair—for personal rather than political reasons—and planned to knock them both off, relenting only because of the countess' frantic pleas. When the explosive device fizzled, the Bug returned to Hollywood.

Bugsy Siegel—shot to death in the home of mob mistress Virginia Hill. The hit almost certainly was carried out on orders of Meyer Lansky, the Bug's lifelong friend, and Lucky Luciano, although both denied responsibility.

His main syndicate business was running the rackets and directing narcotics deals on the West Coast as well as overseeing the delivery of West Coast racing results to East Coast bookmakers. In the process Siegel dreamed up the idea of turning Las Vegas into a legal gambling paradise. He talked the syndicate into investing some $6 million in the construction of the first truly posh legal gambling establishment in the United States, the Flamingo (which was the nickname of Siegel's mistress, Virginia Hill). Unfortunately for Bugsy, he was a man ahead of his time, and the Flamingo proved to be a financial white elephant. Reportedly, the syndicate demanded he make good its losses, but Bugsy was guilty of more serious infractions than just losing the mob's money. He had skimmed off the Flamingo's construction funds and had been dipping into its gambling revenues.

The syndicate passed the death sentence on Siegel, the key vote being cast by Meyer Lansky, Bugsy's lifelong buddy ("I had no choice," Lansky reputedly said later). Lucky Luciano approved the decision at a 1947 conference in Havana, Cuba. On June 20 Siegel was sitting in the living room of the $500,000 Beverly Hills mansion of Virginia Hill, who had been sent on a syndicate mission to Europe, when a killer pumped nine shots through the window. Three hit Siegel in the head, killing him instantly.

Skull, Sally (1813–1867?) multiple murderess

Her name was Sarah Jane Newman, but through a succession of marriages—or as near as it got to that in the Wild West—she became Sarah Jane "Doe"-Robinson-Skull-Doyle-Watkins-Harsdoff. However, she was generally called Sally Skull, the surname of one of her several husbands who came to mysterious and/or violent ends.

In 1821 Pennsylvania-born Sally and her family settled in what would become the state of Texas. By the age of 13 the future Sally Skull had blossomed enough to catch her first husband, whose name is unrecorded. So is his fate. Sally said he went off to fight Indians. Whatever the reason for his departure, he was never seen again. Her second husband was one Jesse Robinson, who married Sally in 1838 and left her bed and board in 1843, describing her as a "common scold" and a woman with a violent temper apt to shoot a little too close to him. Sally found her next husband within a few months, a horse trader named George Skull. He set Sally up on a ranch near Goliad, Tex., where the couple ran a profitable horse business and Sally became one of the area's more colorful sights, sporting her six-gun and bullwhip. George Skull disappeared but no one ever knew exactly when. All of a sudden he just wasn't around and hadn't been for some time. Sally simply said she wasn't going to talk about him. In 1852 John Doyle became another of Sally's ill-fated husbands. Folks said it was kind of predictable what would happen to him after blonde Sally was seen in the company of the famed Mexican bandit chief Juan Cortina. In any event, Doyle took to drinking and one day, presumably liquored up, fell into the Nueces River and drowned. For some reason rumor spread that Sally had drowned him in a barrel of whiskey.

During the Civil War, Sally Skull sported a new husband, whom she referred to as Mr. Watkins, but he didn't last long enough for the locals to learn his first name. Mr. and Mrs. Watkins went on a trip to Corpus Christi, where Mr. Watkins was shot to death by his spouse. There was some dispute about whether Sally had shot him because she thought he was an intruder or out of annoyance at his having the temerity to awaken her. But the lady's account of what had happened was taken and Sally Skull was free to marry again. In 1867 she married William Harsdoff. The couple set off for Mexico on a combination honeymoon and horse-buying trip and were never seen again. Some months later, the badly decomposed body of a woman was found on the road the pair had taken. It was never officially identified as that of Sally Skull, and it may well be that her saga did not end there.

Slade, Joseph "Jack" (1824–1864) murderer

When sober, Jack Slade was a vicious killer; drunk, he was considerably worse. Born in Illinois the son of a congressman, Slade had to flee west after killing a man during an argument. Thereafter, he left a trail of corpses wherever he went. He worked on and off as a stagecoach driver, a station agent for the Central Overland and, finally, a district superintendent for that line. But his main occupation was killing. Some biographers insist that Slade was a regular Jekyll and Hyde, being one of the kindliest men around when sober. The truth is that his killings were only a little less cruel when he was not under the influence. A typical sober killing was that of a teamster named Andrew Farrar, who pulled a gun on Slade one day when the latter entered a saloon. Farrar could have shot him dead at that point, but he let Slade taunt him with the accusation that he was too cowardly to fight with his fists. Farrar rose to the bait and flipped his gun aside. As he was rolling up his sleeves, Slade shot him dead.

Alcohol seemed to make Slade go crazy. He once got intoxicated and shot up the army post at Fort Halleck, Colorado Territory, sending armed soldiers ducking for cover. Worse than that, Slade under the effects of whiskey engaged in acts of unparalleled cruelty. One of his victims was a larcenous Frenchman named Jules Beni, who had tried to kill Slade and made the mistake of failing. Slade caught up with Beni and tied him to a fence post. Between swigs on a bottle of whiskey, he shot Beni full of holes, aiming at his legs and arms to keep his victim alive. When finally he tired of the game, Slade jammed his gun into Beni's mouth and pulled the trigger. He then cut off Beni's ears, one of which he reputedly used as a watch fob. He sold the other as a souvenir for drinking money.

Even Mark Twain recorded some of Slade's exploits in *Roughing It*.

> *Slade was a matchless marksman with a navy revolver. The legends say that one morning at Rocky Ridge, when he was feeling comfortable, he saw a man approaching who had offended him some days before—observe the fine memory he had for matters like that—and, "Gentlemen," said Slade, drawing, "it is a good twenty-five yard shot—I'll clip the third button on his coat!" Which he did. The bystanders all admired it. And they all attended the funeral too.*

Slade had the misfortune of performing some of his unwholesome deeds in Montana vigilante country, where the practitioners of the noose had cleaned out the Plummer gang and were looking to find other guests of honor for their necktie parties. Slade was warned to "get his horse and be gone," but he failed to heed the warnings, apparently figuring his reputation was enough to scare off any attackers. On the night of March 3, 1864 he went on one of his monumental drunks and shot up a good deal of Virginia City.

A group of vigilantes rushed him and tied him up, and within three hours he was convicted and ordered to be hanged forthwith. When the scourge of the West learned his fate, he crawled around on his hands and knees, crying: "My God! My God! Must I die? Oh, my poor wife, my poor wife! My God, men, you can't mean that I'm to die!"

Despite his pleas, Slade was hanged, and by the time his wife got to him, he had been laid out to "cool" in a hotel. The widow packed Slade's body in a tin coffin filled with raw alcohol and set out for Illinois to bury him at his birthplace. By the time the Widow Slade and the coffin got to Salt Lake City, however, the body was decomposing and giving off an awful odor. So Jack Slade was buried in the Mormon Cemetery.

Smith, Edgar Herbert (1933–) murderer

Probably few "wrong man" cases have taken as many twists as that of Edgar Smith, who was sentenced to death for the 1957 bludgeon murder of a 15-year-old New Jersey girl, Victoria Zielinski. Smith established a longevity record on death row, 14 years at Trenton State Prison. During that time he never ceased proclaiming his innocence and soon started a correspondence with conservative columnist William F. Buckley, Jr., which eventually totaled some 2,900 pages. Buckley encouraged Smith to write an impressive book, *Brief Against Death,* in his cell. The book, aided by Buckley's columns, made Smith a national cause celebre. Smith followed up with a second book, *A Reasonable Doubt,* which made belief in his innocence still more compelling.

Finally, in 1971 Smith won a new trial, at which he admitted his guilt and was sentenced to 25 to 30 years for second-degree murder. With time credited for good behavior, he was released on probation. As he left the prison, Smith was picked up by Buckley's car and driven to New York, where before TV cameras he again assured people he was innocent of the killing. His second trial had come about as the result of plea bargaining, which he was convinced was the only way he could get out of prison. "It was a difficult choice," he said, "but I wanted to be free."

Smith set to work writing his third book, *Getting Out,* in which he stated in the prologue:

> *In the Prologue to* Brief Against Death, *I ended with the question: "Did Justice triumph?" Today, four years later, my fight ended and my freedom a reality, that question remains as valid as when it was first asked.*
>
> *Did Justice triumph?*
>
> *Each reader will have to find his own answer.*

As it turned out, readers had to wait until October 1976 to make up their mind. In that month San Diego, Calif. police began a hunt for Smith to answer charges of assault, kidnapping and attempted murder. Smith had forced a young woman into his car at knifepoint, and when she fought him, he stabbed her. The women kept on battling and finally hurled herself out of Smith's car onto the freeway. Smith then drove off.

About a week later, Smith telephoned Buckley from Las Vegas. The columnist was out, so Smith left a number where he could be reached. Buckley promptly notified the FBI and Smith was arrested in a hotel room.

Taken into custody, Smith readily admitted his assault on the San Diego woman and then added a bombshell. He admitted he really had murdered Victoria Zielinski 19 years earlier. "For the first time in my life, I recognized that the devil I had been looking at the last forty-three years was me," he said. "I recognized what I am, and I admitted it."

Smith was sent back to prison for life.

Snyder, Ruth (1895–1928) murderess

Ruth Snyder, a wife who, with her lover, murdered her husband, became probably the most reviled woman of the 1920s; even her death in the electric chair was subjected to indignity. Her sin was not so much being a conspirator in the murder plot but being the active planner and the more active participant in the crime. Her trial was so spectacular that the press contingent included such unlikely personalities as Mary Roberts Rinehart, David Belasco, D. W. Griffith, Billy Sunday, Peggy Hopkins Joyce, Dr. John Roach Straton, Aimee Semple McPherson and even Will Durant, then at the top of the best-seller list with *The Story of Philosophy.*

Albert Snyder never realized how many close calls he had at the hands of Ruth. She had resolved to kill him in 1926, a year after she met corset salesman Judd Gray and found true happiness in an adulterous affair. Gray, not the strongest of personalities, called her "queen," and "my momsie." She referred to him as "lover boy."

Ruth took out a $48,000 life insurance policy on Snyder with a double-indemnity clause. Then she set about trying to kill him, but he seemed to live a charmed life. Twice, she disconnected the gas while Snyder slept and slipped from the room, but both times her husband awoke and saved himself from asphyxiation, never even suspecting his wife. Another time she closed the garage door while he was inside with the automobile's motor running. He nearly fell victim to carbon monoxide poisoning but managed to survive. On two occasions she put bichloride of mercury in his whiskey, but he poured the stuff out, commenting that they had to change bootleggers. Twice she added powerful narcotics to his medicine while he was ill, but he still recovered.

In February 1927 Ruth convinced Gray to help her murder her husband. Gray hid in a bedroom closet before the Snyders returned home one night, and after Snyder fell asleep,

DAILY NEWS FINAL EDITION

NEW YORK'S PICTURE NEWSPAPER

Sunday, 1,357,556 Daily, 1,193,297

Vol. 9. No. 173 36 Pages New York, Friday, January 13, 1928 2 Cents

DEAD!

Story on page 3

CC 79892 CC 79891

Millions of newspaper readers hung on every word in the case of Ruth Snyder and Judd Gray until their execution.

he slipped out and hit him over the head with a sash weight. But the blow woke Snyder up. He struggled with Gray and cried out for his wife to help him. Ruth came to the aid of her lover, picking up the sash weight and hitting her husband again. As he slipped into unconsciousness, Ruth chloroformed him and strangled him with picture wire. Finally, Albert Snyder was dead. Gray then tied Ruth up and when the police arrived, she told them she had been attacked by burglars.

The police became suspicious because her bindings had been tied rather loosely, as though not to cause her discomfort. When they found Gray's name a number of times among her possessions, they decided to tell her Gray had been arrested and had confessed. The trick worked and she talked. Hearing that Ruth had confessed, Gray admitted his part in the murder. Both attempted to make the other the principal party in the murder, but it was well established that the credit belonged to Ruth Snyder.

Both were convicted and sentenced to death in the electric chair, a fate they met on January 22, 1928 at Sing Sing Prison. Just as the executioner pulled the switch on Ruth Snyder, photographer Thomas Howard, sitting in a front-row seat, crossed his legs and snapped a picture with a camera strapped just above his ankle. The next morning the *New York Daily News* devoted the entire front page to the horrifying shot of the current coursing through Ruth Snyder's body, perhaps the most famous picture in tabloid journalism.

Spanish, Johnny (1891–1919) gangster and murderer

Johnny Spanish was one of the bloodiest criminals during the first two decades of the 20th century.

A Spanish Jew (his real name was John Weyler), he is said to have been involved in a murder at the age of 17. For a time he operated as an independent slugger and killer, taking on all assignments, until he finally formed his own gang, which was attached to New York's notorious Five Pointers.

Spanish reportedly always ventured forth with two revolvers stuck in his belt and, on serious missions, two more in his coat pockets. When staging a holdup, he often had an accomplice, a man weighted down with additional guns who acted strictly as a weapons bearer.

Johnny Spanish gained considerable underworld fame for his daring, a classic example being the robbery of a saloon on Norfolk Street belonging to Mersher the Strong Arm. Spanish gave notice that he would appear at a certain time to empty the till, and he turned up on the dot with his trusty gun bearer. The daring Spanish did exactly what he said he would, shooting out the mirror over the bar as he entered and pistol-whipping several customers who objected to contributing their wallets.

In 1909 Spanish became fast friends with Kid Dropper, destined to be for a time the leading gangster in New York. They committed a number of jobs together before becoming deadly enemies when the Dropper stole the affections of Johnny Spanish's girlfriend. In order to provide for the woman of his affections, Spanish determined to take over the stuss games on the Lower East Side, then a popular form of illegal gambling. In his efforts to absorb one such operation with his usual fast shooting, Spanish killed an eight-year-old girl who happened to be playing in the street. He was forced to flee the city for several months until things quieted down. When he returned, he was chagrined to find that the woman he had done the shooting for had left him for Kid Dropper.

Determined to take vengeance, he snatched the woman off the streets one night and drove to a marsh near Maspeth, Long Island. There, he put her up against a tree and fired several shots into her abdomen, which he considered appropriate revenge since she was pregnant at the time. The woman was found alive but unconscious several hours later and, in the meantime, had given birth to a baby with three fingers shot off. For this offense Spanish was sent to prison in 1911 for seven years. His only solace was that about the same time Kid Dropper also was put away for seven years on a robbery count.

Remarkably, when both were freed in late 1917, they hooked up again as partners in crime. However, the inevitable jealousies soon surfaced and the pair and their followers split into separate gangs, each determined to take over what was virtually the sole source of income for organized criminals at the time: labor racketeering and slugging. Each gang sought to service the unions who wanted strikebreakers maimed or killed or the employers who wanted union pickets and organizers eliminated. Both the Dropper and Johnny Spanish fielded large contingents of gunmen to control the rackets and a shooting war broke out that led to dozens of deaths. Johnny Spanish was suspected of carrying out a number of torture-murders himself.

On July 29, 1919 the Dropper forces learned that Spanish was dining in a Second Avenue restaurant without his usual collection of bodyguards. When Spanish stepped into the street, three gunmen, one said to be Kid Dropper himself, emptied their revolvers into his body. With Johnny Spanish's demise, Kid Dropper became the top racketeer in New York City, a position he held until 1923, when he too was assassinated.

Speck, Richard Benjamin (1942–1991)

serial killer

A drifter often high on both alcohol and drugs, Richard Speck was apparently in that condition on July 13, 1966, when he found himself in front of a row house serving as a nurses' dormitory for the South Chicago Community Hospital. After forcing his way into an apartment shared by nine student nurses, he committed one of Chicago's most heinous mass murders. Armed with a knife and a pistol, he trapped six nurses present and tied them up. He waited until three other nurses returned home and bound them also. Then after taking their money, he led eight of the nurses, one at a time, from the room where they were being held and killed them, strangling five and stabbing three. He sexually assaulted one of his victims. The eight were Gloria Jean Davy, Suzanne Bridget Farris, Merlita Gargullo, Mary Ann Jordan, Patricia Ann Matusek, Valentina Pasion, Nina Jo Schmale and Pamela Lee Wilkening. The ninth, 23-year-old Corazon Amurao, managed to hide under a bed and was overlooked. Four hours she cowered there, not knowing what had happened to her roommates or whether the assailant had left. When an alarm clock went off at 5 A.M., the apartment was still. Two hours later, the terror-stricken woman finally crawled out from her hiding place. She found three bodies in the next room and ran screaming from the apartment.

Speck avoided arrest for a number of days until he attempted to slash his wrists and was taken to a hospital, where he was identified as the mass murderer. He was sentenced to the electric chair, but when the Supreme Court voided the death sentence in 1972, he was resentenced to eight consecutive terms of 50 to 150 years. Facing a possible total of 1,200 years in prison, Speck seemed to have received the longest sentence in history. By 1976, however, he was eligible for parole, and although turned down, he was entitled to a review of his case each year thereafter.

Spinelli, Juanita "Duchess" (1889–1941)

murderess

The first woman to be executed legally in California, Juanita Spinelli, dubbed the Duchess of Death by the newspapers, set up a school in California to train young men for crime and masterminded their criminal activities.

Until her middle years Juanita Spinelli's life is shrouded in mystery. She claimed she was born in a hobo jungle to a drifter and a runaway Sioux Indian girl. Her mother died in childbirth and her father disappeared. It is unclear who raised her, but it is known that she was married once or twice.

Her police dossier began in 1935, when she acted as "finger-woman" in a laundry union strike. She informed on a strikebreaker she knew was wanted by the police. At the time, she was living with Michael Simone, a Detroit hoodlum who served as a bodyguard for some of the city's leading gangsters.

While Simone's employers were not directly affected by Juanita's informant role, they felt uncomfortable about having a female stoolpigeon around. Sensing she was not wanted, Juanita moved on to California. There, she struck up an acquaintance with a young San Francisco car thief named Gordon Hawkins, moved in with him and began giving instructions to Hawkins and some of his friends on how to become big-time gangsters. Among her prize pupils were 23-year-old Albert Ives and 18-year-old Robert Sherrard, a fugitive from a mental institution. In time, she brought in Mike Simone from Detroit to act as her chief lieutenant in the gang.

At first, Juanita, now called Duchess by Hawkins, masterminded small operations—auto thefts, easy burglaries, rolling helpless drunks. Then they moved on to stickups. On April 8, 1940 Simone, Hawkins, Ives and Sherrard held up Leland S. Cash, the 55-year-old manager of a roadside barbecue stand. When they announced it was a robbery, Cash, who was hard of hearing, reached for his hearing aid, and Ives, panicking, shot him fatally in the stomach. The quartet escaped with the paper bags Cash was carrying, which they supposed contained the receipts for the day. Actually, the bags only held some extra meat that the victim was taking home.

The Duchess was furious about the needless murder and then even more furious when Sherrard started showing signs of "coming apart." Fearful he would talk about the murder, she ordered him killed. The gang knocked Sherrard out with a Mickey Finn, dressed him in swimming trunks and dumped him off a bridge. According to the Duchess, there was a good chance the police would mark the death down to accidental drowning. To be on the safe side, she moved her brood to Reno, where they pulled a few more jobs. Meanwhile, Ives began getting shaky, and he grew even more nervous when the Duchess started intimating he might be disposed of next. Deciding it was only a matter of time until he too was killed, Ives managed to slip away from the mob long enough to inform the police about the gang's murderous activities.

In the ensuing investigation, every male member of the mob tried to implicate everyone else, especially the Duchess, who sneered at their cowardice. In the end, Duchess Spinelli, Simone and Hawkins were sentenced to die in the gas chamber. Ives was judged insane and committed to a mental institution. He died in 1951.

Duchess Spinelli managed to delay her execution for a year and a half with appeals, including one to Gov. Culbert Olson requesting life imprisonment on the grounds that no woman had ever been legally executed in the state. The governor found the appeal without merit, and the Duchess prepared for death by putting a "curse" on the authorities, the judge and the jurors. She told reporters, "My blood will burn holes in their bodies, and before six months have gone by, my executioners will be punished."

However, an hour before she died on November 21, 1941, the Duchess relented, saying, "I have asked God to forgive them."

Starkweather, Charles (1940–1959)

serial killer

Charley Starkweather, Nebraska's mass murderer of the 1950s, killed his first victim on December 1, 1957. On that day the red-haired youth robbed a gas station attendant, Robert Colvert, at gunpoint in Lincoln, drove him to an open area outside the city and executed him with several shots in the head. He did nothing more for almost two months until January 21, 1958, when he drove to the home of 14-year-old Caril Ann Fugate.

Finding the girl not at home, he sat down to wait for her, toying with a .22 hunting rifle he had brought with him. Caril's mother, Velda Bartlett, yelled at him to stop fooling around with the weapon—whereupon he shot both her and Caril's stepfather, Marion Bartlett. When Caril Ann came home, Starkweather went to her two-year-old sister's bedroom and choked the child to death. He then dragged the parents' bodies outside and put Marion Bartlett's corpse under newspapers and rags in the chicken coop and Velda's in an abandoned outhouse. He dumped the child into a cardboard box and then went into the kitchen, made some sandwiches and joined Caril to watch television.

They put a sign on the door reading: "STAY AWAY. EVERYBODY IS SICK WITH THE FLU. MISS BARTLETT." When Caril's older sister came by and wanted to help, Caril Ann sent her away. Later, Caril Ann's lawyer would argue she had saved her sister from being killed by Starkweather, who was lurking behind the kitchen door as the two sisters talked.

Caril's older sister told her husband, who became suspicious and notified the police. When two officers came to the house to investigate, Caril Ann told them everyone inside was sick. They left. Two days later, Caril turned her grandmother away, and she went to the police. The police returned to the house and found it empty. They then searched the premises and found the three bodies.

An alert went out for Starkweather and the girl, and in the following week of terror, Little Red, the bowlegged teenager who modeled himself after movie star James Dean, played the role of a murderer without a cause, shooting and stabbing seven more people to death. When his car got stuck on a muddy road, a high school couple stopped to lend a hand, Starkweather shot them to death and he and Caril Ann transferred to the victims' car. He then shot a friend, August Meyer, for his guns and ammunition.

Back in Lincoln, Starkweather and Caril Ann entered the house of wealthy steel executive C. Lauer Ward and marched his wife and housekeeper upstairs. The two women were tied up and gagged and then Starkweather stabbed them to death. When Ward returned home, he was murdered before he had time to take off his coat.

The couple took Ward's smooth-running Packard and drove to Wyoming. Twelve miles outside of Douglas, they came upon shoe salesman Merle Collison catnapping in his new Buick at the side of the road. Caril Ann slipped into the backseat while Starkweather walked over to the driver's side of the car and shot the sleeping victim nine times in the head. It was his last killing. Thinking someone was in trouble, an oil company worker named Joe Sprinkle stopped to offer a hand. When Starkweather leveled a rifle at Sprinkle, the oil worker charged him and struggled for possession of the weapon. By luck, a deputy sheriff happened by and Caril Ann ran to him, screaming: "It's Starkweather! He's going to kill me. . . ."

Starkweather managed to break free, jump into the Packard and speed off. After gunning his car to 110 miles an hour and crashing through one roadblock, he was finally stopped when officers shot out his windshield.

Starkweather blandly announced he had killed everyone in "self-defense" and tried to defend Caril Ann. "Don't take it out on the girl. She had no part of it." He claimed she was a hostage. But when the girl started calling him a killer, he changed his attitude. "She could have escaped any time she wanted," he said. "I left her alone lots of times. Sometimes when I would go in and get hamburgers, she would be sitting in the car with all the guns. There would have been nothing to stop her from running away. One time she said that the hamburgers were lousy and we ought to go back and shoot all them people in the restaurant."

"After I shot her folks and killed her baby sister, Caril sat and watched television while I wrapped the bodies up in rags and newspapers. We just cooked up that hostage story between us."

Starkweather was condemned to death and Caril Ann Fugate was sentenced to life imprisonment, tearfully proclaiming her innocence as she left the courtroom. Starkweather went to the electric chair on June 25, 1959, after turning down a request from the Lions Club of Beatrice, Neb., that he donate his eyes to their eye bank following his death.

"Hell no," he said. "No one ever did anything for me. Why in the hell should I do anything for anyone else?" The 19-year-old's execution took four minutes.

Caril Ann Fugate was released on parole in 1977, considered completely rehabilitated.

Struck, Lydia (1833–1879) poisoner

Madame Van der Linden, the Leiden poisoner, between 1869 and 1885 attempted, according to the record, to kill 102 persons and successfully poisoned at least 27. Helen Jegado of France officially did in 26 and may well have finished off another dozen or so. In the United States, Jane Toppan nursed and poisoned at least 31 persons in her care, and her final toll may have been over 100. Lydia Struck had a mere eight confirmed poisonings and three more probables. But while she didn't come close to breaking the record, for sheer callousness Lydia may well be at the head of the list.

Lydia's first victim was her husband of 17 years, a rogue cop fired from the New York City Police Department for cowardice. Edward Struck devoted full time to drinking, and when he drank, he got mean, and when he got mean, he beat Lydia. After one of his tears, Ed Struck grew morose and screamed that he was no good and would kill himself someday. Lydia promptly went out and got some arsenic to use as rat poison. Ed Struck died. Apparently, he had gone out of his mind in a fit of remorse and poisoned himself. All the neighbors said that was what had happened and the police agreed. Even the insurance company that carried a $5,000 policy on him as a policeman paid without question.

Lydia took the four young Struck children to live in Connecticut. Since they reminded her of her unlamented husband, she poisoned each of them. The children's deaths attracted no attention since Lydia claimed no insurance on them and was new to the state. After that, Lydia became a nurse for Dennis Hurlbut, a 75-year-old Bridgeport widower who said that if she married him, he'd leave her his entire estate. They were married and Hurlbut lasted only 14 months. It was arsenic that did him in, but no one suspected that anything other than old age had finished him off.

Lydia's next husband was Horatio Sherman of Derby, Conn. In a way, this was a misstep for Lydia. She was sure Sherman was a man of property and considerable wealth. Only later did she learn that he had married her for her money. Moreover, he drank. Even worse he had two children who drove her crazy. Lydia poisoned the children first. Then she poisoned Sherman as well. There was no profit in these last three murders and Lydia simply moved into the home of an apple farmer as a housekeeper. The arrangement soon turned amorous and Lydia was considering a proposal of marriage when the police located her. Somehow they had gotten suspicious about the deaths of Sherman and his two children happening so close together and had exhumed the man's body. His vital organs were sent to Yale University and found to be loaded with arsenic.

Lydia confessed all eight murders. For some reason she would admit the murders of the six children, Struck and Sherman but not that of old Hurlbut, even though he too had suffered the fatal effects of arsenic. She kept insisting he might well have taken the arsenic "accidentally." Authorities suspected Lydia of dispatching three other men, but she would not confess to those crimes either and there was little point in pursuing the matters. More than enough evidence had been accumulated against her. She was sentenced to life at the Connecticut State Prison at Wethersfield and died there of cancer in 1879, her sixth year of confinement.

Thompson, Miran Edgar "Buddy"
(1917–1948) robber and murderer

Buddy Thompson was one of the most dangerous and daring lone wolf criminals of the late 1930s and early 1940s. A confirmed criminal, Thompson while in his early twenties, left a trail of crimes through his native Oklahoma, Texas, New Mexico, Colorado, Kansas, Mississippi, Alabama and Georgia. Arrested eight times, he engineered eight successful jailbreaks.

His most stunning crime followed the death of his brother, Blackie Thompson, a fugitive from a Texas penitentiary, at the hands of an Amarillo police officer. Thompson sought out the officer and sat waiting for him at the soda counter of a drug store. When the officer noticed Thompson and thought he recognized him from a number of wanted posters, he approached him and asked for identification. Instead, Thompson opened his jacket to reveal an automatic tucked in his belt. He ordered the officer to draw.

It was crazy, something out of a Western movie. "What is this?" the officer asked. "Do I know you or something?"

"No, and you ain't never going to," Thompson said coldly. "You can draw or not, but when I count three I'm going to start shooting. One. Two. Three."

The officer drew but much too slowly. Thompson shot him twice, killing him.

Thompson fled Texas, kidnapping a motorist and forcing the man to drive him to Oklahoma. A month later, he was captured. Found guilty of killing the police officer, Thompson was sentenced to life imprisonment, a light sentence that infuriated Texas officials. They turned him over to federal officers, hoping that under the Lindbergh Law he would get the death sentence for kidnapping. But because the motorist had been released unharmed, Thompson got a 99-year federal sentence and ended up in Alcatraz.

Thompson's reputation preceded him to "the Rock," and Bernie Coy, actively plotting the Alcatraz rebellion-escape, was eager to include a man with a record of eight successful jailbreaks. The Alcatraz break of May 1946 foundered at the last minute because of a single missing key, which prevented the escapees from getting to a police launch that would have taken them to the California mainland, where getaway cars were waiting. When Thompson saw the plot had failed, he realized the only officers who could identify him as being in the break were the nine guards held hostage in two prison cells. Thompson goaded another leading member of the escape team, Dutch Cretzer, a former Public Enemy No. 4, to gun down the nine, against Coy's specific orders. Cretzer did so, and then Thompson slipped back to his cell block, not realizing that Cretzer's fusillade had killed only one officer; the rest were badly wounded or playing dead. After the revolt was crushed and Cretzer and Coy killed, Thompson thought he was home free, only to be accused by the eight surviving guards. Along with Sam Shockley, another participant in the attempted break and a pathetically insane inmate, Thompson was executed in San Quentin's new gas chamber on December 3, 1948, the first to die by that method in California. As the door to the chamber was being pneumatically sealed, Thompson said to Shockley, "I never thought this would really happen."

Toppan, Jane (1857–1938) serial killer

As a mass murderer or murderess, nurse Jane Toppan has never received the recognition which she deserved, although she may well have killed 100 victims. One observer who did give her an appropriate amount of attention was Ellery Sedgwick, the distinguished editor of the *Atlantic Monthly,* who protested: "When it comes to evaluating the histories of famous murderers, Jane Toppan has never received proper recognition. Without the slightest doubt, she outranks both Bluebeard and Jack the Ripper." Sedgwick's interest in Toppan stemmed from the fact that he had been nursed by her through a siege of pneumonia and allowed to live. Many of her other patients did not survive her ministrations.

Nurse Toppan's poor record with patients did not become apparent for about 15 years, since at the time it was considered normal for sick people to die. In fact, Toppan had a reputation among doctors around Lowell, Mass. as one of the community's finest and most capable nurses. She was also for a period head nurse at Massachusetts General Hospital until administrators discovered her certificate was forged and that she was not even a graduate nurse.

Jane Toppan poisoned numerous patients with her own recipe of morphine and atropin, a mixture that prevented doctors from suspecting morphine poisoning because instead of the victim's eye pupils being contracted, as happens with morphine, they would be dilated. Her confession, made after she had taken poison herself in a futile suicide attempt, read: "Everybody trusted me. It was so easy. I felt strange when I watched them die. I was all excited and my blood seemed to sweep madly through my veins. It was the only pleasure I had."

The first step in her usual ritual was to help build up the patient so that the doctor would be encouraged. Then once the physician stopped making regular visits, she would sit at the patient's bedside and feed him or her a little of the poison brew, increasing the dosage each day. The patient's breath would grow short and painful. Then his body would be seized with convulsions, then become lax, then chill and then go into convulsions again. As the climax approached and the patient neared death, Jane would become more and more excited. "It wasn't my fault," she later said. "I had to do it.

They hadn't done anything to me and I gained nothing from their deaths except the excitement of watching them die. I couldn't resist doing it."

Finally traced through some prescriptions she had forged to purchase the necessary ingredients for her poison, Toppan attempted suicide but was saved by quick medical attention. However, she was told that she was dying and, in that belief, made her confession:

> *Yes, I killed them. I'm going to die and I can't face my Maker with this on my conscience. I killed Mattie. Then I killed Annie. I told her father it was suicide. It was poison. I killed Mr. Davis. And I killed Mrs. Mary Gibbs. . . . Oh, I killed so many of them.*

In all, she rattled off the names of 31 victims, whose poisonings were later confirmed. The relatives of several dozen others whom she had nursed until their death refused permission to have autopsies performed, so that it was never determined how many of them were also her victims, although the conventional wisdom put the figure at about 100. At Toppan's trial her pugnacious defense lawyers would concede only 11 murders, but such disclaimers meant little, especially when the defendant told a horrified courtroom, "This is my ambition—to have killed more people—more helpless people—than any man or woman has ever killed."

Finally, the prosecution agreed to accept a plea of not guilty by reason of insanity when the defense consented to a stipulation that no request for parole would ever be made, even if she was pronounced sane at some future time. On June 23, 1902 Jane Toppan was sent to the State Hospital at Taunton, Mass. for the remainder of her natural life. That proved to be another 36 years. She died there in 1938 at the age of 81.

Tri-State Gang

If the Dillinger mob was noted for its members' loyalty to each other, the Tri-State Gang, a more typical criminal combination of the 1930s, won notoriety for the opposite. Based in Philadelphia and led by Robert Mais, Walter Legenza and Anthony Cugino, known as Philadelphia's Public Enemy No. 1, the Tri-Staters became famous for the short-lived careers of many of their members, most of whom were victims of internal assassinations. Cugino was particularly adept at this pastime, killing, at various times, four of his men and two of their girlfriends.

Cugino's career in crime began at the age of 12, when he was sent to a reformatory. In 1919, barely out of his teens, he committed a $35,000 jewel robbery and, when caught, was sent to prison for 15 years. In prison he killed his cellmate, but he drew no added penalty for the act because he successfully claimed he had acted in self-defense. Released in 1930, Cugino hooked up with Mais, Legenza, Salvatore Serpa, Eddie "Cowboy" Wallace, John Zurkorsky and others to form a holdup and counterfeiting gang called the Tri-Staters. Together with Serpa, Wallace and Zurkorsky, Cugino stole a plant payroll and shot down a police officer guarding it.

A few months after the robbery, Cugino and Serpa, suspecting their partners in crime might betray them to the police to save themselves, took Wallace and Zukorsky for a ride. Riddled with bullets, the pair were dumped on a roadside and left for dead. Wallace was dead but Zukorsky staggered upright, hailed a car and was taken to a hospital. From the hospital he called Camden, N. J. police and begged them to go to a rooming house to save two girls with whom he and Wallace had been living. Detectives were too late. They found that the young women, Florence Miller and Ethel Greentree, had just left with two men whose descriptions matched those of Cugino and Serpa. Three weeks later, the bodies of the women were found in a shallow grave in a cornfield near Downington, Pa.

Sometime later, Cugino assassinated another gangster, Johnny Horn, who had two marks against him: Cugino suspected him of possible duplicity and regarded him as a rival for a certain young woman's attention. The only members of the gang Cugino seemed to have any loyalty toward (he later also stabbed Serpa to death in Chicago) were Mais and Legenza. When they were convicted and awaiting execution in Richmond, Va. for killing a mail-truck driver during a robbery, Cugino sent them two pistols hidden in a baked turkey. The pair broke out, murdering a guard in the process, and rejoined Cugino.

Back in business, the Tri-Staters robbed $48,000 from an electric company office in Philadelphia. Soon, Mais and Legenza were scouring the city's underworld for a certain hoodlum they believed had betrayed them, but they were informed on by certain other gang members who feared their vengeance would get out of hand. Returned to Richmond, Mais and Legenza were electrocuted. Meanwhile, Cugino shifted some of his operations from Philadelphia to New York, fearing he too would be betrayed. He still returned to Philadelphia, however, to recruit new Tri-Staters for jobs and to eliminate "weak links" in the operation. He also shot dead Anthony "Musky" Zanghi after a quarrel about how the spoils from a counterfeiting operation were to be divided.

It was the Zanghi murder that doomed Cugino. Convinced that Cugino now believed in nothing but "kill, kill, kill," several gangsters informed Philadelphia police that the gang leader hung around New York's theatrical district a great deal, especially the area of Seventh Avenue and 47th Street. Cugino was captured there just after midnight on September 8, 1935.

Questioned for 15 hours straight, Cugino laughed at police efforts to tie him to a large number of robberies as well as eight murders. Finally, he made some damaging admissions concerning the murder of a New York police detective, James J. Garvey, in 1934. Cugino never paid for any of his crimes, hanging himself in his cell later that night. With his death, the Tri-State Gang, perhaps the most devious and treacherous criminal organization ever, disintegrated.

Tylenol murders 1980s terror

The first victim in Illinois' notorious mystery deaths was seventh grader Mary Kellerman who, suffering from a lingering cold, took some medication so she could go to her suburban Chicago school. She collapsed in the bathroom and was rushed to a hospital, where she was diagnosed with cardiopulmonary collapse.

The next victim—that same day, September 29, 1982—was Adam Janus, who took a painkiller and collapsed into a coma. Adam's younger brother, Stanley, and his wife, Teresa, rushed him to a hospital, telling the attending doctor they could not account for his sudden distress. The deeply troubled coupled returned to Adam's Arlington Heights home to comfort the rest of the family. Stanley, distraught, saw a container of the painkiller Tylenol in the kitchen, took some and fell to the floor suddenly from oxygen starvation of the brain. Stanley's wife, shocked by that event, promptly seized the Tylenol for some relief. She also collapsed. Then a 27-year-old mother of four, Mary Reiner, suffering from the aftereffects of the birth of her latest baby, took some Tylenol and collapsed.

All of the victims died in their respective hospitals except for Teresa, who was in a coma on life support. While these tragic dramas were being played out, an employee at an Illinois Bell Phone Center developed a terrific headache and took some Tylenol—and promptly collapsed and died. And the next day, a United Airlines attendant bought some Extra-Strength Tylenol in a drugstore after her flight from Las Vegas. She took the tablets in her Chicago apartment. Two days later she was found dead. By this time, only Teresa Janus still clung to life.

Within a brief time medical authorities determined all the victims had taken Extra-Strength Tylenol. Bottles collected from the victims' homes all showed some of the capsules were tainted with cyanide.

There was a massive recall of the drug as authorities feared that someone at the maker of the drug, McNeil Consumer Products Co. in Pennsylvania, had tampered with massive amounts of Tylenol shipped recently. Finally it was determined only bottles in the Chicago area had been tampered with, and since the tainted bottles of Tylenol were from different stores it was obvious that someone had gone from store to store, used an eyedropper to add some cyanide to bottles and screwed the lids back on. The victims thus were random selectees in what the press reported as a deadly game of "American roulette." Psychiatrists were quoted as saying that the Tylenol killer was someone who might have a strong personal hatred for someone near him or her, or that the killer was a rather ordinary person who by the poisonings was achieving a measure of fame.

Meanwhile a massive recall was made of the Tylenol lot involved in the poisoning. Several persons near to using the medication did not because of the publicity and saved their own lives. There were a number of reports around the country of "copycat" hoaxers claiming that they too had poisoned Tylenol in their area stores. In the meantime, Teresa Janus was taken off life support and died, the seventh fatal victim.

The killings spurred efforts by the drug industry for sealed containers for many drugs so that tampering could be spotted. However, authorities made no headway in finding the Tylenol poisoner. The only arrest made was that of James Lewis, who sent an extortion letter to the drug maker, demanding $1 million to stop the killings. He was traced by police and given a long prison sentence.

Unabomber terror through the mail

The first terror bombing occurred at Northwestern University on May 25, 1978 when a cigar box packed with thousands of match heads exploded in the hands of a security officer, injuring him and a graduate student. The package sent through the mail was addressed to a professor on campus, but as it developed, he was not the specific target. It was meant simply for whoever opened the package.

The culprit became known as the "Unabomber" after his reign of terror went on for 17 years. In that time three persons would be killed and 29 others injured when innocent-looking packages were opened. The three fatalities were: Thomas Mosser, an advertising executive, killed December 1994 in North Caldwell, New Jersey; Gilbert Murray, a California Forestry Association lobbyist, killed in April 1985 in Sacramento; and Hugh Scrutton, the owner of a computer rental store, also of Sacramento, murdered in December of the same year.

Whoever was victimized by a bomber attack deserved no sympathy as far as the mysterious terrorist was concerned. A brilliant computer science professor at Yale suffered serious injuries, including loss of vision in one eye, the hearing in one ear and part of his right hand. That attack occurred in June 1993 and almost two years later the Unabomber got around to sending the victim, David Gelertner, a taunting letter.

"People with advance degrees," he wrote, "are not as smart as they think they are. If you had any brains you would have realized that there are a lot of people out there who resent bitterly the way technonerds like you are changing the world and you wouldn't have been dumb enough to open an unexpected package from an unknown source." The Unabomber went on to criticize the professor's writings. To further show his contempt for authority, the Unabomber even put a return on one of his letters as the Washington, D.C., address of the FBI.

In June 1995 the Unabomber sent a long manifesto to the *New York Times* and the *Washington Post,* having previously indicated that if it were published, his bomb attacks would cease. The newspapers complied. In his "manifesto" the Unabomber condemned what he called a corrupt technocracy, which was eradicating human freedom for the benefit of corporate and governmental elite.

The important thing was that the bombing stopped.

And even more important, the Unabomber's manifesto led to his unmasking. David Kaczynski, a social worker living with his wife in Schenectady, New York, read the manifesto and recognized much of the phrasings as being the same in letters written by his older brother, Theodore Kaczynski. And when David was packing material in his mother's home in the Chicago suburb of Lombard, Illinois, he came across many more papers written by Ted Kaczynski, with numerous phrasings almost identical to those found in the manifesto. The Kaczynski family shuddered in horror at the thought that Ted was the Unabomber. Ted was a one-time academic, social dropout and now a Montana hermit living in a crude plywood cabin in the remote regions of Stemple Pass.

Kaczynski's younger brother agonized about what to do and finally contacted a lawyer and then went to the FBI. The FBI put Ted Kaczynski under close observation for two months and finally took him into custody. Authorities even hauled away Kaczynski's shack for display at his later trial.

If capturing the Unabomber had been an enormous ordeal, it was probably just as hard to get him convicted. Kaczynski feuded with the FBI, the prosecutor, the judge, and ignored his family. He also fought with his attorneys when they wished to use an insanity defense. He declared it was well known that many of those who refuse to plead insanity are often less insane than those who do.

Kaczynski asked presiding judge Garland Burrell Jr. for the right to dismiss his lawyers. He said he would rather present his own case than listen to his lawyers question his mental health. The judge, in response, ordered the defendant to undergo mental testing to determine if he could stand trial and defend himself.

Later that same evening county prison authorities who were holding Kaczynski reported that it appeared that the prisoner had attempted to hang himself with his underwear. The effort was so poorly made that some officials felt he was merely trying to fake a suicide attempt. In any event Dr. Sally Johnson concluded that Kaczynski was competent to stand trial, and she also agreed with the defense's mental health experts that Kaczynski was a paranoid schizophrenic.

The judge then rejected the defendant's bid to represent himself. Judge Burrell accused Kaczynski of deliberately using disputes with his attorneys to disrupt and delay the trial proceedings. On January 22 the prosecutors and defense attorneys made a deal under which Kaczynski pleaded guilty to the charges filed against him. The only condition was that he be sentenced to life in prison with no possibility of parole rather than the death penalty. At the sentencing phase, Susan Mosser, the widow of victim Thomas Mosser, urged the court to "lock [Kaczynski] so far down that when he dies he will be closer to hell." In his own statement to the court Kaczynski accused federal prosecutors of distorting his motives, that he was an environmentalist crusading against technology.

Kaczynski, then 55, was sentenced to four life prison terms plus 30 years.

In one postscript to the case, David Kaczynski was ordered to pay taxes amounting to $355,000 on the $1 million federal reward he received for turning in his brother. David said he would use part of the reward money to cover the legal expenses he incurred to help his brother avoid the death penalty and give the rest to the victims of his brother's bombings. Many lawmakers of both parties objected to the requirement that taxes be paid, but said they were forced to accept the provision since it was part of an omnibus bill with crucial spending measures that had to be passed.

Unruh, Howard (1921–) serial killer

A quiet 28-year-old Bible reader who had become infatuated with guns while serving in the army, Howard Unruh killed 13 people in 12 minutes because he felt his Camden, N.J. neighbors were laughing at him behind his back.

On September 5, 1949 Unruh stepped from his home at 3202 River Road. Dressed in a tasteful brown tropical-worsted suit, white shirt and striped bow tie, he entered John Pilarchik's shoe repair shop at exactly 9:20 A.M. He approached within three feet of Pilarchik, who was hunched over nailing a heel to a shoe, pulled out a 9-mm Luger and shot him in the chest, killing him instantly.

Holding his pistol at the ready, Unruh calmly stepped back out in the morning sun, turned left and entered Clark Hoover's barber shop next door. Mrs. Edward Smith was in the barber shop with her young son and daughter. Her six-year-old boy, Orris, was sitting on a wooden hobby horse while Hoover cut his hair. Mrs. Smith, her daughter and two other boys waiting to have their hair cut hardly glanced at Unruh, thinking he was another customer. Unruh approached Hoover and said quietly, "I've got something for you, Clarkie."

Then as one would brush a branch aside, Unruh shot the little Smith boy through the head and chest. Now he could see Hoover better and killed him with shots to the head and body. Ignoring the screaming mother clutching the body of her dead son, Unruh turned and walked out to the street. When he didn't find druggist Maurice Cohen in his store, the crazed killer went upstairs to Cohen's living quarters and shot him to death. Unruh also gunned down pedestrians, motorists and three-year-old Tommy Hamilton, who was peeking out a window of his home. He shot 17-year-old Armond Harris in the right arm after slugging him with the pistol barrel. As his potential victim lay senseless, Unruh pulled the trigger again but there was only a harmless click. Although he had more ammunition in his pocket, he simply shrugged and trotted back home. The massacre, which claimed 13 lives, was over by the time police cars skidded to a stop on the street. Sixty policemen and detectives then laid siege to the Unruh home with pistol, rifle and submachine-gun fire. Unruh fired back only a few times. He was otherwise occupied.

During the siege his telephone rang. Unruh picked it up and calmly said, "Hello." At the other end of the line was Philip Buxton, assistant city editor of the *Camden Courier-Post,* who had decided to call the Unruh home after hearing about the rampage. He came up with one of the most bizarre interviews in history.

"Is this Howard?" Buxton asked. He could hear the shooting in the background.

"Yes, this is Howard. What's the last name of the party you want?"

"Unruh."

"Who are you and what do you want?"

"I'm a friend, and I want to know what they're doing to you."

Mass killer Howard Unruh after he surrendered.

Unruh's voice was steady. "Well, they haven't done anything to me yet, but I'm doing plenty to them."

"How many have you killed?"

"I don't know yet—I haven't counted them, but it looks like a pretty good score."

"Why are you killing people?"

"I don't know. I can't answer that yet, I'm too busy. A couple of friends are coming to get me."

Buxton heard the line click. He dialed the number again but there was no answer. Inside the Unruh home, tear gas cannisters were exploding. Unruh parted the curtains, raised his arms and said he was coming out. He walked out to face the muzzles of several dozen guns. "I'm no psycho," Unruh said in a formal tone. "I have a good mind."

His final score fell far short of what Unruh apparently had intended. Except for some ragged shooting by Unruh, the death toll could have been at least 30. There were a lot of people he still wanted to kill. "I'd have killed a thousand if I'd had bullets enough," he said.

Medical experts did not agree with Unruh's evaluation of his mind. Never tried for murder, he was judged incurably insane and committed to a mental institution, where he remains.

Watson, J. P. (1870–1939) bluebeard

As a one-man murder machine, J. P. Watson, America's premier Bluebeard, ranks with the world's worst. He had all the charm and verve of France's Henri Landru, the killing efficiency of Germany's Peter Kurten and the utter lack of morals of Gilles de Rais of the 15th century, who is regarded by historians as the original Bluebeard.

Watson killed more women than most of his European rivals, although the exact number is undetermined. He is known to have married at least 40 women and killed at least 25 of them. The rest got off with just losing all the money they had given to Watson in their blind passion to marry him. Several of his wives followed him from one end of the country to the other, and even after he was sent to prison for murder, they remembered him wistfully for his passionate poetry and the grace with which he had wooed them. They were lucky he had not tired of them, but many others were not so lucky. Watson bashed in about a dozen skulls and wrung an equal number of pretty necks. He hid his victims so well that none were ever found except one, whose whereabouts he eventually revealed voluntarily.

Watson was born Charles Gillam in Paris, Ark. He ran away at the age of 12 and, thereafter, always used the pseudonym of J. P. Watson, varying the first name to whatever struck his fancy. He killed his first woman in 1893, a passionate hillbilly girl who had run off with him and then announced she was pregnant. After she mentioned marriage, Watson fed her poison and took off with her possessions. After that, he never murdered another woman before marrying her. Years later, he said he felt his victims were entitled to a measure of happiness before he separated them from the living.

By 1913 Watson had married 10 women and killed four of them. Then he started getting serious about his calling. To attract victims, he advertised:

> *Gentleman: Neat appearance, courteous disposition, well-connected in business, has quite a little property, also connected with several corporations and has a substantial bank account. Would be pleased to correspond with refined young lady or widow, object matri-*

mony. This advertisement is in good faith, and all answers will be treated with respect.

Watson leafed through hundreds of responses to pick out likely victims. Between about 1915 and 1920 he confined his amorous and murderous activities to the West Coast, from Vancouver, British Columbia to southern California. He dumped wives in such scenic spots as Idaho's Lake Coeur d'Alene and Seattle's Lake Washington. Others went into fast-running rivers. Watson never understood why some murderers had their corpses refloat to the surface. When he weighted a body down, it stayed down. The same was true of the many corpses he buried. He buried them deep, no shallow graves that animals or heavy rains would uncover.

Watson's downfall came about as a result of suspicions that had nothing to do with his murderous activities. One of his wives became suspicious of his constant traveling and, thinking he was two-timing her, hired private detectives to follow him. He was caught by police with a huge amount of loot from previous victims, including at least a dozen diamond rings from different-sized fingers.

Yet, even when the authorities knew they had a master bluebeard on their hands, they could not bring murder charges against Watson. Not a single body could be found. Then while he was in custody in California, the body of a woman turned up in Plum Station, Wash. Watson had done some burying there and he worried that the corpse was one of his victims. So he made a deal with the Los Angeles district attorney to reveal the hiding place of one of his victims provided the DA guarantee him no worse than a life sentence and fight any extradition effort. Since without a body there was no case, the DA consented. The deal was made and Watson led officers out to the desert where he had buried Nina Lee Deloney.

Afterward, Watson confessed to eight other murders and hinted at many more. His confession created a firestorm throughout the country. Dozens of people wrote asking for information on missing loved ones. Watson shunted such requests aside, saying he couldn't be expected to remember every woman he had married or exactly what had become of them.

In 1920 Watson was convicted and drew a life sentence. He died in San Quentin on October 15, 1939. Ironically, his murder confession had been uncalled for; the corpse found in Plum Station proved not to be one of his.

Weeks, Robert (1929–) "romantic" serial killer

While Robert Weeks was definitely a serial killer, he cannot be said to have committed his crimes as a "recreational killer." Rather, he seemed to be a man who couldn't take "no" from a woman after he formed an attachment to her. When a woman tried to break off with him, she either ended up murdered or among the missing.

Weeks put himself through college in Mississippi by working as a mortician and a parachute stuntman. In 1954 he married his first wife, Patricia, in Minneapolis and they moved to Las Vegas the following year. Weeks proved to be a successful businessman, starting the city's first limousine service in 1960. By this time Patricia Weeks found her life a living hell, as her husband kept her a virtual prisoner in his home. Extremely jealous, he would not even allow her to do grocery shopping alone. When Patricia took up the piano, Weeks beat her elderly piano teacher in a jealous rage. In 1968 Patricia insisted on a divorce, and Weeks finally granted her wish. Patricia got the family Cadillac and home as part of the settlement. Shortly thereafter, her car was found abandoned in a local shopping center. Weeks informed his daughters their mother had simply abandoned them.

A few years later Weeks married again, but that marriage ended in divorce in 1974. This wife didn't die for that offense since it was Weeks who had developed a relationship with another woman, Cynthia Jabour. That relationship continued for six years. By late 1980 Cynthia had had enough of Weeks' behavior and wanted out. The couple went on a dinner date, October 5, and Cynthia broke the news to Weeks that they were finished. What Weeks said to her at the time is not known, and Cynthia would never be able to tell. The next day her car was found in a Las Vegas parking lot. Weeks was suspected of murder and at first agreed to take a polygraph test, but instead he vanished, surfacing finally in Chile.

He reappeared in the United States in Houston with a Libyan passport under the name of Robert Smith. He then moved on to San Diego, starting a construction business. While on a business trip to Colorado, he met a 43-year-old divorcée named Carol Riley and convinced her to move to Southern California with him. That relationship came to a mysterious end in April 1986 after the pair had a dinner date. It was known to Carol's friends that she was contemplating breaking off with "Smith" and was going to tell him so. As usual the jilting female's car turned up abandoned in a hotel parking lot.

By the end of the year, "Smith" had become "Charles Stolzenberg," living in Tucson, Arizona. When Weeks-Smith-Stolzenberg was featured on NBC's "Unsolved Mysteries" in May 1987, he was spotted by a number of Tucson viewers.

In April 1988 authorities had sufficient evidence to charge Weeks with the murders of Patricia Weeks and Cynthia Jabour. The case involving Carol Riley was not completed and neither were those involving others with whom it was suspected Weeks had formed short-lived relationships. It is possible those females had survived their apparent encounters with Weeks and chosen not to step forward for fear of unwanted publicity. Or of course there could have been another possible explanation. Few cases of serial murder ever uncover all of their victims. In any event, Weeks was convicted of the two murders he was officially charged with, the jury setting his penalty at life imprisonment without parole.

Weiss, Hymie (1898–1926) gang leader

The man who succeeded the assassinated Dion O'Banion as head of Chicago's North Side Gang during Prohibition, Hymie Weiss continued O'Banion's gang war with the forces of Al Capone. Chicago police credited Weiss with being the one responsible for building O'Banion's bootlegging business into the empire it became. He was more thoughtful, forward-looking and resourceful than the headstrong O'Banion and used reason and bribery more freely than "Deanie" had. Despite the fact that he, like many gangsters, especially members of the North Side mob, regularly attended Mass and was never without crucifixes and rosaries in his pockets, he had a brutal and ugly disposition. He also carried a gun or two and killed without qualm or pity.

Weiss' real name was Earl Wajciechowski, which was soon changed upon his family's arrival in the United States from Poland. He was an accomplished crook in his teens, doing duty as a burglar, car thief, hired slugger and killer for labor unions and as a safecracker. The last skill won him a spot in the O'Banion gang, which specialized in jewel thefts and other safecracking jobs. The Irish gang leader toasted Little Hymie as the "best soup artist in Chicago." With the onset of Prohibition, O'Banion moved into bootlegging, and Weiss acted as his right-hand man in convincing saloon keepers of the value of O'Banion's merchandise.

Weiss wept openly at O'Banion's grave when the latter was buried in November 1924, following his murder by Capone's gunmen. Although Capone boldly appeared at the services with six bodyguards, Weiss kept the O'Banions in line, having promised the Irishman's widow there would be no violence until their beloved Deanie was underground. Besides, there were 100 detectives on hand to maintain the peace. A reporter asked Weiss if he blamed Capone for O'Banion's death. The gangster threw up his hands in mock horror and said: "Blame Capone. Why Al's a real pal. He was Dion's best friend, too."

Weiss maintained the fiction of peace with Capone for almost two months, even banishing Two Gun Alterie from the gang because he kept publicly threatening Capone with vengeance. Meanwhile, Weiss lined up more gunners and bided his time. On January 12, 1925 Weiss, Schemer Drucci and Bugs Moran followed Capone's black limousine until it parked in front of a restaurant at State and Fifty-fifth streets. As they drove slowly by, they raked the vehicle with 26 pistol and shotgun blasts, wounding the chauffeur but missing two bodyguards in the backseat. Capone had stepped into the restaurant 15 seconds earlier.

Weiss' most famous attempt to kill Capone occurred in Cicero on September 20, 1926, when 11 automobiles filled with his gangsters drove past the Hawthorne Inn and poured more than 1,000 bullets and slugs from shotguns, handguns and machine guns into the establishment. A Capone bodyguard and an innocent woman bystander were shot, but Capone again escaped injury.

Three weeks later, on October 11, 1926, Weiss himself was on an undertaker's slab, his wiry body having been ripped open by 10 machine-gun bullets as he crossed the street to his headquarters above O'Banion's flower shop at 738 North State Street. His bodyguard, Paddy Murphy, was killed instantly by the same fusillade, which came from a second-floor room rented by the assassins the day after the Cicero raid. Three others walking with Weiss were wounded.

Weiss was 28 at the time of his death and had a fortune conservatively estimated at $1.3 million. His funeral was lavish, although his wife complained he had only 18 truckloads of flowers while O'Banion had been honored with 26 and a previously departed gangster, Nails Morton, had merited 20. It had to be explained to her that since the onset of the war with Capone, some 30 of Hymie's friends had abruptly departed the world, greatly reducing the number of available flower donors.

See also: ALPHONSE "SCARFACE AL" CAPONE, VINCENT "SCHEMER" DRUCCI, CHARLES DION "DEANIE" O'BANION.

Whitman, Charles (1942–1966) mass murderer

On August 1, 1966, an enthusiastic Charles Whitman, user of guns, concluded 24 hours

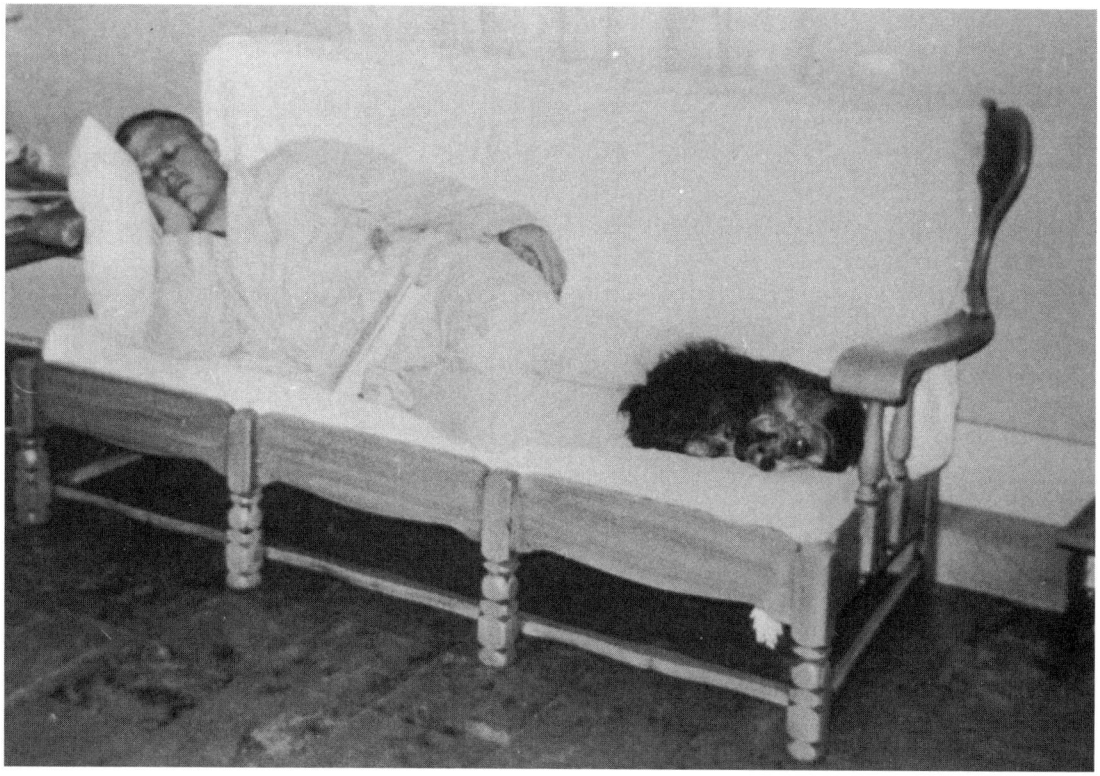

A photo found in a camera belonging to tower murderer Charles Whitman shows him asleep on a couch with his pet dog at his feet. It was believed that his wife took the shot just a few days before his murderous spree.

of killing by turning the University of Texas campus into a shooting gallery from his vantage atop a 307-foot observation tower, murdering a total of 18 people and wounding 30 others in a 96-minute rampage.

Whitman, a crewcut 24-year-old ex-Marine who maintained a near straight-A average at the school, was later described by his psychiatrist as an all-American boy. On July 31 Whitman typed a note declaring: "I am prepared to die. After my death, I wish an autopsy on me to be performed to see if there is any mental disorder." Then he stabbed his mother with a butcher knife and shot her in the back of the head. A few hours later, after feeding the dog, he picked up his wife from her job at the telephone company and brought her home. Sometime during the night he killed her with three knife wounds in the chest.

On August 1 Whitman hauled a footlocker containing a rifle, a shotgun, a revolver, two pistols and 700 rounds of ammunition to the observation tower, killing a woman at the information desk and then two tourists who happened to come along. Now, he prepared to shoot down at the students swarming over the campus during lunch hour. First, though, he set out his other supplies: sandwiches, Spam, fruit cocktail,

Planter's peanuts, water containers, a transistor radio, a roll of toilet paper and a plastic bottle of Mennen spray deodorant.

Then he started shooting. His aim was phenomenal; at a typical distance of about 300 yards, he hit his target on at least one in every three shots. In one case he shot a pregnant student right through her stomach shattering the skull of her unborn baby. Almost 50 persons were hit by Whitman's shots and their bodies lay strewn over the grassy campus. Police efforts to dislodge him failed, as did an attack from a low-flying plane. Finally, officers led by Austin patrolman, Ramiro Martinez, charged up the barricaded stairway and shot Whitman to pieces. Officer Martinez was wounded in the shooting.

Later, an autopsy showed that Whitman had a tumor in the hypothalamus region of the brain, but doctors doubted the condition had caused his violent behavior. Sen. Ralph Yarborough said the man's actions were the result of TV violence, and Gov. John Connally demanded stiffer penalties for insane criminals.

Wilcoxson, Bobby Randell "One-Eye"

(1929–) bank robber and murderer

An efficient and brutal bank robber, One-Eye Wilcoxson was known as the John Dillinger of the 1960s. While both men planned their robberies meticulously, Dillinger carried his off with a certain lightheartedness, but Wilcoxson was deadly serious. Wilcoxson killed cold-bloodedly; whereas it must be said that Dillinger killed only when he felt his own life was in imminent danger. While casing the Kings Highway branch of the Lafayette National Bank in Brooklyn, New York City, Wilcoxson made it a point to talk with the bank guard while he was eating in a diner across the street from the institution. He jokingly asked the guard, 52-year-old Henry Kraus, what he would do "if I walked in to hold up the bank." The guard smiled and said he would shoot him. One-Eye reported to his confederates that the guard should be a danger because he was a "Wyatt Earp type."

Two weeks later, on December 15, 1961, Wilcoxson and a partner, Peter Curry, walked into the bank. Wilcoxson spotted guard Kraus sitting in a chair, stepped up to him and pulled out a revolver. "Well, here I am with a gun," he said and shot the guard in the chest. When Kraus tried to rise, Wilcoxson shot him three more times, killing him. One-Eye then announced it was a stickup, and he and Curry seized more than $32,000. As they were leaving the bank for a getaway car driven by Albert Nussbaum, a police officer, Salvatore Accardi, appeared on the scene and opened fire. The policeman missed, but One-Eye didn't. His first shot hit the officer in the leg and his second penetrated Acardi's badge and sent him hurtling through the bank's outer glass door to the sidewalk. Later, Wilcoxson said he would have continued firing at the policeman except that he thought the cop was dead. Miraculously, the bullet that hit Accardi in the chest had become embedded in the officer's overcoat, and although stunned, he was not seriously hurt.

Born in Duke, Okla., the son of itinerant farmworkers, Wilcoxson had been in trouble most of his life. He lost his right eye sometime during his boyhood but never talked about it. From the age of 10 he worked the California lettuce fields and by 1953 he had become a "boss" fruit picker. At this point in his life Wilcoxson had a wife and daughter and was frequently in trouble with the law for such offenses as wife beating and car theft. He wound up in Chillicothe Prison in Ohio on an auto theft conviction. In prison he met Curry and Nussbaum, and the three teamed up when they were released in 1959. On December 5, 1960 Wilcoxson and Nussbaum held up a bank in Buffalo and followed that up with another robbery in the same city the following month. It is not known how many bank robberies Wilcoxson pulled. He eventually pleaded guilty to the felony-murder of Kraus and seven bank robberies, in which the total loot taken was $205,873.

Wilcoxson's downfall came when Curry surrendered to police after the murder of Kraus, saying he hadn't counted on any killings when he agreed to take part in the bank robbery. Curry identified Nussbaum and Wilcoxson as his confederates. FBI agents captured Nussbaum in Buffalo on November 5, 1962 and learned that Wilcoxson was traveling with a 19-year-old woman and her baby. The agents traced them to Baltimore, where they were living in a rented house directly across the street from one FBI agent and half a block away from another. A week later, Wilcoxson was captured as he was carrying the baby to a station wagon. Suddenly, 30 agents moved in on him and three tackled him, pulling the baby away. Wilcoxson was quickly subdued, unable to draw the gun tucked in his belt.

Wilcoxson and Curry were sentenced to life imprisonment and Nussbaum got 20 years.

Wood, Isaac (?–1858) mass poisoner

The largest all-in-the-family poisoning plot in American history was perpetrated by Isaac Wood at Dansville, N.Y. in the 1850s.

The first to die was Isaac's brother David, who owned a huge estate in the area. David Wood was struck down unexpectedly by a strange malady in May 1855. Before the year was out, his wife Rhoda and his three children had died of the same strange sickness. Isaac Wood had slowly poisoned all five so that he could gain control of the estate; he accomplished that goal by acting as administrator. Isaac then took his wife and child to live in New Jersey, where he murdered them as well. Now a rich man, he moved on to a new life in Illinois.

Before leaving for Illinois allegedly to bear his grief alone, Wood had leased his brother's home to a tenant named Welch. Shortly after the murderer departed, Welch found three packs of arsenic in the barn. The arsenic had been wrapped in legal papers that assigned Isaac Wood full authority over the estate after the death of his brother and his family. That link and the fact that all of Isaac Wood's relatives had died under similar circumstances were sufficient evidence to doom him. Wood was brought back to New York, tried and hanged on July 9, 1858 at Geneseo.

World Trade Center bombing

It came with abrupt suddenness. Shortly before noon on Friday, February 26, 1993, one Mohammad Salameh, a Palestinian living in New York, drove a yellow van into the underground garage of the 110-story World Trade Center in lower Manhattan. At the time, and in fact on any weekday, the twin towers were teeming with 50,000 workers and the usual 80,000 visitors.

Then someone put a lighter to four fuses on a 1,200-pound bomb. The occupant or occupants fled in the yellow van. A scant few

Among those netted in the investigation of the 1993 World Trade Center bombing was Sheik Omar Abdel Rahman, a blind Egyptian cleric known as a fiery fanatic, who was convicted on conspiracy counts for encouraging his followers to engage in violent acts against the United States.

moments later the powerful bomb exploded. Six persons were killed and well over 1,000 injured, as steel beams snapped like toothpicks and cinder blocks disintegrated. Employees in various offices were hurled 10, 20 or 30 feet in the air. Automobiles in the parking level were squashed like tin cans. Much of New York was in a panic, and at first there was no way to estimate the related death and destruction. What was clear was that the bombing was the worst terrorist attack carried out on American soil up to that time.

In hindsight it became apparent that the terrorist attack was neither wholly effective nor for that matter well planned, even though it had been a half-year in the making. The mastermind of the attack was Ramzi Ahmed Yousef, who had entered the country in September 1992 through JFK airport claiming political asylum. He was allowed to enter with Mohammad Salameh, who was providing him with a place to stay in his home.

Immediately the pair went about setting up their plans for the attack, and, it would later be revealed, for many more. Money was sent to them from Europe, and Salameh, under a false name, rented a storage locker in New Jersey and used that address to order various bomb parts. The final step almost six months later was acquisition of compressed hydrogen to add power to explosives. Then the conspirators rented a Ryder van. All was ready for the disaster that took place.

One aspect of the disaster not addressed in its wake was the limited amount of deaths resulting. But if there was a touch of amateurism in the bombing, it was unmatched by the later actions of the bombers. Salameh was most concerned about returning the van to recoup his $200 deposit, a remarkably venal attitude, considering that they were engaged in what was regarded by them a holy enterprise. The conspirators were unaware that the yellow van had attracted attention before the explosion and in its aftermath.

Salameh was taken into custody when he tried to return the Ryder van. The plotters proved unable to contain information about their actions, and soon the New York police received information that led to the apprehension of five suspects who were found with what was called a "witch's brew" of explosives that were intended to be placed under bridges, in tunnels and at New York landmarks, such as the United Nations. It was said other sites around the nation were also targeted.

While Yousef was clearly the mastermind of the World Trade operation, evidence provided by FBI informers revealed the broader nature of the plotters' plans. A number of arrests and trials were held for various offenses. Four involved with the World Trade matter were each sentenced to serve 240 years in prison. Yousef, who was captured in Pakistan, was also sentenced for a deadly bombing of a Philippine Airlines airplane in 1994. He intended his attacks as a test run for blowing up dozens of airliners in the United States. He was later sentenced to life imprisonment plus 240 years. Before his sentence, Yousef ranted, "I am a terrorist and I am proud of it." He told the judge, "Your God is not Allah. You worship death and destruction."

The main trial against a total of 10 accused terrorists was done under a Civil War–era seditious conspiracy law that makes it illegal to wage war against the government. Among those charged was Sheik Omar Abdel Rahman, a blind Egyptian cleric known as a fiery fanatic. Much of the government's case was built on tapes secretly recorded by an undercover FBI informant, Emad Salem. The Rahman defense was built around the claim that he was physically incapable of participating in any of the operational aspects of the plot. However, the courts held the conspiracy counts against the blind cleric were valid and, as a review panel put it in 1999, "evidence showed that Rahman was in constant contact with other members of the conspiracy, that he was looked to as a leader, and that he accepted that role and encouraged his co-conspirators to engage in violent acts against the United States."

The blind cleric and nine others were convicted after a nine-month trial that involved more than 200 witnesses. Among the defendants, all sentenced to life imprisonment, was El Sayyid A. Nosair, accused of the murder of Rabbi Meir Kahane, the militant founder of the Jewish Defense League. He had previously been acquitted of the murder charge by a state court.

Sheik Rahman's conviction was appealed on the grounds that anything he did was no more than an expression of free speech and violated his rights under the Constitution to his freedom of religion. The U.S. Court of Appeals for the Second Circuit ruled, however, that "freedom of speech and of religion do not extend so far as to bar prosecution of one who uses a public speech or a religious ministry to commit crimes. The evidence justifying Rahman's conviction showed beyond a reasonable doubt that he crossed this line."

One example cited by the court was Rahman's conviction for soliciting the murder of Egyptian president Hosni Mubarak on a planned visit to New York, an attack that never was attempted. The evidence showed that the cleric told Emad Salem, the paid FBI informant who had infiltrated the conspiracy, that he "should make up with God" by "turning his rifle's barrel to President Mubarak's chest and killing him."

All the convictions were upheld.

Yellow Henry Gang New Orleans criminals

One of the most vicious gangs in New Orleans during the 1870s and 1880s was a group of murderers, thieves and cutthroats bossed by Yellow Henry Stewart.

Stewart earned his nickname because he was afflicted with malaria, which he was convinced, rightly, would shorten his life span. As a result, he was unbridled in his lawless fury. He would as soon kill a victim as manhandle him, and he was equally feared by other criminals and by the police.

In 1877 Yellow Henry inherited the leadership of the gang that took his name when the former leader, Turpo, went to jail for murder. The new leader brought to his banner some of the most desperate criminals that New Orleans ever produced, including Joe Martin, probably the most expert garroter in the city's history; Crooked Neck Delaney, certainly a top-class performer in the same line as Martin; Tom McDonald, better known as Tom the Dog; Prussian Charley Mader, who wore a false beard and a mask whenever pulling a job; George Sylvester; Garibaldi Bolden; the murderous Haley brothers, Red and Blue; Pat Keeley; and the notorious Frank Lyons, who won fame as a police killer.

Yellow Henry attracted these supporters because of his ability to plan successful capers for the gang, including burglaries, holdups and protection rackets. Finally, Yellow Henry and three of his men were caught and sent to the penitentiary in 1884 for the robbery of a Julia Street sail maker. The brutal gang leader died there of malaria in July 1886.

Frank Lyons, in prison at the time, escaped in 1888 and proceeded to reorganize the Yellow Henry gang. He was apprehended again and returned to prison. In an act incomprehensible but typical of Louisiana in that era, Lyons won a pardon in 1890 from Gov. Francis T. Nicholls. The Yellow Henry gang arose once more, this time until 1892, when Lyons was sentenced to prison for killing a policeman, an act that brought down the full wrath of the police on the Yellow Henrys, breaking them up permanently.

Zelig, Jack (1882–1912) gang leader and murderer

Big Jack Zelig assumed the leadership of the New York criminal empire that had been held first by Monk Eastman and then by Kid Twist. A handsome, brutish killer, Big Jack's services were always available for hire to any bidder, high or low. There is no record of the gang leader ever turning down any job of violence. A Zelig henchman once gave the police Big Jack's price list:

Slash on cheek with knife	$ 1 to $ 10
Shot in leg	$ 1 to $ 25
Shot in arm	$ 5 to $ 25
Throwing a bomb	$ 5 to $ 50
Murder	$10 to $100

If the fee for murder seemed a bit low, it must be remembered that such contracts normally included "fringe benefits," i.e., whatever valuables were found on the victim. Judiciously, Zelig would wait until a businessman, e.g., was making a deposit at the bank before killing him. A common workman would get his on payday. In one case Zelig held off on the murder of a victim until he ventured abroad to do his Christmas shopping.

Zelig, whose real name was William Alberts, was born in Norfolk Street in 1882 to respectable Jewish parents. He ran away at 14 and joined a juvenile gang of pickpockets under the leadership of the colorful Crazy Butch. Zelig soon figured out that the boy pickpockets did all the dangerous work but Crazy Butch took virtually all the loot. He deserted the Fagin and became very successful on his own as a "lush worker," rolling drunken men on the Bowery and in Chatham Square. With his childish face and appearance, he was seldom suspected of pickpocketing. And when his youthful appearance was not enough, Zelig could turn on the tears. One man from whom Zelig had stolen a wallet and a diamond ring was so overcome with remorse at having accused him that he bought the baby-faced thief a new suit of clothes and "forced" money on him.

By the time he was in his twenties, Zelig had moved on to muggings and murder for profit, but he never forgot the virtue of tears.

Whenever he was arraigned—a frequent occurrence—he hired a frail and consumptive girl to come timidly into the courtroom and weepingly plead with the magistrate, "Oh, Judge, for God's sake, don't send my boy husband, the father of my baby, to jail!" The agony in the young "wife's" voice worked wonders for a number of years: Zelig would be released with a warning to go home to his wife and baby, of whom he had neither.

In the early 1900s Zelig attracted the attention of Monk Eastman and soon became one of his most dependable henchmen. When Eastman went to prison a few years later, Zelig remained loyal to Kid Twist, Eastman's successor, carrying out a number of murder assignments. After Kid Twist died in a gangland assassination in 1908, Zelig took over control of a large part of the old Eastman gang, while others left to follow the banner of Chick Tricker or Jack Sirocco. Most of the gangsters went with Zelig because he was a genius at organizing criminal activities and getting the most revenues out of them.

At heart, Zelig remained a bully and a brute. Seeking to impress a new sweetheart although short of cash, he marched into an East Side bordello with her and held up the madam for $80. The madam had the effrontery to complain to the police, and Zelig was arrested. Because of previous arrests, Big Jack faced a long prison term; so he sent word to Tricker and Sirocco to return the money to the madam and frighten her into refusing to testify. The pair deliberately did not carry out his orders, hoping Zelig would be sent away and they would inherit his crime empire. Big Jack finally got another gang leader, Jimmy Kelly, to carry his message to the madam, and when the case came up in court, the woman insisted Zelig looked not a bit like the man who had robbed her. Big Jack was released and vowed war on Tricker and Sirocco.

In the ensuing battles at least a score of gunmen on both sides died. In an awesome display of shooting, Zelig shot and killed a hired gunman, Julie Morrell, sent after him by his foes. Zelig's friends got Morrell drunk and he staggered out onto the dance floor of the Stuyvesant Casino shouting: "Where's that big Yid Zelig? I gotta cook that big Yid!"

Suddenly, Zelig spoke sharply from a table across the dance floor and the dancers scattered. Just then the lights went out and a single shot was fired. When the lights went on, Morrell lay dead on the floor and Zelig was gone. He had shot Morrell through the heart in the dark.

By this time Zelig was offering protection to many of the top gambling clubs in Manhattan. Finally, he was hired by police Lt. Charles E. Becker for a very special job, that of assassinating a gambler named Herman "Beansie" Rosenthal. Becker and Rosenthal had been partners, but when Becker had failed to protect Rosenthal in the way he wished, Rosenthal decided to blow the whistle on the payoffs delivered by the gambling interests of the city to the political and police powers. Zelig collected $2,000 for murdering Rosenthal. In a division of the spoils that was generous for Big Jack, he passed on $1,000 to four of his killers—Gyp the Blood, Whitey Lewis, Dago Frank and Lefty Louie—who did the actual work. After the killings, they appeared to have gotten away clean, since the investigation of the matter was in the hands of Lt. Becker himself. However, a reform district attorney named Charles Whitman launched his own investigation and easily found witnesses who identified the four murderers.

Gyp the Blood soon confessed. He said he had been hired by Big Jack Zelig and named Becker as the man behind the entire operation.

Zelig also broke the underworld code of silence, testifying before the grand jury on Becker's links to the crime. On October 5, 1912, the day before he was to appear in court, Zelig was gunned down on a Manhattan trolley car by Red Phil Davidson. The police department was sure the murder of Zelig was related to his feud with the Sirocco and Tricker forces. Everyone else in New York felt it had something to do with his forthcoming testimony against Becker. As it turned out, even without Zelig's testimony, there was more than enough evidence to convict the four gunmen and Becker as well. All eventually died in the electric chair.

See also: CHARLES E. BECKER, GYP THE BLOOD.

Ziegler, Shotgun George (1897–1934)

gangster

Perhaps the best educated and certainly one of the smartest of the 1930 gangsters, shotgun George Ziegler (whose real name was Fred Goetz) was for a time the mastermind of the Barker-Karpis gang and was a chief planner in the kidnapping of wealthy Edward George Bremer of St. Paul, Minn. in 1934. He was also for a time one of Al Capone's most-trusted trigger men, remaining a prime suspect in the famous St. Valentine's Day Massacre of the Bugs Moran gang.

During World War I, Ziegler had been a second lieutenant and pilot. In 1922 he graduated from the University of Illinois, where he had been a football player and an excellent golfer. Famed FBI agent Melvin H. Purvis said of him, "His character was one of infinite contradictions; well mannered, always polite, he was capable of generous kindnesses and conscienceless cruelty." It may well be that Ziegler became a criminal almost accidentally after being arrested on a rape charge. He jumped bail before his trial and, not wishing his parents to lose the money, decided to get it back quickly. He attempted to hold up a doctor he knew always carried large sums of money. When the physician drew a gun he had permission to carry, Goetz blasted him to death with a shotgun, launching his career as Shotgun George Ziegler.

When next heard of he was a gunman with the Capone mob in Chicago. Besides the St. Valentine's Day killings, Ziegler was credited with six to 10 other mob murders. From time to time he disappeared from the crime scene. During those periods he actually worked as an engineer; he had studied engineering in college. But he regularly departed from the straight life to win fame as one of the best artisans at "cracking a bank" while a member of the Midwest's Keating-Holden gang.

In 1933 Ziegler turned up in the Barker-Karpis mob, where his intelligence soon propelled him into a position of leadership. He picked Bremer as a likely kidnap victim, a caper that netted the gang a $200,000, ransom. Most of the money was turned over to Ziegler, who stashed it in a garage belonging to his wife's uncle, where it was to be left to "cool." That proved to be a fatal error on the Barkers' part. While they trusted Ziegler totally, he was slowly losing his mind. He began to talk wildly in underworld circles, loudly proclaiming credit for the Bremer job. The Barkers realized Ziegler had to be silenced, and on March 22, 1934, just two months after the Bremer kidnapping, four shotguns blasted Ziegler as he stepped out of his favorite cafe in Cicero, Ill. Ziegler fell dead, most of his head blown away. With Ziegler gone, only his widow knew where the ransom money was hidden. Ma Barker was able to cajole the grieving but trusting widow into turning over the money, insisting Ziegler had undoubtedly been killed by enemies from his Capone days. What couldn't be undone was the information the FBI had gained from Ziegler's corpse. On his body were membership cards to the Chicago Yacht Club and the Mohawk Country Club of Bensenville, Ill. Police then found his address and the names and addresses of many members of the Barker-Karpis mob. The Barkers were forced to scatter, all soon to fall victim to the law. Ma Barker and son Fred were killed in a famous shoot-out in Florida the following year.

See also: BARKER BROTHERS.

Zodiac Killer California serial killer

Starting in California in 1966 and extending over the next several years, a weird mass murderer, who became known as Zodiac because of the letters and cryptograms he sent to newspapers, killed a number of victims, mostly young girls, because, he said, he was "collecting slaves for my afterlife." There is considerable dispute over the number of persons Zodiac killed, since he did not claim credit for some murders he definitely committed and the police failed to find the bodies of many he claimed to have killed.

The first murders he acknowledged were those of two high school teenagers, who were parked on a lonely road outside Vallejo, Calif. on December 20, 1968. Carrying a .22-caliber pistol, a lone figure moved to the car and aimed it at the head of 17-year-old David Faraday. Three bullets smashed into Faraday's skull before he could react. Sitting next to the driver, 16-year-old Bettilou Jensen screamed and then bolted from the car. She didn't get far. The attacker dropped her with five bullets. Both youngsters died. The following July 4 Zodiac struck again, killing a young girl sitting in a parked car in a public park near Vallejo. Her 19-year-old companion survived despite four bullet wounds. The killer had shined a flashlight into their car, temporarily blinding the youth, so that he could give only a sketchy identification of the attacker: a fairly heavy man with glasses.

In one of Zodiac's more gruesome killings, he stabbed Cecelia Shepard in the back 24 times, cutting the outline of a bloody cross. The best description of Zodiac was obtained when he killed a part-time college student working as a cab driver in San Francisco. He had shot him from the backseat and set about cleaning up the taxi, presumably to eradicate his fingerprints. Then he cut off a piece of the victim's bloody shirt—to enclose in a future letter to a newspaper—before leaving. Zodiac was seen by witnesses, and with their aid the police put out a composite description of him: a man of 35 to 45, five foot eight inches with short brown-reddish hair and wearing thick glasses.

Zodiac's letters to the police and to the newspapers continued throughout the early 1970s, although some were believed to be fakes. The San Francisco police attributed no more than six murders to Zodiac, although his own count eventually reached 37. A possible confirmation of Zodiac's total came in 1975 from Don Striepeke, sheriff of Sonoma County. Striepeke used a computer study of murder records in the state attorney general's office as the basis for a theory that about 40 murders in four western states could be traced to one killer, perhaps Zodiac. The officer found in these murders what he regarded as threads of similarity, and he even theorized that the murderer was using a huge letter "Z" mapped over several western states as a blueprint for where to commit his crimes. Since the mid-1970s nothing more has been heard from Zodiac, the most common police theory being that he is either dead or confined in some mental institution.

PHOTO CREDITS

(Numbers refer to page.)

Wide World 40, 73, 81, 104, 139, 154, 166, 170, 184, 189

New York Daily News 6, 13, 59, 74, 152

Library of Congress 37, 195

National Archives 16, 20, 45, 54, 83, 85, 210, 215

Corbis/Bettmann-UPI 48

Corbis/Reuters 113

Author's collection 5, 9, 27, 64, 68, 79, 93, 95, 117, 191, 218

BIBLIOGRAPHY

Hundreds of sources were utilized for this work. What follows is a bibliography of selected sources. Many works consulted in reference to individual entries are mentioned in the text or in "Further Reading" sections that follow those items.

Adams, Ramon F. *Burs Under the Saddle*. Norman: University of Oklahoma Press, 1964.

Adler, Polly. *A House Is Not a Home*. New York: Popular Library, 1954.

Allen, Frederick Lewis. *Only Yesterday, An Informal History of the Nineteen Twenties*. New York: Harper & Bros., 1931.

———. *Since Yesterday*. New York: Harper & Bros., 1940.

Asbury, Herbert. *The Gangs of New York*. New York: Alfred A. Knopf, Inc., 1927.

———. *The Barbary Coast, An Informal History of the San Francisco Underworld*. Garden City, N.Y.: Garden City Publishing Company, Inc., 1933.

———. *Sucker's Progress*. New York: Dodd, Mead and Company, Inc., 1938.

———. *Gem of the Prairie*. New York: Alfred A. Knopf, Inc., 1940.

———. *The French Quarter, An Informal History of the New Orleans Underworld*. New York: Alfred A. Knopf, Inc., 1940.

———. *The Great Illusion: An Informal History of Prohibition*. New York: Doubleday & Co., 1950.

Berger, Meyer. *The Eighty Million*. New York: Simon & Schuster, 1942.

Block, Eugene B. *The Wizard of Berkeley*. New York: Coward-McCann, 1958.

———. *Great Train Robberies of the West*. New York: Coward-McCann, 1959.

———. *Great Stagecoach Robbers in the West*. New York: Doubleday & Co., Inc. 1962.

———. *Fifteen Clues*. Garden City, N.Y.: Doubleday & Co., Inc., 1968.

Bolitho, William. *Murder for Profit*. New York: Harper & Bros., 1926.

Bonanno, Joseph. *A Man of Honor, The Autobiography of Joseph Bonanno*. New York: Simon & Schuster, 1983.

Boswell, Charles, and Lewis Thompson. *The Girls in Nightmare House*. New York: Gold Medal, 1955.

———. *Practitioners of Murder*. New York: Collier, 1962.

Brynes, Thomas. *Professional Criminals in America*. New York: Chelsea House, 1969.

Burns, Walter Noble. *The One-Way Ride*. Garden City, N.Y.: Doubleday, Doran & Company, 1931.

Caesar, Gene. *Incredible Detective: The Biography of William J. Burns*. Englewood Clifs, N.J.: Prentice-Hall, 1968.

Chandler, David. *Brothers in Blood: The Rise of the Criminal Brotherhoods*. New York: Dutton, 1975.

Churchill, Allen. *A Pictorial History of American Crime.* New York: Holt, Rinehart & Winston, 1964.

Coates, Robert M. *The Outlaw Years: The History of the Land Pirates of the Natchez Trace.* New York: The Literary Guild of America, 1930.

Collins, Ted, ed. *New York Murders.* New York: Sloan & Pearce, 1944.

Crouse, Russell. *Murder Won't Out.* New York: Pennant Books, 1953.

Croy, Homer. *He Hanged Them High.* New York: Duell, Sloan & Pearce, 1952.

DeFord, Miriam Allen. *Murders Sane & Mad.* New York: Abelard-Schuman, Ltd., 1965.

Demaris, Ovid. *Captive City.* New York: Lyle Stuart, Inc., 1969.

DeVol, George. *Forty Years a Gambler on the Mississippi.* New York: H. Holt & Company, 1926.

Drago, Harry Sinclair. *Outlaws on Horseback.* New York: Dodd, Mead & Company, 1964.

Eisenberg, Dennis; Uri Dan; and Eli Landau. *Meyer Lansky, Mogul of the Mob.* New York & London: Paddington Press Ltd., 1979.

Elman, Robert. *Fired in Anger.* Garden City, N.Y.: Doubleday & Company, Inc., 1968.

Emrich, Duncan. *It's an Old Wild West Custom.* New York: The Vanguard Press, Inc., 1949.

Emery, Edward Van. *Sins of New York.* New York: Frederick A. Stokes, 1930.

———. *Sins of America as "Exposed" by the Police Gazette.* New York, Fredrick A. Stokes Co., 1931.

Frank, Judge Jerome, and Barbara Frank. *Not Guilty.* Garden City, N.Y., Doubleday & Company, Inc., 1957.

Godwin, John. *Alcatraz 1868–1963.* New York: Doubleday & Co., 1963.

———. *Murder USA.* New York: Ballantine Books 1978.

Gosch, Martin A., and Richard Hammer. *The Last Testament of Lucky Luciano.* Boston: Little, Brown, 1975.

Hammer, Richard. *Playboy's Illustrated History of Organized Crime.* Chicago: Playboy Press, 1975.

Hecht, Ben. *A Child of the Century.* New York: Simon & Schuster, 1954.

———. *Charlie, The Improbable Life and Times of Charles MacArthur.* New York: Harper & Bros., 1957.

Horan, James D. *Desperate Men.* New York: G. P. Putnam Sons, 1949.

———. *Pictorial History of the Wild West.* New York: Crown Publishers, Inc. 1954.

———. *The Desperate Years.* New York: Crown Publishers, Inc., 1962.

———. *The Pinkertons, The Detective Dynasty That Made History.* New York: Crown Publishers, Inc. 1967.

Hynd, Alan. *Murder, Mayhem and Mystery.* New York: A. S. Barnes & Co., 1958.

Jackson, Joseph Henry. *San Francisco Murders.* New York: Duell, Sloan and Pearce, 1947.

Johnston, James A. *Alcatraz Island Prison.* New York: Charles Scribner's Sons, 1949.

Karpis, Alvin, with Bill Trent. *The Alvin Karpis Story.* New York: Coward McCann & Geoghegan, Inc., 1971.

Katcher, Leo. *The Big Bankroll, The Life and Times of Arnold Rothstein.* New York: Harper & Bros., 1959.

Katz, Leonard. *Uncle Frank: The Biography of Frank Costello.* New York: Drake, 1973.

Kefauver, Estes. *Crime in America.* New York: Doubleday & Co., 1951.

Kilgallen, Dorothy. *Murder One.* New York: Random House, 1967.

Klein, Alexander, ed. *Grand Deception.* New York: J. B. Lippincott & Company, 1955.

———. *The Double Dealers.* Philadelphia and New York: J. B. Lippincott & Company, 1958.

Kobler, John. *Capone.* New York: G. P. Putnam's Sons, 1971.

Kohn, George C. *Encyclopedia of American Scandal.* New York: Facts On File, 1989.

Lawes, Warden Lewis Edward. *Twenty Thousand Years in Sing Sing.* New York: R. Long & R. R. Smith, Inc., 1932.

Lewis, Alfred Henry. *The Apaches of New York.* New York: G. W. Dillingham Company, 1912.

———. *Nation-Famous New York Murders.* G. W. Dillingham Company, 1914.

McLoughlin, Denis. *Wild and Wooly.* Garden City, N.Y.: Doubleday & Company, Inc., 1975.

Maas, Peter. *The Valachi Papers.* New York: G. P. Putnam's Sons, 1968.

Messick, Hank. *Lansky.* New York: G. P. Putnam's Sons, 1971.

Morrel, Ed. *The Twenty-fifth Man.* Montclair, N.J.: New Era Publishing Co., 1924.

Murray, George. *The Legacy of Al Capone.* New York: G. P. Putnam's Sons, 1975.

Ness, Eliot, with Oscar Fraley. *The Untouchables.* New York: Julian Messner, 1957.
Newton, Michael. *Hunting Humans.* New York: Avon Books, 1992.
Pearson, Edmund L. *Studies in Murder.* New York: MacMillan Company, 1926.
———. *More Studies in Murder.* New York: Harrison Smith & Robert Haas, Pub., 1936.
Peterson, Virgil. *Barbarians in Our Midst.* Boston: Little, Brown & Co., 1936.
———. *The Mob.* Ottawa, Ill.: Green Hill Publishers, Inc., 1983.
Radin, Edward D. *12 Against the Law.* New York: Bantam Books, 1952.
———. *12 Against Crime.* New York: Collier Books, 1961.
Reid, Ed. *Mafia.* New York: Random House, 1952.
———. *The Grim Reapers.* Chicago: Henry Regnery Co., 1969.
Reid, Ed, and Ovid Demaris. *The Green Felt Jungle.* New York: Trident Press, 1963.
Rodell, Marie F. *New York Murders.* New York: Duell, Sloan and Pearce, 1944.
Salerno, Ralph, and John Tompkins. *The Crime Confederation.* New York: Doubleday & Co., 1969.
Sann, Paul. *The Lawless Decade.* New York: Crown Publishers, Inc., 1957.
Scott, Gini Graham. *Homicide: 100 Years of Murder in America.* Lincolnwood, Ill.: Roxbury Park, 1998.
Smith, Alton. *Syndicate City.* Chicago: Henry Regnery Co., 1954.
Sondern, Frederic, Jr. *Brotherhood of Evil: The Mafia.* New York: Farrar, Straus & Cudahy, 1959.
Stone, Irving. *Clarence Darrow for the Defense.* New York: Doubleday & Co., 1941.
Tallant, Robert. *Ready to Hang.* New York: Harper & Bros., 1952.
Teresa, Vincent, with Thomas C. Renner. *My Life in the Mafia.* Garden City, N. Y.: Doubleday & Company, 1973.
Teresa, Vincent. *Teresa's Mafia.* Garden City, New York: Doubleday & Company, Inc., 1975.
Toland, John. *The Dillinger Days.* New York: Random House, 1963.
Touhy, Roger, with Ray Brennan. *The Stolen Years.* Cleveland: Pennington Press, Inc., 1959.
Turkus, Burton B., and Sid Feder. *Murder, Inc.: The Story of the Syndicate.* Farrar, Straus & Young Co., 1951.
Turner, Wallace. *Gambler's Money.* Boston: Houghton Mifflin Co., 1965.
Wendt, Lloyd, and Herman Kogen. *Lords of the Levee.* New York: Bobbs-Merrill, 1943.
Wilson, Frank J., and Beth Day. *Special Agent.* New York: Holt, Rinehart & Winston, 1965.
Whitehead, Don. *The F.B.I. Story.* New York: Random House, 1956.
Wolf, Marvin J., and Katherine Mader. *L.A. Crime.* New York: Facts On File, 1986.
Wooldridge, Clifton R. *Hands Up! In the World of Crime or Twelve Years a Detective.* Chicago: Police Publishing Co., 1901.

Index

Boldface page numbers indicate main headings.

A

Abbandando, Frank "the Dasher" **3**, 162, 183, 184
Abrams, Big Mike **4**
Abriel, Pedro 31–32
Accardi, Salvatore 216
Accardo, Anthony Joseph **4–6**
Adonis, Joe **6–7**
Aiello, Andrew 7, 52
Aiello, Antonio 7, 52
Aiello, Dominick 7, 52
Aiello, Joseph **7**, 52–53
Aiuppa, Joe 6
Alberts, William. *See* Zelig, Jack
Alcatraz Penitentiary
  Barker, Doc at 30
  Capone, Al at 55
  Thompson, Buddy at 202–203
Alderisio, Felix "Milwaukee Phil" **7**
Alfred P. Murrah Federal Building 172
Allen, Bill **7–8**
Allen, Kathleen 145
Allison, Clay **8–10**
Allman, John "Bad" **10–11**, 173–174
Alterie, Louis "Two Gun" **11–12**, 170, 214
Amatuna, Samuzzo "Samoots" viii–ix, **12–13**, 107
Amberg, Joe 13–14, 15
Amberg, Louis "Pretty" viii, **13–15**
American 170
American Mining Co. 76
American Revolution 72
Amurao, Corazon 197
Anastasia, Albert **15–18**
  Adonis, Joe and 6
  Gotti, John and 113
  Lepke, Louis and 46
  Masseria, Giuseppe and 159
  Murder, Inc. and 161, 162
  murder of 13, 105, 108, 109
  Reles, Abe and 183, 185
Anastasia, Tough Tony 15
Anderson, Dutch 61–62, 63
Anderson, Jesse 80
Annenberg, Maxie 170
Annenberg, Moe 170
Anselmi, Albert **18–20**, 55, 107, 108, 150, 172
Anti-Coolie Clubs 66
Anton, Theodore "the Greek" 92
Apache Kid **20–21**, 68
Apalachin Conference 109
Arizona State Prison 188
Army, Confederate 8, 25
Army, U.S. 10, 25
Arthur, Chester A. 65
artichoke racket 74–75
Asbury, Herbert 95
asphyxiation victims 22–24
Atascadero State Hospital 142
Atlanta Centennial Park bombing **21–22**
Atlanta children **22–24**
Atlanta Penitentiary
  Capone, Al at 55
  Chapman, Gerald at 62
  Cohen, Mickey at 71
  Coppola, Trigger Mike at 75
  Costello, Frank at 109
  Genovese, Vito at 109
Atlantic Monthly viii, 203
Auburn Prison 61
Aynesworth, Hugh 146

B

Baker, Cullen M. **25**
Ball, Joe vii, **26**
Bananas, Joe 104, 105
bank robbers
  Anderson, Dutch 62
  Barker-Karpis gang 27–30
  Chapman, Gerald 62
  Clark, Russell 86
  Crowley, Francis "Two Gun" 77
  Curry, Peter 216–217
  Dietrich, Walter 86
  Dillinger, John 84–91
  Drucci, Schemer 91–92
  Five Points gang 52
  Hamilton, John 86, 89
  Hedgepeth, Marion 134
  Makley, Far Charley 86
  Meter, Homer Van 86, 89
  Nelson, Baby Face 165–168
  Pierpont, Harry 86, 89
  Sutton, Willie 17
  Wilcoxson, One-Eye 216–217
Banner, Virginia 77
Barelli, Vincent 71–72
Barker, Arizona Clark "Kate" or "Ma" **26–28**, 29, 30, 224
Barker, Arthur or "Doc" or "Dock" 27–28, **29–30**, 165
Barker, Fred 27, 28, **29**, **30**, 224
Barker, George 27, 29, 30
Barker, Herman 27, **29**, **30**, 165
Barker, Lloyd 27, **29**, 30
Barker-Karpis gang 27–30, 43, 223–224
Barnes, Leroy "Nicky" 105
barrel murders **30–31**
Barrie, Wendy 191
Barrow, Blanche 40, 41
Barrow, Buck 40, 41
Barrow, Clyde **39–42**, 43, 165
Bartlett, Marion 199
Bartlett, Velda 199
Barton, James R. 102
Barton, William 99
Bass, Sam 51
Batista, Fulgencio 17
Battaglia, Sam "Teets" **31**
Baum, W. Carter 89, 167
Bayonne, Vincent 31–32
Bayonne-Abriel gang **31–32**
Bean, Roy 65
Beck, Martha viii, **32–33**
Beck, Rosemarie Ann 186
Becker, Charles E. **33–34**, 120, 222, 223
Beeber, Fred 173
Beecher, Henry Ward 65
Belasco, David 195
Belcastro, Jimmmy 4
Bell, Shannon 175
Belleville State Hospital 125
Bender family viii, **34–36**
Beni, Jules 193
Berger, Meyer 188
Berman, Otto "Abbadabba" 188, 190
Bianchi, Kenneth **130–131**
Big Greenie 191

Big Harpe **124–125**, 157, 158
Billington, John **36**
Billy the Kid 77, 134
Bilotti, Tommy 58, 60
Bioff, Willie 52
Biograph Theater 90
Bittaker, Lawrence Sigmund 186
Black, Bob **141–142**
Blackbeard **36–38**
Black Hand gang 56, 107, 147–148
Blonde Alibi 150
Bloody Mama. *See* Barker, Arizona Clark "Kate" or "Ma"
Bluebeard viii, 203, 211
Bolber, Morris **38–39**
Bolden, Garibaldi 220
bombers
  Giancana, Sam 110
  Graham, John Gilbert 115–116
  Gyp the Blood 120
  Madden, Owney 152–154
  McVeigh, Timothy 172–173
  Unabomber 207–209
bombings
  abortion clinic 22
  airplanes 115–116, 219
  Atlanta Centennial Park 21–22
  gay and lesbian bar 22
  Hawthorne, Alice 21
  Uzanyol, Melih 21
  World Trade Center 217–219
Bonnie. *See* Parker, Bonnie
bootleggers
  Adonis, Joe 6, 159
  Alterie, Louis "Two Gun" 11–12
  Amberg, Louis "Pretty" 14
  Ball, Joe 26
  Capone, Al 54
  Coll, Peter 71, 72
  Coll, Vince 71–72
  Diamond, Legs 82–83
  Drucci, Schemer 91–92
  Eastman, Monk 97
  Gordon, Waxey 84
  Lansky, Meyer 159, 190
  Luciano, Lucky 159
  Madden, Owney 152–154
  Masseria, Giuseppe "Joe the Boss" 158–160
  O'Banion, Dion 11, 169–172
  Schultz, Dutch 14, 15, 71, 188–190
  Siegel, Bugsy 159, 190–192
  Terrible Gennas 12, 18
  Torrio, Johnny 54, 171
  Weiss, Hymie 213–214
Boston Strangler **81–82**
Botkin, Cordelia **42–43**
bounty hunter 10–11
Bowen, John "Chick" 160
Bowman, Mace 9
Bowman, Margaret 49, 50
Boyd, Isadore 32
Boyd, Percy 41
Brady, Al 43
Brady gang **43**
Branch Davidians 172, 173
Brandeis, Louis 173
Bremer, Edward George 28, 30, 223
Bridewell Prison 170
Bridgeport, Shirley 111
Brief Against Death (Smith) 194
Briggen, Joseph **44**
Broadway Mob 6
Brock, Leonard 51
Brock, Will 51
Brooklyn Eagle 15, 185
Brooks, David 75, 76
Brown, Frances 127–128
Bruns, Richard 187–188
Buccieri, Fiore "Fifi" **44–45**
Buccieri, Frank 45
Buchalter, Louis "Lepke" 15–16, **45–47**. *See also* Lepke, Louis
Buckley, William F., Jr. 194
Budd, Grace 100
Bug and Meyer gang 190
Bundy, Carol Mary 69–70, 131
Bundy, Ted **47–51**, 69, 70, 118
Bunty Kate 148, 149
Buono, Angelo **130–131**
burglars. *See also* gangsters; robbers; thieves
  Abriel, Pedro 31–32
  Bayonne, Vincent 31–32
  Gallo, Crazy Joe 105–106
  Giancana, Sam 110
  Harvey, Donald 126
  Lake, Leonard 143–145
  Ng, Charles Chitat 143–145
Burrell, Garland, Jr. 208
Burrow, Jim 51
Burrow, Rube **51**
Burton, Elijah 128
Bush, George H. W. 22
Buxton, Philip 209

C

Calhoun, Clay 10, 173, 174
Camden Courier-Post 209
Campagna, Louis "Little New York" **52–53**
Campbell, Caryn 49
Campione, Frank 57
cannibals
  Dahmer, Jeffrey 79–80
  Fish, Albert viii, 100–101
  Gecht, Robin 186
  Helm, Boone 128–129
  Packer, Alfred viii, 175–176
  ripper gangs 186
Cantellops, Nelson 109
Capezio, Tough Tony 4
capital punishment. *See* death penalty
Capone, Alphonse "Scarface Al" **53–55**
  Accardo, Anthony Joseph and 4, 5
  Aiello brothers and 7, 52
  Alterie, Louis "Two Gun" and 11
  Amatuna, Samoots and 12, 13
  Anselmi, Albert and 19
  Campagna, Louis "Little New York" and 52, 53
  Capone, Frank and 56
  Drucci, Schemer and 92
  in Five Points gang 95
  Genna brothers and 107, 108
  Giancana, Sam and 110
  Luciano, Lucky and 53
  Maranzano, Salvatore and 155, 157
  McGurn, Machine Gun Jack and 150, 151
  Nelson, Baby Face and 166
  O'Banion, Dion and 11, 92, 171, 172
  Scalise, John and 19
  Weiss, Hymie and 11, 19, 92, 171, 172, 213, 214
  Ziegler, Shotgun George and 223, 224
Capone, Frank **55–56**
Capone, Louis 47, 162, 180, 184
Carbo, Frankie 191
Cardinella, Salvatore "Sam" **56–57**
Carnera, Primo 153
Carpenter, Richard **57–58**
Carroll, Mike 145
Carroll, Tommy 89, 167
Carson, Kit, III 98
Cash, Leland S. 198
Cassidy, Butch 135
Cassidy, Red 83
Castellammarese War 72, 156
Castellano, Paul **58–61**, 114, 115, 117
Castro, Fidel 6, 110
Catena, Jerry 105
Cater, Nathaniel 23
Cavalry Killer 173–174
Cejnar, Jack 89
Central Park Casino 14
Chandler, Cynthia 69
Chapman, Gerald **61–63**
Chapman, Grace F. 62
Charley, Long 137
Chase, John Paul 167–168
Cherokee Bill **63–64**
Chessman, Caryl 130
Chicago Tribune 56, 170
Chillicothe Prison 217
Chinese riots **64–68**
Choir Boy 57
Christgen, Eric 127
Christie, Ned **68–69**
Churchill, James 127
CIA (Central Intelligence Agency) 6, 45, 110
Ciano, Count 108
Cincinnati V.A. Medical Center 126
Civil Conservation Corps (CCC) 89
Civil War 9, 77, 91, 141–142, 192
Clark, Douglas Daniel **69–70**, 131
Clark, Ed 21
Clark, George Rogers 157

Clark, Russell 86, 87, 88, 89, 167
Cleveland, Grover 20
Cline, Alfred L. vii, **70**
Clinton, Bill 22
Clyde. *See* Barrow, Clyde
coal racket 153
Cohen, Maurice 209
Cohen, Mickey **70–71**
coin machine racket 179
Colbert, Chunk 8, 9
Colby, William 110
Coll, Peter 71
Coll, Vincent (Vince) "Mad Dog" **71–72,** 157, 189
Collins, Ellen 138
Collins, Morgan 169
Collison, Merle 199
Colombo, Joe, Sr. 105
Colonel Plug **72–73**
Colorado Volunteers 97
Colosimo, Big Jim 54, 56
Columbia Correctional Center 80
Colvert, Robert 199
Compton, Veronica Lynn 131
Connally, John 216
Connecticut State Prison 201
Cook, Bill 63
Cook, Jim 63
Cook, William "Billy" **73–74**
Cooper, Gary 191
Coppola, Ann 75
Coppola, Michael "Trigger Mike" **74–75**
Corll, Dean vii, **75–76**
Corona, Juan vii, **76**
Cortina, Juan 192
Cosa Nostra. *See* Mafia; Murder, Inc.
Cosner, Paul 145
Costello, Frank 60
  Adonis, Joe and 6
  Anastasia, Albert and 16, 17
  Coll, Vincent and 71
  Gallo, Crazy Joe and 105
  Gambino, Carlo and 18
  Genovese, Vito and 108, 109–110
  Lansky, Meyer and 190
  Lepke, Louis and 46
  Luciano, Lucky and 156
  Madden, Owney and 153
  Maranzano, Salvatore and 157
  Masseria, Giuseppe and 159
  Murder, Inc. and 162
  Reles, Abe and 185
  Schultz, Dutch and 190
  Siegel, Bugsy and 190
counterfeiters
  Cugino, Anthony 205
  Lupo the Wolf 158
  Zanghi, Anthony "Musky" 205
Courtright, Longhair Jim **76–77**
Cowley, Sam 90, 167
Coy, Bernie 202–203
Coy, Jacob 101
Coy, Wayne 86
Crane, Stephen 33
Cretzer, Dutch 203
Crowley, Francis "Two Gun" **77–78**
Crown Point Jail 89
Cugino, Anthony 204, 205
cult leader 154–155
Cumpanis, Ana 90
Curry, Peter 216, 217
Cusick, William 56

D

Dahmer, Jeffrey vii, **79–80**
Dalhover, James 43
Dalitz, Moe 161
Dallas Times-Herald 146
Dalton gang 27
Daniels, Murl **80–81**
Dannemora Prison 46
Davidson, Red Phil 223
Davis, Dixie 189
Davis, Floyd 173
Davis, Sammy, Jr. 23
Davis, Sarah Eliza 35
Davis, Volney 29
Davy, Gloria Jean 197
Deane, Mrs. Joshua 43
death penalty. *See also* electrocution; execution; hanging
  Bundy, Ted 118
  Clark, Douglas 70
  Gilmore, Gary Mark 110–111
  Gohl, Billy 113
  Judd, Winnie Ruth 139
  Kokoraleis, Andrew 186
  Manson, Charles family 155
  McVeigh, Timothy 173
  Ng, Charles Chitat 145
  Panzram, Carl 176
  Supreme Court on 63, 110, 111, 155, 173, 188, 197
Degnan, Suzanne 128
Delaney, Crooked Neck 220
Dellacroce, Aniello 59, 113–114
Deloney, Nina Lee 212
Democratic Party
  Capone, Frank and 55–56
  murder victims in viii
  O'Banion, Dion in 169
  Packer, Alfred and 175, 176
Demon in the Belfry **93–94**
De Mora, James. *See* McGurn, Machine Gun Jack
Department of Justice, U.S. 22
Depression
  Crowley, Francis "Two Gun" during 78
  Dillinger, John during 84, 86
  McGurn, Machine Gun Jack during 151
  murder ring during 38
  Pittsburgh Phil during 178
DeSalvo, Albert H. **81–82**
Dever, William E. 11
Devil's Island. *See* Alcatraz Penitentiary
Dewey, Robert 74
Dewey, Thomas E. 45, 46, 47, 162, 189–190
Diamond, Alice 82
Diamond, Jack "Legs" 14, 71, 72, **82–84,** 189
Díaz, Porfirio 101
Dick, Leroy 35
Diehl, Billy 21
Dietrich, Walter 86
diFrasso, Dorothy 191
Dillinger, John Herbert 40, **84–91,** 204
  FBI and 43
  Nelson, Baby Face and 165, 166–167
  Purvis, Melvin and 30
  Wilcoxson, One-Eye and 216
Dirty Dozen 85
Doherty, Jim 12
Dolak, Frank 15
Dolan, Dandy, Johnny **91**
Doto, Joseph. *See* Adonis, Joe
Dowling, Tom 10
Downer, George 35
Downing, Delphine 32
Doyle, Chief 8
Doyle, John 192
Doyle, Little Patsy 153
Dragna, Jack 70
Driscoll, Danny **91**
Drucci, Vincent "Schemer" 11, 12, **91–92,** 170, 172, 214
Dubs, Deborah 144–145
Dubs, Harvey 144–145
Duchess of Death 197–199
Dull, Judy 111
Dundee, Vince 10
Dunlop, Arthur 28
Dunning, John Presley 42
Dunning, Mary 42–43
Durant, Will 195
Duringer, Rudolph 77
Durrant, William Henry Theodore **93–94**

E

Eastman, Monk **95–97,** 120, 221, 222
Eden, Charles 37, 38
electrocution
  of Abbandando, Frank "the Dasher" 3, 162
  of Beck, Martha 32
  of Becker, Charles E. 34, 223
  of Bundy, Ted 50–51
  of Capone, Louis 47, 162, 180
  of Carpenter, Richard 58
  of Crowley, Francis "Two Gun" 78
  of Daniels, Murl 80–81
  of Fernandez, Raymond Martez 32
  of Fish, Albert 100–101
  of Frank, Dago 223
  of Gacy, John Wayne 103
  of Goldstein, Buggsy 180
  of Gray, Judd 196
  of Gyp the Blood 120, 223
  of Hahn, Anna 121–122
  of Hamilton, Ray 41
  of Legenza, Walter 205
  of Lepke, Louis 45–47, 162, 180
  of Lewis, Whitey 223

of Louie, Lefty 223
of Maione, Happy 162
of Mais, Robert 205
of Makley, Far Charley 89
of Pierpont, Harry 89, 91
of Pittsburgh Phil 162, 180
of Snyder, Ruth 194, 196
of Starkweather, Charles 200
of Weiss, Mendy 47, 162, 180
Encyclopedia of American Crime viii
Entratta, Charles 83
Epps, Billy 10
Espinosa, Felipe **97–98**
Espinosa, Julián **97–98**
Espinosa, Victorio **97–98**
Examiner 94
execution. *See also* death penalty; electrocution; hanging
of Big Harpe 124, 158
of Cardinella, Sam 57
of Cook, William "Billy" 74
of Dalhover, James 43
of Gilmore, Gary Mark 110–111
of Glatman, Harvey Murray 112
of Graham, John Gilbert 116
of Hawkins, Gordon 198
of Petrillo, Herman 39
of Petrillo, Paul 39
of Rees, Melvin David 182
of Shockley, Sam 203
of Simone, Michael 198
of Spinelli, Duchess 198–199
of Thompson, Buddy 203
Executioner's Song (Mailer) 111
extortionists
Battaglia, Sam "Teets" 31
Campagna, Louis "Little New York" 52–53
Genna brothers 107
Lepke, Louis 45–47, 178
Lewis, James 206
Lupo the Wolf 147–148, 158
Madden, Owney 152–154
Masseria, Giuseppe "Joe the Boss" 158–160

F

Fagin, Crazy Butch 221
Faraday, David 224
Farrar, Andrew 193
Farrington, Hilary **99**
Farrington, Levi **99–100**
Farris, Suzanne Bridget 197
Favato, Carino 39
Fay, Janet 32
Fay, Joey 84
FBI (Federal Bureau of Investigation)
on Aiuppa, Joe 6
on Atlanta children 23
on Barker, Doc 30
on Barker, Fred 30
on Barker, Ma 27, 28, 30
on Brady gang 43
on Bundy, Ted 50
on Castellano, Paul 60
Cook, William "Billy" and 74
Dillinger, John and 89, 90, 167, 168
Gambino, Carlo and 114, 118
on Gotti, John 115
on Graham, John Gilbert 116
Green, Eddie and 90
on Jewell, Richard 22
on Karpis, Alvin "Creepy" 43
Nelson, Baby Face and 89, 90, 167–168
Nussbaum, Albert and 217
on Smith, Edgar Herbert 194
Unabomber and 207, 208
Wilcoxson, One-Eye and 217
on World Trade Center bombing 218, 219
on Ziegler, Shotgun George 223, 224
Feinstein, Puggy 179–180, 184
Ferguson, Miriam "Ma" 41
Fernandez, Raymond Martinez 32
Fischetti, Charles 56
Fish, Albert viii, **100–101**
Fisher, John King **101–102**
Five Points gang 52, 53, 91, 95, 96, 196
Flamingo 192
Flegenheimer, Arthur. *See* Schultz, Dutch
Fleury, Laurent 138
Flores, Juan **102**
Floyd, Pretty Boy 39–40, 43, 165
Fluger. *See* Colonel Plug
Folger, Abigail 154
Folsom Prison 70
Fontes, Andrés 102
Ford, Bob 27
Ford, John 10
forgers
Cline, Alfred L. 70
Holmes, H. H. 132–134
Manson, Charles 155
Forrest, Earle F. 21
Forsyth, Red 4
Fort Leavenworth Prison 176. *See also* Leavenworth Penitentiary
42 gang 31
Foster, Belle 25
Foster, Joe 101
Frank, Dago 33, 120, 222
Franse, Steve 108
Frazier, D. M. 66
Frechette, Evelyn "Billie" 87, 88, 89
Freeman, William 127
French, Mary 187, 188
Fritz, Gretchen 187–188
Fritz, Wendy 187–188
Frykowski, Voyteck 154
Fugate, Caril Ann 199

G

Gable, Clark 191
Gacy, John Wayne **103**, 126
Gagliano, Tom 159
Galante, Carmine **103–105**, 108
Gallagher, Jack 129
Gallo, Crazy Joe **105–106**
Galluccio, Frank 53, 54
Gambino, Carlo
Castellano, Paul and 58–59, 117
Gallo, Crazy Joe and 105
Genovese, Vito and 17, 18, 109
Gotti, John and 113, 114, 115, 116, 117–118
Gravano, Sammy "the Bull" and 117
Masseria, Giuseppe and 159
gamblers, gambling
Adonis, Joe 7
Alterie, Louis "Two Gun" 11–12
Anastasia, Albert 109
Battaglia, Sam "Teets" 31
Becker, Charles E. 222
Capone, Al 54
Cohen, Mickey 70–71
Coppola, Trigger Mike 74–75
Courtright, Longhair Jim 77
in Cuba 110
Eastman, Monk 95–97
Feinstein, Puggy 184
Lansky, Meyer 17, 190
Murder, Inc. and 161
O'Banion, 11
Rosenthal, Herman 33, 222
Schultz, Dutch 188–190
Siegel, Bugsy 190–192
Spanish, Johnny 196–197
Zelig, Jack 222
gangs
Barker-Karpis 27–30, 43, 223–224
Bayonne-Abriel 31–32
Black Hand 107, 147–148
Brady 43
Bug and Meyer 190
Burrow 51
Dalton 27
Dirty Dozen 85
Fagin 221
Five Points 52, 53, 95, 196
42ers 45
Genna 150, 151
Gophers 152
Hudson Dusters 153
Innocents 129, 141
James Street 53
Lenox Avenuers 120
Live Oak 137
North Side 91–92, 213
O'Banion 11, 12, 19, 151

Plummer 193
Purple gang 179
ripper 185–186
Terrible Gennas 107–108
Tri-State 204–205
Whyos 91, 95, 148
Yellow Henry 220
gangsters. *See also* mob leaders; murderers; robbers
Adonis, Joe 6
Aiello, Joseph 7
Alterie, Louis "Two Gun" 11–12
Amatuna, Samoots 12–13
Amberg, Louis "Pretty" 13–15
Anselmi, Albert 18–20
Barelli, Vincent 71–72
Barrow, Clyde 39–42
Battaglia, Sam "Teets" 31
Bioff, Willie 52
Bolden, Garibaldi 220
Brady, Al 43
Buccieri, Fiore "Fifi" 44–45
Campagna, Louis "Little New York" 52–53
Cassidy, Red 83
Cohen, Mickey 70–71
Coll, Vince 71–72
Coppola, Trigger Mike 74–75
Cretzer, Dutch 203
Cugino, Anthony 204, 205
Dalhover, James 43
Davis, Volney 29
Delaney, Crooked Neck 220
Diamond, Legs 82–84
Dillinger, John 84–91
Dolan, Dandy Johnny 91
Eastman, Monk 95–97, 221, 222
Frank, Dago 120, 222
Goldstein, Abe "Bummy" 12
Gyp the Blood 120, 222, 223
Haley, Blue 220
Haley, Red 220
Harris, William J. 29
Hawkins, Gordon 198
Holden, Tommy 28
Horn, Johnny 205
Ives, Albert 198
Jackson, Humpty 96
Karpis, Alvin "Creepy" 28, 29
Keating, Francis 28
Keeley, Pat 220
Kelly, Jimmy 222
Kelly, Paul 95
Kid Dropper 196–197
Kid Twist 221, 222
Legenza, Walter 204, 205
Lewis, Whitey 120
Louie, Lefty 120, 222
Lucchese, Tommy 46
Lyons, Danny 91
Lyons, Frank 220
Madden, Owney 152–154
Mader, Charley 220
Mais, Robert 204, 205
Martin, Joe 220
McCarthy, Johnny 91
McDonald, Tom 220
Miller, John 137, 138
Morton, Nails 11, 170, 214
Nash, Frank 28
Nelson, Baby Face 165–168
O'Banion, Dion 169–172
Parker, Bonnie viii, 39–42, 43, 165
Peifer, Jack 30
Profaci, Joe 17, 18
Reiser, Charles "the Ox" 182–183
Sawyer, Harry 30
Scalise, John 18–20
Serpa, Salvatore 204, 205
Shaffer, Clarence 43
Sherrard, Robert 198
Simone, Michael 198
Sirocco, Jack 222, 223
Spanish, Johnny 196–197
Spencer, Al 28
Stewart, Yellow Henry 220
Stompanato, Johnny 71
Sylvester, George 220
Terrill, Ray 28
Thayer, Earl 28
Torrio, Johnny 53, 54
Tricker, Chick 222, 223
Turpo 220
Van Meter, Homer 85
Wallace, Eddie "Cowboy" 204
Weaver, Bill 29
Weiss, Hymie 213–214
Zanghi, Anthony "Musky" 205
Zelig, Jack 33, 221–223
Ziegler, Shotgun George 223–224
Zion, Eddie 12
Zukorsky, John 204–205
Gargullo, Merlita 197
garment industry 45–46, 47
Garrity, Breezy 91
Garvey, James J. 205
Gavin, Michael 56
Gecht, Robin 185, 186
Gein, Edward **106–107**
Gein, Henry 106
Gelertner, David 207
Genna brothers 12, 18, 19, **107–108,** 150, 151. *See also* Terrible Gennas
Genovese, Vito **108–110**
Adonis, Joe and 6
Anastasia, Albert and 17
Castellano, Paul and 114
Coll, Vince and 71
Coppola, Trigger Mike and 74
Galante, Carmine and 103–104
Gambino, Carlo and 18
Maranzano, Salvatore and 157
Masseria, Giuseppe and 159
Tieri, Funzi and 59–60
Gentle Maggie 148, 149
Gentry, Doc 102
Geronimo 134
Getting Out (Smith) 194
Giancana, Sam "Momo" 4, 5–6, 44, 45, **110**
Gillam, Charles. *See* Watson, J. P.
Gillis, Lester J. *See* Nelson, George "Baby Face"
Gilmore, Gary Mark **110–111**
Giscobbe, Anthony 38–39
Giscobbe, Anthony, Mrs. 38–39
Glatman, Harvey Murray vii, **111–112**
Goebbels, Joseph 191
Goering, Hermann 191
Goetz, Fred. *See* Ziegler, Shotgun George
Gohl, Billy vii, **112–113**
Goldsby, Clarence 63
Goldsby, Crawford. *See* Cherokee Bill
Goldstein, Abe "Bummy" 12, 13
Goldstein, Buggsy 14, 162, 180, 183, 184
Gophers 152
Gordon, Waxey 84, 153
Gotthardt, Minnie Mae 26
Gotti, John 59, 60–61, **113–115,** 116–118
Gotti, John, Jr. 115
Graham, John Gilbert vii, **115–116**
Grant, Cary 191
Grasso, Arthur 17
Gravano, Sammy "the Bull" 115, **116–118**
Gray, Judd 195–196
Green, Eddie 89, 90, 167
Greenberg, Harry 191
Greenberg, Lou 170
Green River Killer **118**
Greentree, Ethel 205
Griffith, Almira 35
Griffith, D. W. 195
Groat, Dave 10
Gsellman, George 121
Guardian Angels 144
Guinta, Joseph "Hop Toad" 19, 55, 150
gunfighters
Allison, Clay 8–10
Bowman, Mace 9
Colbert, Chunk 8–10
Fisher, John King 101–102
Hardin, John Wesley 123–124
Gunness, Belle viii, **118–119**
Gunness, Peter 119
Gurino, Vito "Chicken Head" 162, 183
Gusenberg, Frank 170
Guzik, Jake 4
Gyp the Blood 33, **120,** 222, 223

H

Hahn, Anna viii, **121–122**
Hahn, Philip 121
Haley, Blue 220
Haley, Red 220
Half Moon Hotel 184–185
Hamer, Frank 42
Hamilton, John 86, 89

Hamilton, Polly 90
Hamilton, Ray 41, 42
Hamilton, Tommy 209
Hamm, William A., Jr. 28, 30
Hance, Ben 63
"handshake hit" 18–19
Hangar, Charles 173
hanging
of Abriel, Pedro 32
of Bayonne, Vincent 32
of Chapman, Gerald 63
of Cherokee Bill 63–64
of Chinese 66–67
of Dolan, Dandy Johnny 91
of Driscoll, Danny 91
of Durrant, William Henry Theodore 94
of Espinosa, Victorio 97
of Farrington, Levi 100
of Flores, Juan 102
of Gallagher, Jack 129
of Helm, Boone 129
of Hoch, Johann 132
of Holmes, H. H. 134
of Horn, Tom 136, 160
of Keene, John 142
of Lane, George 129
of Little Harpe 125
of Longley, William P. 124
of Lyons, Danny 91, 148
of Mays, Sam 125
of Nelson, Earle Leonard 165
of Panzram, Carl 176
of Piper, Thomas W. 177
of Slade, Jack 194
of Tong, Gene 66
Hanging Judge 63–64, 68
Hansen, Robert vii, viii, **122–123**
Hardin, John Wesley **123–124**
Hardsdoff, William 192
Hargrave Secret Service 88
Harker 35, 36
Harlow, Jean 191
Harold, Margaret 181, 182
Harpe, Micajah **124–125**. *See also* Big Harpe
Harpe, Wiley **124–125**. *See also* Little Harpe
Harris, Armond 209
Harris, Jack 101
Harris (Mansfield Reformatory guard) 81
Harrison, Lester **125**
Harrison, William J. 29
Harvey, Donald **126**
Hatcher, Charles **127**
Hawkins, Gordon 198
Hawthorne, Alice 21
Hawthorne Inn 214
Hawthorne Smoke Shop 92
Healy, Dan 92
Hearst, Patricia 71
Hearst, William Randolph 94, 170
Hedgepeth, Marion 134
Hedlin, Dave 56
Heirens, William **127–128**
Heiss, George 121–122
Hell Benders **34–36**
Hell's Kitchen
Coll, Vince in 71
Madden, Owney in 153
Helm, Boone **128–129**
Henley, Elmer Wayne 75, 76
Henshaw, William 153
Hickok, Wild Bill 123
Hicks, Jeffrey Joe **129–130**
Hill, Edwin B. 21
Hill, Virginia 192
Hillman, Sidney 47
"Hillside Stranglers" vii, **130–131**
Hines, Jimmy 153, 189
Hip Sing Tong 4
Hirsch, Frederick 77
hit men. *See also* Mafia; Murder, Inc.; murderers
Alderisio, Felix "Milwaukee Phil" 7
Buccieri, Fiore "Fifi" 44–45
Capone, Louis 47
Entratta, Charles 83
Frank, Dago 33
Galante, Carmine 108
Giancana, Sam 110
Gyp the Blood 33
Louie, Lefty 33
McGurn, Machine Gun Jack 150–151
Pittsburgh Phil viii, 177–180
Strauss, Pittsburgh Phil 47
Viana, Nicholas 57
Weiss, Mendy 47
Whitey Lewis 33
Yale, Frankie 54
Hoch, Johann **131–132**
Hoeweler, Carl 126
Hogan, Mary 106
Holden, Tommy 28
Holinsky, Benny 15
Holley, Lillian 88
Hollis, Herman E. 167
Holmes, Bill 21
Holmes, H. H. **132–134**, 163
Hoover, Clark 209
Hoover, Herbert 54, 176
Hoover, J. Edgar
on Barker-Karpis gang 27, 28, 29, 30
Dillinger, John and 90
Lepke, Louis and 45, 46–47
Mafia and 156–157
on Nelson, Baby Face 168
Senate on 43
Horn, Johnny 205
Horn, Tom **134–136**, 160
Horner, Freda 153
Horrowitz, Harry. *See* Gyp the Blood
Hotsy Totsy Club 83
Houston, Sequoyah 63
Howard, Thomas 196
How to Be a Detective 89
Hudgens, Raymond 188
Hudson Dusters 153
Hunt, Sam "Golf Bag" 4
Hunter, Dick 173
Hurlbut, Dennis 201

I

Il Diavolo **56–57**
Illinois Bell Phone Center 206
Immigration Bureau 90
Indiana State Police 86
Indiana State Reformatory 86
Innocents 129, 141
Inside Detective 129
Internal Revenue Service 71
International News Service 89
Irvine, William 135
Ives, Albert 198

J

Jabour, Cynthia 213
Jackson, Carroll 181
Jackson, Humpty 96
Jackson, Mary Jane "Bricktop" viii, **137–138**
Jackson, Maynard 23
Jackson, Mrs. Carroll 181, 182
Jackson, William "Action" 5, 44
Jack the Ripper viii, 203
James, Frank 27, 99
James, Jesse 27, 51, 84, 99
James Street gang 53
Janus, Adam 205
Janus, Stanley 205–206
Janus, Teresa 205, 206
Jarecki, Edmund K. 56
Jegado, Helen 200
Jensen, Bettilou 224
Jewell, Richard 21–22
Jewish Defense League 219
Johnson, Charles 36–37
Johnson, Jerome A. 105
Johnson, Sally 208
Joliet Prison 147
Jones, William Daniel 41
Jordan, Mary Ann 197
Jorgensen, Christine 106
Joyce, Peggy Hopkins 195
Judd, Winnie Ruth **138–140**

K

Kaczynski, David 208–209
Kaczynski, Theodore "Ted" 208
Kahane, Rabbi Meir 219
Kaplan, Nathan 82. *See also* Kid Dropper
Karpis, Alvin "Creepy" 28, 29, 30, 43
Keating, Francis 28
Keating, Lawrence 63
Keating-Holden gang 223
Keeley, Pat 220
Keene, John **141–142**
Kefauver Committee
Adonis, Joe and 6, 7
on Cohen, Mickey 70–71
on Costello, Frank 109
Kellerman, Mary 205
Kelly, Jimmy 222
Kelly, Paul 95
Kemper, Edmund Emil, III **142**
Kennedy, Robert F. 75
Keppel, Robert 48
Kerr, Clarence 58
Kid Dropper 82, 196–197
kidnappers
Allman, John 10–11
Baker, Cullen M. 25
Barker, Doc 30

Barker, Fred 30
Barker, Ma 28
Barrow, Clyde 41
Capone, Frank 56
Coll, Vince 71–72, 153
Cook, William "Billy" 73–74
Drucci, Schemer 91–92
Flores, Juan 102
Gallo, Crazy Joe 105–106
Hatcher, Charles 127
Heirens, William 127–128
Hudgens, Raymond 188
Karpis, Alvin "Creepy" 30
Lake, Leonard 142–145
McBratney, James 114
Ng, Charles Chitat 142–145
Parker, Bonnie 41
Schmid, Charles Howard 187–188
Smith, Edgar Herbert 194
Spanish, Johnny 196–197
Thompson, Buddy 202–203
Ziegler, Shotgun George 223–224
kidnap victims
Boyd, Percy 41
Bremer, Edward George 28, 30, 223
Coppola, Ann 75
Degnan, Suzanne 128
Hamm, William A., Jr. 28, 30
Jones, William Daniel 41
Orr, Thomas 25
Phengle, Ida 10
Walsh, Adam 146
Kid Twist 221, 222. *See also* Reles, Abe "Kid Twist"
killers, serial
Abbandando, "the Dasher" 3
Abrams, Big Mike 4
Allman, John "Bad" 10–11
Ball, Joe vii
Barrow, Clyde 39–42
Bianchi, Kenneth 130–131
Bluebeard viii, 203, 211
Bolber, Morris 38–39
Bundy, Carol Mary 69–70
Bundy, Ted 47–51, 118
Buono, Angelo 130–131
Clark, Douglas 69–70
Cline, Alfred vii
Corll, Dean vii
Dahmer, Jeffrey 79–80
Favato, Carino 39
Glatman, Harvey vii
Gohl, Billy vii
Goldstein, Buggsy 14
Graham, John vii
Green River Killer 118
Hansen, Robert vii, viii, 122–123
Harrison, Lester 125
Harvey, Donald 126
Hatcher, Charles 127
Jack the Ripper viii, 203
Lake, Leonard vii, 143–145
Lucas, Henry Lee 145–147
Ng, Charles Chitat vii, 143–145
Petrillo, Herman 38–39
Petrillo, Paul 38–39
ripper gangs 185–186
Speck, Richard Benjamin vii, 197
Starkweather, Charles 199–200
Toppan, Jane viii, 118, 200, 203–204
Unruh, Howard 209–210
Watson, J. P. vii
Weeks, Robert 212–213
Whitman, Charles 25
Zodiac 224–225
Kinder, Mary 87, 88
King, Daisy 115–116
King of the Bombers 4
Kiss of Death Girl 178, 180
Koch, Ernest 121
Kokoraleis, Andrew 186
Korad, Steve 44
Krakel, Dean 136
Kraus, Henry 216, 217
Krenwinkel, Patricia 154
Kurten, Peter 211

L

La Bianca, Leno 155
La Bianca, Rosemary 155
labor racketeers
Campagna, Louis "Little New York 52–53
Kid Dropper 197
Lepke, Louis 82–83, 161
Murder, Inc. and 161
Orgen, Little Augie 46, 82–83
Shapiro, Jacob "Gurrah" 46, 82–83
Spanish, Johnny 197
Lafayette National Bank 216
LaGuardia, Fiorello 46
Lake, Leonard vii, **143–145**
Lamm, Baron 84
Lamont, Blanche 93, 94
L'Amphere, Roy 118, 119
Landau, Abe 190
Landregan, Bridget 177
Landru, Henri 211
Lane, George 129
Lansky, Meyer
Adonis, Joe and 6–7
Amberg, Louis "Pretty" and 15
Anastasia, Albert and 17
Gambino, Carlo and 18
Genovese, Vito and 109
Jewish gangsterism and 105
Lepke, Louis and 46
Madden, Owney and 153
Maranzano, Salvatore and 157
Masseria, Giuseppe and 159, 160
Murder, Inc. and 161, 162
Schultz, Dutch and 189, 190
Siegel, Bugsy and 190, 192
Lawes, Lewis E. 78
Lawrence, Jimmy. *See* Dillinger, John Herbert
Leach, Kimberly 49–50
Leach, Matt 86, 87, 88–89
Leavenworth Penitentiary. *See also* Fort Leavenworth Prison
Barker, Lloyd at 29
Carroll, Mike at 145
Hicks, Jeffrey Joe at 129, 130
Lepke, Louis at 47
Ng, Charles Chitat at 143
Lefors, Joe 135, 136
Legenza, Walter 204, 205
Lehman, Herbert 189–190
Leibowitz, Samuel 72
Lenox Avenuers 120
Lepke, Louis. *See also* Buchalter, Louis "Lepke"
Diamond, Legs 83
Madden, Owney and 153
Murder, Inc. and 161, 162
Reles, Abe and 180, 183, 184
Rudnick, George and 178
Schultz, Dutch and 190
LeRoi, Agnes 138–139
Leslie, Harry 87, 90
Levy, Lisa 49, 50
Lewis, James 206
Lewis, Joe E. 151
Lewis, Whitey 33, 120, 222
Life of John Wesley Hardin, The (Hardin) 124
Lindbergh Law 202
Ling Tchen 4
Linn, William 151
Little Bohemia Resort 167
Little Harpe **124–125**, 157, 158
Little Red **199–200**
Live Oak gang 137
Lizzie the Dove 148, 149
loansharks
Amberg, Joe 13–14, 15
Amberg, Louis "Pretty 13–15
Battaglia, Sam "Teets" 31
Murder, Inc. and 161
Rudnick, Whitey 184
Loeber, Charley 61–62
Logan (rancher) 77
Lombardo, Tony 12, 13
Lonely Hearts Killers 32–33
Lone War Trail of Apache Kid (Forrest and Hill) 21
Longley, William P. "Wild Bill" 25, 124
Lorenzo (roofer) 39
Lorre, Catherine 131
Lorre, Peter 131
Louie, Lefty 33, 120, 222
Lucas, Henry Lee **145–147**

Lucchese, Tommy 46, 157, 159, 190
Luciano, Lucky 18, 60
  Adonis, Joe and 6, 7
  Amberg, Louis "Pretty" and 15
  Anastasia, Albert and 16–17
  Capone, Al and 53
  Coll, Vince and 71
  Coppola, Trigger Mike and 74
  Costello, Frank and 185
  Dewey, Thomas and 46
  in Five Points gang 95
  Gambino, Carlo and 59
  Genovese, Vito and 108, 109, 110
  Lansky, Meyer and 190
  Lucchese, Tommy and 46
  Madden, Owney and 153
  Maranzano, Salvatore and 156, 157
  Masseria, Giuseppe and 159–160
  Murder, Inc. and 161, 162
  Schultz, Dutch and 188, 189, 190
  Siegel, Bugsy and 190, 192
Luertgert, Adolph Louis **147**
Luertgert, Louise 147
Lupo the Wolf **147–148**, 158
Lutz, Philip, Jr. 88
Lyons, Danny 91, **148–149**
Lyons, Frank 220

M

Madden, Owney "the Killer" 14, 71, 72, **152–154**
Mad Dog **71–72**, 153
Mader, Charley 220
Mad Hatter **15–18**
Mafia. *See also* mob leaders; Murder, Inc.; *specific mob leaders*
  Accardo, Tony in 5
  Anastasia, Albert in 16–17
  barrel murders and 30–31
  Castellammarese War and 72, 156
  Castellano, Paul in 60, 61
  Galante, Carmine in 103–105
  Gallo, Crazy Joe in 105–106
  Genovese, Vito in 108–110
  Giancana, Sam in 110
  Gotti, John in 113–115
  Gravano, Sammy "the Bull" in 116–118
  Lupo the Wolf in 148
  Maranzano, Salvatore in 155–157
  Masseria, Giuseppe "Joe the Boss" in 158–160
  Siegel, Bugsy in 190–192
  Terrible Gennas in 12
Maggie: A Girl of the Streets (Crane) 33
Magoon, Blue Jaw 162
Mahoney, John 182–183
Mailer, Norman 111
Maione, Happy 162, 178, 180, 183, 184
Mais, Robert 204, 205
Makley, Far Charley 86, 87, 88, 89, 90–91, 167
Malone, Owen 24
Mangano, Phil 16
Mangano, Vincent 16
Mansfield Reformatory 80, 81
Manson, Charles **154–155**
Maples, Dan 68
Maranzano, Salvatore 16, 71, **155–157**, 158, 191
Marten, Edward 178
Martin, Joe 220
Martinez, Ramiro 216
Mason, Samuel 124, **157–158**
Massachusetts General Hospital 203
Masseria, Giuseppe "Joe the Boss" 16, 156, **158–160**, 191
mass murderers
  Ball, Joe 26
  Bender, John 34, 35
  Bender, Kate 34, 35
  Bender, Ma 34, 35
  Bender, Old Man 34, 35, 36
  Boston Strangler 81–82
  Briggen, Joseph 44
  Cook, William 73–74
  Corll, Dean 75–76
  Corona, Juan 76
  Daniels, Murl 80–81
  Fish, Albert 100–101
  Gacy, John Wayne 103
  Gohl, Billy 112–113
  Graham, John Gilbert 115–116
  Hoch, Johann 131–132
  Holmes, H. H. 132–134
  Mullin, Herbert 161
  Murrel, John A. 163
  Nelson, Earle Leonard 164–165
  Panzram, Carl 176
  Piper, Thomas W. 177
  Rees, Melvin David 181–182
  Schmid, Charles Howard 187–188
  West, John Coulter 80–81
  Whitman, Charles 214–216
Matusek, Patricia Ann 197
Mayflower 36
Maynard, Robert 38
Mays, Sam 124–125, 158
McBratney, James 114
McCarthy, Dapper Dan 170
McCarthy, Johnny 91
McDonald, Tom 220
McGovern's Cabaret 169
McGown, Kitty 148, 149
McGurn, Machine Gun Jack 4, **150–151**
McKinney, James **151–152**
McNeil Consumer Products Co. 206
McNutt, Paul V. 86, 87, 88, 90
McPherson, Aimee Semple 195
McPherson, Angus 129
McVeigh, Timothy **172–173**
Meldrum, Robert **160**
Mercado, Ruth Rita 111
Merlo, Mike 12, 171–172
Mersher the Strong Arm 196
Meter, Homer Van 86
Methvin, Henry 42
Mexican War 97
Meyer, August 199
Miles, Nelson 134
Miller, Florence 205
Miller, Frank 175
Miller, John 137, 138
Millman, Harry 179
Mittleman, Evelyn 178, 180
mob leaders. *See also* gangsters
  Accardo, Anthony Joseph 4–6
  Amatuna, Samoots 12–13
  Anastasia, Albert 6, 15–18
  Battaglia, Sam "Teets" 31
  Capone, Al 53–55
  Castellano, Paul 58–61
  Costello, Frank 6, 16, 17
  Galante, Carmine 103–105
  Gallo, Crazy Joe 105–106
  Gambino, Carlo 17
  Genna, Bloody Angelo 12
  Genovese, Vito 6, 17, 108–110
  Giancana, Sam 4, 5, 110
  Giunta, Hop Toad 19
  Gotti, John 113–115
  Lansky, Meyer 6–7, 15, 17, 105
  Lepke, Louis and 45–47
  Luciano, Lucky 6, 15, 16–17
  Maranzano, Salvatore 16, 155–157
  Masseria, Giuseppe "Joe the Boss" 16, 158–160
  Merlo, Mike 12
  O'Banion, Dion 11
  Rothstein, Arnold 84
  Schultz, Dutch 188–190
  Siegel, Bugsy viii, 190–192
  Trafficante, Santo 17
  Weiss, Hymie 11
Montana State Training School 176
moonshiners
  Genna brothers 107–108
  Giancana, Sam 110
  O'Banion, Dion 171
Moore, Screwy John 4
Moran, Bugs
  Alterie, Louis "Two Gun" and 11, 12

Capone, Al and 55, 214
McGurn, Machine Gun Jack and 151
in O'Banion gang 170, 172
Reiser, Charles "the Ox" and 182
Ziegler, Shotgun George and 223
Morello, Giuseppi 30, 148
Moretti, Willie
Genovese, Vito and 108
Maranzano, Salvatore and 157
Masseria, Giuseppe and 159
Morgan, B. F. 85
Morrell, Julie 222
Morton, Nails 11, 170, 214
Mosser, Carl 73–74
Mosser, Susan 208
Mosser, Thelma 73–74
Mosser, Thomas 207, 208
Mubarak, Hosni 219
Mudgett, Herman Webster. *See* Holmes, H. H.
Mullin, Herbert **161**
Murder, Inc. **161–163**. *See also* Mafia
Abbandando, "the Dasher" in 3
Anastasia, Albert in 15–16, 46
Buchalter, Louis "Lepke" in 15–16, 45, 46, 47
Gotti, John in 113
Pittsburgh Phil in viii, 177–180
Reles, Abe "Kid Twist" in 6, 14, 47, 183–185
Siegel, Bugsy in 190–192
murderers. *See also* cannibals; gangsters; killers, serial; mass murderers; outlaws; poisoners
Abriel, Pedro 31–32
Allen, Bill 7–8
Amatuna, Samoots 12–13
Amberg, Joe 13
Amberg, Louis "Pretty" viii, 13–15
Anastasia, Albert 15–18
Anderson, Jesse 80
Anselmi, Albert 18–20
Apache Kid 20–21
Atkins, Susan 154
Baker, Cullen M. 25
Barker, Doc 29
Barker, Herman 28
Battaglia, Sam "Teets" 31
Bayonne, Vincent 31–32
Beck, Martha 32–33
Becker, Charles E. 33–34
Billington, John 36
Burrow, Rube 51
Cardinella, Sam 56–57
Carpenter, Richard 57–58
Carroll, Mike 145
Chapman, Gerald 61–63
Cherokee Bill 63–64
Christie, Ned 68–69
Cline, Alfred L. 70
Coll, Vincent 71–72, 153
Cook, Bill 63
Cook, Jim 63
Courtright, Longhair Jim 76–77
Crowley, Francis "Two Gun" 77–78
Dellacroce, Aniello 59
Diamond, Legs 82–84
Doherty, Jim 12
Dolan, Dandy Johnny 91
Driscoll, Danny 91
Drucci, Schemer 12, 91–92
Durrant, William Henry Theodore 92–93
Espinosa, Felipe 97–98
Espinosa, Julián 97–98
Espinosa, Victorio 97–98
Fernandez, Raymond Martinez 32
Flores, Juan 102
Gallo brothers 18
Gein, Edward 106–107
Gentle Maggie 148, 149
Gilmore, Gary Mark 110–111
Glatman, Harvey Murray 111–112
Gray, Judd 195–196
Gunness, Belle 118–119
Gyp the Blood 120
Hamilton, Ray 41
Hardin, John Wesley 123–124
Heirens, William 127–128
Helm, Boone 128–129
Hicks, Jeffrey Joe 129–130
Horn, Tom 134–136
Hudgens, Raymond 188
Jackson, Mary Jane "Bricktop" viii, 137–138
Johnson, Jerome A. 105
Keene, John 141–142
Kemper, Edmund Emil, III 142
Kid Dropper 196–197
Krenwinkel, Patricia 154
Lepke, Louis 15–16, 45–47
Luetgert, Adolph Louis 147
Lupo the Wolf 147–148
Lyons, Danny 91, 148–149
Madden, Owney 152–154
Manson, Charles 154–155
Mason, Sam 124, 157–158
McBratney, James 114
McKinney, James 151–152
Meldrum, Robert 160
Reiser, Charles "the Ox" 182–183
Reles, Abe 183–185
Scalise, John 18–20
Searver, Christopher 80
Skull, Sally 192–193
Slade, Jack 193–194
Smith, Edgar Herbert 194
Snyder, Ruth 194–196
Spanish, Johnny 196–197
Spinelli, Duchess 197–199
Tannenbaum, Allie 191
Terrible Gennas 18, 19
Thompson, Ben 101–102
Thompson, Buddy 202–203
Toole, Ottis 145–146
Van Houten, Leslie 154
Watson, J. P. 211–212
Watson, Tex 154, 155
Wilcoxson, One-Eye 216–217
Williams, Wayne B. 23–24
Zelig, Jack 221–223
Murder Stable 148, 158
murder victims vii–ix. *See also* asphyxiation victims; strangulation victims
Abrams, Big Mike 4
Allman, John 10–11
Alterie, Louis "Two Gun" 12
Amatuna, Samoots 12–13
Amberg, Joe 15
Amberg, Louis "Pretty" 15
Anastasia, Albert 13, 15–18, 108, 109
Anselmi, Albert 18–20, 150
Atlanta children 22–24
Barker, Fred 27, 28
Barker, Lloyd 30
Barker, Ma 26–28
barrel 30–31
Bartlett, Marion 199
Bartlett, Velda 199
Bell, Shannon 175–176
Beni, Jules 193
Blackbeard 38
Boston strangler 81–82
Bowen, Chick 160
Brown, Frances 127–128
Budd, Grace 100
Burton, Elijah 128
Campbell, Caryn 49
Carroll, Mike 145
Cater, Nathaniel 23
Chandler, Cynthia 69
Charley, Long 137
Chinese 4, 64–68
Churchill, James 127
Cohen, Maurice 209
Colbert, Chunk 8, 9
Coll, Peter 72
Coll, Vince 71–72, 189
Collison, Merle 199
Colosimo, Big Jim 54

Colvert, Robert 199
Corll, Dean 75–76
Cosner, Paul 145
Davy, Gloria Jean 197
Degnan, Suzanne 128
Dewey, Robert 74
Diamond, Legs 189
Diehl, Billy 21
Dolak, Frank 15
Dowling, Tom 10
Downing, Delphine 32
Doyle, Little Patsy 153
Drucci, Vince 172
Dundee, Vince 10
Epps, Billy 10
Faraday, David 224
Farrar, Andrew 193
Farris, Suzanne Bridget 197
Fay, Janet 32
Feinstein, Puggy 179–180
Fellers, Mary Elizabeth 182
Flelury, Laurent 138
Folger, Abigail 154
Franse, Steve 108
Frazier, D. M. 66
Freeman, William 127
Frykowski, Voyteck 154
Gallo, Crazy Joe 105–106
Gargullo, Merlita 197
Garvey, James J. 205
Genna, Bloody Angelo 108
Giancana, Sam 5
Giscobbe, Anthony 38–39
Giunta, Hop Toad 150
Goldstein, Abe "Bummy" 13
Greenberg, Harry 191
Greentree, Ethel 205
Groat, Dave 10
Gsellman, George 121
Hamilton, Tommy 209
Harold, Margaret 181, 182
Harpe, Micajah 124
Harris, William J. 29
Henshaw, William 153
Holinsky, Benny 15
Holmes, Bill 21
Hoover, Clark 209
Horn, Johnny 205
Houston, Sequoyah 63
Hurlbut, Dennis 201
Jabour, Cynthia 213
Jackson, Carroll 181
Jackson, Mrs. Carroll 181, 182
Jackson, William "Action" 5
James, Jesse 27
Janus, Adam 206
Janus, Stanley 206
Janus, Teresa 206
Jensen, Bettilou 224
Jordan, Mary Ann 197
Kaplan, Nathan 82
Keating, Lawrence 63
Kellerman, Mary 205
Kerr, Clarence 58
Kid Dropper 197
Kid Twist 222
Koch, Ernest 121
Kraus, Henry 216, 217
La Bianca, Rosemary 155
La Bianca, Leno 155
Landregan, Bridget 177
Leach, Kimberly 49–50
LeRoi, Agnes 138–139
Ling Tchen 4
Lizzie the Dove 148, 149
Lorenzo (roofer) 39
Mahoney, John 182–183
Mangano, Phil 16
Maples, Dan 68
Maranzano, Salvatore 71, 155–157
Mason, Sam 157–158
Matusek, Patricia Ann 197
McGurn, Machine Gun Jack 150–151
McPherson, Angus 129
Meyer, August 199
Miller, Florence 205
Miller, Frank 175
Miller, John 138
Moretti, Willie 108
Morgan, B. F. 85
Morrell, Julie 222
Mosser, Carl 73–74
Mosser, Thelma 73–74
Mosser, Theodore 207
Murphy, Paddy 214
Murray, Gilbert 207
Murray, John Robert 69, 70
Narano, Gina 69
Newcomen, John 36
Newman, Clara 164–165
Nickell, Willie 135
Nielssen, Fred 113
Noon, George 175
O'Banion, Dion 11, 19, 54, 172
Obendoerfer, George 122
O'Connor, Brenda 144
Packard, Jess 152
Palmer, Albert 121
Parent, Steven Earl 154
Pasion, Valentina 197
Payne, Jimmy Ray 23
Pilarchik, John 209
Pitzel, Benjamin F. 134
Powell, John 126
Quinn, Joseph 148, 149
Reiner, Mary 206
Reynolds, Glen 21
Riley, Carol 213
Roberts, Ed 10
Rogers, Ike 63
Rosen, Joe 47
Rosenthal, Herman 33, 222
Ross, Josephine 127, 128
Rudnick, George 178
Ryan, Ann 182
Samuelson, Hedvig 138–139
Sarber, Jess 89
Scalise, John 18–20, 150
Schmale, Nina Jo 197
Schultz, Dutch 15, 157, 162, 190
Schuster, Arnold 17
Scrutton, Hugh 207
Sears 151
Sebring, Jay 154
Serpa, Salvatore 205
Shepard, Cecelia 224
Sherman, Horatio 201
Sherrard, Robert 198
Shommettee, Marie 182
Siegel, Bugsy 190, 192
Slater, Harry 141
Smith, Orris 209
Snyder, Albert 194, 195
Spanish, Johnny 197
Stapely, Robin 144
Steele, Michelle 127
Struck, Edward 200
Swan, Israel 175
Tate, Sharon 154
Tibbett, William 152
Tresca, Carlo 108
Venable, Shelby Jean 182
Wagner, Jacob 121
Walcker, Marie 132
Wallace, Eddie "Cowboy" 204, 205
Walsh, Adam 146
Ward, C. Lauer 199
Watkins, Mr. 192
Weeks, Patricia 212–213
Weinberg, Bo 189
Weiss, Hymie 172, 214
White, Clarence 182
Wilkening, Pamela Lee 197
Williams, Minnie 93–94
Wood, David 217
Wood, Rhoda 217
Wright, Clarence E. 7
Young, Mabel Hood 177
Zanghi, Anthony "Musky" 205
Zelig, Jack 33, 223
Ziegler, Shotgun George 224
Zielinski, Victoria 194
Zion, Eddie 13
Murieta, Joaquin 102
Murman, George 128
Murphy, Archie 137
Murphy, Paddy 214
Murray, Gilbert 207
Murray, John Robert 69, 70
Murrel, John A. **163**
Mussolini, Benito 104, 108, 191
"Mustache Petes" 155, 159, 190–191

N

Narano, Gina 69
narcotics
Accardo, Anthony Joseph on 5
Diamond, Legs in 82–83
Eastman, Monk in 97
Galante, Carmine in 104
Genovese, Vito in 18, 108–110
Lepke, Louis in 46
Murder, Inc. and 161
Siegel, Bugsy in 191
Nash, Frank 28
necrophilias
Clark, Douglas Daniel 131

Compton, Veronica Lynn 131
Dahmer, Jeffrey 79–80
Nelson, Earle Leonard **164–165**
Nelson, George "Baby Face" 39, 43, 89, 90, **165–168**
Nelson, Helen 167–168
Nerone, Giuseppe "the Cavalier" 107, 108
Newcomen, John 36
New Irving Hall 95–96
Newman, Clara 164–165
Newman, Sarah Jane. *See* Skull, Sally
New York Daily News 196
New York Mirror 47
New York Police Department 162–163
New York Times
on Chapman, Gerald 61, 62
on Gravano, Sammy "the Bull" 118
on Schultz, Dutch 188–189
Unabomber and 207–208
New York World 33
Ng, Charles Chitat vii, **143–145**
Nicholls, Francis T. 220
Nichols, Terry 173
Nickell, Willie 135
Niebel, John Elmer 81
Nielssen, Fred 113
nightclub racketeers
Diamond, Legs 82–84
Fay, Joey 84
Nitti, Frank 4
Noe, James H. 91
Noon, George 175
Norris, Roy Lewis 186
North Side gang. *See also* O'Banion, Charles Dion "Deanie"; O'Banion gang
Capone, Al and 54–55
Drucci, Schemer in 91–92
Genna brothers and 107–108
Torrio, Johnny and 54
Weiss, Hymie and 213
Northwestern University 207
Norton, John 57
Nosair, El Sayyid A. 219
Nuova Villa Tammaro 159
Nussbaum, Albert 216, 217

O

O'Banion, Charles Dion "Deanie" **169–172**
Alterie, Louis "Two Gun" and 11–12
Amatuna, Samoots and 12
Drucci, Schemer and 91–92
murder of 19, 54
Reiser, Charles "the Ox" and 182
Weiss, Hymie and 213, 214
O'Banion gang 11, 54–55, 107, 108, 151. *See also* North Side gang
Obendoerfer, George 122
O'Connell, Pat 99
O'Connor, Brenda 144
O'Dwyer, William 177, 178, 185
Ohio State Prison 90
Oklahoma City bombing **172–173**
Oklahoma State Penitentiary 29
Olson, Culbert 198
Olympic Games 21–22
Oregon State Prison 176
Orgen, "Little Augie" 46, 82–83
Orr, Thomas 25
Ouray, Chief 175
Outlaw Exterminators, Inc. 10, **173–174**
outlaws
Baker, Cullen M. 25
Barker, Ma 26–28
Barton, William 99
Christie, Ned 68–69
Farrington, Hilary 99
Farrington, Levi 99–100
Flores, Juan 102
Harpe brothers 124–125
Mason, Sam 124, 157–158
Taylor, William 99
Wilkinson, Noah 160

P

Packard, Jess 152
Packer, Alfred viii, **175–176**
Palace Chop House and Tavern 190
Palmer, Albert 121
Panzram, Carl **176**
Pappas, Carole 186
pardon
of Barker, Doc 29
of Barrow, Buck 41
of Barrow, Clyde 40
of Blackbeard 38
by Cleveland, Grover 20
of Cumpanis, Ana 90
of Eastman, Monk 97
of Fisher, John King 101
of Hardin, John Wesley 124
of Jackson, Mary Jane "Bricktop" 138
of Lyons, Frank 220
Parent, Steven Earl 154
Parish Prison 138
Parker, Bonnie viii, **39–42,** 43, 165
Parker, Isaac 63–64, 68
Park Sheraton Hotel 17
Pasion, Valentina 197
Paterson, Emily 165
Payne, Jimmy Ray 23
Pecorara, Rose 12
Peifer, Jack 30
Penthouse 146
People's Temple 146
Petrillo, Herman **38, 39**
Petrillo, Paul **38–39**
Pflaum, William K. 56
Phengle, Ida 10
Philippine Airlines 219
Pico, Don Andrés 102
Pied Piper of Tucson 187–188
Pierpont, Harry 86, 87, 88, 89, 90–91, 167
Piest, Robert 103
Pilarchik, John 209
Pinkerton, William 99–100
Pinkerton Detective Agency 134
Piper, Thomas W. **177**
Piquett, Louis 88
pirates
Blackbeard 36–38
Colonel Plug 72–73
Pittsburgh Phil viii, 47, 162, 163, **177–180,** 183, 184
Pitzel, Benjamin F. 134
Playboy 45
Plummer, Henry 129, 193
poisoners
Bolber-Petrillo murder ring 39
Botkin, Cordelia 42–43
Hahn, Anna 121–122
Harvey, Donald 126
Hoch, Johann 131–132
Jegado, Helen 200
Struck, Lydia 200–201
Toppan, Jane viii, 118, 200, 203–204
Van der Linden, Madame 200
Watson, J. P. 211–212
Wood, Isaac 217
Polanski, Roman 154
Powell, John 126
Profaci, Joe 17, 18, 105
Prohibition
Adonis, Joe during 6–7
Amberg, Louis "Pretty" during 13–15
Capone, Al during 53–55
Cardinella, Sam during 56–57
Eastman, Monk during 97
Genna brothers during during 107–108
Masseria, Giuseppe "Joe the Boss" during 158–160
Murder, Inc. during 161
O'Banion, Dion during 11, 169–172
Schultz, Dutch during 188–190
Weiss, Hymie during 213–214
prostitution
Barker brothers and 28
Battaglia, Sam "Teets" and 31
Capone, Al and 54
Colosimo, Big Jim and 54
Eastman, Monk and 95–97
Lyons, Danny and 148
Murder, Inc. and 161
O'Banion, Dion and 171
Schmid, Charles Howard and 187
Psycho (film) 106
Purple gang 179
Purvis, Melvin H. 30, 90, 223

Q

Quantrill 99
Quinn, Joseph 148, 149

R

Raft, George 191
Rahman, Sheik Omar Abdel *218,* 219
Rais, Gilles de 211
rape victims
  Campbell, Caryn 49
  Chandler, Cynthia 69
  Fritz, Gretchen 187–188
  Fritz, Wendy 187–188
  Jackson, Mrs. Carroll 181, 182
  Narano, Gina 69
  at New Irving Hall 95–96
  Newman, Clara 164–165
  Paterson, Emily 165
  Phengle, Ida 10
  Ryan, Ann 182
  Shomettee, Marie 182
  Steele, Michelle 127
rapists
  Alllman, John 10–11
  Apache Kid 20–21
  Bianchi, Kenneth 130–131
  Boston Strangler 81–82
  Bundy, Ted 48–51
  Buono, Angelo 130
  Chessman, Caryl 130
  Clark, Douglas 69–70
  Glatman, Harvey Murray 111–112
  Hansen, Robert 122–123
  Hatcher, Charles 127
  Lake, Leonard 142–145
  Nelson, Earle Leonard 164–165
  Ng, Charles Chitat 142–145
  Piper, Thomas W. 177
  Rees, Melvin David 181–182
  Schmid, Charles Howard 187–188
  Speck, Richard Benjamin 197
  Ziegler, Shotgun George 223
Rastelli, Phil 105
Reagan, Ronald 22, 140
Reasonable Doubt, A (Smith) 194
Red Light Bandit 130
Rees, Melvin David **181–182**
Reid, Ed 185
Reiner, Mary 206
Reiser, Charles "the Ox" 170, **182–183**
Reiser-Shopes, Mrs. 183
Reles, Abe "Kid Twist" 178, **183–185**
  Abbandando, "the Dasher" and 3
  Adonis, Joe and 6
  Amberg, Louis "Pretty" and 14
  Anastasia, Albert and 162
  death of 47, 162–163
  Pittsburgh Phil and 179–180
  Siegel, Bugsy and 162
Republican Party viii
  Bundy, Ted in 48
  Capone, Al in 56
  Capone, Frank in 55–56
  Leslie, Harry in 87
  O'Banion, Dion in 169
  Packer, Alfred in 176
  Scottoriggio, Joseph in 75
  Whitman, Charles S. in 33
Reynolds, Glen 21
Reynolds, Melvin 127
Richards, W. A. 135
RICO statutes 115, 117
Riley, Carol 213
Rinehart, Mary Roberts 195
riots, Chinese 64–68
ripper gangs **185–186**
robbers. *See also* burglars; gangsters; thieves
  Anderson, Dutch 61–62
  Apache Kid 20–21
  Barker, Doc 27, 29–30
  Barker, Fred 27, 30
  Barker, Herman 27, 28, 29
  Barker, Lloyd 27, 29
  Barker, Ma 28
  Barton, William 99
  Battaglia, Sam "Teets" 31
  Beck, Martha 32–33
  Bender family 34–36
  Brock, Leonard 51
  Brock, Will 51
  Burrow, Jim 51
  Burrow, Rube 51
  Chapman, Gerald 61–63
  Cherokee Bill 63–64
  Chessman, Caryl 130
  Crowley, Francis "Two Gun" 77
  Daniels, Murl 80–81
  Dillinger, John Herbert 84–91
  Espinosa, Felipe 97–98
  Espinosa, Julián 97–98
  Espinosa, Victorio 97–98
  Farrington, Hilary 99
  Farrington, Levi 99–100
  Fernandez, Raymond Martinez 32
  Fisher, John King 101–102
  Harrison, Lester 125
  Hoch, Johann 131–132
  Karpis, Alvin "Creepy" 30
  Kid Dropper 196–197
  Loeber, Charley 61–62
  Lucas, Henry Lee 145–147
  Mobile and Ohio flyer and 99
  Panzram, Carl 176
  Reiser, Charles "the Ox" 182–183
  Reles, Abe 183–185
  Rogers, Ike 63
  Scales, Clint 63
  Searver, Christopher 80
  Singleton, Ed 85
  Spanish, Johnny 196–197
  Starkweather, Charles 199–200
  Taylor, William 99
  Thompson, Buddy 202–203
  Toole, Ottis 145–146
  West, John Coulter 80–81
Roberts, Ed 10
Roberts, Kiki 82, 84
Robinson, Jesse 192
Rock Springs Independent 67
Rogers, Ike 63, 64
Rogers, Will 89
Rolfe, Louise 150–151
Roosevelt, Eleanor 139
Roosevelt, Franklin D. 47, 61
Rosen, Joseph 47, 184
Rosenkrantz, Lulu 190
Rosenthal, Herman 33, 34, 120, 222
Ross, Josephine 127, 128
Rothstein, Arnold 84
Roughing It (Twain) 193
Rowe, Alleen 187
Rudnick, George 178
Rudnick, Whitey 184
Rudolph, Eric Robert 22
Runyon, Damon viii, 13, 14
Ryan, Ann 182

S

safecrackers
  Mahoney, John 182–183
  O'Banion, Dion 170, 182
  Reiser, Charles "the Ox" 170, 182–183
  Weiss, Hymie 214
Saga of Tom Horn, The (Krakel) 136
Sage, Anna 90
Sage, Walter 179
Saietta, Ignazio. *See* Lupo the Wolf
Salameh, Mohammad 217, 218
Salem, Emad 219
Samuelson, Hedvig 138–139
San Carlos Indian Reservation 134
San Quentin Penitentiary
  Botkin, Cordelia at 43
  Briggen, Joseph at 44
  Clark, Douglas at 131
  Cook, William "Billy" at 73, 74
  Flores, Juan at 102
  Glatman, Harvey Murray at 112
  McKinney, James at 151
  Thompson, Buddy at 203
  Watson, J. P. at 212
Sarber, Jess 87, 88, 89
Sassy Sam 4
Saunders, John 187
Savage, Chief 177
Sawyer, Harry 30
Sbarbaro, John A. 92
Scales, Clint 63
Scalise, John **18–20,** 55, 107, 108, 150, 172
Scarpato, Gerardo 159
Schleuter, August 113

Schmale, Nina Jo 197
Schmid, Charles Howard **187–188**
Schultz, Dutch **188–190**
  Amberg, Louis "Pretty" and 14, 15
  Coll, Vince and 71, 72
  Diamond, Legs 83–84
  Lepke, Louis and 46
  Madden, Owney and 153
  Maranzano, Salvatore and 157
  Masseria, Giuseppe and 159
  Murder, Inc. and 162
  Workman, Charlie and 184
Schuster, Arnold 17
Scottoriggio, Joseph 75
Scrutton, Hugh 207
Searver, Christopher 80
Sebring, Jay 154
Secret Service, U.S. 148
Sedgwick, Ellery viii, 203
Seidensahl, Joe 138
Selman, John 124
Senate, U.S. 4
serial killers. *See* killers, serial
Serpa, Salvatore 204, 205
Setton 124–125
Sex Beast 182
Shaffer, Clarence 43
Shapiro, Jacob "Gurrah" 46, 83
Shean, Walter J. 62, 63
Shepard, Cecelia 224
Shepley, George F. 138
Sherman, Horatio 201
Sherrard, Robert 198
Shockley, Sam 203
Shoemaker, William 92
Shomettee, Marie 182
Shopes, Charles "the Ox" **182–183**
Short, Luke 77
Sieber, Al 20, 134
Siegel, Benjamin "Bugsy" viii, **190–192**
  Cohen, Mickey and 70
  Madden, Owney and 153
  Masseria, Giuseppe and 159
  Reles, Abe "Kid Twist" and 162, 185
Simms, Billy 101
Simone, Michael 198
Sinatra, Frank 23
Singleton, Ed 85
Sing Sing Penitentiary
  Beck, Martha at 32
  Becker, Charles E. at 34
  Crowley, Francis "Two Gun" at 78
  Eastman, Monk at 97
  Madden, Owney at 153
  Snyder, Ruth at 196
Sirocco, Jack 222, 223
Skull, George 192
Skull, Sally **192–193**
Slack, Ben 173
Slade, Joseph "Jack" **193–194**
Slater, Harry 141
Slesers, Anna 81
Smith, Al 97
Smith, Carmine 71
Smith, Edgar Herbert **194**
Smith, Mary 71–72
Smith, Mrs. Edward 209
Smith, Orris 209
Smith, Robert. *See* Weeks, Robert
Smuggler Union Mine 160
Snyder, Albert 194, 195
Snyder, Ruth **194–196**
Society for the Abolishment of Capital Punishment 176
Sorenson, Widow. *See* Gunness, Belle
Spanish, Johnny **196–197**
Spanish-American War 42, 68
Sparks Steak House 60
Speck, Richard Benjamin vii, **197**
Spencer, Al 28
Spinelli, Juanita "Duchess" viii, **197–199**
Spotswood, Alexander 38
Sprinkle, Joe 199
St. Valentine's Day Massacre 19, *54*, 55, 150, 151, 172, 223
Standard Oil Co. 182
Standish, Miles 36
Stapely, Robin 144
Stark, George 35
Starkweather, Charles **199–200**
Steele, Michelle 127
Sterling, Ross 40
Stevenson, E. A. 67
Stewart, Virgil 163
Stewart, Yellow Henry 220
Stockyard Bluebeard. *See* Hoch, Johann
Stolzenberg, Charles. *See* Weeks, Robert
Stompanato, Johnny 71
Story of Philosophy, The (Durant) 195
strangulation victims
  Atlanta children 22–24
  Bowman, Margaret 49, 50
  Bridgeport, Shirley 111
  Dull, Judy 111
  Fritz, Gretchen 187–188
  Fritz, Wendy 187–188
  Lamont, Blanche 93
  Levy, Lisa 49, 50
  Mercado, Ruth Rita 111
  Paterson, Emily 165
  Piest, Robert 103
  Rudnick, Whitey 184
  Slesers, Anna 81
  Snyder, Albert 195
  Wilcox, Leann 118
Straton, John Roach 195
Strauss, Harry. *See* Pittsburgh Phil
Striepeke, Don 224
Struck, Edward 200
Struck, Lydia viii, **200–201**
suicide
  of Ball, Joe 26
  of Barker, Herman 28, 29
  of Coppola, Ann 75
  of Cugino, Anthony 205
  of Hatcher, Charles 127
  of Lake, Leonard 145
  of Nitti, Frank 4
Sullivan, Tim 33
Sullivan Law 72
Sundance Kid 135
Sunday, Billy 195
Sunset Slayer **69–70**, 131
Supreme Court, U.S. 63, 110, 111, 155, 173, 188, 197
Sutton, Willie 17
Swan, Israel 175
swindlers
  Anderson, Dutch 61
  Beck, Martha 32–33
  Chapman, Gerald 61
  Fernandez, Raymond Martinez 32
  Holmes, H. H. 132–134
  Pitzel, Benjamin F. 134
Swope, Herbert Bayard 33
Sylvester, George 220

T

Tammany Hall
  Eastman, Monk and 96, 97
  Madden, Owney and 153
  Schultz, Dutch and 189
  Sullivan, Tim and 33
Tannenbaum, Allie 191
Tate, Sharon 154
tax evaders
  Capone, Al 55, 151
  Cohen, Mickey 71
  Coppola, Trigger Mike 75
  Costello, Frank 109
  Genovese, Vito 109
  Schultz, Dutch 189
Taylor, William 99
Teach, Edward. *See* Blackbeard
Terrible Gennas 12, 18, 19, **107–108**, 171. *See also* Genna brothers
Terrill, Ray 28
terrorists
  Nosair, El Sayyid A. 219
  Rahman, Sheik Omar Abdel *218*, 219
  Salameh, Mohammad 218
  Unabomber 207–209
  Yousef, Ranmzi Ahmed 218, 219
terrorists, suspected
  Jewell, Richard 21–22
  Rudolph, Eric Robert 22
Texas Highway Patrol 42
Texas Rangers
  on Ball, Joe 26
  on Fisher, John King 101
  on Hardin, John Wesley 124
  Lucas, Henry Lee and 146
Thack, Edward. *See* Blackbeard
Thatch, Edward. *See* Blackbeard
Thayer, Earl 28

thieves. *See also* burglars; gangsters; robbers
Adonis, Joe 7
Barker, Fred 29
Barrow, Clyde 39–42
Diamond, Legs 82–83
Dillinger, John 85
Hamilton, Ray 41
Heirens, William 127–128
Holmes, H. H. 132–134
Lansky, Meyer 190
Parker, Bonnie 39–42
Siegel, Bugsy 190–192
Weaver, Bill 29
Wilcoxson, One-Eye 216–217
Thomas, Heck 68
Thompson, Ben 101–102
Thompson, Blackie 202
Thompson, Miran Edgar "Buddy" **202–203**
Thompson, William Hale 92
Thompson, William Hale, Mrs. 31
Thornton, Roy 40
Tibbett, Lawrence 152
Tibbett, William 152
T.I.C. Commercial Detective Agency 77
Tieri, Frank 105
Tieri, Funzi 59–60
Tiger Woman **138–140**
Tobey, Charles 70
Tobin, Tom 97–98
Todd, George 99
Tolbert, Paden 68
Tombs 91
Tom the Dog 220
Tong, Gene 66
Tony the Aristocrat 107, 108
Toole, Ottis 145–146
Toppan, Jane viii, 118, 200, **203–204**
Torrio, Johnny
Capone, Al and 53, 54, 55–56, 171, 172
in Five Points gang 95
Genna brothers and 107
Touhy, Roger 28
Trafficante, Santo 17, 105
Trenton State Prison 194
Tresca, Carlo 104, 108
Tricker, Chick 222, 223
Tri-State gang **204–205**
Turner, Julia 26
Turner, Lana 71
Turpo 220
Twain, Mark 193
Tylenol murders **205–206**

U

Ullman, Sheriff 10
Umberto's Clam House 105
Unabomber **207–209**
Underboss (Gravano) 117
Unione Siciliana 12, 13, 19, 171
Union Pacific 65, 67
United Airlines 206
University of California 142
University of Illinois 223
University of Texas 215
Unruh, Howard **209–210**
Unsolved Mysteries (TV program) 213
Utah State Prison 110
Uzanyol, Melih 21

V

Valachi, Joe 109, 183
Valenti, Umberto 158
Valentine, Lewis J. 46, 178
Valentino, Rudolph 151
Van der Linden, Madame 200
Van Houten, Leslie 154
Van Meter, Homer 85, 89, 90, 165, 167
Vaudeville Variety Theater 101–102
Veitch, Arthur 191
Venable, Shelby Jean 182
Vengalli, Michael 72
Verain, Leland. *See* Alterie, Louis "Two Gun"
Viana, Nicholas 57
Vigil, Lorraine 111–112

W

Wagner, Jacob 121
Wajciechowski, Earl. *See* Weiss, Hymie
Walcker, Marie 132
Waldo, Rhinelander 33
Waldrip, Louis 51
Walker, James J. 14
Wallace, Eddie "Cowboy" 204
Wallace, Mike 70
Wallapai Scouts 21
Walpole State Prison 82
Walsh, Helen 77
Ward, C. Lauer 199
Washington Post 207–208
Watkins, Mr. 192
Watson, Charles "Tex" 154, 155
Watson, J. P. vii, **211–212**
Wayne, John 10
Weaver, Bill 29
Webb, Charley 124
Webb, Del 162, 190
Webster, William H. 23
Weeks, Patricia 212–213
Weeks, Robert **212–213**
Weinberg, Bo 189
Weiss, Hymie **213–214**
Capone, Al and 11, 19, 92, 171, 172
in O'Banion gang 170, 171, 172
Reiser, Charles "the Ox" and 182
Weiss, Mendy 47, 162, 180, 184
Welch (tenant) 217
Wertham, Frederic 100
West, John Coulter 80–81
Western Electric Co. 56
Weyler, John. *See* Spanish, Johnny
Wheeler, John 8
White, Clarence 182
Whitman, Charles vii, **214–216**, 222–223
Whitman, Charles S. 33–34, 120
Whyos 91, 95, 148
Wilcox, Leann 118
Wilcoxson, Bobby Randell "One-Eye" **216–217**
Wilkening, Pamela Lee 197
Wilkinson, Noah 160
Williams, America 138
Williams, Minnie 93–94
Williams, Wayne B. 23–24
Wilson, Bully 72
Wilson, Roger. *See* Nelson, Earle Leonard
Winchell, Walter 47
Witch, the 39
Wolensky, Moe "Dimples" 46
Wood, David 217
Wood, Isaac **217**
Wood, Rhoda 217
Worden, Bernice 106
Workman, Charles "the Bug" 184, 190
World Trade Center bombing **217–219**
World War I
Eastman, Monk during 97
Reiser, Charles "the Ox" during 182
Ziegler, Shotgun George during 223
World War II 110
Wright, Clarence E. 7–8
Wyoming Cattlemen's Association 135

Y

Yale, Frankie 54, 95, 172
Yale University 201
Yarborough, Ralph 216
Yellow Henry gang **220**
York, A. M. 34–35
York, William H. 34, 35
Young, Mabel Hood 177
Youngblood, Herbert 88, 89
Young Turks 59, 71, 161
Yousef, Ramzi Ahmed 218, 219

Z

Zanghi, Anthony "Musky" 205
Zelig, Jack 33, 120, **221–223**
Ziegler, Mrs. George 224
Ziegler, Shotgun George **223–224**
Zielinski, Victoria 194
Zion, Eddie 12, 13
Zlenha, Joseph Z. 56
Zodiac Killer 76, **224–225**
Zurkorsky, John 204–205
Zwillman, Longy 15